C000261483

Duncan Redford is Senior Research Fellow in Modern Naval History at the National Museum of the Royal Navy (NMRN). He previously held a Leverhulme Early Career Research Fellowship at the Centre for Maritime Historical Studies, University of Exeter, and is the author of *The Submarine: A Cultural History from the Great War to Nuclear Combat* (I.B.Tauris).

Philip D. Grove is Subject Matter Expert in Strategic Studies at Britannia Royal Naval College for the University of Plymouth. He has taught at the University, RNEC Manadon and CTC RM Lympstone as well as various Royal Navy establishments and ships. He has published widely and is the author of *The Second World War: The War at Sea* (with Mark J. Grove and Alastair Finlan) and *The Battle of Midway.*

THE

ROYAL NAVY

A History Since 1900

Duncan Redford
and
Philip D. Grove

in association with

Published in 2014 by
I.B.Tauris & Co. Ltd
London • New York
Reprinted 2016
www.ibtauris.com

ISBN: 978 1 78076 782 6
eISBN: 978 0 85773 507 2
ePDF: 978 0 85772 346 8

A full CIP record for this book is available from the British Library
A full CIP record is available from the Library of Congress

Library of Congress Catalog Card Number: available

Typeset in Perpetua by A. & D. Worthington, Newmarket, Suffolk
Printed and bound by CPI Group (UK) Ltd, Croydon, CR0 4YY

Contents

Tables and Figures

Tables

Figures

Colour Plates

Series Foreword

The Royal Navy has for centuries played a vital if sometimes misunderstood or even at times unsung part in Britain's history. Often it has been the principal, sometimes the only, means of defending British interests around the world. In peacetime the Royal Navy carries out a multitude of tasks as part of government policy – showing the flag, or naval diplomacy as it is now often called. In wartime, as the senior service of Britain's armed forces, the Navy has taken the war to the enemy, by battle, by economic blockade or by attacking hostile territory from the sea. Adversaries have changed over the centuries. Old rivals have become today's alliance partners; the types of ship, the weapons within them and the technology – the 'how' of naval combat – have also changed. But fundamentally what the Navy does has not changed. It exists to serve Britain's government and its people, to protect them and their interests wherever they might be threatened in the world.

This series, through the numerous individual books within it, throws new light on almost every aspect of Britain's Royal Navy: its ships, its people, the technology, the wars and peacetime operations too, from the birth of the modern navy following the restoration of Charles II to the throne in the late seventeenth century to the war on terror in the early twenty-first century.

The series consists of three chronologically themed books covering the sailing navy from the 1660s until 1815, the Navy in the nineteenth century from the end of the Napoleonic Wars, and the Navy since 1900. These are complemented by a number of slightly shorter books which examine the Navy's part in particular wars, such as the Seven Years' War, the American Revolution, the Napoleonic Wars, World War I, World War II and the Cold War, or particular aspects of the service: the Navy and empire, the Women's Royal Naval Service, the Royal Marines, naval aviation and the submarine service. The books are standalone works in their own right, but when taken as a series present the most comprehensive and readable history of the Royal Navy.

Duncan Redford
National Museum of the Royal Navy

'The role in Britain's history of the Royal Navy is all too easily and too often overlooked; this series will go a long way to redressing the balance. Anyone with an interest in British history in general or the Royal Navy in particular will find this series an invaluable and enjoyable resource.'

Tim Benbow
Defence Studies Department,
King's College London at the
Defence Academy of the UK

Acknowledgements

Producing this book has been a considerable undertaking, with tight deadlines. With this in mind, my thanks go to my good friend Phil Grove, who agreed to write the chapters dealing with the Navy's history after 1945, and in doing so removed a considerable burden from my shoulders. However, writing a book is very much a team effort and more people are involved than just those named on the cover. My sincerest thanks go to the Leverhulme Trust, who between 2008 and 2011 funded my research and provided me with the support I needed to immerse myself in naval history in its widest sense; the fruits of their generosity underpin this book. I should also like to record my deep thanks to Matthew Sheldon, the Head of NMRN Portsmouth's curatorial team, and Dominic Tweddle, the NMRN's Director General, whose fantastic support made this book and the accompanying series on the history of the Royal Navy a possibility. I should also like to thank the many NMRN staff at all its various museums, especially Stephen Courtney, who have assisted Phil and me by supplying us with many wonderful pictures from which to chose the illustrations for this book. Thanks also go to the NMRN's library staff, Allison, Heather and Maggie, for giving excellent support in obtaining obscure books and journals at very short notice; Jenny Wraight at the Naval Historical Branch was also a tower of strength. Gratitude is also due to the nameless archival staff in museums, archives and universities dotted around the UK who promptly supplied me with documents to further my research. Finally, and above all, I want to thank my partner Katie for her unswerving support and encouragement — this book could not have been written without her.

Duncan Redford

I should like to echo Duncan wholeheartedly, but would also mention Peter Barr and Gill Smith, our librarians at the Britannia Royal Naval College, who have provided great support for my work. Thanks also go to Richard Kennell, our former Head Librarian, for all his help in supporting so many lectures that I have given here, some of which have found their way into this book. Additionally the young officers passing through our gates have also been instrumental with their questions, thoughts and open minds. And finally like Duncan, but never ever last, I should like to thank my family, Alayna, Amber and Aiden, for the tremendous support they have always given me. I am so proud of them. Without their encouragement I would never have taken Duncan up on his offer.

Philip Grove

Introduction

On 26 June 1897 thousands travelled to Portsmouth on specially provided trains to witness the spectacle of 165 Royal Navy ships, together with invited representative vessels from 14 other navies, drawn up in five long lines at Spithead to celebrate the Diamond Jubilee of Queen Victoria. The beaches and piers along the waterfront were crammed with day-trippers. The anchorage was a teeming mass of craft, each jammed with spectators sweating in the June sun, jostling around the black painted hulls, white superstructures and buff-painted funnels of the anchored British warships. Only the presence of the royal yacht, *Victoria and Albert*, restored some sort of order, but once the royal party had passed, the pleasure craft returned and bobbed in its wake. An unofficial display of speed was provided by the experimental steam-turbine-powered launch *Turbinia*, which Sir Charles Parsons, the developer of the marine steam turbine, hoped would persuade the Royal Navy to take up his invention. Such was the *Turbinia*'s impact that 'from a technical point of view, there would have been no important step forward to chronicle if the *Turbinia* had not made her brilliant appearance'. After sunset, at 20:45, the entire fleet, British and foreign ships alike, were illuminated in outline, masts, tops and turrets all picked out by the most modern and novel of methods – electric light bulbs.[1]

It was, everyone agreed, an awe-inspiring sight. No clearer example of seapower could be conceived. Britons were justly proud of their fleet – the most powerful collection of warships ever seen – drawn up for a royal review by the Prince of Wales to celebrate Queen Victoria's Diamond Jubilee. The press gushed appreciation, believing that if the British taxpayer 'does not feel more than a thrill of satisfaction at a sight so splendid and so inspiring, he is no patriot and no true citizen'. Some felt that 'at night the illumination of the fleet was a spectacle which surpassed all anticipation'. *The Illustrated London News* called it 'one more beautiful of its kind than human eye had previously looked upon' and thought that the illumination was the most popular feature of the day. Even the normally sober and conservative *Naval Annual* enthused that 'Nothing could have been more beautiful than the effect of the fleet illuminated on the night of June 26th', while the *Saturday Review* called it 'enchanting and enthralling'. Even after the illumination ceased on the stroke of midnight, those who remained watching from the shore could still see the anchor lights of the great fleet gleaming in the darkness.[2]

Much was made of the fact that no Royal Navy vessels had been recalled from either the Mediterranean or any overseas squadron and that the fleet was almost completely made up of modern vessels, a welcome note given the less than enthusiastic response to the Navy which had been placed on public display at the 1887 Golden Jubilee Review. Fortunately the Royal Navy had been comprehensively expanded and rebuilt between 1884 and 1897. Indeed the expansion of the Navy was, in 1897, still on-going.[3]

The twentieth century must have looked like it would be the Navy's century, as indeed the eighteenth and nineteenth centuries had been beforehand. Britain was an island – protected by its navy it was invulnerable to invasion. Britain was also at the centre of a globalized maritime trading network of formal empire – the Dominions and colonies that made up the British Empire – as well as an informal empire of economic and political influence that stretched far beyond those territories that Britain had claimed for itself.

However, with the dawn of the twentieth century came a problem that has stayed with the Royal Navy ever since – affordability. As a result, one of the key issues facing the Navy has been to do more with less – fewer ships, fewer sailors, less money. In the period before World War I the emphasis was to save more by making the Navy more efficient – shaking it out of its Victorian lethargy – and to use cutting-edge technology and strategy to reduce the cost of naval defence while increasing the utility of the fleet. In the inter-war period it was to reduce the costs of naval defence by using international agreements to reduce the size of many navies, not just Britain's. In the post-war period it has been a tale of an ever smaller navy as defence budgets have come under pressure, even before the 'peace dividend' at the end of the Cold War.

Yet despite the financial parsimony that has underpinned much of its history since 1900, the Royal Navy has not been found want-ing when Britain has been forced into war. Indeed the experience of both world wars shows how much Britain has relied on its navy, even if Britons may now have forgotten the roles their Navy was carrying out, or even never fully understood what was happening in the first place. World War I may not have been the quick 'second Battle of Trafalgar' that many people were hoping for, and when the great clash of Dreadnoughts occurred at Jutland in 1916 it may not have been the decisive victory that Britain wanted, but the Navy not only did not lose the war for Britain but actively helped to win it. Jutland showed the Germans that they could not beat the British Grand Fleet, and the economic blockade that the Royal Navy was instrumental in enforcing helped crush German war-making poten-tial and morale in 1917 and 1918, forcing Germany to the negotiat-ing table.

In World War II, the Royal Navy's now unsung contributions ensured again that Britain was not defeated and could, in time, take the war first to Italy, then Germany and finally Japan. In 1940 the Navy deterred the Germans from launching an invasion of Britain. Then it ensured that Britain could not be starved out of the war. Finally it would be able to support not just a bombing campaign against Germany, by escorting convoys of vital supplies across the Atlantic, but also launch invasions to liberate Europe and parts of North Africa from the tyranny of fascism and Nazism.

Even in that violent peace which came to be called the Cold War, the Royal Navy was at the forefront in defending Britain's interests or facing down aggression, from Korea to the Falklands. And with the end of the Cold War, its tasks did not end: there was the First and Second Gulf Wars, interventions in Bosnia and Kosovo, in Sierra Leone, Libya and Afghanistan.

The empire that the Royal Navy protected has been gone for decades, but Britain's global interests and the Navy's global presence, much reduced though it now is, have not. Quite simply, wherever British interests have been threatened or perceived to be at risk the Royal Navy has been on hand to deter, to coerce or to fight if needed, and is still carrying out these global tasks and helping to police a globalized economy based on a maritime trading system just as it was doing in 1900. The world has changed but the need to protect Britain from those who would do it harm has not.

The twentieth century has also been one of rapid technological change, change which challenged assumptions, altered the way the Royal Navy could fight when needed and influenced the way sailors lived and worked at sea. Since 1900 it has had to assimilate submarines, aircraft, computers, missiles, nuclear weapons, sonar and radar, to name but a few of the wide range of technological advancements that have seen service at sea. At the same time the rum ration has ended, thanks in part to the advancing technological requirements of a sailors' day-to-day work. Coal-fired boilers have gone too, replaced by cleaner and less manpower-intensive diesel engines and gas turbines. Hammocks have been replaced by bunks and the food supplied to sailors has improved immeasurably, as have pay and conditions of service.

As a result of these and other changes, the Royal Navy of today is very different from that of 1900. The dreadnought battleships are no more, and aircraft carriers have gone too as a result of the 2010 Strategic Defence and Security Review, but politicians have promised the Navy two new aircraft carriers by 2020 – although whether there will be any aircraft to fly from them is not so clear. But despite being smaller, despite the lack of interest in the Navy by politicians and the public, today's Royal Navy has capabilities that were undreamed of at the start of the twentieth century. Nuclear-powered hunter-killer submarines can remain submerged for months and circumnavigate the globe without stopping; their Tomahawk cruise missiles can strike at targets hundreds of miles inland. Missile-armed destroyers have an anti-aircraft capability that would have astounded Cunningham's Mediterranean Fleet in the summer of 1941 as it suffered under the lash of German airpower. The Navy's minesweepers and amphibious shipping, especially its ability to mount helicopter assaults, would have been greeted with joy by the commanders tasked with seizing the Dardanelles in 1915.

The Navy at the start of the twenty-first century might not be the size and shape it perhaps needs to be in order to meet the roles and expectations that will be thrust upon it the next time the call comes, but Britain is still an island, is still part of a globalized maritime trading system and still has political and economic interests around the world that will have to be defended. And as the twentieth century has shown, the best, most effective and most cost-effective way – if not the popular way – has been to use the Navy. This is the Royal Navy's story of Britain's most recent maritime century: the Navy in the twentieth century and after.

CHAPTER 1

The Last Years of Pax Britannica

In mid-December 1899 the news of British defeats at the hands of Boer forces at Stormberg, Magersfontein, and on the Tugela river at Colenso erupted in the press. The British Army's defeats during this 'Black week' were described in the press as 'inexplicable blunders', and that 'disaster ensued through absolute neglect of ordinary precautions'.[1] However, the army was not alone in this war; it was supported by the Royal Navy which at sea was trying to prevent the importation of arms via Portuguese East Africa, while on land it was solving one of the army's most pressing problems – a lack of artillery.

Quite simply the army lacked modern long-range artillery to counter the Boers' own guns. General Sir George White, commander of the threatened garrison at Ladysmith, asked the Royal Navy to help. Unfortunately the light guns the Navy used to support its own landing parties – when such operations were needed – were just as inadequate. The answer was to dismount 4.7-inch and long 12-pounder quick-firing guns from the cruisers HMS *Terrible* and HMS *Powerful* and design gun carriages for them. Happily the commanding officer of HMS *Terrible*, Captain Percy Scott, was something of an enthusiast for naval gunnery, on ship or not. He rapidly designed and built the necessary gun carriages. Naval guns, together with sailors to operate them, and more sailors and Royal Marines to protect them, were then dispatched to various army formations. Soon the Navy was heavily involved in some of the most

Fig. 1.1. The Naval Brigade from HMS *Terrible* moving through Durban
with a 4.7-inch gun on one of Captain Percy Scott's gun carriages.

famous (or notorious) sieges and engagements of the war. In all, the
Royal Navy and Royal Marines supplied 1,400 men and over 60
guns, ranging from the 6-inch gun on field gun carriage designed
and built by the Navy in Durban (a Scott design), to Scott's 4.7-inch
and 12-pounder guns and the more standard naval landing party
guns, to the construction of an armoured train (Scott again).[2]

In particular, the Navy's improvised field guns quickly grasped
the public imagination:

> We hear much of the 4.7 and 12 pdr naval gun. They inspire awe and
> wonder in the uninitiated, and the music halls cheer the men who
>> Work their way to heaven
>> To the tune of four point seven.[3]

Nor was the Boer War the Royal Navy's only operation as the
twentieth century opened. Nine thousand miles away, between
May and August 1900, more British 'naval brigades' were defeating
the Boxer uprising in China. HMS *Terrible* was again to the fore –

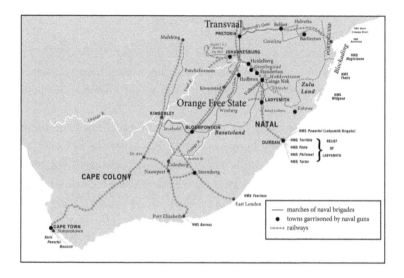

Fig. 1.2. The Royal Navy's involvement and
operations in the Second Boer War.

the Navy's ability to rapidly move ships and men from one area to another, thousands of miles away, a clear demonstration of the strategic mobility of seapower. Again Scott's designs for gun carriages ensured that the Navy was able to provide invaluable long-range artillery support on land to the international naval force which relieved the besieged legations in Peking in August, leading to the collapse of the Boxer rebellion. It might be a new century, but the sort of naval operation that it opened with would have been recognizable to those serving 40 years earlier.

But would this type of naval operation – indeed naval attitudes from the previous century – be needed or even useful in the new one? Were new enemies waiting for Britannia to neglect her trident and was there within the Navy's fleets the means of shaking itself out of its peacetime lethargy and attitudes to become vigorous, modern and efficient as well as fully attuned to the technological advances that were taking place?

Sir John Fisher's navy

There was one senior officer who was dedicated to dragging the Royal Navy into the new century whether some of his colleagues wanted to or not – Vice Admiral, soon to be Admiral, Sir John Fisher.

In 1900 Fisher was the Commander in Chief Mediterranean Fleet – the Royal Navy's premier command – where he had invigorated his fleet. Professionally Fisher was closely involved first with gunnery and then the new field of torpedoes (then a catch-all term that had more to do with mines than the modern self-propelled torpedo) and the naval applications of electricity. However, Fisher's main talents lay as an administrator, and a radical one at that, acting as the Director of Naval Ordnance, Admiral Superintendent of Portsmouth Dockyard and then Controller of the Navy (and member of the Admiralty Board) responsible for the Navy's materiel, before being appointed in 1897 as the Commander in Chief North America and West Indies Station, before gaining the Navy's most prestigious command, that of the Mediterranean Fleet in 1899.[4]

In June 1902 Fisher was appointed Second Sea Lord, responsible for issues such as pay, training and welfare. Training, or more accurately education, was an area which had come to Fisher's attention some months earlier. The Navy had already recognized that the education and training given to its most junior officers at HMS *Britannia*, a retired three-deck sail-powered battleship moored in the river at Dartmouth, was not adequate for the rapid technological advances that were occurring. In 1896 the decision had been made to build a shore-based college – Britannia Royal Naval College – on a hill outside Dartmouth; the foundation stone was laid by King Edward VII on 2 March 1902. Fisher, as Second Sea Lord, was essentially presented with a blank canvas on which to sketch out a new way of educating and training the Navy's officer cadets.[5]

The training and education scheme for junior officers that Fisher devised – named the Selborne scheme after the First Lord of the Admiralty – was a radical solution to the problems the Navy was facing. Fisher's plan proposed a common training scheme for all

Fig. 1.3. Britannia Royal Naval College,
Dartmouth, seen soon after opening.

officer cadets, irrespective of branch. This meant that engineers,
paymasters (the logistics branch), Royal Marines and the executive
branch would receive common training and education to the point
where they passed their lieutenant's exams. The intention was that
technical education would be properly integrated, that the status
of engineers would improve, that the various differences in training and education depending on method of entry into the officer
corps would be removed and that the officer corps would become
more flexible. The scheme, however, would take up to 20 years to
reach fruition and ensure that sufficient officers had passed through
the programme to allow it to function as intended. Given the technological, material and strategic uncertainties the Royal Navy was
facing, the attempt to produce a well-educated but flexible officer
corps had to be the right step to take.[6]

The scheme, especially the new possibility that engineers could
achieve command of ships, previously a privilege of the executive
branch, was opposed by many inside and outside the Navy. As a
result the plans for an effectively interchangeable officer corps were

scaled back. Nor could the scheme cope with the rapid expansion of the Navy, which occurred as Anglo-German naval rivalry increased. A range of new methods of entry had to be introduced in the years immediately before World War I to help ameliorate the officer shortage. The scheme's greatest failing was that it could not satisfactorily meet the differing requirements for executive, engineer and Royal Marine training. The Royal Marine officers were never absorbed under the Selborne scheme, and having closed the Royal Naval Engineering College in 1910, it reopened in 1913 to deal with the new 'special entry' engineer cadets who, like their executive branch special cadet brothers, were joining the Navy at 18 in order to alleviate the officer shortage that had developed as a result of the increasing size of the Navy.[7]

Co-incident with the Selborne scheme, the engineering branch was brought into line with their sailor colleagues; the old titles for engineering officers, such as inspector of machinery, were swept away and instead they used the same ranks as the executive branch, giving them new titles such as engineer rear admirals, engineer captains and engineer commanders, all the way down to engineer cadets. The ratings of the stoker branch were also aligned with their sailor colleagues.

There were also significant reforms to the treatment of ratings. Newspapers developed by a former sailor, Lionel Yexley, first the *Bluejacket* in 1898 and then the *Fleet* in 1905, provided a vehicle for sailors to make complaints without falling foul of naval discipline. The first target for reform was food. The official ration was one pound of meat and half a pound of vegetables per man per day, to form the main meal at noon, and a breakfast and supper each of one pint of tea or cocoa and a portion of dry bread or ship's biscuit without butter. Additionally, each mess, or individual, could buy ingredients and treats from the ship's canteen to supplement and improve their meals. Canteen prices, however, were usually high owing to the corruption involved in getting the canteen contract or to the expectation that equipment and supplies that really should have been supplied by the Navy, such as oilskin coats for bad weather, had to be paid for out of canteen profits.

Fig. 1.4. A seamen's mess deck on HMS *Jupiter*, a *Majestic* class battleship around the turn of the century.

The Rice and then the Login Committees examined the food issue in 1900 and 1906. The first introduced two new meals: one at 'standeasy' – the short break in the middle of each morning – and one at 7.30 in the evening. It also added a few small items such as coffee, jam and condensed milk to the ration. Yexley, however, had a clear package of reforms by 1906 which won the support, first, of Fisher, now First Sea Lord, and then of the Login Committee. The result was that the package of reforms essentially amounted to a pay rise of around 3d per man per day – a considerable sum.

Other reforms soon followed. Fisher and Yexley, joined later by Winston Churchill as First Lord of the Admiralty, worked in concert to reduce the cost and number of uniform items sailors were expected to have in their kit. Birching for boy sailors was suspended in 1906 and tighter controls on caning introduced. Flogging, which had only been suspended in 1881, was formally abolished. Naval prisons were reformed too. In 1909 it was decided to replace naval prisons with detention quarters by 1911; the men remained in uniform, not prison clothes, and underwent a mix of drill and physical training rather than the old punishments such as picking oakum. In 1912 the Brock Committee looked into the issue of summary punishments (those meted out by senior ratings and officers, as opposed to serious offences which were tried by court martial). It advised wide-ranging changes to the type of punishments that could be imposed and what offences could be punished summarily. Churchill went further, limiting the powers of commanding officers to disrate sailors – demoting them to a lower rank as punishment. Pay was increased too as a result of Yexley's continual pressure on the subject and marriage allowances were under consideration by the Admiralty and Treasury when war broke out in August 1914.

The final area of disquiet was the promotion (or lack of it) from the lower deck to the wardroom. During the nineteenth century the avenues for ratings to be promoted to officer rank had been shut off. It was noted that in the 84 years before 1902 only five men had been promoted from the lower deck to the wardroom. The initial solution to the growing pressure from ratings for increased promotion opportunities was Fisher's decision to advance 100 senior warrant officers to the rank of lieutenant. This only involved men nearing retirement and gave no avenue for promotion beyond lieutenant nor did it provide any opportunities for intelligent and capable younger ratings to be promoted. Yexley's continual pressure on the subject allowed Churchill to propose a 'Mate' scheme in 1912. Antipathy on the part of the then Second Sea Lord, Prince Louis of Battenberg, and outright opposition from other senior officers meant the scheme did not go as far as either Churchill or Yexley desired and it was almost impossible for men promoted under the scheme to get beyond the rank of commander.[8]

The reforms may not have been perfect but perhaps they were just enough to equip and sustain officers and men as they dealt with the wave of naval technology on which the Royal Navy's superiority floated.

New technology, new opportunities

The period 1900–14 saw the introduction or perfection of a great deal of new equipment. First on the scene was the submarine. Originally seen as part of Fisher's flotilla defence plans, the submarine was developed rapidly by the Royal Navy and by the outbreak of war was far more capable than the 1901 *Holland* type submarines. By 1914 the *E* class had a reasonable torpedo armament, a deck gun, wireless with which to communicate with shore headquarters and the ability to operate at a considerable distance from a base. The Navy was also keen to exploit the use of the submarine within the battlefleet, driving hard for a submarine that had the speed to keep up with the battlefleet and would be capable of playing a part in the expected 'second Trafalgar' decisive battle.[9]

While the adoption of the submarine was a very visible indication of rapidly improving naval technology, other improvements such as the use of wireless telegraphy – radios – or improvement in the control and accuracy of heavy guns were less obvious to the casual observer. Wireless had the most profound impact on naval warfare of almost any single new technology in the twentieth

Fig. 1.5. British submarines, 1901: *Holland* 2, the Royal Navy's second submarine to enter service.

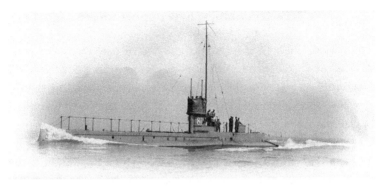

Fig. 1.6. British submarines, 1913: *E* class submarine *E7*.
Note the radio mast mounted on the conning tower.

century. Previously the fastest way the Admiralty, the controlling hub of the Royal Navy's administration and operations, had to
communicate globally with its bases and distant commanders was
to use a network of telegraph cables laid on the seabed and across
British territory. Messages could be securely and quickly transmitted from the Admiralty to any port on the British cable network –
for example, Hong Kong, Bombay, Gibraltar or Malta. The problem
was there was no means of getting these messages to a fleet once it
had left port except by a ship. Nor was there any means of commu-
nicating between ships that were out of sight of each other. Wireless
telegraphy, developed by Marconi and a Royal Navy officer, Henry
Jackson, using Morse code, changed this.

Table 1.1. Distribution of wireless sets in the Royal Navy, 1900.[10]

	Marconi sets	Jackson sets
Channel Squadron	6	2
Mediterranean Fleet	4	3 (and one spare)
Reserve Fleet	3	3
Training Squadron	4	0
HMS *Vernon* (Torpedo school)	2	2 (and one spare
HMS *Defiance* (Torpedo school)	2	2 (and one spare)

China Fleet	3	3 (and one spare)
Shore stations	3	0
Awaiting installation	5	0

The decision to adopt wireless technology came as early as 23 February 1900, but by 1904 only about half of the fleet had been fitted with wireless sets, only Malta had a shore-to-ship wireless capability, wireless coverage of the English Channel was incomplete and the Admiralty itself did not have a set. However, arrangements had been made with Lloyds of London to fit transmitters in their global network of signal stations which were to be taken over by the Navy in the event of war. Fisher accelerated the wireless programme; from 1906 the Admiralty could use wireless to send orders to ships anywhere in home waters and the Mediterranean. By 1909 the Admiralty had upgraded all the shore wireless stations with sets that could be heard over at least 500 nautical miles and some were given sets with a 1,000-mile range.[11]

The steady improvements in wireless technology allowed the Admiralty to function effectively as a clearing house for intelligence which it could then disseminate quickly to commanders around the globe. It also allowed it to take a far more hands-on approach to the operations of its fleets, squadrons and even individual ships. From 1905 at the heart of this new system of controlling the Navy's ships was a 'plot' or 'War Room' where the Naval Intelligence Department and the Trade Section pooled their information to track foreign warships – even in peacetime. The Navy also anticipated making use of wireless sets on merchant vessels which would in wartime allow the Admiralty and British warships to be alerted almost instantaneously to an attack on a civilian vessel by an enemy cruiser, allowing the position of such a raider to be localized and a search area established. This ability to quickly respond to new information collected on a global scale was at the centre of Fisher's subsequent strategic reforms – the fleet redistribution, flotilla defence and the fleet unit for Imperial defence.

The Navy even ventured into the air, establishing a naval wing of the newly formed Royal Flying Corps (RFC) specifically to deal with maritime aviation with airships, seaplanes and land planes (for more information see *A History of the Royal Navy: Air Power and British Naval Aviation* by Ben Jones). Even before the formal founding of a naval air wing, the Admiralty had started experiments in 1909 with Zeppelins. Unfortunately the product of this, a Vickers airship dubbed the *Mayfly*, did not live up to its name. By early 1912 the Navy had succeeded in launching a biplane from HMS *Africa*. Soon after the formation of the RFC in 1912 the naval wing started showing a distinct appetite for independence and imaginative thinking; the Admiralty started producing seaplane carriers to allow aircraft to support the fleet at sea in 1914 and on 1 July 1914 the Royal Naval Air Service – a separate entity from the RFC – was born.[12]

There were advances in gunnery too. Captain Percy Scott of Boer War fame had developed a number of techniques that improved accuracy and the range at which gunfire was likely to be effective. However, his greatest innovation was the 1905 development of the director firing system which, when combined with mechanical computers to predict where a target would be when the shells landed some seconds later, gave a ship the means to calculate an enemy's range, course and speed while ensuring that information was fed into the ship's gun sights. Unfortunately there were two competing mechanical computers, one developed by a naval officer, Frederick Dreyer, and one by a private inventor, Arthur Pollen. An acrimonious dispute grew up between Pollen and the Admiralty over secrecy, contracts, Pollen's views of several senior officers and the effectiveness of the equipment Pollen was demonstrating which only the outbreak of war in 1914 halted. In 1906, following the improvements in long-range gunnery, came the most visible sign of the changes in naval technology – the dreadnought.[13]

The *Dreadnought* was a new type of battleship. Its main armament was large 12-inch guns unlike the mixed heavy and medium guns of previous battleships. It was faster than all previous battleships thanks to its use of steam turbine engines rather than triple expansion engines. It was quite simply revolutionary, making all existing

Fig. 1.7. HMS *Temeraire*, Britain's third *Dreadnought* class battleship.

battleships – now pre-dreadnoughts – obsolete. It was the ultimate
symbol of technological process as well as naval power. And the
British public loved it. The *Dreadnought* (and her successors) seized
the public imagination like no other ship. On souvenir charts of
naval reviews, dreadnoughts were even coloured differently so that
the public could easily spot them. Ironically Fisher, the man who
had conceived of the dreadnought, preferred his follow-up design of
dreadnought style fast armoured cruisers which in time came to be
known as battlecruisers.[14]

The dreadnoughts were also a symbol of how Fisher intended
to maintain peace – by deterrence. First, it was a deliberate decision to start an arms race to make hostile states think twice about
competing with Britain. When the *Dreadnought* was launched, other
naval powers simply stopped building battleships while they tried
to work out what to do; during that time the British built another
ten! Only the Germans and Americans really took up the challenge
– the French and Russians did not build a dreadnought until 1913 –
and even the Germans stopped trying to complete after 1912 and

instead concentrated on getting their army ready to beat the French. Second, it gave the impression of overwhelming power – something the Royal Navy did quite well, especially through its internationally reported spectacles such as the fleet reviews at Spithead and elsewhere – and of course these new powerful dreadnought battleships helped contribute to the Navy's aura of invincibility. Fisher was using technology to create not just a more efficient navy but also one that through deterrence was strategically more effective.[15]

New friends, new enemies

Strategically the period 1900–14 saw significant change. Throughout the nineteenth century Britain's (and hence the Royal Navy's) main strategic threat, real or imagined, came from France – sometimes partnered with Russia, sometimes not. War scares with France occurred in the 1840s, the late 1850s (despite Britain having had an alliance of convenience with France against Russia in the Crimean War), in 1888 and again in 1898, and of course the 1884 'Truth about the Navy' furore was very much about the relative naval superiority of Britain over rivals like France and Russia. Indeed it was the British fear of a strategic alliance of France and Russia that many saw as the root of the 1889 Naval Defence Act, which enshrined the principle that the Royal Navy should be bigger than the next two naval powers combined.

Towards the end of the nineteenth century a new potential naval threat emerged. In 1898 Imperial Germany passed its first naval law. This allowed for the construction of an additional seven battleships, two large and seven light cruisers by 1 April 1904, taking the German fleet to a total of 19 battleships, eight armoured cruisers, 12 large cruisers and 30 light cruisers. This was hardly a threat to the Royal Navy, but it was enough to launch limited naval offensives against France and Russia. However, the German naval expansion, thanks to its architect Admiral Alfred von Tirpitz, was firmly aimed at challenging Britain – just not yet. The German navy's plan was for staged growth. In 1900 Germany passed the second naval law which authorized a doubling of the German fleet to 38 battleships plus a full cast of supporting cruisers. The British press warned of the increasing German naval threat, especially given German support for the Boers, but cooler and more calculating heads within government were also starting to consider the strategic impact of increased German naval spending. The Director of Naval Intelligence, Captain Reginald Custance RN, the Admiralty's Parliamentary and Financial Secretary, H.O. Arnold-Forster, and the First Lord of the Admiralty, Lord Selborne, all expressed increasing concerns about the German threat within naval and political circles; yet others, such as the First Sea Lord, Lord Walter Kerr, played down the issue.[16]

The problem the British faced was that maintaining a 'two-power' naval standard was increasingly expensive as it involved having a navy superior to the combination of the next two biggest navies in the world, which at the start of the twentieth century meant France and Russia. Expanding to a 'three power' standard to include Germany as well was prohibitively expensive. Also the army estimates had surged out of control after 1900 due to the cost of the Boer War, threatening to unbalance Britain's defence finances.

One possible answer was to reduce the costs of defence by seeking allies, allowing Britain to reduce or possibly eliminate naval expenditure in certain regions. In 1902 Britain and Japan concluded an alliance that was essentially naval in character and would deal with a potential Franco-Russian combination in the Far East which could have pitched a force of up to nine battleships and 20 cruisers against the Royal Navy's China Fleet of four battleships and 16 cruisers. Then between 1904 and 1905 the Russians removed themselves from Britain's list of strategic threats following their humiliating defeat by Japan in the Russo-Japanese War and the destruction of much of Russia's naval force. Finally in 1904 France and Britain concluded a series of agreements that resolved nagging tensions and territorial issues – the Entente Cordiale. This agreement between old enemies was partially in response to the danger of being drawn into the Russo-Japanese War and also due to the fact that France feared Germany far more than she did Britain. Yet the agreement did not actually commit Britain to assisting France in the event of a new Franco-German war.[17]

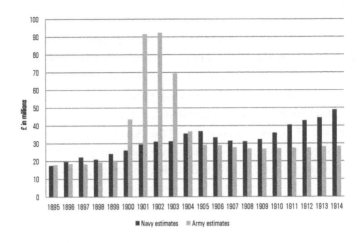

Fig. 1.8. British defence spending 1895–1914.

Another solution to the problem was to cut spending on the Navy and army. This was very much why Fisher had been appointed as First Sea Lord in 1904. He was convinced that not only could the efficiency of the Navy be improved but that a more efficient and effective navy would cost less. That said, Fisher during his time as First Sea Lord was vehemently opposed to any increase in spending on the army at the expense of the Navy. The ferocious disputes over the security of Britain from invasion were as much about the army trying to poach money that might be spent on the Navy as a difference of strategic opinion.

Irrespective of the actual enemy, the Royal Navy had a number of goals that it had to achieve. The first was to prevent invasion; the second to ensure the security of British seaborne trade, closely intertwined with which was the defence of the empire from marauding naval squadrons who might prey on British trade. Finally there was the need to take the offensive against the enemy in order to defeat them.

The invasion bogeyman was one that had regularly exercised the British public and politicians from the earliest days of the British state. Indeed the twentieth century opened with an invasion panic that swept the country – the somewhat illogical fear that failings by the British army in South Africa would lead to an invasion of the United Kingdom (illogical indeed, as by 1900 the British public and politicians should have become accustomed to British military incompetence). The scare was given weight by apparently suspicious activity by the French and Russian navies, such as buying British steam coal as well as the previously announced visit of the French Mediterranean Fleet to the Levant, even though Whitehall viewed the threat of invasion as laughable. Agitation by the National Service League, who wanted to introduce that most un-British of concepts – conscription in peacetime – in order to create a continental-style army, ensured that the possibility of invasion remained a live issue for the government in the years after the Boer War.[18]

In 1903 the Committee of Imperial Defence (CID) investigated the invasion issue and decided that a force of over 70,000 men would be needed by an invader to have any chance of success, but that it was impossible for the French to collect shipping for such a force in their Atlantic and Channel ports. Even if France had such shipping the preparations could not be disguised, giving the British time to prepare. Furthermore, an invasion would require at least two days of good weather and no molestation by the Royal Navy. In short the Navy had, during the course of the enquiry, comprehensively demolished the army's case for a large home army to guard against invasion. The prime minister, Arthur Balfour, even dismissed the possibility of an invasion by France to the Cabinet Defence Committee the next year. Yet by 1907 the National Service League succeeded in bringing the invasion bogey back to the CID. The invasion mongers argued that as the likely aggressor was now Germany, the previous analysis of the possibility of invasion was invalid as it was based on France, but the argument essentially remained unchanged – while there was a Royal Navy the invasion of Britain was impossible.[19]

Traditionally the Navy had contained any threat of invasion, real or imagined, by a combination of means. First, enemy ports could be blockaded to physically prevent an invasion force and its escorting fleet from getting to sea. Second, the Navy could seek the destruction of the enemy fleet at sea in a decisive battle to achieve 'command of the sea' and thus deter an invasion force from sailing with no friendly fleet to protect it. Finally, there were coastal attack operations to destroy enemy forces while still in port as well as disrupting their support infrastructure. Of these, seeking a decisive battle was by far the most popular option within the service. It allowed the Royal Navy to dream of emulating the totemic example of Nelson at Trafalgar. Admiral Sir Cyprian Bridge considered command of the sea to be 'the main object in naval warfare'. Indeed the whole emphasis within British naval thinking on decisive battle and command of the sea had received a significant fillip in the early 1890s when a US Navy officer, Captain Alfred Thayer Mahan, published the first of three books dealing with British seapower. *The Influence of Seapower upon History* was an instant hit in the USA, in Britain and elsewhere – even Germany. It explained that national greatness was due to the use of seapower and in particular it stressed the importance of obtaining command of the sea by defeating an enemy fleet in battle. Then, Mahan argued, the state holding command of the sea could use that power in any way it saw fit.[20]

Unfortunately experience had shown that enemies were reluctant to die gloriously just to add to the Royal Navy's tradition of victory. Instead enemies preferred to skulk in harbour, which explains the British development in the nineteenth century of a coastal attack strategy to go into the ports of recalcitrant navies and destroy them. However, the development of the torpedo and the torpedo boat made both coastal attack and close blockade increasingly difficult from the 1880s onwards – despite numerous British efforts to perfect close blockade in peacetime manoeuvres. It also meant that a considerable part of the Royal Navy's fleet was tied to defending Britain from invasion.

Fisher, once he became First Sea Lord on 20 October 1904, proposed a solution that he felt would both prevent invasion *and* restore strategic mobility to the battlefleet, allowing it to go wherever it might be needed to support national strategy. This was the idea of flotilla defence. While Fisher had been Commander in Chief Portsmouth during 1903 and 1904, he had been able to observe the performance and development of the Royal Navy's latest weapon system, the submarine, which had been adopted in 1901 (for more information see *A History of the Royal Navy: The Submarine* by **Duncan Redford**). Flotilla defence envisaged using large numbers of torpedo boats, destroyers and possibly small cruisers as well as the new submarines to make it impossible for an enemy force to get close enough to British shores to launch an invasion without being detected and destroyed by this mass of 'flotilla' craft. Importantly it released the battlefleet from the task of anti-invasion duties, thereby restoring the Navy's strategic mobility to act on a global scale. By making it impossible for an enemy to command the sea, flotilla defence denied them use of the sea. This 'sea denial' strategy was the antithesis of command of the sea and the decisive battle, and was thus intensely unpopular within the service. It is likely that flotilla defence exacerbated the poor personal relations between Fisher and Admiral Lord Charles Beresford, the leader of the anti-Fisher faction, who wished to succeed Fisher as First Sea Lord. Unfortunately Beresford was a poor strategist and clearly did not understand – or want to understand – what Fisher's reforms allowed.

Closely linked to the idea of flotilla defence was Fisher's 1904 plan to redistribute the Navy's fleets and their ships. Hitherto there had been four principal fleets equipped with battleships and cruisers: the Channel Squadron with eight battleships, the Home Fleet with eight, the Mediterranean Fleet with 12 and the China Fleet with five battleships to support the Navy's overseas commands and stations with their collection of smaller vessels for Imperial and trade defence. This organization was itself very new – the Home Fleet had been created in 1902–3 to deal with the problem of home defence – actual or perceived – if the Channel Fleet was sent to the Mediterranean in the event of a war with France. After the 1904 reorganization the Channel Squadron was renamed the Atlantic Fleet, its strength maintained at eight battleships and its base moved to Gibraltar, where a large investment in dry docks and associated naval facilities since the late 1890s was reaching fruition with the opening of the King Edward VII Dry Dock – one of three being built there. The Home Fleet was renamed the Channel Fleet and its strength increased to 12 battleships. The Mediterranean Fleet would be reduced to eight battleships and a decision on the strength of the China Fleet deferred until the outcome of the Russo-Japanese War was clear. The armoured cruiser squadrons that had been attached to the old fleets were also reorganized into three flying squadrons able to be sent anywhere in the world for Imperial and trade defence duties.[21]

This re-disposition of assets was not 'bringing the legions' home to deal with the German threat. Instead it was an outward-looking posture that was flexible enough to deal with a highly fluid strategic situation in 1904 where the enemy might come from a number of different directions – Germany, France or Russia. As a result of the plan the number of battleships in home waters was to fall from 16 battleships in two fleets to 12 in one. Additionally, there were two aspects to the plan that gave it a global focus and not a European one. First, the newly formed Atlantic Fleet at Gibraltar could be used to reinforce the Channel Fleet (against France, Germany, Russia or a combination thereof) and also the Mediterranean (France and Russia) or China Fleets (France and Russia). Second, the decision to strip out the armoured cruiser squadrons from the various fleets and concentrate them into three flying squadrons gave the Navy, thanks to its network of coaling stations and telegraph network, the ability to operate in almost any part of the world's seas for trade defence, Imperial defence or defending Britain's wider political and economic interests – its 'informal' empire. For all the noise during the period 1900–14 regarding invasion, as Fisher himself pointed out, Britain's real threat was from starvation if Britain's seaborne trade were to be attacked.[22]

However, there were many within the Navy who still felt that the protection of trade and the closely related issue of Imperial defence could also be addressed by the pursuit of command of the sea. The 1902 Colonial Conference was told, 'The primary object of the British Navy is not to defend anything, but to attack the fleets of the enemy, and by defeating them to afford protection to British Dominions, supplies and commerce.' Convoy, the traditional method of protecting trade in war, had fallen out of use in the 1870s and the legislation repealed due to opposition from within the Navy (it was felt to be too defensive) and the shipping companies (who did not want to have their ships delayed). Trade defence therefore rested on command of the sea, blockading enemy commerce raiders, and offensive patrolling by British cruisers which were being built in some numbers for trade protection and Imperial defence duties. Such was the importance of the issue of food supply that in 1903 the government convened a royal commission on the question.[25]

The development of exceptionally fast liners by German shipping companies such as the Hamburg-Amerika Line and Norddeutscher Lloyd, some of which had won the Blue Riband for the fastest crossing of the Atlantic by a passenger ship, raised the possibility of the Germans converting these ships into Armed Merchant Cruisers (AMCs) in time of war. Such exceptionally fast ships would be able to prey upon British shipping and outrun hunting British cruisers. The British response was to subsidize the Cunard Steamship Company to build two massive and extremely fast liners, the *Lusitania* and the *Mauritania*, which could be easily converted into AMCs if and when war was declared.[24]

The real solution to the problem, however, was not to use AMCs but to develop a warship that could catch and outgun even the fastest of German armed liners. Co-incident with the development of the more famous all-big-gun battleship HMS *Dreadnought*, Fisher also saw the need for a fast, all-big-gun armoured cruiser and clearly felt that the fast armoured cruiser equipped with 12-inch guns was superior to his new *Dreadnought* class battleships. Fisher even went as far as arguing, with relatively little success, that the battleship itself was obsolete. Combining the roles of armoured cruiser and battleship held out the possibility of significant savings in both money and manpower – both pressing issues for the Edwardian Royal Navy. It also meant that the Navy was itself none too sure of how to use these new vessels, especially after Fisher stood down as First Sea Lord in 1910. More importantly the fast armoured cruiser was seen as solving the trade defence problem caused by the possibility of the Germans using large, fast Atlantic passenger liners as AMCs.[25]

Fig. 1.9. Fisher's preferred ship, the all-big-gun armed fast armoured cruiser, or battlecruiser. HMS *Inflexible*, the second of the *Invincible* class, entered service in 1908.

The new fast armoured cruisers such as HMS *Invincible* also had an Imperial defence role. The development of Dominion navies, notably by the Australians and Canadians in 1901 and 1910 respectively and given 'Royal' status in 1911, was welcomed by Britain as a way of getting the Dominions to pay a more proportional cost of their naval defence. At the same time, the development of Dominion navies and the ships for them provided an outlet for the navalism and expressions of national consciousness that were increasing in fervour. The fast armoured cruiser – or battlecruiser as it came to be called – provided such an outlet and contributed to Imperial defence in two ways. First, there was the decision by Australia and New Zealand (and later the Federation of Malaya) to pay for capital ships for the Royal Navy. In 1909 – when a naval scare over the strength of the Royal Navy was rocking Britain and the empire – Australia paid for the *Indefatigable* class battlecruiser HMS *Australia* and New Zealand the *Indefatigable* class battlecruiser HMS *New Zealand*. It was also hoped that Canada would make a serious contribution to Imperial naval defence by also sponsoring battleships or battlecruisers, but this dream foundered on the rocks of Canadian domestic politics whose politicians said they were 'more interested in boxcars [i.e. railways] than in battleships'.[26]

The second way was to act as the physical focus for navies built by the Dominions, which could slowly grow and shoulder more of the Imperial defence burden, with a battlecruiser at the heart of these 'fleet units'. The 'fleet units' were conceived in July 1909 and were a way round the Dominions' habit of looking at their naval forces in prestige rather than practical terms – 'sentimental navies' according to the Admiralty – and the Admiralty's refusal to have anything to do with such weak and inconsequential forces. At the Imperial Conference in July, the Admiralty proposed that those Dominions seeking a navy should base it around a battlecruiser and 12 smaller ships of specific types – three light cruisers, six destroyers and three submarines. Significantly, while the costs were greater than the Dominions had hoped, the fleet units were cheaper than the existing arrangements in the Pacific. All in all, the Admiralty hoped for four fleet units in the Pacific region – one Australian, one Canadian and two British (one of which was to be partially subsidized by New Zealand) – all operating independently in peacetime, but in war acting as a multi-national Imperial navy. Unfortunately once Fisher and the First Lord of the Admiralty, Reginald McKenna, who had developed and sold the plan to the Dominions, had been forced out of office in 1910 and 1911 respectively, their replacements, especially the new First Lord, Winston Churchill, quickly scrapped the fleet unit concept in an effort to reduce the cost of the Royal Navy and to concentrate its resources on being able to take the offensive in a future war with Germany.[27]

For many inside the Navy, in parliament and members of the public, the Royal Navy's ability to take offensive action, often through seeking a decisive battle – a second Trafalgar – to obtain command of the sea, was all that mattered. This simplistic view of naval warfare was challenged regularly by one of Fisher's most important civilian colleagues, the historian and strategist Julian Corbett. Corbett constantly reminded the Navy and politicians that what mattered was not command of the sea but what Britain, in terms of national strategy, could do with it. Many in the Navy and elsewhere were wont to confuse the means (command of the sea) with the ends (winning a war). People, Corbett noted in his important 1911 study of naval and national policy, *Some Principles of Maritime Strategy*, live on the land not the sea; therefore what is important is what your navy allows you to do to, or on, the land.[28]

With the move away from coastal attack operations during the 1880s owing to the fear of the torpedo, and vile relations between the Navy and the army ensuring that cooperation in the field of amphibious warfare was impossible, only economic warfare was a possibility as to what to do with command of the sea in order to win a future war. Economic warfare was an area embraced with enthusiasm by the Fisher regime – although again against a great deal of internal opposition from Admirals like Sir Arthur Wilson, VC, and from the army which would have no role other than that of an Imperial constabulary force.

World trade and the interconnectedness of economies had vastly increased in the period after 1870. If Britain was vulnerable to a blow aimed at its trade as outlined by the French *Jeune École* in the 1880s, so too was Germany in the 1900s. In particular British control of over half the world's shipping, the global shipping insurance market and the global credit market meant that other states were vulnerable to Britain interdicting their trade at sea and in the marketplace. Indeed the amount of spare capacity in neutral shipping was considered insufficient to meet the needs of Germany and still maintain neutral imports to other states and exports in the event of a war between Britain and Germany. Quite simply the pre-war statistics indicated that Britain's refusal to allow British merchant vessels to carry German goods would cause severe economic and financial hardship that could cause sufficient social unrest to force Germany out of a war. The Admiralty's plans may have horrified the Foreign Office, the Board of Trade and the City of London, but there was a great deal of determination to force through the plans within the Admiralty and the Committee of Imperial Defence – especially as the alternative after 1904 was the politically contentious War Office plans to create a large enough army to be able to fight in France as part of an formal alliance.

Fisher has often been criticized for his decision to scrap 154 old and obsolete vessels that were scattered around the globe on Imperial policing duties, as some people at the time and subsequently have thought that these ships could have been useful for trade defence purposes. As the Admiralty analysis of the risks posed by German AMCs shows, such slow and under-armed vessels would have been a liability. Quite simply having large numbers of old obsolete vessels was a waste of money and manpower and, additionally, would not deal with the problems the Navy faced. Only the linked ideas of flotilla defence and the fast armoured cruisers restoring strategic mobility of the fleet could. Also the idea that such vessels would be useful in a future war as convoy escorts was nonsensical, as the Royal Navy and British shipping companies had rejected convoy as a trade defence tool 30 years earlier. Furthermore, the scrapping of such inefficient and manpower-intensive ships freed up crews to increase the readiness of the most modern parts of the reserve fleet through the nucleus crew scheme. This scheme made the most of Britain's large fleet by ensuring that most modern ships in the reserve had sufficient key crew members (normally two-fifths) to be able to go to sea for exercises and drills without being mobilized, thus speeding mobilization when it occurred and raising the efficiency of the fleet.

After Fisher

Unfortunately while Fisher's Admiralty was very much attached to the idea of economic warfare as an offensive weapon against Germany, this cannot be said for his successors. Nor does it seem that these successors – naval and political – understood either the interconnected nature of Fisher's policies or the impact of new weapons and technology on a future naval war. Fleet redistribution, the use of flotilla defence, the scrapping of older vessels, the reforms of the reserve fleet and the nucleus crew scheme were all part of one bold plan to carry out the Royal Navy's key roles, neutralize its strategic rivals and reduce spending on defence by increasing efficiency.

The reforms, however, were often poorly understood by politicians, the public and a professionally ill-educated officer corps, leading to considerable opposition from both inside and outside the Navy. Fisher's most outspoken critic was the man who had been his former while he commanded the Mediterranean Fleet, Admiral the Lord Charles Beresford. Beresford had been moved to command the Channel Fleet in 1907 and proved to be a constant thorn in the side of Fisher's administration, probably due to a poisonous combination of thwarted ambition, personal animosity and strategic incomprehension. As a former Conservative MP with significant political and social links throughout the British establishment, Beresford was doubly dangerous after 1906 when the Liberals were in government as he could act as a focus for dissent not just over naval policy but against the Liberal government generally.

On 24 March 1909, unable to put up with Beresford's insubordination, the Admiralty ordered him to give up his command of the Channel Fleet. Beresford immediately retaliated by writing to the prime minister, Herbert Asquith, accusing the Admiralty of strategic incompetence, failing to provide sufficient small craft and not having any formed plans in the event of war. Beresford's accusations came just after the height of the 1909 naval scare when the Liberal government (which was responsible for the shortage of flotilla craft Beresford was complaining about) had been forced by a public panic about British naval superiority over Germany into building more dreadnoughts than it wished to. The scare had been surreptitiously egged on by the Admiralty in order to avoid meeting the Cabinet's demands for cuts in battleship construction. Asquith leapt at the chance to have someone else act as the means of clipping the Admiralty's (and Fisher's) wings following their earlier machinations. Just to make sure the right answer was arrived at, Asquith ensured that members of the Committee of Imperial Defence (CID) who supported Fisher were excluded from the sub-committee he had set up under his personal direction to investigate the charges.

The inquiry was a disaster for Beresford's credibility. He was shown to be incoherent and strategically incompetent. Unfortunately it was a pyrrhic victory for Fisher, which was probably Asquith's intention all along – after all Asquith had approved the Admiralty decision to sack Beresford and then failed to publicly back Fisher by dismissing Beresford's complaints. Fisher and McKenna felt that Asquith was trying to get rid of them. In October 1909

Fisher decided to resign. Fearing that Asquith would use the forthcoming general election to replace McKenna as well as appointing a more amenable officer as Fisher's successor, if the Liberals won as expected, Fisher ensured that his replacement was in office before the election. But would Fisher's reforms and strategic intentions be maintained by his successor?

Certainly this was the plan. Admiral Wilson, untainted by the Fisher–Beresford feud, was called out of retirement to take up the post of First Sea Lord and was expected to be a safe pair of hands and not undo Fisher's work. Unfortunately Wilson was habitually abrasive, almost always ignored advice and was incapable of delegation. He also decided that a close blockade of Germany and obtaining a decisive battle between the British and German fleets was the way ahead rather than relying on the combination of flotilla defence and economic pressure.

Matters were brought to a head in August 1911 when at a CID meeting to discuss plans if war broke out between France, Britain and Germany over Germany's hostile moves towards establishing a foothold in Morocco, Admiral Wilson shocked not only the CID but also his own service by advocating a close blockade of Germany and an assault on Heligoland while the army was held as a mobile reserve for amphibious operations. Compared to the slick army presentation that persuaded observers to believe that a few British divisions placed on the extreme left of the massive French army would have a decisive result, Wilson's plan would have seemed laughable. Asquith, under pressure from the War Office, resolved to shake up the Admiralty. In mid-October McKenna was replaced as First Lord of the Admiralty by Winston Churchill who immediately set about getting rid of Wilson, replacing him with Admiral Sir Francis Bridgeman on 29 November. Bridgeman did not long survive Churchill's meddling in naval policy and administration, however. On 28 November 1912 Churchill suggested that Bridgeman should retire due to ill health. When Bridgeman pointed out that he felt quite well thank you, Churchill insisted on his resignation on 2 December, to be replaced by the person he had wanted all along, Prince Louis of Battenberg. Behind Churchill's meddling and possibly bullying manner – even his own party considered him an opportunist and totally devoid of integrity – was Fisher, trying to shape Churchill's non-existent grasp of maritime strategy.

The result of Fisher's behind-the-scenes advice to Churchill was that flotilla defence and the complete Fisher strategic approach for dealing with Germany were supported and consideration was given to cutting battleship construction in order to fund more flotilla craft, including submarines. But events rapidly forced Churchill away from the path Fisher had set out for him. The passing of the new German Naval Law (the Novelle) in early 1912 promised a German battlefleet of over 24 battleships in commission. Politically it was impossible for the British to rely on flotilla defence in the face of such a challenge.

For the public, nearly all politicians and a distressingly high number of senior Royal Navy officers, naval strength and capability had been equated with battleships since before the 1889 Naval Defence Act and the public adoption of a two-power standard. The new dreadnoughts had only made matters worse; these new powerful warships had seized the public's imagination, while many in the Navy had been very sceptical about Fisher's idea that the battleship was no longer the absolute arbiter of naval power. Everyone liked a navy that looked impressive, with its lines of battleships – now dreadnoughts – at naval reviews. It looked like a navy that was unbeatable, even if the strategic rationale for decisive battle in the North Sea was highly questionable in a time of long-range torpedoes, destroyers, submarines and mines. This combination of strategic misconceptions and emotional thinking about naval power compelled Churchill to continue building dreadnoughts. More significantly, such were the escalating costs that the two-power standard was nominally abandoned and a measure of 60 per cent above that of Germany used instead – although a 60 per cent margin over Germany effectively gave Britain a two-power standard against any other pair of naval powers. The crews for these new dreadnoughts had to come from the flotilla vessels earmarked for flotilla defence, reducing the effectiveness of the sea denial strategy. At the same time, the increasing size of the battlefleet – soon to be called the Grand Fleet of Battle or just the Grand Fleet — and the desire for a decisive clash of dreadnoughts in the mid-North Sea meant there were ever increasing calls for cruisers and destroyers to protect the battleships from torpedo attack, further denuding the resources available for Fisher's grand strategic concept.

Fisher might have based his thinking on the use of technology, strategic change and deterrence to avoid war, in the process transforming and dividing the Navy, but all too many of his peers — all heirs to the memory of Nelson — were fixated on getting their own Trafalgar. They should have remembered to be careful what they wished for.

CHAPTER 2

Waiting for the Next Trafalgar

World War I at Sea from the Outbreak
of War to the Eve of Jutland

The Royal Navy goes to war

In July 1914 the Royal Navy held one of those maritime pageants
at which it excelled – a review of the fleet for royalty and the great
and the good. No royal coronation or jubilee had gone by without
a review of the fleet at Spithead since 1887. Significant political
events were celebrated too: the Entente Cordiale with France and
visits of colonial and Dominion politicians. The Navy was anxious
to show parliament and the public what good use was being made
of the money voted each year for the service. This time there was
neither royal event to celebrate nor any major political visit, but it
still generated much public interest – even the *Tatler* (a society and
stage magazine) sent a photographer to cover it. The inspection by
the King was part of a wider test mobilization that had been mooted
much earlier in the year – ostensibly to save money by not having
the normal summer manoeuvres.[1]

As the mobilization exercise concluded, the international situation took a turn for the worse. On 26 July came the Serbian reply
to the Austrian ultimatum following the assassination of Archduke
Ferdinand. The First Sea Lord, Admiral Prince Louis of Battenberg,
was faced with the decision to allow the fleet currently assembled
to disperse and the reservists to be demobilized – risking a surprise
attack – or to order their continued service – effectively a mobilization. The First Lord of the Admiralty, Winston Churchill, was out of

London for the weekend, visiting his sick wife in Norfolk, and when contacted by telephone placed the decision in Battenberg's hands. Prince Louis decided to order the fleet to remain concentrated and the reservists be retained. The crisis worsened. Overnight on 29 July the First Fleet passed through the Straits of Dover en route to its war stations – the battleships to Scapa Flow and Cromarty Firth, the battlecruisers to Rosyth, with the Second Fleet concentrated at Portland. On 1 August the Admiralty's 'War Room' and its oceanic plots of all enemy vessels was activated. The chance of a surprise attack on the Royal Navy had passed.[2]

With naval mobilization under way, British attention quickly focused on the German ships that were at sea in the Mediterranean, the battlecruiser *Goeben* and the light cruiser *Breslau*. The Commander in Chief Mediterranean Fleet, Admiral Sir Archibald Berkley Milne, was not one of the Royal Navy's stars. With his fleet were three battlecruisers of the 2nd Battlecruiser Squadron, HMS *Inflexible*, HMS *Indefatigable* and HMS *Indomitable*, and a squadron of cruisers under the command of Rear Admiral Ernest Troubridge – a good leader but not a particularly creative thinker. Milne's fleet should have been able to deal with the German ships, yet they slipped away and into Turkish waters. The reason was straightforward: Milne had been ordered to give priority to safeguarding the move of French army units from North Africa to France, and only then to seek out and shadow the *Goeben* and *Breslau*. Furthermore, the Admiralty had ordered that Milne's ships were not to be brought to action by superior forces and to respect Italian neutrality, which prevented the British from following the Germans into Messina before the outbreak of hostilities.

Once the war between Germany and Britain had started at 11pm on 4 August, the bulk of Milne's forces lay in the central and western Mediterranean, as per Admiralty instructions. Only Troubridge's cruiser squadron lay to the east, blocking the entrance to the Adriatic. When the German ships left Messina and headed first south and then east, they were seen and shadowed by the light cruiser HMS *Gloucester*, which signalled Troubridge and Milne with updates of the Germans' position, course and speed. Troubridge, however, viewed his force as inferior to that of the *Goeben* and *Breslau* – probably rightly – and in view of the Admiralty instructions to avoid action with a superior force, broke off the pursuit. Before Milne could move his battlecruisers east the Germans had escaped to Turkish waters.

Troubridge's failure to seek an action was greeted with shock. The hunt for a scapegoat was on – Milne was relieved of his command and Troubridge was court martialled, but acquitted. Unsurprisingly Churchill was less than willing to publicize the Admiralty's part in the debacle. The escape of the *Goeben* and the subsequent Troubridge court martial left a bad taste in British mouths. It was down to the Grand Fleet to give the British the naval victory they so badly wanted.

The Grand Fleet

When the Royal Navy's ships in home waters reached their war stations and the fleet's reserves were mobilized, a new organization came into being – the Grand Fleet, formed of the Navy's most modern ships. Churchill, however, felt, with some justification, that its designated commander, Admiral Sir George Callaghan, was too old and that he should be replaced with the Second Sea Lord, Admiral Sir John Jellicoe. Despite Jellicoe's protests, the change of command took place and not only did the Navy have a new fleet to fight its longed for second Trafalgar, but a new admiral in command to take up the mantle of Nelson.[3]

The first British shot of the war may well have been fired by the Royal Navy, when the destroyers *Lance* and *Landrail* attacked the German minelayer *Konigin Luise* on 5 August. But unfortunately for the Navy and the British public, the expected clash of dreadnoughts in the southern North Sea on the outbreak of war did not occur. One reason why there had not been a decisive battle between the Grand Fleet and the German High Seas Fleet was the different strategic approaches of each side. The Germans expected the British to establish the traditional close blockade with cruisers backed up by battleships in the Heligoland Bight. The British, however, had no intention of doing so, preferring a policy of patrolling squadrons of destroyers and cruisers across a wide swathe of the central North Sea, as well as submarines closer to the German coast, with the Grand Fleet normally operating above 54°N, keeping the valuable dreadnoughts away from what they considered would be mine- and submarine-infested waters in the southern North Sea. Indeed during August 1914 the Grand Fleet stayed between 58°N (about level with Aberdeen) and 61°N (level with the northern tip of the Shetland Islands) except for an occasional sweep further south.[4]

Another reason for there not being a naval clash on the outbreak of war was that the Royal Navy had been tasked with getting the British Expeditionary Force safely to France. Between 9 and 23 August the Navy transported 80,000 infantry and 12,000 cavalry – four infantry divisions, a cavalry division and support troops – to France without a single loss. The close protection was provided by the pre-dreadnoughts formerly of the Second and Third Fleets of the Home Fleet, now titled the Channel Fleet, while to the north the Grand Fleet was ready to intercept any sortie by the Germans.[5]

Despite the move of the BEF to France it is clear that the Navy remained the Cabinet's weapon of choice in the war and it seems that the opening of a continental commitment was inadvertent. After all, national strategy was not – and is not – synonymous with whatever the army's general staff wants.[6]

The nub of the issue – that Britain did not actually need a second Trafalgar – rather escaped many observers, including Churchill. Geography and the Navy's distant blockade could, through economic pressure, starve Germany into submission. But this meant a long war that would definitely not be over by Christmas. The maritime economic war kicked off the day after the declaration of hostilities. Trading with Germany by British subjects was made a treasonable act. Ship owners were threatened with forfeiture if they carried contraband between foreign ports, and exporters were warned off selling contraband or war-like stores to any foreign buyers – even Allied powers. Patrolling cruisers in the western approaches and in the northern limits of the North Sea examined every neutral ship suspected of carrying contraband they could find. However, pressure soon mounted from within the Liberal party and from neutrals for the British to scale back the extent of the Admiralty's economic war against Germany. By the end of 1914 the Navy's plans to starve Germany through the control of merchant shipping had been supplanted by ineffectual diplomatic efforts by the Foreign Office to limit contraband entering Germany via neutrals; every effort made by the Navy to try to change the policy was ignored.[7]

Fisher's return as First Sea Lord in 1914 saw increased attempts to invigorate British economic warfare, but often plans fell foul of Churchill, who was very concerned about accusations that the Navy was doing nothing and that it needed to support the army more. He seemed unable to understand that through economic warfare the Navy was not only doing something but doing the one thing that was likely to force Germany out of the war. The tensions between Fisher and Churchill over strategy and economic warfare in the North Sea undoubtedly contributed to their breach over Churchill's Dardanelles adventure. Throughout 1915 increasingly loud voices from the Grand Fleet, from within the Admiralty, in the press and in parliament called for a tightening of the economic blockade, which in turn led to an increasing willingness to disregard neutral opinion. The creation of the Ministry of Blockade in February 1916 provided a means to tighten national economic warfare, of which the naval blockade and the command of the sea provided by the Royal Navy were the chief weapons.

Blockade work, however, was hard for the Navy. The Northern Patrol, blocking the entrances to the North Sea and by default the Baltic between Shetland and Norway, had perhaps the hardest task thanks to the combination of massive patrol areas and utterly vile weather, making the job exceedingly dangerous. In January 1915 the AMC *Viknor* struck a German mine and sank; there were no survivors. The next month the *Clan MacNaughton* capsized in a storm and in August the AMC *India* was torpedoed by a U-boat off Norway. But the blockade work and economic warfare were unglamorous and from the outset political and public attention was focused on the Grand Fleet.[8]

The first major sea battle occurred on 28 August 1914.

Fig. 2.1. The German light cruiser *Mainz* with two of her three funnels
blown away, sinking at the battle of Heligoland
Bight. Seen from HMS *Southampton*.

Submarines, cruisers and destroyers of the Harwich Force, which
was tasked with patrolling the southern North Sea, blocking the
exit into the Channel and defending East Anglia from attack, carried
out a raid on German warships in the Heligoland Bight. Admiral
David Beatty's battlecruiser force had been sent south to support
the operation, but while Commodore Reginald Tyrwhitt knew of
this, Commodore Roger Keyes (commanding the British submarines
during the battle) did not. Keyes' and Tyrwhitt's forces encountered
German cruisers and the day was saved only by Beatty's force charg-
ing in – apparently to the surprise and shock of both sides. Three
German cruisers and a destroyer were sunk, and the battle was
portrayed as a great victory. In reality it was not and did not deter
the German High Seas Fleet from devising an audacious attack on
the British mainland itself.[9]

At 07:00 on 3 November 1914 11-inch shells started falling
on Great Yarmouth's beach, fortunately doing little damage to

the town. At almost the same time, a patrol boat, HMS *Halcyon*, signalled by wireless that she was under attack by a superior enemy force. There had been no indications from the Admiralty's code-breaking organization, Room 40, that some sort of operation was in the offing as it was only just starting to break the German naval cyphers. As the reports from the *Halcyon* and other ships in the area started to come in, the Navy scrambled to respond, trying to get battlecruisers to intercept the retreating German force of three battlecruisers, the armoured cruiser *Blucher* and three light cruisers. Mines laid by the German ships sank the submarine *D5* as she and other submarines sailed from Great Yarmouth to attack the Germans. Time and distance were against the Grand Fleet, and the Germans were able to reach the safety of their defensive minefields in the Heligoland Bight.[10]

The following month the Germans struck again, bombarding Scarborough and Hartlepool. This time the whole High Seas Fleet was involved. The actual bombardment was carried out by the 1st Scouting Group – the German battlecruiser force commanded by Admiral Franz von Hipper – while the High Seas Fleet loitered out in the North Sea, hoping to ambush and destroy part of the Grand Fleet – most likely Beatty's battlecruisers – or lead them over a new minefield if they charged south to try to catch their German opposite numbers. Between about 08:00 and 09:15 on 16 December the German battlecruisers shelled Scarborough, Hartlepool and Whitby. Only Hartlepool had any form of defence – a battery of coastal defence guns – the other towns were undefended; 137 people were killed and nearly 600 wounded, mostly civilians, prompting outrage against both the Germans and the failure of the Royal Navy to defend British civilians. It was the sort of attack that Fisher's flotilla defence strategy was supposed to prevent, but the light cruiser and destroyer force that was needed to make it work had been sucked into the Grand Fleet. The forces that were available were not enough to do the job.[11]

The Royal Navy, thanks to Room 40's decryption of German wireless messages, had known that an operation was going to be mounted. As a result, both Beatty's battlecruisers and the Grand

Fleet's 2nd Battle Squadron of six dreadnoughts, which were the most powerful and fastest the Navy had, together with their cruiser and destroyer escorts, were at sea to intercept the German battle-cruisers. The British force, commanded by Vice Admiral Sir George Warrander, was to be off the south-east corner of Dogger Bank at dawn on 16 December so as to be between the German battle-cruisers and their base. However, the British did not know that the German High Seas Fleet was also at sea. It was exactly the situation the Germans had been hoping for: an opportunity to destroy part of the Grand Fleet, reducing the Royal Navy to effective parity with Germany and changing the strategic situation in one stroke.

But the battle was not what either side was expecting.

The British destroyers which had become separated from the main body during the night blundered into the German High Seas Fleet's escort screen before dawn on 16 December. A confused and vicious close-quarters fight between destroyers ensued in the dark-ness. The German commander, Admiral Friedrich von Ingenohl, thought he was facing the entire Grand Fleet and turned his force for home (leaving his own battlecruisers to look after themselves following their bombardment), losing his chance of destroying Beatty's battlecruisers or Warrander's dreadnoughts. When reports of the bombardment of Scarborough started filtering through to Beatty he took his battlecruisers back towards the British coast, followed a little later by Warrander's 2nd Battle Squadron. The two British forces were now separated but in a good position to catch the German battlecruisers as they withdrew. The southern tip of Beatty's light cruiser screen sighted a German light cruiser and destroyers and attacked them. A poorly worded signal from Beatty meant that his light cruisers broke off the engagement and the German battlecruisers slipped past unseen by either British force in the mist and rain that was blanketing the area.[12]

A signalling error was to cost Beatty a resounding victory the following month when on 24 January 1915 British and German battlecruisers clashed near Dogger Bank. Room 40 again gave warn-ing of the German plan and the Admiralty ordered Beatty to sail with all the available battlecruisers from Rosyth, together with

Commodore Tyrwhitt's Harwich Force, to intercept and destroy the German battlecruisers commanded by Admiral Hipper. The rest of the Grand Fleet was also ordered to sea by the Admiralty, but a delay in making the decision to alert Jellicoe at Scapa Flow meant that they could not reach the intercept point until sometime after Beatty. At 07:20, as dawn was breaking, one of Tyrwhitt's cruisers, the *Aurora*, sighted German ships and opened fire. The gun flashes attracted Beatty's battlecruisers and a chase developed. The British slowly overhauled the German force, opening fire after 09:00 at a range of 20,000 yards. When the Germans returned fire they concentrated on Beatty's flagship HMS *Lion*. At 10:18 *Lion* was hit by a shell that reduced her speed. A false report of a U-boat sighting caused the British to turn away briefly, and then the signalling error that was to cost the British their victory occurred.

HMS *Lion* was still dropping astern of the fight and Beatty ordered his ships back on to a north-easterly course to resume the chase, and exhorted his captains to attack the rear of the enemy. However, his flag lieutenant, who was responsible for translating Beatty's orders into intelligible signals, left the course north-east signal flying and the other ships read the signal as 'attack the rear of the enemy bearing north-east'. The only ship to the north-east was the German armoured cruiser *Blücher* which, badly damaged earlier in the battle, was limping away. The British ships pounced on her, delivering a heavy fire at close range until she sank. By the time Beatty transferred to a destroyer and regained control of his ships the other German battlecruisers were too far off. The Dogger Bank action was over. A German armoured cruiser (in fact the British had always classified it as a battlecruiser because it was so powerful) had been sunk, but it was not the victory it should have been. The British would not get another chance to attack the High Seas Fleet or its battlecruisers for over a year.[13]

The threat of underwater weapons – the submarine and the mine – were the chief constraints in British naval efforts to get at the Germans. Together these weapons made the Admiralty fear that shallow waters like the southern North Sea were too dangerous for major warships like the dreadnought battleships and battlecruisers.

Only the flotilla forces, the fast light cruisers and destroyers, could stand a chance of operating successfully in such areas and were indeed expendable.

While minesweeping was all very well when the position of a minefield was known, it was not much use when it was unknown. The waters around the United Kingdom and the North Sea were just too big to be swept regularly enough to ensure there were no mines posing a threat. Prior to the war mines had tended to be used defensively to protect harbours, estuaries and other points from attack. But World War I saw heavy use of offensive mining – the sowing of minefields in enemy waters to disrupt trade and sink both warships and merchant vessels. The British, however, were slow to embrace offensive minelaying, particularly because of a lack of suitable ships to lay the mines, partly through a lack of suitable mines and partly through a general reluctance to undertake such action. The first British offensive minefield in the Heligoland Bight was not laid until January 1915 with two other minefields being laid there in May.[14]

The Germans, however, were quick to make use of offensive minelaying from the outset of the war. Submarines, warships and converted auxiliaries were all used as minelayers. The liner *Berlin* was converted to an armed merchant cruiser and minelayer at the outbreak of the war and on 23 October 1914 laid 200 mines off Tory Island. Four days later the Grand Fleet's 2nd Battle Squadron, unaware of the minefield, sailed into it during training exercises. The battleship HMS *Audacious* hit a mine, and such were the Grand Fleet's jitters about submarine attack that it was feared that a U-boat, not a minefield, was responsible. Despite efforts to save the ship through counter-flooding to correct the list and to get it into harbour, first under her own steam and then by towing, the *Audacious* sank.

That very month the Navy received a suggestion about how ships could protect themselves against mines. Lieutenant Charles Dennistoun Burney put forward plans for 'paravanes' which would cut a mine's mooring rope, allowing it to float to the surface and be destroyed with gunfire before it could hit a ship. Mines, however,

Fig. 2.2. The battleship HMS *Audacious* sinking off Tory
Island after hitting a mine, 27 October 1914.

were not the only underwater weapon the Grand Fleet had to cope
with; there were also submarines.[15]

The submarine threat proved to be just as dangerous as pre-war
exercises and discussions suggested it might be. There were numerous submarine scares that plagued the Grand Fleet in its Scapa
Flow anchorage. Jellicoe was so worried about the lack of adequate
defences around his base that on 5 September 1914 he moved the
Grand Fleet to a temporary anchorage at Loch Ewe on the west
coast of Scotland which was far from German U-boats but also
from the High Seas Fleet if it left its German North Sea harbours.
The first warship to fall victim to the U-boats was the light cruiser
HMS *Pathfinder*. Hit by a single torpedo fired by *U-21*, *Pathfinder*
sank in four minutes in the freezing waters off St Abbs Head, ten
miles north of Berwick-on-Tweed; most of her crew were drowned.
Worse was to come.

On 22 September three obsolescent armoured cruisers, HMS
Aboukir, HMS *Hogue* and HMS *Cressy* of the 7th Cruiser Squadron,
were patrolling an area off the Dutch coast known as the Broad
Fourteens. The ships were about two miles apart in line abreast,
moving at a leisurely ten knots and not zigzagging. Just before

06:30 an explosion rocked the *Aboukir*, which capsized after about 25 minutes – it was thought at first that she had hit a mine. As the *Hogue* went to pick up the *Abourkir*'s survivors who were struggling in the water, she suffered two massive explosions and a submarine was seen to broach off her port quarter. The cause was now clear: submarines and torpedoes, not mines. As the *Hogue* quickly sank, the *Cressy*, which had also stopped to pick up survivors despite the obvious danger of torpedo attack, called for assistance on her radio. At almost the same time as the radio message was being transmitted, she was hit in quick succession by two torpedoes. Within 15 minutes the *Cressy* had capsized and sank, leaving thousands of men struggling in the water.

This was a terrible blow. Three armoured cruisers – albeit ones bordering on obsolescence and manned by reservists – had been sunk by a single equally obsolescent submarine, the *U-9*. The loss of life was massive: 1,459 men were killed out of 2,200 and it was this loss that was the real issue, not that of three old cruisers – trained men were in short supply. Three weeks later the *U-9* struck again, sinking the armoured cruiser *Hawke* with the loss of nearly all her crew off Aberdeen.

One of the main reasons why the loss of life was so heavy in these incidents was that there were not enough lifejackets for everyone on board. Pre-war policy had been to have one 'life-belt' for every ten crew up to a maximum of 40 lifejackets, but there had to be enough to equip two ships' cutter crews. The massive loss of life from the *Aboukir*, *Hogue*, and *Cressy* prompted a deluge of suggestions about the most suitable lifejackets, the effects of immersion in cold water and the value of things such as hammocks as floatation aids (the answer in this particular case was not much). Sir Alfred Yarrow, owner of Yarrow & Co, Ltd, one of the major suppliers of destroyers to the Royal Navy, even went as far as to donate 'Miranda' lifejackets to the crew of every British warship his company had constructed. However, improving a sailor's chance of survival once a ship had been sunk did not solve the submarine problem.[16]

The problem the Admiralty faced was threefold. First, how to find submarines. Despite having operated submarines for 14 years, by the autumn of 1914 the Royal Navy was no closer to finding a solution. Many of the solutions put forward by naval officers were strong on imagination but weak on the science required to achieve them.

Second, it had very limited experience of working with scientists – its recent experience of inventors such as Arthur Pollen was less than happy. However, during autumn 1914, a Commander Ryan, a retired officer and wireless genius who had been recalled to the Navy on the outbreak of war, was experimenting with the possibility of detecting the noise a submarine made. He persevered in the face of official indifference until early in 1915 when the Admiralty started to pay attention. Resources started to be made available to Ryan, and by December 1915 the Admiralty had established an underwater acoustics research centre at Hawkcraig, Scotland. Unfortunately Ryan's work and the work of civilian scientists at Hawkcraig and other rapidly established research bases would not bear fruit for many months.[17]

Third, having found a submarine, how could it be destroyed? At the start of the war and for many months afterwards there were only four choices, two of which relied on the submarine being on the surface – ramming it or attacking it with gunfire. A third option was to lay minefields that would either prevent a submarine gaining access to an area or destroy it if it tried. Such minefields, aided by nets that would indicate a submerged submarine's position to patrol boats or destroyers, was the basis of British and French attempts using the Dover Patrol to block the eastern entrance to the English Channel to German U-boats. Unfortunately the British mine until late in the war (when the Navy started making direct copies of captured German models) was highly unreliable. The fourth choice, the use of explosive sweeps towed behind a destroyer or trawler, was quite literally a hit-or-miss affair, since, without any means of locating a dived U-boat, getting the explosive sweep in the same bit of sea and at the same time as a U-boat was really down to luck. It is no surprise therefore that the Royal Navy had few successes against the submarine. Between August and December 1914 the Germans lost only five U-boats, two to ramming by warships and three to mines.

Table 2.1. German U-boat losses by cause, 4 August 1914–31 May 1916.

Rammed by warship	3
Gunfire/surface ship	8
Torpedoed by British submarine	3
Mines	7
Own forces	1
Accidental	3
Marine	3
Not known	3

The Navy therefore had to rely on passive defensive measures against the submarine. Speed was the best defence. The faster a warship went the harder it was to score a torpedo hit. Zigzagging regularly was also an effective measure, as frequent and irregular alterations of course would make an attack hard if not impossible. Unfortunately for the Navy it was not just its warships that were threatened by the submarine and the mine – Britain's merchant fleet, on which she relied for imports, exports and the war effort as a whole, was also at risk.

The Navy's battles in the air and on shore

In the mobile warfare that occurred in the late summer and early autumn of 1914, before the Allied and German lines stretched from the Swiss border to the North Sea coast, the Royal Naval Air Service (RNAS) entered the fray. With the dispatch of the Royal Flying Corps to France, the RNAS was made responsible for the air defence of Britain from 3 September 1914, mirroring the Navy's responsibility as the first and last line of home defence.

In addition to this vital role, the RNAS had been tasked with destroying German Zeppelins, which, although used initially as reconnaissance units for the High Seas Fleet, could be used to bomb Britain – a possibility which had caused a major panic in 1912. To get at the Zeppelin bases and factories in Germany the RNAS needed bases in Belgium. It was from these early bases near the Belgian coast that the RNAS began in September to use aircraft, improvised armoured cars and supporting Royal Marine light infantry in lorries to mount raids against German lines of communication as their Schlieffen Plan took them across south-east Belgium and deep into France. On 22 September the RNAS made an attempt on the Zeppelin sheds in Cologne and Düsseldorf. Bad weather over the target prevented the pair of aircraft attacking Cologne from finding their target, but in Düsseldorf one of the two attackers managed to find the Zeppelin shed through the clouds and dropped two 20lb bombs which either did not go off or missed the target. All four aircraft returned to the Antwerp area where an advanced refuelling base had been established. Another raid was mounted in early October as the Germans threatened the airstrip near Antwerp. The raid was a partial success. The solitary aircraft sent to bomb the Cologne Zeppelin shed failed to find it and bombed the railway station instead, causing little or no damage, but the aeroplane attacking the Düsseldorf shed not only found its target but also hit it, destroying Army Zeppelin Z IX, to the delight of the British press and public.[18]

With the fall of Antwerp the attention of the anti-Zeppelin campaign moved to airfields in eastern France which would allow aircraft to attack the Zeppelin works on the shores of Lake Constance on the Swiss/German border. The attack was unsuccessful and the Germans moved their factory to Potsdam, well out of attack range. The RNAS campaign against the Zeppelin then moved north and on to the sea. A plan was devised to use seaplanes, carried by ships to within range of the German North Sea coast, to attack the Zeppelin sheds at Cuxhaven on Christmas Day 1914. The raid was not a success. Few aircraft managed to take off from the sea and no damage was done to the Zeppelin base. On the other hand, it was an impressive statement of intent.[19]

Nor were operations to support the fleet forgotten: the liner *Campania* was converted to a seaplane carrier for the Grand Fleet, and the *Ark Royal* was dispatched to provide air support for the Dardanelles campaign. Far more significantly, in 1915 attention fixed on the use of aeroplanes to carry torpedoes to allow an attack on the German High Seas Fleet while it was in harbour, hinting at a solution to the Navy's age-old problem – what to do when an enemy refuses to come out and be beaten. However, there were problems to solve before such a raid could be mounted – aircraft reliability, range, and how to get enough aircraft to a flying-off point for an attack to be effective. Again this was an important statement of intent, as was the reaction to the escalation in submarine warfare. When the Germans started unrestricted submarine warfare, the RNAS force in Flanders attacked the U-boat base at Zeebrugge and anti-submarine patrols using airships, seaplanes and land planes were soon established. But without an effective weapon, aircraft were not yet submarine killers.

The possibility of using seapower to mount amphibious assaults in unexpected or vulnerable areas away from the battlefront was one that was attractive to both politicians and many naval officers. At the outbreak of war Churchill decreed that all surplus naval personnel not required for sea service, together with the Royal Marines, were to be formed into a Royal Naval Division. The division's first taste of battle was in October 1914 when it was rushed to defend Antwerp from German forces. On 2 October a crisis meeting in London between Lord Kitchener (War Office) and Churchill heard that the Belgians were planning to evacuate the post city of Antwerp at the head of the Scheldt estuary, which the Germans had been besieging since 28 September.

The loss of Antwerp and the Belgian coast along the Scheldt was seen as a matter of national importance for Britain, threatening the cross-Channel links further south and providing a launching point for an invasion if the Germans so desired. Indeed if they got as far as the Pas de Calais area German aircraft could attack Britain. The British government had been highly sensitive about who controlled the Low Countries since the time of William and Mary; Napoleon described the Scheldt as 'a pistol aimed at the heart of England'. The result was that Churchill himself went to Antwerp to be the Cabinet's man on the spot. It was also decided to send the Navy's Royal Marine Brigade, which arrived in Antwerp on 4 October, and,

at Churchill's express request, the 1st and 2nd Royal Naval Brigades
– reservists untrained in modern land war tactics. Churchill even
offered to take command of British forces in Antwerp, provoking
guffaws of laughter in Cabinet when his telegram was read out. The
presence of the Royal Naval Division prolonged the siege for seven
days, and on 10 October the city surrendered. The division's losses
were 1,500 men interned in Holland after crossing the border to
avoid surrendering and 1,000 missing. Churchill claimed that the
extra week gave the Allies time to prepare the area between Calais
and Dunkirk for defence.[20]

The Antwerp episode increased criticism of Churchill and the
Admiralty over the failure of force, the long-hoped-for second
Trafalgar battle with the Germans, the loss of the *Cressy*, *Hogue* and
Aboukir to a single German submarine in just over an hour, and the
depredations of the German surface raiders around the globe. The
blood price was the resignation of the First Sea Lord, Prince Louis
of Battenberg, on 28 October – something that also helped appease
the British public's rabid anti-German sentiment. Jackie Fisher,
called out of retirement, replaced him. But for the Royal Naval
Division, its war was over, at least until another Churchillian plan
was put into operation – the attack on the Dardanelles.[21]

There is a great deal of confusion over the Dardanelles debacle, because there were actually two different plans. The first plan
was for a naval 'demonstration' off the Dardanelles to cause Turkey
to transfer troops away from the Caucasus which would relieve
the pressure on Russia; it had the support of naval officers in the
Admiralty, from Lord Kitchener and the Cabinet. The idea was that
if opposition was greater than expected the British could withdraw
without loss of face, or ships or men. The other plan – Churchill's
– was to get a fleet to Constantinople and force Turkey out of the
war. Churchill wanted a massive naval attack on Turkey which his
advisers had said would be impossible to achieve without support
from land, but this had been specifically ruled out by the War
Office (Kitchener) and the Cabinet. To get his own way Churchill
prevented his naval advisors – Fisher and others– from speaking in
the Cabinet's War Council except to answer a direct question put

to them, and no such question came. Churchill was thus the only conduit for naval advice to get to the wider government. He also sent disingenuous messages to the commander of the Mediterranean Fleet, Vice Admiral Sackville Carden, which suggested that the orders had come from the Admiralty with the support of Fisher as First Sea Lord, when they did not. Churchill also ignored Carden's repeated requests for proper minesweepers to allow the battleships to get close enough to the forts to destroy them.[22]

On 28 January 1915 the naval demonstration was authorized, but Churchill ordered Carden to carry out the full-scale naval attack which went in on 19 February 1915. On 20 February Churchill made a major press announcement which, as well as giving away the objectives of the attack to the Germans and the Turks, also had the effect of ensuring that if the Cabinet ordered a disengagement, it could only do so while suffering a massive loss of prestige, as Britain's much vaunted navy would have been beaten by a third-rate *non-European* power. It made the continuation and escalation of the Dardanelles campaign a certainty.

The naval attack went badly. Although the outer forts did not present too much of a problem, this was not true of those in the narrows. Carden informed Churchill of the difficulties faced, indeed the impossibility of the task, information that did not reach the War Council. The forts and modern batteries guarding the narrows were protected by over 300 mines laid in lines across the Dardanelles. The Turkish guns were able to inflict massive damage on the former trawlers and their fisherman crews being used as minesweepers. This meant that the battleships could not get close enough to be sure of hitting the gun embrasures in the forts or the small field guns and howitzers the Turks also employed along the coast. Faced with Churchill's demands for results and the impossibility of achieving them Carden suffered a nervous breakdown and was replaced by his deputy, Rear Admiral John de Robeck, on 17 March. On 18 March the fleet made a full-scale attack. It was a disaster; two British pre-dreadnoughts, HMS *Ocean* and HMS *Irresistible*, and one French pre-dreadnought, the *Bouvert*, were sunk; the battlecruiser HMS *Inflexible* was severely damaged by a mine and had to be beached on the island of Tenedos. On 23 March de Robeck telegraphed the Admiralty that land forces were needed to clear the coast to allow the straits to be forced by the Navy. Now the Royal Naval Division's time had come.

The Royal Naval Division had not completed its concentration and refit at Blandford before it was moved to the Mediterranean to support operations in the Dardanelles, together with a number of British, French and Australian/New Zealand divisions. The landings on the Gallipoli peninsula started on 25 April, but the RND, despite its imagined role as an amphibious force, did not take part in the initial landings. Instead the division was employed piecemeal by the army as beach parties to support the army units making the main attack. Despite this, the division was involved in the thick of the fighting. At V Beach, Cape Helles, Sub-Lieutenant Arthur Tisdall, Anson Battalion, won the Victoria Cross for rescuing men under heavy fire – one of six Victoria Crosses awarded to naval personnel supporting the landings from the *River Clyde* steamer which had been deliberately run aground on V Beach with a load of infantry in its holds in the face of heavy machine-gun fire. The other VCs went to the *River Clyde*'s captain, Commander Edward Unwin, Midshipman George Drewry, Midshipman Wilfred Malleson, Able Seaman William Williams and Able Seaman George Samson.

Once the beachhead was established the RND moved into the line, but again was not employed as a whole division, battalions and brigades being used as supports for army units. It was in one such deployment at Anzac Cove, fighting alongside the Australian and New Zealand troops, that Lance Corporal Walter Parker, Royal Marines, Portsmouth RM Battalion, won a Victoria Cross for extreme courage when assisting the wounded and bringing up supplies. From mid-May the RND was concentrated on the Cape Helles front, and at the end of the month was joined by its last three battalions – Hawke, Benbow and Collingwood Battalions – which had arrived from the UK. The division then fought a bitter engagement at the third battle of Krithia.

The fighting at Gallipoli was by now that of trench warfare and the RND was involved in several attacks in June and July, until on 25 July the division, now down to about half its nominal strength owing to battle casualties and disease, was withdrawn. In June 1916, after discussions about its future, the RND moved to France to fight on the Western Front.

The Navy, however, continued to provide gunfire support for the army units and ensure the safety of supplies and the sea routes across the Mediterranean. More importantly British submarines were active, penetrating the straits and operating in the Sea of Marmara in an effort to cut off Turkish supplies (for more information see *A History of the Royal Navy: The Submarine* by Duncan Redford). This was not new. In December 1914 submarine *B-11* sank the Turkish battleship *Mesudiye*. Vice Admiral Carden, before his breakdown, had asked for modern *E* class submarines and these became available during the Dardanelles operations, with *E-14* carrying out the first patrol by an *E* class submarine. The commander of the second *E* class submarine to operate in the Dardanelles, Lieutenant Commander Martin Nasmith of *E-14*, was awarded the Victoria Cross after destroying or damaging 11 ships, including one alongside in Constantinople, which sparked panic in the area. Unfortunately Nasmith did not succeed in locating either the *Goeben* or the *Breslau*.

On 6 August the Navy landed army divisions at a fresh site at Suvla Bay in the hope that this would break the stalemate of the trenches at Cape Helles and Anzac. Unlike the oared cutters that had been used for the landings at Anzac and Cape Helles, the Suvla landings were made using a force of purpose-built armoured landing craft led by Commander Unwin, VC, of *River Clyde* fame. The landing was unopposed, but in what was one of the most inept displays of generalship, the army units failed to take advantage of this to get inland. The Turks rushed units to the area and succeeded in pinning the British in a shallow beachhead. With the generals out of ideas and the continuance of the campaign in doubt following the failure at Suvla, evacuation was only a matter of time. Anzac and Suvla were evacuated in December by the Royal Navy; Cape Helles followed in January. Despite the efforts of the enemy, the evacuation ironically was the greatest success of the campaign; the military and naval losses were minimal and the Turks were unable to interfere.

The campaign, however, cost Fisher and Churchill their jobs and brought down the Liberal government. With the failure of the naval attack and the start of the land campaign, Churchill demanded reinforcements from home waters to support the expanding operation. By mid-May 1915 Fisher, worried about the distorting impact the campaign was having, wished for limits on the numbers and types of ships sent as reinforcements to the Dardanelles and on 14 May, following a meeting of the War Council, a compromise was negotiated. The next morning Fisher found several minutes from Churchill waiting for him that demanded even more ships than had originally been envisaged and far in excess of the compromise they had reached the previous afternoon. It must have seemed to Fisher that Churchill would not accept any attempts to temper his policy towards the Dardanelles, and given Fisher's intense dislike of the way Churchill had, Fisher felt, exceeded his position as political head to interfere in operational matters, he resigned. Of course Fisher had threatened to resign before – by some counts this was his ninth such threat – but this time he meant it. On the morning of Saturday 15 May he left the Admiralty, dropping by to see Lloyd George in the Treasury to let him know what had happened. Fisher's resignation was greeted with widespread dismay as the news leaked out, but his failure to return to the Admiralty to take charge on 17 May when it seemed that a sortie by the High Seas Fleet was in the offing cost him much of his support. On 22 May, after receiving some impossible demands from Fisher in order for him to stay on as First Sea Lord, Asquith finally accepted his resignation.[23]

The Dardanelles failure, Fisher's resignation, the breaking news of a shell shortage for the army and the resulting need to form a coalition with the Conservatives in order to keep a stable majority made Churchill's future at the Admiralty a bleak one. The new coalition partners would not tolerate him in such an important role, especially as it seemed no one was able to control him. On 21 May 1915 Churchill accepted Asquith's decision that he too would have to go. Arthur Balfour, the Conservative leader, was appointed First Lord of the Admiralty, and Admiral Sir Henry Jackson First Sea Lord. Unfortunately this pairing of politician and professional, while very amiable, was far from dynamic; the lack of direction in the Admiralty would be a major bar to dealing effectively with the German attack on British trade.

The defence of trade and the economic war

The geographical position of Britain ensured there was a highly effective barrier to German efforts to destroy British overseas trade. Only by passing through the Straits of Dover in the south, or passing out of the top of the North Sea, round the far north of Scotland, then down the west coast of Scotland and then Ireland could German commerce raiders reach the mass of shipping that passed in and out of the south-western approaches to Britain. The Dover and English Channel passage was blockaded by the Royal Navy's local forces of the Nore Command, backed up by the pre-dreadnoughts of the Channel Fleet which were drawn from the older battleships of the first and second fleets. The route up the North Sea and then round the top of Scotland was almost as difficult, as it required a German raider to avoid the naval patrols in the southern and central areas of the North Sea and the Grand Fleet with its supporting cruisers based at Scapa Flow in the Orkneys which guarded the 200-mile gap between the tip of Scotland and Norway. The Royal Navy had, therefore, a built-in advantage over the Germans – provided that they kept a good watch on the northern and southern exits from the North Sea, and no German ships were already at sea on the outbreak of war.

Unfortunately for the British, not only were the *Goeben* and *Breslau* at large in the Mediterranean but there were also a number of other German warships at sea throughout the world. On the outbreak of the war the most significant German force was the ships of Admiral Maximilian von Spee's Pacific Squadron – the armoured cruisers *Scharnhorst* and *Gneisenau*, plus the light cruiser *Nurnberg* – in the Caroline Islands in the western Pacific. Additionally, the German light cruiser *Leipzig* was off the Mexican Pacific coast, the light cruiser *Emden* was patrolling off Japan, the light cruiser *Konigsberg* was at sea in the Indian Ocean and the light cruiser

Karlsruhe was at sea to the north of the Bahamas heading out into the Atlantic.

Finally, there was the longstanding British concern that the Germans would convert fast liners into commerce raiders at sea or in foreign ports. Certainly there were German liners scattered across the globe: the *Cap Trafalgar* at Montevideo, the *Kronprinz Wilhelm* off the US Atlantic coast, the *Prinz Eitel Friedrich* at Shanghai and finally the *Kaiser Wilhelm Der Grosse* at Bremerhaven. The *Cap Trafalgar* and the *Kronprinz Wilhelm* were both converted to commerce raiders while at sea shortly after war broke out, using weapons supplied by German warships and supply vessels that were already beyond the British blockade. The *Prinz Eitel Friedrich* was converted at the German base at Tsingtao, where she was soon joined by a Russian liner captured by the *Emden* which was then converted into a commerce raider, the *Cormoran*. Only the *Kaiser Wilhelm Der Grosse* had been converted in a German port just before the outbreak of the war and had to break through the British patrols across the top of the North Sea, which she did successfully during 4 and 5 August 1914.[24]

In all, these 11 commerce raiders destroyed or captured over 300,000 tons of British or Allied shipping. To catch them the British relied on a system of patrolling cruisers and auxiliary merchant cruisers (converted merchant ships – often the faster liners), but not convoy, using the ships of the Grand Fleet or those allocated to the Royal Navy's overseas command, supported in the Indian Ocean and Pacific by the ships of the Royal Australian Navy, the New Zealand naval forces and the Imperial Japanese Navy. The effort required was massive; by the end of August the Royal Navy had 12 cruisers and three auxiliary merchant cruisers searching the West Indies and South Atlantic, just to try to find the light cruiser *Karlsruhe*. More worryingly, shipping movements outside the North Atlantic and home waters had almost ceased by the end of August due to the fear caused by German surface raiders. Only the introduction of the British War Risks Insurance Scheme got trade moving again, but at a reduced level. The first British anti-raider success came on 26 August 1914 when HMS *Highflyer* surprised the

Kaiser Wilhelm Der Grosse while she was at anchor in the Azores and sank her. Just under three weeks later, on 14 September, the *Cap Trafalgar* was engaged and sunk by the British auxiliary merchant cruiser *Carmania* at the Brazilian Trinadade Islands around 500 miles out into the South Atlantic, where the Germans had established a secret supply anchorage. In the Indian Ocean the cruiser *Koenigsberg* was trapped in the Rufiji river. Then it was the Royal Australian Navy's turn: the cruiser HMAS *Sydney* caught the German light cruiser *Emden* at the Cocos Islands on 9 November 1914 and sank her after a brisk gun battle.[25]

The Admiralty's chief concern, however, was the powerful German Pacific Squadron commanded by Admiral von Spee, who had headed across the Pacific to attack British trade along the Chilean coast. To catch him, the Admiralty had sent Admiral Sir Christopher Cradock and a force of cruisers round Cape Horn into Chilean waters. Cradock's force of the armoured cruisers HMS *Good Hope* and HMS *Monmouth*, the light cruiser HMS *Glasgow* and the auxiliary merchant cruiser HMS *Otranto* was inferior in strength to the German force. Cradock protested that his force was weaker than Spee's but all he was sent was the elderly pre-dreadnought HMS *Canopus*. On 5 October an intercepted message from Spee allowed the Admiralty to inform Cradock that the German squadron was definitely heading for South America. On 22 October Cradock left his base at the Falklands and passed round Cape Horn into the Pacific.

It seems likely that the court martial of Rear Admiral Troubridge in September for his failure to attack the stronger German force of the *Goeben* and *Breslau* would have left little doubt in Cradock's mind what would happen to him if he continued questioning the Admiralty and failed to engage Spee's ships. Wireless intercepts by HMS *Glasgow* during 31 October suggested a German cruiser – probably the light cruiser *Leipzig* – was close by and the next day Craddock formed his force into a search line (except the *Canopus* which was to the south escorting Craddock's supply ships) and headed north to find the enemy.

At 16:30 on 1 November 1914 HMS *Glasgow* sighted the German ships and closed on Cradock's flagship, HMS *Good Hope*, and the rest of the force as quickly as possible. By 17:47 the British battle-line was ready. Cradock was between the Germans and the setting sun and he intended to quickly close the range and get to grips with the enemy to prevent the Germans' longer-ranged guns having too much effect. However, Spee's ships were faster as well as having better guns, so Spee was able to keep out of range of Cradock's ships until 19:00 when the sun had set and Cradock's advantage had gone. Now the British ships were silhouetted by the sun's afterglow while the German ships were hidden in the growing dusk. The result was a disaster for the British. The *Good Hope* and *Monmouth* were sunk, having received terrible punishment in the opening few minutes of the battle; there were no survivors. The *Glasgow* and *Otranto* fled in the darkness. It was a dreadful blow to the Navy and to its prestige at home and abroad.[26]

To avenge this disaster, the Admiralty – now with Fisher back at the helm as First Sea Lord – assembled a strong force of battlecruisers and armoured cruisers in the South Atlantic. Their commander was Admiral Sir Doveton Sturdee, who had been chief of the Admiralty's war staff and whom Fisher blamed for the Coronel debacle. Sturdee was also a strong supporter of Beresford, another reason for Fisher to get him as far from the Admiralty as possible. On 7 December Sturdee's force reached Port Stanley in the Falkland Islands and found the *Canopus*. The *Canopus* and the settlement at Port Stanley had been expecting an attack by Spee's cruisers since 25 November when they received word that the Germans had passed Cape Horn and entered the Atlantic. The arrival of Sturdee's powerful squadron of two battlecruisers and five cruisers was therefore very welcome. At 07:50 on 8 December 1914, as the British ships were filling their coal bunkers, a lookout post on a mountain overlooking Port Stanley reported two strange warships approaching from the south. Spee had arrived.

The shocked British force quickly raised steam and put to sea, although they were not as shocked as Spee, who found himself facing the battlecruisers *Invincible* and *Inflexible*, which he thought were in the Mediterranean. At Coronel the Germans had had the advantage of speed and longer-ranged guns. Now the British had an unassailable advantage; it was just the sort of battle that Fisher had designed his large armoured cruisers for. After a chase of nearly three hours the British opened fire on the rearmost German ship, the *Leipzig*. To give his light cruisers a chance to escape, Spee ordered *Scharnhorst* and *Gneisenau* to turn around and engage the British force. His plan was only partially successful as the British light cruisers chased after their German counterparts with almost no let-up, while the battlecruisers destroyed the *Scharnhorst* and *Gneisenau*. At 16:17, having been reduced to a blazing wreck, the *Scharnhorst* rolled over and sank; at around 17:45 the *Gneisenau* followed her. Of the three German light cruisers, only the *Dresden* got away; HMS *Kent* sunk the *Nurnberg* at 19:27, while the *Glasgow* and *Cornwall* disposed of the *Leipzig* at 20:35; HMS *Bristol* sank two out of the three colliers that were with the German force. The *Dresden*'s escape was not permanent; she was found at Juan Fernandez Island in March 1915 by HMS *Glasgow* and sunk.[27]

With the destruction of Spee's squadron British efforts to find the remaining commerce raiders continued, but it was the Royal Navy's coincidental seizures of German merchant ships which were supplying the raiders with coal that ensured their fate. The German merchant raiders *Prinz Eitel Friedrich*, *Kronprinz Wilhelm*, and the *Cormoran* had to seek refuge in US territory for want of coal in March, April and December 1915 respectively. Germany's last cruiser at large, the *Karlsruhe*, had been destroyed by an internal explosion on 4 November 1914, although the British remained ignorant of this for some time and continued extensive searches for her. The global surface raider threat to British and Allied trade was over – but not that of the submarine.[28]

During the opening months of the war much naval attention was understandably focused on dealing with the surface raider threat; during the first four months of the war 55 British, Allied and neutral merchant ships of 222,432 tons were sunk by German surface raiders compared to 42 ships (78,152 tons) sunk by mines and just three ships of 2,950 tons by submarine. However, as the Royal Navy eradicated the initial German surface threat, mines and submarines came

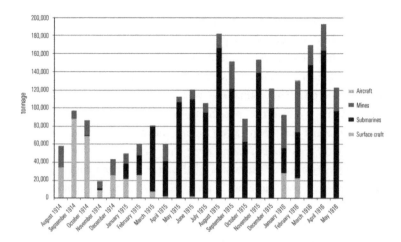

Fig. 2.3. British, Allied and neutral merchant vessels destroyed by enemy action, 4 August 1914–31 May 1916.[29]

to play an increasing role in the German attack on British trade. By the end of May 1916 mines had sunk 418,746 tons of British, Allied and neutral shipping while the U-boats had sunk 1,537,664 tons. Against mines, there was little more the British could do on top of their existing minesweeping efforts, except commission more mine-sweepers, but until the end of June 1916 the number of mines swept per ship sunk was largely unchanged at between 10.6 and 8.9 mines. Submarines, despite inconsequential successes against freighters during 1914, would rapidly become the most significant threat to merchant ships as well as warships.[30]

The reason for the U-boats' lack of success in 1914 was very simple – the Germans deliberately chose not to use them against merchant shipping, partly because of U-boat crews' feelings that such action was dishonourable, but also for fear of the reaction of neutrals – especially the USA – to their shipping being attacked as they traded with or near the Allies. However, by early 1915, the decision had been taken for a deliberate and determined subma-rine attack on any ship in a declared danger area – 'unrestricted' warfare. This meant that the pre-war Hague conventions, of the prize rules requiring ships to be stopped and searched before being either taken into a port as a prize or sunk having ensured the safety of crew and passengers, would be ignored.

The British considered that attacks on merchant ships – private property crewed by civilians – was an almost inconceivable level of brutality. When the possibility of submarines being used in such a manner had been raised before the war by people like Lord Fisher and Sir Arthur Conan Doyle they were shouted down. The British experience at the hands of the U-boats from mid-February 1915 onwards was therefore a profound and dreadful shock; many compared it to piracy.[31]

The outcome of the new German attitude to a commerce war was clear. In January 1915, before the start of the Germans' first unrestricted submarine campaign, U-boats sank seven merchant ships of 17,126 tons; in February – when the unrestricted campaign was declared – nine ships of 22,784. In March 1915, the first full month of the campaign, 23 merchantmen of 72,441 tons were sunk. The British countermeasures to this sudden and effective submarine attack met with mixed success. Minefields across the Straits of Dover proved to be less effective than the British imagined; nets to entangle a submarine also produced mixed results. Decoy ships – Q-ships – which were made to look like innocent and vulnerable merchant vessels while actually bristling with hidden guns scored some successes, but also made U-boats very wary of stopping and searching any vessels. The Auxiliary patrol which watched the British coast from converted yachts, trawlers and drifters worked even harder and more aggressively, but with limited impact on U-boat operations. However, a new anti-submarine weapon, the depth-charge, did complete its development and started entering service in small numbers, but still the problem of locating a dived U-boat remained.

It was the attitude of the USA that was the key to curtailing the German's first attempt to use U-boats to strangle Britain. The sinking of the Cunard liner *Lusitania* on 7 May 1915 by *U-20* produced violent diplomatic protests from America over the loss of 128 of its citizens among the 1,198 passengers and crew who drowned as

Fig. 2.4. An example of the British reaction to the German
unrestricted U-boat campaign: *Punch*, 7 April 1915.

the ship sank in 20 minutes. In August the liner *Arabic* was sunk by
U-24 off Ireland and three more Americans were among the dead.
This time the USA gave Germany an ultimatum as well as a protest.
The Germans ended their unrestricted campaign but allowed their
U-boats to continue operating against British and Allied shipping

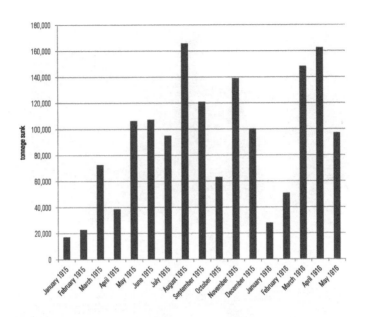

Fig. 2.5. British, Allied and neutral merchant ships sunk by U-boats,
January 1915–May 1916.

provided they tried to keep within the prize rules and avoided all
US ships and liners of any nationality. Only the small U-boats based
in the captured Belgian ports of Ostend, Zeebrugge and Bruges
continued to make war, if nominally within the rules, on Allied
supply lines. Many of the German U-boats – the *UC* type – were
switched to minelaying operations, while those allocated to the
High Seas Fleet went back to playing a subordinate role – to assist
with the plans to wear down the Grand Fleet, plans that would lead
to the greatest sea battle of the dreadnought age – Jutland.

CHAPTER 3

A Second Trafalgar?

Jutland and its Aftermath:
The War at Sea 1916–18

The clash of the dreadnoughts

Around 14:15 on 31 May 1916 a signal flashed out that the Battlecruiser Fleet had been waiting to hear for over a year (and longer for the Grand Fleet) – 'enemy in sight'. HMS *Galatea*, one of the Battlecruiser Fleet's reconnaissance screen, had spotted a small steamer to the east which was blowing off steam – a sign that it was stopped. Within seconds, the lookouts and officers on the bridge of the *Galatea* had seen that a two-funnelled ship was close by the stopped steamer. As the *Galatea* and her fellow light cruisers of the 1st Light Cruiser Squadron approached these strange ships to investigate, it became clear that they were cruisers.

As soon as Beatty, commanding the Battlecruiser Fleet (BCF), received the 'enemy in sight' signal he immediately turned his ships off their northerly course, which had been taking them towards a rendezvous with the rest of the Grand Fleet under Admiral Sir John Jellicoe some miles to the north, and headed south-east to cut off the escape of the enemy ships. Beatty's force was also accompanied by the seaplane carrier *Engadine* and there were frantic but successful efforts to get a seaplane into the air. Unfortunately for the British things now started to go wrong.

The signal to turn to the south-east was missed by the 5th Battle Squadron (5BS) which Beatty had stationed about five miles to his north-west. The 5BS was the most powerful unit in the Grand

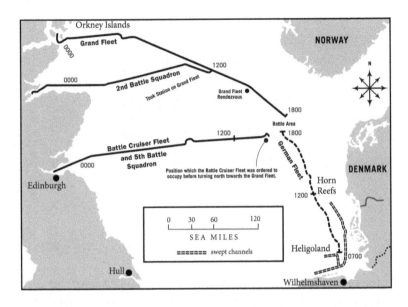

Fig. 3.1. The fleets' approach to Jutland. Thanks to the Admiralty's code breakers, the British put to sea hours before the Germans sailed.

Fleet, consisting of four of the five super-dreadnoughts of the *Queen Elizabeth* class – HMS *Barham*, HMS *Warspite*, HMS *Valiant* and HMS *Malaya*, all armed with eight 15-inch guns and with their oil-fired steam turbines, almost as fast as Beatty's coal powered battlecruisers. After much nagging 5BS had been lent to Beatty while one of his battlecruiser squadrons was away at Scapa Flow getting badly needed gunnery practice. But thanks to the missed signal 5BS was now heading in almost the opposite direction to Beatty's battlecruisers. By the time that the mistake was rectified, 5BS was about ten miles behind the BCF.

As *Barham* and the super-dreadnoughts of 5BS belatedly altered course to follow the BCF another signal was arcing across the wireless system: HMS *Galatea* had sighted a large amount of smoke to the north-east, in fact so much smoke that it could only be from an enemy fleet. The Germans had sailed. Of course the Admiralty, thanks to Room 40, knew the whole High Seas Fleet was going to mount an operation – it was why the Grand Fleet and BCF had been ordered to sea and to patrol the area of Jutland bank. But for the Grand Fleet and the BCF, as they sailed across a dull flat sea on the morning of 31 May, it seemed that this sortie was shaping up to be like so many sweeps of the North Sea before it – no sign of the enemy, no action and then back to base.

The indistinct shapes on the horizon soon solidified into the battlecruisers of Hipper's 1st Scouting Group, and it was the Germans who opened fire first at 15:45 as both sides charged south. The reason for the German course was simple – they were trying to draw the BCF onto the guns of the rest of the High Seas Fleet, while Beatty had the dual task of trying to destroy Hipper's force and tell Jellicoe the position of the German main fleet. Unfortunately for the British, the German gunnery was far more accurate than that of the BCF. In the first 12 minutes of the battle the BCF was hit by perhaps 15 heavy shells, the Germans by just four. Then at 16:00 Beatty's flagship, HMS *Lion*, was hit on Q turret. The shell penetrated the armoured roof of the turret and exploded, destroying the turret and sending flames lancing down towards the magazines, feeding on cordite charges waiting in the turret trunking to be fired and sending a plume of flames high into the air. Only the order to flood the magazines, apparently given by Major Francis Harvey of the Royal Marines as he was dying, stopped a catastrophic explosion that would have destroyed the ship, an act which saw him awarded a posthumous Victoria Cross. Minutes later several heavy shells hit HMS *Indefatigable* and after a delay of perhaps 30 seconds she blew up; there were just two survivors. However, 5BS had been slowly closing the gap and at 16:08 they were able to open fire on the rearmost German battlecruiser *Von Der Tann*. Soon the rearmost of Hipper's ships, *Von Der Tann* and *Moltke*, were being hit – and hit hard – by 15-inch salvos from the *Queen Elizabeth* class super-dreadnoughts. The battle continued for 24 minutes after the destruction of HMS *Indefatigable* when HMS *Queen Mary*, which had been targeted by the *Derfflinger* and the *Seydlitz*, seemed to be hit almost simultaneously by a large number of shells and she disintegrated. All Beatty could say was, 'There seems to be something wrong with our bloody ships today.'

Fig. 3.2. HMS *Queen Mary* exploding. HMS *Lion* is on the left
surrounded by shell splashes. Picture taken from HMS *Lydiard*.

At almost the same moment that the *Queen Mary* exploded,
Commodore William Goodenough's 2nd Light Cruiser Squadron,
which had been working hard to get back ahead of the BCF during
the opening stages of the battle, sighted numerous masts together
with a great deal of funnel smoke ahead. Minutes later at 16:47 he
was wirelessing that he had sighted the main enemy battlefleet.
Beatty had been drawn onto the guns of the High Seas Fleet by
Hipper, as the Germans had intended.

Beatty's reaction was to try and turn the tables on the Germans
by turning around and trying to lead them into the arms of the
Grand Fleet coming down from the north. But now a combination
of poor tactical decision making by Beatty and more poor signalling meant that as Beatty headed north he passed 5BS heading south,
and he allowed it to continue south for some time before ordering
a reverse of course to escape the trap. This made 5BS the centre
of attention for the Germans and it was deluged with shells, with
several of the super-dreadnoughts being hit as they turned around.
During the run north the BCF pulled out of range, but 5BS, further
behind, fought on alone against the combined German forces for at
least 30 minutes.

Jellicoe, away to the north and moving south to support Beatty, had been wondering where exactly the enemy was since the sighting reports at around 16:45. The position, course and speed of the enemy were vital information if the Grand Fleet was to deploy from its cruising formation to line-of-battle in the right direction and at the right time. Quite simply Beatty failed to ensure his commander in chief had good information about what was happening over the horizon and where the High Seas Fleet was going. The first indication as to the direction of the enemy came as Beatty's ships raced into sight at about 18:00. After some pointed signals, Beatty finally remembered what he was there for and sent a barely adequate indication of the enemy course and direction. But Jellicoe had already worked it out in his head and ordered the deployment of his fleet at 18:16 in the direction that would ensure Admiral Reinhard Scheer's High Seas Fleet had a very unpleasant shock.

As Beatty's and Jellicoe's forces met, the battlecruisers headed for the front of the British line, while 5BS, still some distance behind Beatty's ships, headed for the rear of the British battle-line. The mass of cruisers and destroyers manoeuvring to try and take their correct station as the Grand Fleet dreadnoughts turned into a single line of 24 ships, six miles long, across the path of the German Fleet caused a great deal of rapid course changes – with enemy shell fire adding to the excitement. For reasons best known to himself, Rear Admiral Sir Robert Arbuthnot, commanding four obsolescent, large armoured cruisers, moved with HMS *Defence* and HMS *Warrior* (the other two ships were unable to follow him because of the onrushing British fleet) into the gap between the opposing fleets to reach his allocated position rather than go behind the British fleet. His ships set upon a disabled German cruiser, *Wiesbaden*, just as Scheer's dreadnoughts and Hipper's battlecruisers loomed out of the murk. *Defence* exploded under the weight of heavy shell hits, and then *Warrior* was comprehensively wrecked by shell fire but managed to limp out of the way. *Warrior* was saved by the antics of HMS *Warspite* (5BS) whose steering gear chose this moment to jam and she steered two complete circles between the British fleet and enemy, the centre of attention for the entire High Seas Fleet, and suffered for it. By the time *Warspite*'s recalcitrant steering gear was brought to heel, she had been hit many times and, despite trying to remain in the battle-line, was too badly damaged, forcing her to retire from the battle.

At the head of the British line the 3rd Battlecruiser Squadron, which had positioned itself in front of Beatty's battlecruisers, was treated to the sight of Hipper's battlecruisers at a range of 9,000 yards and opened a heavy fire on them at about 18:21. The *Lutzow* and the *Derfflinger* were particularly heavily hit by the shell fire from HMS *Invincible*, HMS *Inflexible* and HMS *Indomitable*. But then the mists blocking the German view cleared and HMS *Invincible* felt the full weight of Hipper's ships' fire. Hit on her centre turret, the middle of the ship disintegrated, leaving the bow and astern jutting up from the seabed and six survivors out of a ship's company of 1,032 clinging to the wreckage.

As the Grand Fleet's dreadnoughts turned into line at one-minute intervals after Jellicoe's 18:16 order to deploy, they opened fire on the head of the approaching German line. The crescent of gun flashes across the horizon told Scheer exactly what he had blundered into – the very thing he had to avoid, the Grand Fleet. He then ordered a 'battle emergency turn away' which involved the rear ship turning first, then each successive ship turning once it saw the ships astern starting to turn. The result was that just as the Grand Fleet's gunners were getting into their stride, the German fleet seemed to disappear in the mist. By 18:45 the British guns were falling silent.

Once Scheer had made some distance to the south-west, he made the mistake of turning back in order to try and cut across the rear of the British. But all he succeeded in doing was to blunder into the middle of the Grand Fleet, which again poured fire onto him. A second, far more disorganized emergency turnaway occurred in the worsening visibility as the Germans desperately tried to escape. Hipper's battlecruisers were ordered at 19:14 to attack the head of the British line while the German destroyers launched a mass torpedo attack to cover the flight of the High Seas Fleet. The torpedo attack led to the Grand Fleet turning away to avoid the torpedoes running towards it, with the result that contact was lost with the German heavy units.

The Grand Fleet, after the torpedo attack, slowly edged south. The High Seas Fleet tried to avoid being pushed further west and came round towards the south-east. The visibility was very poor and the sun was setting so that there were sporadic outbreaks of gunfire as the opposition was glimpsed, but Jellicoe had no firm idea where the enemy fleet was or the course it was taking. In the darkness that followed, both fleets bumped against each other as the Germans tried to pass round the Grand Fleet and head back to base. Vicious fighting occurred between each side's flotilla forces; in the darkness the armoured cruiser HMS *Black Prince* blundered into the path of German battleships and was destroyed, leaving no survivors. The British, however, were not trained in night fighting, so the dreadnoughts did not force an action. By dawn the High Seas Fleet had escaped and was safe behind its defensive minefields.[1]

The aftermath

The Germans, having reached port first, claimed a victory and their propaganda machine went into overdrive with the neutral press. The British ships, getting back to base 24 hours and more after the Germans, were greeted with a degree of dismay that the Germans had not been utterly destroyed. Propaganda aside and despite their losses (which the British could afford) the failings the Royal Navy experienced with their shells, their command and control – especially the desire of senior officers to get to grips with the enemy without waiting for orders to do so – and their lack of training for night fighting, the British had managed to achieve a strategic victory as well as tactical win too – even if it was somewhat more of a pyrrhic victory than was comfortable. That the British were dissatisfied with the result of the battle does not mean that they lost.

The Germans had attempted to destroy a significant part of the Grand Fleet in isolation and had failed in their aim. They had not destroyed enough of the Grand Fleet to make British command of the sea untenable. The British economic blockade was still in place, as were the British Army's supply lines across the Channel to the

Western Front. In addition, the German fleet suffered proportionally more damage than the British. Indeed, apart from their propaganda victory, the Germans had very little to show for the battle and their fleet's morale had received a severe shock. Tactically the Germans were in much worse shape than the British during and after the battle. Their commander, Scheer, had made a number of potentially fatal errors which only British cack-handedness allowed him to get away with.

Table 3.1. Ships sunk or damaged (and suffering casualties to crew) as a result of the battle of Jutland.[2]

	British			German		
	Total present	Sunk	Damaged and suffering crew casualties	Total present	Sunk	Damaged and suffering crew casualties
Dreadnoughts	28	0	6	16	0	10
Pre-dreadnoughts	0	0	0	6	1	2
Battlecruisers	9	3	3	5	1	4
Armoured cruisers	8	3	0	0	0	0
Light cruisers	26	0	6	11	4	5
Destroyers	79	8	11	61	5	9

The battle and the Royal Navy's perceived failures were, however, to cast a long shadow throughout the reminder of the war and well into peacetime. Many of the more obvious defects at a tactical and materiel level were quickly addressed; others to do with the Navy's own corporate culture were harder to change. In particular the Navy was consumed with infighting between the supporters of Jellicoe and those of Beatty as to whose fault the Germans' escape was. In many respects apportioning blame is irrelevant. The chief failing – command and control – was caused by a corporate culture stretching back decades that stifled initiative and where obedience to orders was paramount. With regard to the loss of three battlecruisers, again much of the blame must be laid at the Navy's own confusion as to what fast armoured cruisers were actually for – either as trade defence or as a high-speed section of the battle-line. Also the poor magazine safety standards that were endemic within the BCF cannot escape some of the blame, and for that Beatty, who had tried to compensate for his force's reputation for poor gunnery by rapid firing and less attention of safety, must shoulder much of the responsibility.

Nor did Jutland mark the end of the Grand Fleet's efforts to bring the High Seas Fleet to battle, but all such efforts were ultimately unsuccessful, and after August 1916 the Germans showed increasing reluctance to risk meeting the Grand Fleet at sea. Indeed, after a sortie in October 1916, the High Seas Fleet did not put to sea again as a whole until April 1918. The result was months of boredom for the Grand Fleet and fruitless sweeps of the North Sea. Unlike the Germans, and possibly owing to the remoteness of the main fleet anchorage in Scapa Flow, the British put a great deal of effort into improving the recreational facilities – sports, regattas and concerts – available to its sailors. Finally on 12 April 1918 the Grand Fleet was concentrated at the Battle Cruiser Fleet's base at Rosyth, which, being on the opposite side of the Firth of Forth to Edinburgh, made leave taking and finding recreational pursuits much easier for those who had previously suffered the delights of Scapa Flow.[3]

The efforts to keep up morale in the Grand Fleet were generally successful and discipline was not a particular problem. However, dissatisfaction within the lower deck over issues like pay was on the rise. Indeed, the lower deck agitation for better pay and conditions had been given a boost by the recruitment of a large number of hostilities-only ratings who were used to trade union representation as part of their peacetime jobs. At the same time, there were increasing calls for the welfare societies to take a more active and collective role – essentially the unionization of the service. Understandably the officers took a very dim view of such agitation and successfully resisted such calls, but with varying degrees of understanding depending on the officer, especially after the revolutions in Russia during 1917 and 1918, with the Labour movement and 'socialism' cast as the villain. It is hard not to see the Navy being appalled by the prospect that the level of industrial unrest and days lost to strikes in the UK during the later stages of the war could be visited on their service. While the total days lost per year during the war were lower than the pre-war period, this has to be seen in the context that Britain was at war. Given the events of 1917, the massive jump in industrial disputes in 1917 compared to 1916 must have been alarming – almost twice as many days were lost to disputes in 1917 than 1916; in 1918 the number was slightly higher.

The pressure on the Navy for improved conditions did, however, bear fruit, despite the resistance to the more radical demands: pay was increased in 1917. Fortunately the calls from some senior officers to repress the lower deck societies were not heeded and the concessions over pay, plus the fact that the Navy had a strong system to deal with grievances as well as seeing to the welfare of its sailors, took the heat out of the agitations.[4]

One issue that affected the Navy after Jutland, and which contributed to a significant social change, was the manpower shortage. The scarcity of males of military age meant that women had to be used on a wide range of tasks. The Navy, like the army and later the RAF, formed a women's service to manage their activities – the Women's Royal Naval Service or WRNS. The widespread use of female labour, especially in industry and the production of munitions, as well as the use of women in the armed forces, undoubtedly contributed to the 1918 decision to extend the vote to women over the age of 30.[5]

What a state or a navy does with its seapower is the important issue. The German High Seas Fleet was impotent – or should have been if flotilla defence had been properly implemented – and remained impotent after Jutland. However, the British had been unable to wean themselves off the image of the battleship and then the dreadnought as being the sole arbiter of seapower, with the result that they wanted a second Trafalgar, even if strategically one was perhaps not necessary to neutralize German naval power in the North Sea. For both sides, Jutland signalled a change in the war at sea.

The economic blockade – starving Germany

The most significant impact of the battle of Jutland was that the British economic blockade of Germany could continue unchallenged. While the blockade in the early years of the war had not been enforced as rigorously as the Admiralty wanted, by the end of 1916 it had become much tighter. However, the Germans could and did receive goods and foodstuffs via neighbouring neutral states, but thanks to the efforts of the Ministry of Blockade, diplomatic pressure had ramped up against neutral trading with Germany.

An area that remained an almost constant concern was Germany's ability to import iron ore from Sweden across the Baltic and avoid Britain's economic blockade. By the end of 1915 the British had succeeded in getting five *E* class submarines past the defences of the Skagerrak, Kattegat and the Sound and into the Baltic. Originally the first two boats, *E-1* and *E-9*, were to target any units of the High Seas Fleet found operating in the Baltic and the German naval sea training organization. However, attention was soon turned to the Swedish iron-ore trade. Later *E-8*, *E-18* and *E-19* all passed successfully into the Baltic and made a series of successful attacks against iron-ore ships in 1915, but it is worth noting that the British submarines continued to operate within the prize rules even after the German use of unrestricted submarine warfare. Unfortunately German measures in 1916 and 1917 to combat the submarine threat in the Baltic, together with deterring a German assault on Riga – a priority for British submarines – saw a falling off in the attempts to interdict the iron-ore trade. However, as the route through the Kattegat into the Baltic was now effectively closed by German and neutral navies, there was an imaginative scheme to tow four *C* class submarines to Archangel and then by barge along rivers, canals and lakes to the Baltic in a 17-day journey. It took time to ready the *C* class submarines, not least because the batteries, which had been shipped separately, were found to be very badly damaged in transit and only *C-32* and *C-35* managed short patrols before the winter ice brought operations to a halt. When the ice melted in 1917 the British submarines were again directed against German moves along the coast, not against the iron-ore trade. With the Russian capitulation after the March revolution in 1918, the decision was made to destroy the *C* class submarines rather than surrender them to the Germans, while the *E* class boats were to try to escape out of the Baltic using Swedish waters, or intern themselves in Sweden if this proved impossible. The attempt to blockade Germany in the Baltic was finally over.[6]

Table 3.2. German imports of foodstuffs (in thousands of tonnes).[7]

		Average net imports 1912–13	Imported 1917	% decrease
Breads/cereals		5538	17.6	99.7
Animal fats		161.6	5.2	96.7
Fish		361.3	161	55.4
Eggs		169	40	76.3
Leguminous vegetables		310.8	1.7	99.5
Fruits		850	220	74.1
Vegetable fats & oils		155.3	Not given	
Oilseeds		1595.4	17.1	98.9
Cattle foods	- oilseeds	1571.9	14.8	99.1
(not including pig fodders	- ban	1744.9	10.2	99.4
like maize)	- oilcake	532.5	2	99.6
	- other	359.2	18.6	94.8

The increasing effectiveness of the blockade, both through diplomatic measures and continuing navy patrols as well as the day-to-day interception of neutral vessels to ensure that they were not carrying contraband, meant that in the winter of 1916–17 Germany experienced real food shortages. Before the war the average calorie intake per person per day in Germany was 3,215; by autumn 1916 it had fallen to 1,344 before rising very slightly in November to 1,431 calories when an average working man would need about

2,500 to remain healthy and those involved in heavy manual labour might need up to 4,000. Around 763,000 people died prematurely in Germany as a result of the economic blockade.

The shortage of fertilizers and fodders which had been previously imported and were now covered by the blockade only made the German situation worse. The Germans had also experienced poor weather and a poor harvest during 1916, which was exacerbated by a lack of agricultural labour. Indeed the restrictions on fertilizers would continue to compound German woes; the crops of wheat, oats and potatoes in 1918–19 were only half what they had been in 1912–13. The successful British efforts to starve the enemy out of the war encouraged the Germans to revisit a mode of warfare that neutral pressure earlier in the conflict had forced them to abandon – unrestricted submarine warfare.

The economic blockade – starving Britain

If Jutland ended German enthusiasm for ambushing parts of the Grand Fleet, it did not end their attempts to impose an economic blockade on Britain. Despite the destruction or internment of the first wave of German surface raiders during 1914 and early 1915, a new wave of disguised merchant raiders sortied in 1916. Two raiders were sunk trying to break out of the North Sea. The *Greif* was engaged on 29 February 1916 by the AMC HMS *Alcantara*; both ships subsequently sank as a result of the damage they had received, while the *Leopard* was sunk by the cruiser HMS *Achilles* on 16 March 1917. On the other hand, the *Moewe*, *Wolf* and *Seeadler* all operated successfully against Allied shipping during 1916 and 1917 (the *Moewe* making two cruises) and only the *Seeadler* was lost, wrecked on a reef in French Polynesia. The *Moewe* and *Wolf* returned safely to Germany. However, the main threat to Allied shipping was not from surface raiders or mines in the months after Jutland – it was the submarine.

Despite the German move back to restricted submarine warfare, Allied losses rapidly increased after June 1916. In October (the worst month of 1916) 314,239 tons of shipping was lost to U-boats;

from September to the end of the year over 200,000 tons of shipping was sunk by enemy submarines per month. Worse still was the lack of success of anti-submarine measures. From 1 June to the end of 1916 only 15 U-boats (in all theatres) were sunk by Allied countermeasures, of which mines were the most effective. British submarines were almost as effective as surface ships, sinking two U-boats, while surface ships sank two with depth-charges and one was sunk by a Q-ship. It was obvious that the Royal Navy had not managed to find a solution to the submarine problem, and the established countermeasures – patrolling shipping routes and focal points, diverting shipping, laying minefields, giving merchant ships defensive guns, deploying Q-ships and the Dover barrage with its nets, mines and surface patrols – were not coping with German submarines.

The submarine threat was vexing the Grand Fleet too. After the failure of the Grand Fleet to bring Scheer's force to action at the cost of two cruisers sunk by U-boats – thanks to Scheer chasing erroneous reports of the BCF – when the High Seas Fleet sortied on 19 August 1916 it was decided that the Grand Fleet would not come south of 55°30'N (roughly midway between the Tyne and Berwick on Tweed) or east of 4°E unless there were exceptional circumstances, a decision approved by the Admiralty in September. In October 1916 Jellicoe as commander in chief of the Grand Fleet told the First Lord of the Admiralty, Arthur Balfour, and the First Sea Lord, Henry Jackson, that 'the very serious and ever-increasing menace of the enemy's submarine attack on trade is by far the most pressing question at the present time'. A few days later, Jellicoe was mooting the possibility that 'we are risking all the advantages we may gain by successes on shore if we are forced to conclude peace because we cannot feed the country'.[8]

The inability of the Jackson–Balfour administration to get on top of the submarine menace was one of the chief reasons for their removal – Jackson, worn out by over work and unable to delegate effectively, in November; Balfour in December. The other chief reason for the loss of confidence was the repeated German destroyer raids on the Dover barrage, despite Balfour's promises that after the raid in October 1916 any subsequent incursion would be severely

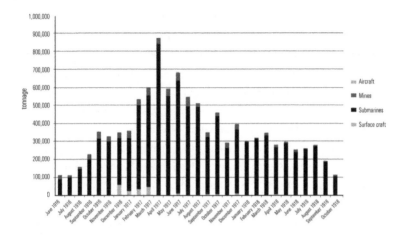

Fig. 3.3. British, Allied and neutral merchant vessels destroyed
by enemy action, 1 June 1916–31 October 1918.[9]

dealt with by the Navy. That the Germans raided the Dover barrage
and its patrols the next month, suffering no damage in return,
was a severe blow to confidence in Balfour. It was hoped that their
replacements, Jellicoe as First Sea Lord (Beatty got the command he
had lusted after – the Grand Fleet) and Sir Edward Carson as First
Lord of the Admiralty, would be able to get a grip on the submarine
problem. And there was hope for improvement: hydrophones were
getting better, giving a means of locating (eventually) a submerged
U-boat, and the entry into service of depth-charges gave warships a
more effective weapon against a dived submarine than bludgeoning
it to death with their bows.

Since Jutland, however, the Germans had been discussing how
to prosecute the war against Britain and had come to the conclusion that their only hope lay in resuming unrestricted submarine
warfare. This they did on 1 February 1917 and the results were
dreadful for the British. In February 1917 464,599 tons of Allied
shipping was sunk by U-boats and by the end of April the monthly
tonnage lost had risen to a horrifying 834,549 tons; for the rest
of the year the monthly tonnage lost never fell below 300,000.
As Allied shipping was massacred between February and April, it

seemed to Jellicoe and others that Britain would be starved out of the war. Certainly Jellicoe, exhausted after years of shouldering the burden of command of the Grand Fleet, was extremely pessimistic about Britain's ability to continue the war into 1918 unless a solution was found. On the other hand, American outrage over the German resumption of unrestricted submarine warfare contributed to their decision to join the war on the Allies' side at the start of April 1917.

One aspect of the problem that particularly exercised the Admiralty was the German use of Ostend, Zeebrugge and the inland port of Bruges, which was connected to Zeebrugge and Ostend by ship canals, as a base for U-boats preying on Allied shipping in the North Sea, English Channel and the western approaches, as well as the destroyer flotillas that had been making such a nuisance of themselves raiding the Dover barrage and patrols.

Fortunately – at least as far as the Dover Patrol was concerned – the German destroyers based at Zeebrugge–Ostend–Bruges were taken out of the equation on 21–21 April 1917 when a German destroyer raid literally ran into HMS *Broke*. *Broke* and her counterpart HMS *Swift* were patrolling the barrage overnight on 20–21 April, with *Swift* in the lead. At about 00:45 both ships sighted a line of five or six enemy destroyers. Both opened fire on the enemy and *Swift* attempted to ram one of the German ships but missed and in so doing passed through the line of German destroyers under heavy fire. As she did so, her own gunfire did serious damage and she managed to launch a torpedo which appeared to hit one of the German destroyers; the *Swift* then chased after another destroyer. *Broke* also decided to ram yet another German destroyer and did so most successfully. In fact the *Broke* was a little too successful: German crewmen clambered from their badly damaged ship, *G42*, onto the *Broke* where a hand-to-hand fight started, with the *Broke*'s crew using cutlasses, rifles and bayonets to repel borders. The German destroyer sank by the stern as the *Broke* slowly drove her under, but unfortunately *Broke* had been hit hard by German gunfire and was burning, with all but one of her guns out of action. When the *Broke* and *Swift* were reunited about 30 minutes after the start of the fighting, they closed on a stationary burning German destroyer

(*G85*) which, having fired on them again, was sunk by torpedo and gunfire. The Germans did not dare launch another destroyer raid on the Dover barrage for nearly a year; instead they contented themselves with operations against the French coast around Dunkirk.[10]

Despite the bloody nose given to Germany's Zeebrugge destroyer force, the U-boat problem was still not resolved. A definite step in the right direction had been taken when, shortly after becoming First Sea Lord, Jellicoe formed an Anti-Submarine Division within the Naval Staff to generate and coordinate anti-U-boat plans which previously had been run by several different staff divisions. It allowed for the first time concentrated and deliberate thought on how to beat the U-boat. However, many of the suggestions – such as using sound impulses through the water, first achieved against a British submarine in Harwich harbour in the spring of 1918 and not perfected until after the end of the war – would take a great deal of time to develop. Anti-submarine warfare was very much a matter of a large number of cumulative measures in the Admiralty view.

With the unbelievable shipping losses after February 1917 and Jellicoe's deep pessimism that a solution could not be found, it was clear that something completely different would have to be tried. However, questions were being asked as to whether Jellicoe was the man to lead the Navy in view of his gloomy outlook during the spring and his clear exhaustion from overwork. The First Lord, Carson, was replaced by Sir Eric Geddes in July 1917 in order to liven up the Admiralty, but in the end Geddes decided that Jellicoe had to go and he was sacked in a most shameful way on Christmas Eve 1917, to be replaced by Admiral Sir Rosslyn Wemyss.[11]

One solution to the U-boat problem was to try convoy – something the Navy and ship owners had been saying for decades was unfeasible as a trade defence measure. Another possibility was to do something about the U-boat and destroyer bases in Flanders – Ostend, Zeebrugge and Bruges.

Convoy had been suggested as a solution – or at least part of the solution – to the U-boat problem in October 1916 by the 10th Cruiser Squadron engaged on the northern patrol and by numerous officers in the Grand Fleet in November 1916 when they were asked for ideas; yet at a meeting between the naval staff and ship owners in late February 1917 the notion was dismissed. The Admiralty had numerous objections: that they did not have enough ships to act as escorts, that there was little experience of convoy work – overlooking the fact that they had years of experience of ships sailing in close company with an escort (they just called it the Grand Fleet) – and that there were too many merchant ships to convoy, an idea which analysis in the Admiralty soon proved to be incorrect. But despite its opposition to convoy, the Admiralty had already introduced convoy for the UK–Holland trade route in July 1916 and only three ships had been sunk. Also, the French were so worried about their coal imports from Britain that in December they had sent a naval officer to set up a system of convoy in conjunction with the Admiralty. The first convoys from this scheme sailed on 6 February 1917, it having been decided in January that the convoys were not to be called convoys in case it provoked the Germans to attack the neutral vessels that made up about half the vessels engaged in the trade; instead the convoys were called 'controlled sailings'. That these controlled sailings began after the Germans had already resumed unrestricted submarine warfare at the start of February seems to have been overlooked by the Admiralty. Perhaps the most significant reason why convoy was not tried earlier was that it was perceived as being defensive: the Navy would have to wait for U-boats to come to the convoy rather than seeking out and destroying them through offensive action (patrols) in a most dashing and satisfying manner.

Finally, on 21 April 1917, a trial of convoy between the Humber and Norway via Lerwick in the Shetlands was agreed. Much of the delay over introducing convoy was because the Admiralty feared it did not have the ships to provide escorts and still carry out offensive patrols, when in fact the patrols were effectively irrelevant to the problem. But the entry of the USA into the war meant that escorts were no longer in quite such short supply – US Navy destroyers could now be used to help provide escorts. Once convoy started its slow introduction the Admiralty found it did not need as many escorts as it imagined and that the issue was really one of using resources effectively (or not) rather than having insufficient resources. Far more important was the realization that the actual number of ocean-going merchant ships that would need to be convoyed each week was not over 2,000 but a far more manageable 120–140. During April the Admiralty was slowly coming round to the idea of a convoy system. On 26 April Rear Admiral Alexander Duff, the director of the Anti-Submarine Division, produced a plan for introducing ocean convoys. Jellicoe approved the plan the next day and the orders to start a convoy from Gibraltar went out almost immediately. Convoy was thus already part of the Navy's arsenal against the U-boat when, three days later, Lloyd George visited the Admiralty and claimed to have forced a hidebound navy to embark on convoying against its wishes. Nothing could have been further from the truth.

Convoy did not, however, end the losses. Indeed shipping losses only fell slowly for the rest of the year as more trade routes were run on the basis of convoys. But the convoy did help solve one problem: where to find U-boats. In order to sink convoyed merchant ships, U-boats had to be within torpedo range. The Allies could now reduce their search areas from millions of square miles to just a few around each convoy. Instead of being defensive, as had been alleged by many officers since 1870, convoys were actually the basis for anti-submarine forces to take the offensive against the U-boats on a ground of their choosing. Escorts, despite not having an effective means of detecting submerged U-boats with enough accuracy to make an attack, found that it was now much easier to find and attack them; aircraft too were more effective and able to concentrate on where U-boats *had* to be if they wanted to sink a merchant ship rather than where they might be.

The other possibility, that of doing something about the U-boat and destroyer bases at Ostend, Zeebrugge and Bruges, was also given much thought by the Navy. The desire to close these ports led directly to the decision to mount an operation to block the harbour mouths by sinking old ships which would also mean that the canals to Bruges would be closed. The attack went in on 22–23 April 1918 – St George's Day – and was led by the new commander of the Dover Patrol, Admiral Roger Keyes. Both Zeebrugge and Ostend

Fig. 3.4. The block ships for the Zeebrugge raid. Bottom: HMS *Intrepid*;
middle: HMS *Iphigenia*; top: HMS *Thetis*. The entrance to
the canal was only partially blocked at Zeebrugge.

had to be blocked if the Germans were to be trapped in Bruges,
otherwise they could use the canal network to escape through
whichever port remained open. Despite heroic bravery by the landing parties from HMS *Vindictive*, which placed itself alongside the
mole, they were not able to silence gun batteries in the harbours
with the result that the blockships came under heavy fire and were
not able to sink themselves in the correct positions. Thus the raid
was only a partial success, while the attack on Ostend was a failure.
The attack, however, was a major fillip to British morale, coming as
it did at a time when the British army was reeling under a series of
attacks from the Germans that wiped out all the Allied territorial
gains of 1917 *and* 1916 on the Western Front.

The other way of doing something about Ostend, Zeebrugge and
Bruges and the U-boats based there was to clear the Germans physically from the Belgian coast. From the middle of 1916 the Admiralty
was asking the army to do just that. By 1917, with the shipping situation deteriorating, calls for the army to launch an attack increased.

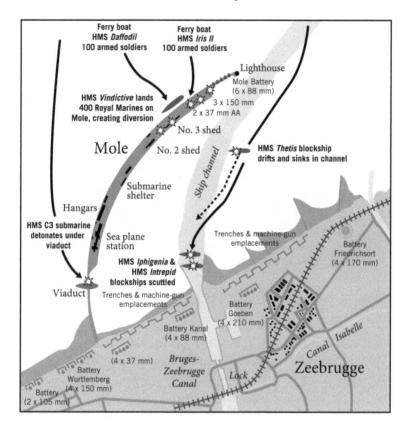

Fig. 3.5. The attack on Zeebrugge, 23 April 1918.

Fortunately for the Navy, the army was already looking at plans to make the Belgian coat untenable for the Germans with an attack out of the salient at Ypres in 1917 – the third battle of Ypres, or Passchendaele.

The Navy and the Western Front

On 26 October 1917, in the final phase of the third battle of Ypres, the Royal Naval Division (RND) attacked in support of the Canadian Corps' efforts to capture the wrecked village of Passchendaele. The weather had broken, the battlefield was a morass – the drainage systems had broken down under the weight of shell fire in the Ypres

Fig. 3.6. HMS *Vindictive* seen after the raid on Zeebrugge. The mass of
mangled metal in the centre of the ship was the special gangways
that were built to allow her landing force to get onto the
mole and attack German guns.

salient and the water could not drain away quickly from the low-
lying areas that formed the British lines. The conditions were atro-
cious and very few gains were made in the initial attack and in the
next assault on 30 October. A change of tactics and the use of night
attacks to prevent the German pillboxes providing mutual support
during assaults ensured that all the objectives were gained over the
next four days with very little loss. On 5 November the RND was
pulled out of the line and when the Canadians finally slithered over
the last few yards of mud to capture and hold Passchendaele village
and its ridge on 10 November, the battle was shut down.

There was another naval dimension to Passchendaele. If the
attacks from July onwards had been as successful as had been
planned and reached the key railway junction of Roulers, it was
intended to launch an amphibious assault on the Belgian coast in the
vicinity of Middelkerke as part of an assault along the coast from the

Allied positions on the River Yser north of Ypres. Admiral Reginald Bacon, commanding the Dover Patrol, provided much of the planning and in the end it was envisaged that the landing would be made by a division supported by tanks. Great efforts were put into developing suitable landing craft that could land the assaulting tanks and infantry quickly, including the development of specialized equipment to allow the British armour to climb over the sea wall – shades of the methods used on D-Day in 1944! The landing was planned for 8 August but was postponed until 6 September, as the initial 5th Army attack at Ypres made very little headway. In fact it seems that the need to conform to the conditions for the landing contributed to General Hubert Gough's 5th Army rushing its preparations to renew their attacks. The plan for the landing and advance along the coast kept being deferred as the 5th and then from 25 August the 2nd Army attacks failed to break though the German position and reach Roulers. Finally on 21 October the division which had been specially trained for the amphibious attack left its camp and the plan was abandoned. However, the unit in question was the 1st Division, not as might have been expected the RND which had been formed back in 1914 for just this sort of operation.[12]

After withdrawal from Gallipoli and refitting in Britain, the RND had been moved to France to fight on the Western Front in June 1916. Now the division was up to full strength with three brigades (including an army one) and for the first time its own supporting chorus of artillery, engineers, logistics units and the like – just like any other division. It even got a number to go with its name – the 63rd – and on 19 June 1916 it came under full army operational control while still being owned by the Admiralty.

After training and experience in quiet sectors, the RND's first engagement as a complete division on the Western Front was in the battle of the Ancre (13–19 November 1916), the final battle of the Somme campaign. The battle was fought on exactly the same ground that the British had failed to capture on the very first day of the battle of the Somme, but this time the attack was a success and the extremely strong German position was captured. The RND on the right of the attack fought very well despite heavy casualties, and Lieutenant Colonel Bernard Freyberg was awarded a Victoria Cross for his gallantry and leadership.[13]

The battle of the Somme also saw the first use of a new land weapon that the Navy, especially the Royal Naval Air Service (RNAS), could claim credit for – the tank. The RNAS had developed armoured cars when involved around the fighting for Antwerp in 1914 and had been using them in a variety of other theatres subsequently, such as the Middle-East. With the development of trench warfare and the RNAS expertise in armoured cars, it seems that Churchill decided to explore ways of making all-terrain armoured vehicles overcome the shortcomings of wheeled armoured cars. As a result, in February 1915 the Admiralty convened a 'landships' committee to investigate proposals at around the same time that Major Ernest Swinton was trying (and failing) to interest the War Office in a similar idea. In June 1915 the landships committee was reformed as a joint Admiralty and War Office venture following some very pointed criticism of the War Office by the commander in chief of the British Expeditionary Force in France. Indeed Arthur Balfour, as First Lord of the Admiralty, so distrusted the attitude of the War Office to tank development that he ensured that the Admiralty retained one armoured car squadron for experimental work after it had been decided that all others should be transferred to the army. By early 1916 prototypes were being demonstrated and then rushed into production. On 15 September 1916 36 tanks went into action for the first time at the battle of Flers-Courcelette, part of the larger Somme offensive.[14]

The RND, however, did not at first have an easy relationship with the army. The generals found its naval ranks, ratings and mannerisms distinctly odd and the RND's lack of enthusiasm for, and skill at, parade-ground drill caused a great deal of hostility from senior army officers who set much store by such achievements. On 14 October 1916 the RND got a 'proper soldier' as its commanding officer following the wounding of Major General Archibald Paris of the Royal Marines – the division's commander since before Gallipoli. The new commanding officer, Major General Sir Cameron Shute, was determined to beat the naval ways out of his new unit, and he wrote a number of highly critical reports on the RND which alleged it was not battle ready, despite his division's excellent performance in the battle of the Ancre. Shute rapidly became exceedingly unpopular within the RND and the division's feelings towards him were salaciously and scatologically summed up by one of its junior officers, the writer and satirist A.P. Herbert:

The General inspecting the trenches
Exclaimed with a horrified shout
'I refuse to command a division
Which leaves its excreta about.'

But nobody took any notice
No one was prepared to refute,
That the presence of shit was congenial
Compared to the presence of Shute.

And certain responsible critics
Made haste to reply to his words
Observing that his staff advisors
Consisted entirely of turds.

For shit may be shot at odd corners
And paper supplied there to suit,
But a shit would be shot without mourners
If somebody shot that shit Shute.

Shute was not, in the end, shot. In February 1917 the army had tried to wrest the RND away from the Admiralty and received a bloody nose for its pains. Shute was just transferred away from the RND shortly after this bureaucratic battle and replaced by a more congenial commander.

The next major attack for the division was in April 1917 after the German retreat to the Hindenburg Line. Here the RND was involved in heavy fighting for the village of Gavrelle; from 14 to 29 April it was in almost continuous action. When the division came out of the line its next big test would be Passchendaele. Nor did the end of the third Ypres/Passchendaele campaign mean the end of the

RND fighting in 1917. Following the German counterattack in the wake of the Cambrai limited offensive in late November 1917, the RND was tasked in mid-December with holding the Flesiquieres salient. However, on 30 December the Germans launched a very heavy attack to pinch out the British position which the RND successfully fought off.[15]

In and out of the line in the first three months of 1918, the RND was back in the Flesiquieres salient when the Germans launched their massive spring offensive on 21 March 1918. The 5th Army, the next army along the line from the 3rd, of which the RND was a part, almost ceased to exist as a fighting force, while the centre and right of 3rd Army was thrown back. But unlike some of the other divisions that disintegrated under the devastatingly heavy German attack, the RND kept some cohesion and managed to conduct a fighting retreat until the British position stabilized almost on what had been the front line before the 1916 Somme offensive.

Following on from the massive German defeat in August at the battle of Amiens, the RND fought at the battle of Albert, 21–28 August 1918. The division was then involved in breaching the Hindenburg Line on 2–4 September on the Canal du Nord and then again on 27–30 September when they advanced seven miles and breached the Hindenburg support line position. By 1 October the

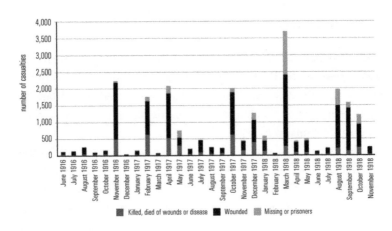

Fig. 3.7. 3rd (Royal Naval) Division casualties, June 1916–November 1918.[16]

RND had advanced to the outskirts of Cambrai and was employed in taking out a key part of the German defences there on 8 October, allowing the town to be captured two days later. This was the last major battle for the RND. Between 9 October and 6 November the division was rested well away from the front, and when it returned to action in early November it was engaged in pursuit rather than set-piece battles. As one of the elite divisions on the Western Front, the RND was used to crack open the German defences. As a result it suffered heavy casualties: just fewer than 30,000 in all during its time on the Western Front; of these, 4,659 were killed or died of wounds, disease or other causes.[17]

The Navy and the air war

The Navy was also fighting above as well as on the Western Front, thanks to the presence of the RNAS. Although the RNAS units in France were nominally involved in either strategic bombing of Germany, attacks on Ostend, Zeebrugge and Bruges, or supporting the Navy at sea, the army successfully argued that they should also help the Royal Flying Corps during the battle of the Somme and during 1917 when German airpower seemed to be getting the upper hand over the trenches. Ironically the reason the RFC was doing so badly was that it had got itself into a vicious circle over what it felt was offensive activity. For the RFC, getting 20 miles beyond the German front line was considered twice as offensive as just getting ten miles, rather than making the enemy air force the target or enabling air support of the ground war to be their objective. As a result RFC losses increased, made worse by the decision to shorten the training of fighter pilots in order to maintain front-line strength, which in turn merely added to the losses as inexperienced pilots fell prey to German fighters.[18]

Another reason for the army's enthusiastic encouragement of the RNAS to work with the RFC over the trenches was due to well-grounded fears that the Admiralty, through its longstanding experience of working with industry, was getting better and more aircraft for its air force than the army was. The RNAS was indeed leading the way in aeronautical research and development, thanks to the Navy's close ties with industry. By April 1918 the RNAS had developed all of the tools needed for long-range flight that were in use in World War II – drift predictors, a bombsight that allowed the target to be approached from any direction not just into or down wind, navigation protractors and, above all, the use of direction-finding wireless telegraphy for navigation purposes.[19]

Aside from assisting the RFC with its problems over the Somme in 1916 and more generally along the front in 1917, these products of RNAS research and development were being put to great use in three main areas. The use of aircraft for anti-submarine warfare received – unsurprisingly – a great deal of support within the Navy, and although aircraft were not yet a formidable anti-submarine weapon, they were a significant deterrent to U-boats. The RNAS was a heavy user of both airships and aircraft for anti-submarine work; the aircraft were faster, but the airships, with their very long range, were perfect for working with convoys, and even hydrophones were fitted to both types. One of the results of the RNAS's investment in research was the development of the 'spider's web' patrol scheme which allowed the systematic search of 4,000 square miles of sea by a single 'flying boat' aircraft such as the Curtis 'Large American'. The RNAS also recognized that while sinking submarines was difficult, keeping them submerged, where their speed was substantially reduced, was almost as good. As a result much emphasis was placed on continuous anti-submarine air patrols in places like the English Channel. Indeed the Navy found the combination of convoy and an air as well as surface escort to be almost unmatched in preventing U-boat attacks. In 1918 only three ships were sunk in convoys that had an air escort in addition to the normal warship escort.[20]

The second area of RNAS activity was an extension of their pre-Jutland effort to dislocate German Zeppelin raids by attacking their bases and factories. Now the interest was wider, with the aim of using bombing raids to undermine the German economy – it was the birth of British strategic bombing. However, given the Navy's deep interest in economic warfare, this should perhaps be seen as an extension of the economic war rather than the development of what

Fig. 3.8. A Felixstowe Flying Boat used for anti-submarine patrols.
Note that the hull of the aircraft is dazzlepainted.

has come to be known as strategic bombing – the idea that airpower alone can bomb a country out of a war. The RFC was ambivalent about the development of a long-range bomber force and as a result the Admiralty carried on alone. The RNAS long-range bombing force (the reformed No. 3 Wing) was deployed behind the French to stop the British army finding out about what it was doing there. But when the War Office got wind of the Navy's plans they tried to get the force disbanded, the army's ambivalence having turned to open hostility. In the end, after months of bitter inter-service disputes, the Admiralty agreed to wind up No. 3 Wing from February 1917 and night-time strategic bombing petered out during the spring, just as the force was taking delivery of the new Hadley Page 0/100 heavy bombers. The RNAS Dunkirk Force, however, continued its operations – strategic and tactical – using light and heavy bombers for day and night attacks.[21]

The third area of significant development between 1916 and 1918 was the desire to use the RNAS as a ship-borne weapon against an enemy fleet at sea or, more likely, one in harbour that

Fig. 3.9. The Handley Page 0/100 bomber developed for the Royal
Naval Air Service's strategic bombing attacks on
German industry and infrastructure.

was stubbornly refusing to put to sea just to give the Royal Navy the
chance of putting right what it got wrong at Jutland. The problems
with the early seaplanes that HMS *Engadine* had struggled to launch
at Jutland were twofold. First, the ability to hoist out a seaplane onto
the water and for it to then get airborne, land on water afterwards
and be recovered back onto the ship was very weather dependent –
the bigger the waves, the less likely the seaplane would get airborne.
Second, the act of taking off or landing on the water required large
floats in place of wheels. The weight of the floats and the drag they
exerted meant that the performance of seaplanes tended to be inferior to landplanes of a similar size and engine power.

After Jutland, the numbers of aircraft within the Grand Fleet
rapidly increased. At the start of 1917 the Grand Fleet had three
seaplane carriers carrying 23 aircraft; soon HMS *Nairana* and HMS
Pegasus, converted ferries, entered service, although Beatty was still
unhappy at the level of air support he had available. In March 1917
the fleet was joined by HMS *Furious* which had been fitted with a
flying-off deck on her bow in place of her gun turret and could
carry three reconnaissance planes and five fighters. Not only were

there more seaplane tenders, but many warships also carried landplanes for anti-Zeppelin work that were launched from runways
on top of the gun turrets of battlecruisers or the forecastles of the
cruisers. The first light cruiser so fitted took her Sopwith Pup to sea
on an operational sweep in August 1917 and successfully launched
the aircraft in order to shoot down Zeppelin *L-23*. By 1 April 1918
seven battlecruisers and ten light cruisers had launching platforms
fitted and aircraft embarked. Once the landplanes had carried out
their task they would then ditch by their parent ship, and the pilot
(and sometimes the plane) be recovered.[22]

A better solution was to find some way of allowing the aircraft
to land back on the warship so that they could be readied for use
again. In 1917 Squadron Commander Edwin Dunning, RNAS,
realized that the stalling speed of aircraft like the Sopwith Pup

Fig. 3.10. HMS *Caroline*, a *C* class light cruiser, with an aircraft and launching
platform fitted above her forward gun turret. HMS *Caroline*, having fought
at the battle of Jutland, was converted into a Royal Naval Volunteer Reserve
Drill Ship in the 1920s. She performed this role until the early twenty-first
century before being preserved for the nation in Belfast as the last surviving
warship from the battle of Jutland.

was so low that if a ship were to steam quickly into the wind, the aircraft would to all intents and purposes hover above the deck. On 2 August 1917 Dunning demonstrated that it would be possible to land on the aircraft launching deck of HMS *Furious*. He approached the ship from astern, side-slipped round the masts and funnels until he was over the launching deck and then reduced his engine power, allowing his aircraft to sink down onto the deck where it was held in place by members of the crew. It was the first time an aircraft had been launched from, and landed on, the same ship. It would change naval aviation – and navies – forever. Sadly Dunning was killed on 7 August when he attempted to repeat his achievement and his plane was blown over the side of the ship by a gust of wind.

HMS *Furious* soon sprouted a landing deck on her stern to complement the flying-off deck on her bow, but there still remained the obstacle of her masts and funnels which caused considerable turbulence over the landing area. What was needed was a continuous deck for launching and landing aircraft that was unobstructed for its entire length. Fortunately an Italian liner whose construction had been halted at the start of the war was purchased by the Admiralty in September 1916 and by March 1918 had been converted into HMS *Argus* with a full unobstructed flightdeck. Also at the start of 1918 a new aircraft carrier was ordered, based on the incomplete hull of the battleship that had been being built at the Armstrong yard for the Chilean navy, while at the same time a new purpose-built aircraft carrier – to become HMS *Hermes* – had been mooted by the Admiralty. In September 1918 HMS *Argus* joined the Grand Fleet and the next month received 12 of the slowly arriving Sopwith Cuckoo torpedo bombers.[23]

What Beatty wanted all these aircraft – and more – for was to launch an air attack on the German High Seas Fleet at its base at Wilhelmshaven using the new torpedo bombers, the Grand Fleet having become somewhat exasperated by the refusal of the Germans to come out and fight. The Admiralty had reservations over the resources and time needed to produce a large enough attack force and the ships to launch them. When in October 1917 Beatty tried to interest the Admiralty again, the plan was rejected but with the proviso that it might be considered in the future. Resources, not imagination, were what the Navy lacked for a successful air attack.[24]

Unfortunately, there was a great deal of governmental disquiet over the organization of the air services, as well as a great deal of dissatisfaction within the RNAS itself. In particular, the lack of effective air defence against German air raids by Zeppelins and ordinary aircraft gave a great deal of ammunition to those arguing for one centrally controlled air force, at just the time when resources and technology were allowing the use of aircraft as a fleet-based weapon. As a result of the political pressure – and with hindsight, very appropriate timing – a single air service, the Royal Air Force (RAF), came into being on 1 April 1918, combining the resources and personnel of both the RNAS and the army's Royal Flying Corps.

There was no immediate change for the Navy; the RNAS personnel and aircraft that were transferred to the RAF carried on doing the same jobs as before. The RAF continued to support the Navy's efforts to deal with the U-boat and to get at the High Seas Fleet with torpedo aircraft. However, the new service was much more closely aligned to the ethos, character and goals of the old RFC; after all, the RNAS personnel only numbered 55,000, while the RFC transferred over 200,000 to the new RAF. Indeed in a few short years the new RAF would be making similar doctrinal errors to the old RFC, confusing means with ends – not really surprising given that the officer who had made the error, Hugh Trenchard, was now running the RAF. Of course, the RFC and RAF were not alone in this regard; many in the Navy had in the years running up to the war spectacularly confused means with ends – hence the obsession with seeking a decisive battle. The key difference was that the Navy had a breadth of roles, specializations and experience that when allied with (admittedly civilian) intellectual analysis, allowed such doctrinaire views to be challenged to a greater or lesser extent from within. Any challenge over how the aircraft were used to support the Navy under the new arrangements could only result in arguments between the services. Nor did the new service have the research and development resources of the Admiralty, perhaps compounding the problems the new service faced in working out what would and what would not be possible with the improving aircraft technology in the years ahead. The new service might be able to live off the RNAS expertise for a short while, but at some point trouble would erupt between the services over how aircraft were to be used and indeed over who really protected Britain.

Peace?

On 29 October 1918 disturbances rocked the High Seas Fleet. The German navy was preparing itself for one final sortie against the Grand Fleet, to go down fighting rather than embrace the calls for an armistice that their army's leaders had successfully pressed for after a loss of nerve at the start of the month. But the German sailors had other ideas. By 6 November sailors were in control of Lubeck, Travemunde, Bremen, Cuxhaven, Wilhelmshaven and Hamburg. The rest of Germany was in revolt too, also led by mutinous sailors. Unrestricted submarine warfare had been called off on 16 October as the German government complied with US President Woodrow Wilson's second note. Bulgaria had surrendered on 29 September; Austro-Hungary and Turkey capitulated on 30 October. The Central Powers had collapsed under the weight of their losses and economic warfare, and to prevent occupation were surrendering. On 11 November at 11:00, the armistice between Germany and the Allied powers came into force. The Great War was over.

Now the Navy had to face the peace and the new world order.

CHAPTER 4

Disarmament and Rearmament

The Interwar Period

On the morning of 21 November 1919, HMS *Cardiff* met the German High Seas Fleet and led them towards the Grand Fleet; in Versailles the victorious Allies debated what to do with the German ships. Forty miles east of May Island in the Firth of Forth, the two fleets met. Not since 31 May 1916, off Jutland, had these two massive symbols of national power and pride met; then it was in anger, now it was as part of the armistice.

As the German High Seas Fleet approached it met the full might of the Grand Fleet, representative warships from Allied navies and all the British home naval commands, drawn up in two long columns six miles apart, which shaped courses to pass either side of the dirty and demoralized German ships. All in all, there were 13 squadrons of battleships, battlecruisers, armoured and light cruisers and the obligatory screen of destroyers – some 370 ships to take the Germans into custody. The British were not taking any chances: the Grand Fleet was at action stations ready to react if the Germans showed the slightest hostile intent. Then, on a command from the Grand Fleet's flagship HMS *Queen Elizabeth* – the signal ML – the British fleet turned through 180 degrees to take station on either side of the German ships, conveying them to their anchorage in the Firth of Forth. Admiral Beatty, the Grand Fleet's commander, ordered that 'The German flag will be hauled down at sunset today, Thursday, and will not be hoisted again without permission.' Such was the importance of the event that *The Graphic* even produced a souvenir issue of the surrender of the High Seas Fleet, calling it the 'most striking symbol of Germany's utter failure to attain that World Power for which she really undertook the Great War on August, 1914'.[1]

The German ships remained anchored off Rosyth for only a few days before they were transferred in small groups to the Grand Fleet's main wartime anchorage at Scapa Flow. There they sat and waited, quietly rusting away in isolation while the negotiations to turn the armistice into a treaty to end the war dragged on at the peace conference in Paris. The deadline for the treaty to be signed was noon on 21 June 1919 (although it was extended at the last minute by a couple of days). However, it seems that the German officers at Scapa Flow were determined to avoid handing over their ships to the Allies for either destruction or use by Allied navies. At 10:00 on 21 June, before the nominal expiration of the deadline, the Germans put into action a well-organized plan to scuttle their ships. All bar one of the battleships and battlecruisers, over half the cruisers and 32 out of 50 destroyers were successfully scuttled. The German High Seas Fleet had ceased to exist, but the Royal Navy's Grand Fleet was no longer around to witness the event: early in 1919 it had been broken up into the Atlantic, Home and Reserve Fleets.

Demobilization and retrenchment

At the end of the war the Royal Navy's strength was 37,636 officers and 4,000,975 enlisted men (excluding the Royal Naval Air Service which had been transferred to the Air Ministry as part of the RAF on 1 April 1918); pre-war it had had just 150,000 officers and men. Clearly the Navy was going to have to shrink both in terms of its size and the amount of money spent on it. At the same time, the men who had volunteered for service during the war – both reservists and hostilities-only personnel – needed to be returned to their peacetime employment, not only to reduce the cost of the Navy but also to start the process of returning the wider economy to a peacetime footing.[2]

In what was perhaps an all too rare appreciation of possible feelings within the lower deck, the Admiralty was at pains to explain to the fleet the demobilization scheme and to help men prepare for civilian life before the order to demobilize was given in mid-January 1919. The Admiralty even produced a pamphlet for prospective employers of ex-naval personnel, explaining the ranks and rates of different specializations and what general skills a man of a particular rate and specialization might have, such as experience of managing men, or particular machine-tool skills. In the highly charged political atmosphere of late 1918 and early 1919, where industrial unrest was rife, where troops had been used against strikers in Glasgow and civil and military militancy was widespread, demobilization and lower-deck pay and other issues were extremely important. If it were mismanaged in any way, mutinies and disorder, such as those suffered by the British army and Dominion army units in Calais, Southampton, Folkestone, Rhyl and Cardiff, might follow, or worse – sailors had been at the centre of the Russian and German revolutions after all.

Fortunately the Admiralty moved quickly to deal with lower-deck concerns. Pay and pensions were increased (despite opposition from the other services and the Treasury), demobilization went smoothly on the whole and, in order to forestall the development of a ratings union, the Admiralty developed a welfare committee system to provide an outlet for grievances. As a result, unrest in the Navy was slight, and even the most serious events – auxiliary service crews refusing orders or the raising of the red flag on the patrol boat *Kilbride* in Milford Haven – were isolated acts.

The knife was wielded quickly on the uncompleted war emergency construction programmes too, as defence spending was slashed. One of three *E* class light cruisers was cancelled, as were 38 modified *V & W* class destroyers, two *S* class destroyers, and 33 submarines during 1918–19. Three out of the four *Hood* class battle-cruisers, whose construction had been suspended in 1917, were scrapped on the slipways. However, new ships would be needed if the strength of the Navy was to be maintained. Naval airpower demanded new ships and rebuilds of existing ones – 'aircraft carriers' – to operate aircraft in support of fleet operations. Much of the existing fleet was worn out by war service or was obsolescent, hence the Admiralty's demands to keep most of the *D* and *E* class cruisers under construction and the proposals in 1920 for four new battleships.

There was also the rather tricky problem of excess officers in the Navy. Too many had been recruited as a result of the pre-war naval expansion and by the habit of offering regular commissions to officers who joined during the war. In 1920 a voluntary redundancy scheme was implemented; the Admiralty hoped that 650 officers of lieutenant commander rank and below would take advantage of the scheme, but in the end only 407 did so. Nor did the Admiralty – rather hypocritically – do anything about the size of the flag officers' list. The shortfall in the 1920 scheme meant that in 1922 there was another attempt to reduce officer numbers – the 'Geddes Axe'. This scheme saw 200 lieutenants retire voluntarily and another 350 made redundant. But even this was not enough as the Navy continued to reduce in size through the 1920s; in 1926 and 1929 retirement inducements were offered to lieutenant commanders. On the whole the redundancy packages were generally sympathetically dealt with by the Treasury; only when the Admiralty, in a self-serving moment, tried to get better terms for the most senior officers did the Treasury dig its heels in. Ratings pay, too, was examined in the 1920s as the cost of living continued to fall. In 1925 it was decided that a new lower pay scale would be used for all men joining the Navy from October 1925, but that the 1919 pay rates would remain for those already serving.[3]

It was also clear that once demobilization had been completed there would not be a return to 1914 levels of spending on the Navy. Instead the Cabinet decided in August 1919 that given the lack of potential enemies and the impact of the war, no major conflict was likely for the next ten years. This was the now notorious 'Ten Year Rule'. It was straightforward and, it has to be admitted, not the cause of any British unreadiness for war in 1939. Put simply, the Ten Year Rule told all three branches of the armed forces that for the next decade there was no likelihood of major war and that they should prepare their budgets accordingly. However, it also meant

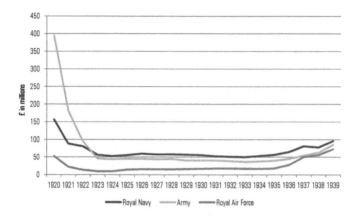

Fig. 4.1. Defence spending, 1920–39.[4]

that at the end of the ten-year period, the armed forces should be ready to fight a major war. It was a financial, and even strategic, planning tool that should have allowed the armed forces to absorb the lessons from the previous war and tailor their procurement plans and doctrine accordingly to ensure that military readiness and reconstruction after the war were achieved in a reasonable time period.

The problems with the Ten Year Rule started in 1925 following the Admiralty's successful campaign to get a cruiser construction programme past the Treasury and Cabinet. As a result of this, Winston Churchill, now Chancellor of the Exchequer, managed to persuade the Committee for Imperial Defence that the Admiralty was not to make preparations to base a fleet at Singapore that was equal to that of Japan's. This effectively extended the Ten Year Rule to cover a war with Japan up to 1935. Then three years later – again as a direct result of the Admiralty's success in getting funding approved by the Cabinet – Churchill, with the approval of his Cabinet colleagues, decreed that the Ten Year Rule would now become self-repeating and would reset itself after each year to year zero. The impact of this was clear, straightforward and devastating. Instead of being at a point where all three armed services were just three years from when they had to be ready to fight a major war, overnight they were returned, in financial and procurement terms, to 1919. Procurement plans were dashed, and work on the improved base at Singapore was retarded, as was the modernization programme for battleships.[5]

The result was that the low point in spending on the Navy was not in the early 1920s, as the service contracted after the Great War, but in 1932, owing to the twin impacts of the self-perpetuating Ten Year Rule and further government retrenchment thanks to the collapsing economic situation. The immediate result on the Navy of this further retrenchment in the early 1930s was the mutiny of the Atlantic Fleet in September 1931 at Invergordon.

The mutiny at Invergordon started on 12 September with meetings in canteens ashore after news broke that the 1925 pay scales would be extended to those who joined under the 1919 regulations. Worse, the cut in officers' pay was only 11 per cent compared to the 25 per cent faced by many of their men; the ratings' pensions would be affected too. There was a clear sense of betrayal by both the Admiralty as the cuts were not equal, but also by the politicians who had repeatedly promised during the 1920s that the 1919 pay scales would not be cut. Sailors decided that they would refuse orders to sail the ships of the Atlantic Fleet on the morning of Tuesday 15 September – if the crew of HMS *Valiant* set the ball rolling. As the ships readied themselves to sail on 15 September, only HMS *Hood*, HMS *Norfolk* and HMS *York* reported that their crews had presented themselves for work. The Admiralty was told of the problems by 09:30 and those ships that had managed to get to sea were recalled and exercises cancelled at 09:31.

A quick response by the Admiralty might have defused the situation but none was forthcoming. Instead the mutiny – the strike – continued with the men feeling increasingly nervous due to their physical isolation at Invergordon and the lack of news – from anyone – and anxious to be presented with a way out of their predicament. But still nothing came from either the government or the Admiralty. The strikers (it seems unfair to call a pay dispute a mutiny) decided to return to work during the evening of 16 September and by 21:30

that day the mutiny (or strike) was effectively over and the fleet was ordered to return to its base ports. The Admiralty promised investigations into the impact of the cuts on the worse-affected ratings and the House of Commons held an emergency debate on the issue on 17 September. Owing to fear of further action within the fleet it was decided that the pay cut would be restricted to 10 per cent. The mutiny helped destroy international confidence in the British fiscal situation, forcing Britain off the Gold Standard. Seven weeks after the mutiny two dozen ratings were dismissed for their parts in the strike; members of the Admiralty Board who were felt to have given poor advice had their careers blighted. The First Lord of the Admiralty, Austin Chamberlain, was replaced after the National Government won the general election in late October. The new First Lord, Sir Bolton Eyres-Monsell, was, somewhat unusually, a retired naval officer. His understanding of the Navy as an institution and his political skill not only helped restore the Navy internally – although the mutiny cast a long shadow – but also and more importantly rebuilt the service's battered image with the public and parliament after a long and fractious decade of which Invergordon was just the latest piece of trouble.

A violent peace and the need for a new enemy

Nor could it be said that the armistice of 11 November 1918 and then the formal treaties that brought the Great War to a close actually ended war or the possibility of it. There was a nasty little undeclared war going on in Russia between the Bolsheviks and the 'White' Russians (who were supported by almost everyone else, including Britain, making the civil war an international affair). There was also an ongoing crisis in the Near East caused by the collapse of the Ottoman Empire.

With the end of the war against Germany and the Central Powers, Britain had to decide which line to take in the Russian civil war between the Bolsheviks and the non-Bolshevik (or White Russian) forces. At the end of November the Cabinet decided to intervene on the side of the White Russian forces and a cruiser squadron together with a destroyer flotilla was dispatched to the Baltic. Torpedo-armed Coastal Motor Boats (CMBs) were sent over-land to the Caspian Sea, while HMS *Suffolk* at Vladivostok fitted out and manned an armoured train which supported the anti-Bolshe-vik forces in central Siberia along the Trans-Siberian Railway near Omsk – about as far from the sea as it is possible to get.

The main British effort was, however, in the Baltic, where not only were White Russian forces supported but the establishment of independent Baltic states overseen and the German forces in the area compelled to leave the Baltic states and Russian territory as demanded by the armistice. The initial British force of five *C* class cruisers, nine *V & W* class destroyers and seven minesweep-ers suffered an early loss when the light cruiser HMS *Cassandra* struck a mine in the Baltic and sank, thankfully with only very light casualties. Soon submarines joined the naval forces and two CMBs commanded by Lieutenant Augustus Agar were also dispatched to the region by MI6 to run agents in and out of the 'Red' areas. Agar soon got fed up with the relative impunity that minefields gave the Red warships while they shelled 'White' forces in the forts near Kronstadt. He decided to exceed his orders and on the night of 16–17 June 1919 torpedoed and sank the Bolshevik armoured cruiser *Oleg*; he was awarded a Victoria Cross for his bravery and initiative.[6]

Agar's private war delighted the anti-Bolshevik forces in the region as well as Admiral Rosslyn Wemyss (the First Sea Lord) and Admiral Walter Cowan, commander of the British naval forces, who thought it an excellent demonstration of what the Navy should be doing and argued as much to the government. The government was less impressed, but Wemyss got permission for a more offen-sive posture and Cowan received reinforcements: the aircraft carrier HMS *Vindictive*, more minesweepers and eight large CMBs. Cowan did not wait for long before launching his forces at the Bolsheviks in Kronstadt. In the early morning of 18 August 1919, under cover of an air raid launched by *Vindictive*'s aircraft, seven of the large CMBs, and Lieutenant Agar in a smaller CMB, penetrated the harbour at Kronstadt and caused mayhem.

Fig. 4.2. CMB 4 being readied for the attack on Kronstadt.

The crisis in the Near East was a complex affair. Naval gunboat diplomacy was used in 1919 to persuade a reluctant Ottoman regime to sign a peace treaty with the Allied powers – the Treaty of Sèvres. The Greek invasion of Asia Minor was given tacit support too. Yet the naval presence also helped shore up the Ottoman regime in the face of internal opposition from the nationalist uprising led by Kemal Atatürk. When in 1922 the Greeks threatened Constantinople, against the wishes of the other Allies, the Royal Navy concentrated forces off the port in support of the French army units protecting the city. The Greeks, very aware of their vulnerable supply lines to their forces in Asia Minor, backed down.

The Kemalist forces were, however, beating the Greeks in Asia Minor. By September the nationalists were threatening the city of Smyrna, which, despite its location in the Ottoman Empire, had a large Greek population and character. The Mediterranean Fleet stood off the port and British citizens were evacuated by the Navy in commandeered merchant ships, but its efforts to achieve an orderly surrender of Smyrna to Kemal's troops failed when the city caught fire and was largely burnt to the ground. The nationalist forces then threatened the Dardanelles, which under the terms of the Treaty of Sèvres had been demilitarized and declared neutral. When Kemal's forces approached Charnack on the eastern shore of the Dardanelles, war threatened. The Mediterranean Fleet was sent to the region to support the few Allied troops in the area and stop Kemal's forces crossing the straits. Careful diplomacy on the ground prevented any escalation and eventually a new treaty was signed at Lausanne in 1923 to replace that of Sèvres. However, the threat of war in the Near East had made Conservative backbench MPs in Lloyd George's wartime coalition government, which was still clinging to power, take a long hard look at what being in bed with a politician like Lloyd George meant. They decided that they were not impressed with the future outlook and forced the Conservative party to leave the coalition, consigning Lloyd George to the political wilderness.

For the rest of the interwar period the Navy was involved in an almost continuous round of naval diplomacy, foreign visits, anti-piracy work, disaster relief and the protection of British citizens and interests around the globe. In 1923–24 a Special Service Squadron toured the globe. In the late 1930s the Navy patrolled Spanish waters to deal with 'pirate' submarines operated by the Italians for Franco and to try to prevent the shipment of arms to either side in the civil war. Yet these were effectively side issues when compared to the big question of where and against whom would the next war be fought.

The terms of the Versailles Treaty, notwithstanding the demise of the High Seas Fleet at Scapa Flow, meant that a new German navy was limited to 15,000 men, six 'battleships' no bigger than 10,000 tons, six cruisers no larger than 6,000 tons, 12 destroyers, 12 smaller torpedo boats and no submarines at all – in short a force that could contest control of the Baltic with Russia but was not a threat to Britain. The Admiralty felt that the US Navy was the fleet that should be used to set the size of the Royal Navy. However, when this idea was floated in Cabinet in August 1919 by the First Lord of the Admiralty, Walter Long, it only succeeded in provoking the Cabinet to declare a few days later that 'It should be assumed ... that the British Empire will not be engaged in any great war during the next ten years, and that no Expeditionary Force is required for this purpose.' Nor could the Admiralty use conflict with the USA as the basis for its war plans and the size of the Navy.[7]

Fortunately the Admiralty did, after much argument, manage to get the agreement of the government that the Royal Navy should not be inferior to any other navy – a 'one-power' standard that included the USA. As a result, Cabinet approval for the construction of four new battleships was given in 1920. But before work could commence, the Americans proposed a naval arms limitations conference. This did not, however, solve the problem of whom the Royal Navy should be preparing to fight – even if the government had decided that any such war would be in ten years' time.

Table 4.1. Naval strength at the end of World War I.[8]

	Britain	USA	France	Germany	Japan	Italy
Battleships	61	39	20	40	13	14
Battlecruisers	9	-	-	5	7	-
Cruisers	30	16	21	3	10	7
Light cruisers	90	19	8	32	16	10
Flotilla leaders	23	-	-	-	-	8
Destroyers	443	131	91	200	67	44
Submarines	147	86	63	162	16	78
Aircraft and seaplane carriers	4	-	-	-	-	-

The quest for naval arms limitation

The Great War was seen by many as the war to end all wars. To make sure that this was indeed the case, many people asked why the war had started. The answer, felt many in Britain and the USA, was not political determination to meet national aims even at the risk of a war, but the arms race before the war – particularly the *naval* arms race. Such a view may well have been erroneous but it was a common one. There was also a more general aversion to war as a political tool. In July 1921 'No More War' demonstrations took place across Europe on the anniversary of the outbreak of war; the rallies continued in Britain until 1924. The year 1921 also saw the foundation of the 'No More War Movement'. In the *Morning Post* it was reported that at the 'Women against War' meeting on 11 November 1921, to loud cheers, Lady Frances Balfour had declared that:

> It is not a choice between good and evil: it is the choice between life and death to the world. Wars have miserably failed. It is for the women of the world to say, with one voice: "Let's scrap the old battle-ships and launch a new order of things".[9]

For the British public the American call for a naval arms limitation conference was popular. It was also popular with the government, as it was a means of avoiding an expensive arms race. The government may have decided that cuts in naval strength were needed to help the economy, but what was communicated in the press was the need for arms reduction, not for economy but for peace.

The Washington Naval Conference of 1921–22 was a turning point in British maritime history. Britain gave up the naval superiority it had had since 1815 and more recently enshrined in the 'two-power' standard. Instead parity or a 'one-power' standard was accepted with America, the latest challenger to British maritime pre-eminence. The Washington Treaty ushered in 15 years of naval arms limitation, only ending with Britain's (at first secret) rearmament after 1933 and the failure of the 1936 London Naval Conference.

The 1922 Washington Naval Treaty did indeed see the USA, Britain, France, Japan and Italy all agree to limit the size and composition of their navies for the next ten years and suspend the construction of new battleships for the same period of time. Additionally, the total displacement of the battleship and aircraft carrier force, as well as the maximum size of each ship, was limited. This meant that while Britain was limited to a maximum displacement of its entire battleship force of 525,000 tons, no one ship could be larger than 35,000 tons or have guns greater in calibre than 14 inches. Furthermore, no new battleships were to be built for ten years. As a special consideration given the age of the Royal Navy's battleships and the more recent building programmes of the USA and Japan, Britain was allowed to build two new battleships which could have nine 16-inch guns. These two ships – HMS *Rodney* and HMS *Nelson* – finally entered service in 1927. The amounts set aside for aircraft carriers were smaller: only 135,000 tons with no one ship greater than 27,000 tons. The key to the treaty was the ratio between the powers: 5, 5, 3, 1.75, 1.75 in the order Britain, USA, Japan, France and Italy, ensuring that Japan, for example, could have only a battleship or aircraft carrier force three-fifths the size of that of Britain or the USA. Cruisers were given a maximum size of 10,000 tons displacement per ship and forbidden to have guns larger than 8-inch calibre, but the controlling ratio for battleships and aircraft carriers was not extended to cruisers and other warships.

At a stroke, Britain had accepted what was effectively naval parity with the United States, but the treaty still gave a two-power standard against the next two biggest naval powers – as long as everybody kept to the agreement. Perhaps surprisingly, given the strength of popular interest in the Royal Navy before the war, and a clear example of how the Great War had changed expectations inside and outside parliament, there was very little opposition to the treaty. Even the Navy League, the pre-war staunch defender of British naval supremacy, proclaimed itself in favour of naval arms limitation and then found itself under attack from its own members for placing its faith in collective security and international treaties rather than in the strength of British seapower. Both the prospect of a treaty and the final agreement were seen as entirely reasonable: 'The only hope of putting an end to a rivalry which is unhealthy and dangerous lies in the adoption of a policy of limitation.' The *Daily Telegraph* told its readers that 'with the approval, as we believe, of the mass of the people, we have announced that we shall be satisfied if in future our Navy is not inferior to that of any other country.' The *Scotsman* concurred, stating that 'Agreement is, indeed, the only way out; and this country has shown by the moderation of its policy that it has no desire to resume naval rivalry.'[10]

However, the Royal Navy and Britain also benefited from this attempt to impose international limits on naval armaments. First, they had avoided an arms race with the USA and, at the cost of parity with the US Navy (someone they were not prepared politically to fight), prevented the Americans and Japanese producing fleets based on more modern ships than the Royal Navy. Second, the Royal Navy alone had emerged with permission to build two new battleships – the Americans and Japanese at best could look forward to completing a couple of ships that had already been started, with the implication that the Royal Navy would be able to build in lessons from the recent war far better than its closest rivals and help preserve shipbuilding capacity from the full force of the treaty's battleship-building holiday. Third, it had prevented the Washington ratios being extended to cruisers and lesser warships; yes cruisers were limited in size and gun-power, but there was no total tonnage limit, or limit on hull numbers, ensuring that for as long as Britain was prepared to spend money, it could protect its trade and maritime empire. Fourth, parity with the USA might have been accepted, but Britain still had the largest navy and the Washington ratios also gave Britain a two-power standard against Japan and any European naval power that had signed the treaty or was bound by Versailles. More importantly the Royal Navy succeeded in replacing much of its cruiser force during the 1920s, a feat that was largely due to Beatty's adept political manoeuvring as First Sea Lord.

The flaw in the treaty concept was that the Washington agreement was supposed to herald a series of international agreements that could cover land and air warfare. However, these were never pursued. After all, the single most powerful land army and air force belonged to France, who thanks to the Versailles Treaty and an absence of a rival land or airpower with whom to compete saw no need for such treaties. Worse, the decision to do away with the Anglo-Japanese treaty in favour of the Washington process turned an ally into a potential rival in the Far East. The other flaw in the Washington process was that it relied on states obeying the rules and not cheating, something that became problematic in the 1930s. Britain's desire to avoid an expensive naval arms race in the early 1920s made the Washington Treaty possible, not the promise of global arms reduction.

The pressure for disarmament continued during this 'Washington period' with an unsuccessful attempt at Geneva in 1927 to produce an agreement that extended the Washington ratios to cruisers. Then in 1930, there was the London Naval Treaty. This saw the British Labour government extend the battleship-building holiday to 1936, scrap more of the Navy's older battle-ships and, despite howls of protest from the Admiralty, reduce the number of cruisers from 70 to 50 – the same number as the Americans. The Admiralty protests were backed up by a vocal campaign by the British Navy League (who, in the aftermath of the Washington process, had decided that they weren't that in favour of disarmament after all). Between them, Britain, Japan and the USA scrapped another nine old battleships as part of the new treaty. The most potentially damaging aspect of the treaty for the Royal Navy was not the arbitrary cruiser reduction but the extension of the battleship-building holiday. The ten years after Washington had been bad enough for the armour plate manufacturers, gun makers and shipbuilders capable of constructing battleships, but they had adjusted, merged and survived. But they had no fat left to see them through the now barren years until 1937 and Britain's ability to build large warships started to shrink. Another Jutland and the clash of dreadnoughts seemed a long way off.[11]

The long, stormy legacy of Jutland and the Great War

The battle of Jutland had been a deep disappointment to both the Royal Navy and the British. Instead of the long-hoped-for decisive battle that would destroy German seapower and give the British a victory to compare with Trafalgar, the Navy lost three of its prestigious battlecruisers – HMS *Indefatigable*, HMS *Queen Mary* and HMS *Invincible* – all to horrendous magazine explosions. Three older armoured cruisers and eight destroyers were also lost. The Germans, on the other hand, lost just one battlecruiser, one obsolescent pre-dreadnought, four light cruisers and five torpedo boats. The Germans may have suffered a strategic defeat but to casual observers it looked awfully like a British loss. The legacy of the battle not only influenced debates during the war but long into the peace.

The failure of the Navy to meet public as well as its own expectations as to what would happen when the Grand Fleet actually managed to meet the German High Seas Fleet in battle resulted in a round of inquiries and reports to try to find out what went wrong, why and what was to be done about it. Throughout the 1920s the Navy's staff college, its tactical school in Portsmouth, senior officers, the naval staff in the Admiralty and the staffs of the various commanders in chief afloat all pored over the battle in an effort to make sure all the ills were identified and corrected. To call the battle of Jutland an obsession for the Royal Navy during much of the interwar period is not an overstatement.

The obsessions with the battle did cause some desirable changes and improvements that might be considered overdue. The ideas that fighting at night between capital ships – the battleships and battlecruisers – was to be avoided at all costs and that destroyers fighting at night should pursue a defensive action were rejected. Indeed a great deal of theoretical and practical effort was put into getting the Navy to feel happy with the idea of fighting aggressively and offensively at night – the payback for this investment was the crushing defeat inflicted on the Italian navy at night during the battle of Matapan in 1941. The command and control problems that Jutland had highlighted were also addressed by developing 'divided tactics' – a means of allowing decentralization of command within the battle fleet, thus reducing the communication problem Jellicoe and Beatty had faced while ensuring better coordination of efforts by subordinate commanders. Allowing officers to use their initiative was encouraged not disparaged.[12]

The fuses in the Navy's large-calibre shells and the shells themselves, which had failed when the British warships had actually managed to score a hit and which had thus been highlighted as one of the main reasons why the German's losses were not heavier, were improved. This, however, had an unfortunate side effect. By concentrating attention on the reliability of shells, the inaccuracy of British gunnery during the war was in part disguised. What made the problem worse was that poor gunnery was a particular problem in Beatty's Battlecruiser Fleet, which being based at Rosyth during the war did not have easy access to the gunnery ranges that had been established in the Orkneys and were regularly used by the Grand Fleet. After the war revised fire-control systems to control long-range gunnery duels were developed. This itself was an avenue for dispute, given the Admiralty's poor pre-war relations with Arthur Pollen and his accusations that Frederick Dryer had stolen his ideas for mechanical fire-control computers. Pollen took his case to the Royal Commission on Awards to Inventors in 1920 and 1923, which did not find in his favour, and had his case re-heard in 1925 where again it was rejected – he only succeeded with regard to one part of his system, the Argo 'Clock'. The Navy's new fire-control systems – the Admiralty Fire Control Table marks 1–7 – which were fitted into all new cruisers and battleships from the mid-1920s onwards, were very much developments of the Dryer system, although in part influenced by the Argo 'Clock'.

Unsurprisingly after the war Beatty, now First Sea Lord (he had intrigued against Jellicoe's successor in the post, Admiral Wemyss, and forced him out), was highly sensitive to any suggestion that failures at Jutland were down to him or the efficiency of his ships. The result was that the efforts to find out what went wrong and what went right ended up being construed in personal terms. The

Navy and indeed politicians were divided over it. Was Jellicoe, as the then commander of the Grand Fleet, or his subordinate, Beatty, as the then commander of the BCF, and their different approaches to gunnery, command and control and their tactical handling of the battle more at fault? This dispute, which started soon after the battle, limped on well into the interwar period and polarized the Navy's officer corps, just as the Fisher–Beresford feud had divided the Edwardian navy. The decision by Jellicoe's successor as First Sea Lord, Admiral Sir Rosslyn Wemyss, to commission an official account of the battle, based solely on the documentary evidence available, within a few weeks of the end of the war provided a continual focus for antagonism between Jellicoe's and Beatty's supporters. This 'Harper record', so named after its chief author Captain J.E.T. Harper, may have been started under Wemyss's tenure as the professional head of the Royal Navy, but was finished under his successor as First Sea Lord, Admiral Sir David Beatty – the former commander of the BCF at Jutland.

Beatty took great exception to Harper's draft of the official account and the positions shown on the accompanying charts of the battle which either did not tally with his recollections of the battle or that he felt portrayed the BCF (and by inference him as its commander) in a less than attractive light. Some of Beatty's senior staff had also been with him at Jutland and they too opposed Harper's account. Admiral Ernle Chatfield disagreed strongly with the contention that it was the BCF's poor gunnery rather than faulty shells that had resulted in so little damage to the German ships. Chatfield had been Beatty's flag captain at Jutland and so was hardly impartial. Harper tried to resist the pressure to change areas which he had documentary support for, but in the end had to give in to Beatty's wishes. This upset Jellicoe who had not seen either the official account or the amendments Beatty had insisted on, and when he did see them he objected most strongly. In fact Jellicoe refused to leave Britain to take up his post as governor general of New Zealand unless it was guaranteed that the published work would not contain the passages *he* objected to. Unable to reconcile the wishes of Beatty and Jellicoe and aware of the rumours that were circulating about the official account around the Navy and in the gentlemen's clubs of St James's, the Admiralty shelved the project indefinitely.

The Jutland controversy rumbled on through the early 1920s as Beatty's Admiralty made various attempts to get its version of events published and was opposed by Jellicoe and his supporters. The controversy even enveloped the official Cabinet Office history of the war at sea, as the author, Sir Julian Corbett, had the temerity to criticize Beatty and by default side with Jellicoe. However, almost as soon as the volume of Corbett's official history that dealt with Jutland was finished, the author died, preventing Beatty from getting any changes through. The Admiralty had to be satisfied with a preface that stated they disagreed with the author's opinions.

As the 1920s moved forward the Jutland controversy would occasionally spark into life as memoirs were published by various politicians and retired admirals. In the end the controversy died away with Beatty's retirement from the post of First Sea Lord in 1927 and the appointment of a perceived Jellicoe supporter, Admiral Sir Charles Madden, as Beatty's successor. Jutland may have been the source of much-needed change in the Navy, making sure its performance in World War II was much better, but it was also an open sore that was slow to heal.

The very centrality of the battleship, and indeed battles like Jutland, was also questioned. First the Post War Questions Committee in 1919 and then the Bonar Law Committee between 1920 and 1921 considered the alleged vulnerability of battleships to torpedo attack and later air attack, to the accompaniment of a vigorous and at times bad-tempered public debate carried out on the correspondence pages of *The Times*. In the end the committee was split between those who advocated economy by reducing the numbers of battleships built and those in favour of new construction.[13]

The other significant lesson learnt as a result of the Great War was in the field of trade defence. The pre-war thinking on this had been proved to be wrong and that convoy should be the mainstay of any future set of measures to protect trade, especially if an enemy were to use unrestricted submarine warfare again. However, such an event was perhaps unlikely as the Germans had been banned from having submarines under the terms of the Versailles Treaty. Convoy was only part of the solution to the anti-submarine problem. The Royal Navy had enjoyed some successes in sinking U-boats that were trying to attack convoys in 1917 and 1918, despite not having an effective and easy means of locating a submerged submarine. Therefore, hand in glove with the rediscovery of convoy as a trade-protection measure, came the development and implementation of new technology to locate a submarine accurately enough for the new depth-charges, which had been so effective in the war, to be accurately dropped.

Mastering new technology: submarines

Submarines and aeroplanes, like all new technology, threw up two broad problems for the Royal Navy: first, how to deploy and manage their own use of the technology to best effect; second, how to frustrate the efforts of those who would seek to use the technology against Britain.

With regard to submarines, there was an awful lot to consider. The Navy had ended the war with several types of submarine: small coastal ones (the *C*, *H*, and *V* classes), larger 'overseas' or 'patrol' submarines (the *E*, *G*, *J*, and *L* classes), 'fleet' submarines (the *K* class), minelaying submarines (some of the *E* class), 'monitor' submarines equipped with a 12-inch gun as well as torpedo tubes (the *M* class) and the unique *R* class anti-submarine submarine. By the mid-1920s the Navy decided to concentrate on three broad types: fleet submarines, patrol submarines (including some fitted for minelaying), and – a new concept – the 'cruiser' submarine; the other types were scrapped, sold or used for experimental and training purposes.

Fleet submarines, despite the Navy's enthusiasm for them in the immediate pre-war period and the development of the steam- and battery-powered large (and fast – at least on the surface) *K* class during the latter half of the war, were not a success. There were two principal problems that the Navy was unable to solve during the interwar period. First, there was the need for a very high surface speed in order to operate with the main battle fleet. Diesel engines just were not powerful enough, so in the K class steam turbines had been tried with mixed results. The K class, thanks to its steam turbines, had large numbers of openings in the hull that had to be closed correctly if the submarine were not to permanently sink rather than dive and be able to return to the surface (as happened to K-13 on her builder's trials in January 1917). The other problem was that the command and control facilities of the boats – the ability to pass and receive tactical messages, normally by signal flags or signal lights – was poor, and there was no way at all of passing messages to the submarines once they had dived to make their attacks. Despite the K class's shortcomings some of them stayed in service until 1926.

The concept of fleet submarines working as an integral, tactical part of the battle fleet was clearly very important to the Navy, as they kept trying to perfect the idea after the war. In 1923 an 'improved' K class, K-26, was completed and was not sold until 1931 and a final effort was made with the Thames class of three fleet submarines in the early 1930s – although they were powered on the surface by diesels not steam turbines and were too slow to keep up with the fleet as a result.[14]

The cruiser submarine also proved to be less than successful, although not due to the state of technology at the time. The cruiser submarine concept arose in the Royal Navy because of the need to find a way to use the submarine effectively in a future maritime economic war that was acceptable to the British public. Of course, thanks to the experience of the recent war, the British viewed unrestricted submarine warfare as beyond condemnation, so submarines had to be used within the prize rules, stopping, searching and capturing – not sinking without warning – enemy merchant ships. The result was X-1, a submarine that in addition to the normal suite of torpedoes also had a gun armament (two twin 5.2-inch guns with full fire-control systems) that was better than most destroyers. The idea was that X-1 would carry sufficient spare crew to form a prize crew for the first merchant ship captured. This

Fig. 4.3. *X-1*.

ship would be used to accommodate the crews of successive ships captured and sunk. When this prison ship was full it would be given a course to the nearest land, the prize crew re-embarked and the whole operation started again somewhere else. It was the perfect way for the British to use submarines in a future economic war, but for one small problem: Britain, as the owner of the largest merchant fleet and the largest maritime trading empire, had the most to lose with the perfection of the cruiser submarine concept. As the Naval Staff's director of the Tactical Division pointed out, 'it is a matter of utmost importance that Great Britain should refrain from advertising the utility of such a craft to the world at large'. *X-1* remained as the only example of her type.[15]

On the other hand, the patrol submarine proved to be a very successful concept, building as it did on the experience of both the war and the Navy's pre-war experience of using overseas type submarines. Furthermore, when the first post-war patrol submarine design – the *O* class – was being considered, it was felt that submarines were now sufficiently important to warrant names rather than numbers. By the end of the 1930s the Navy's largest patrol submarines, the new *T* class, had a massive ten-torpedo bow salvo, compared to the normal six. They were deliberate battleship killers: a ten-weapon salvo was sufficient to ensure enough hits to immobilize if not destroy even the most modern of battleships.[16]

Frustrating the efforts of enemy submarines depended on being able to locate them accurately enough for a successful depth-charge attack. The hydrophones (passive sonar) developed during the war which listened for the noises of a submarine moving through the water only gave bearings. For a single ship to make an attack, both bearing and range were needed. Fortunately early theoretical and practical work on active sonar – ASDIC in the Royal Navy's parlance – had started in the later stages of the war, and almost as soon as the armistice came into force a prototype set was ready. By 1922 a set suitable for destroyers was being tested and was soon being refitted into the Navy's destroyer force. The sonar dome for the ASDIC transducer was also quickly improved, the fixed dome being streamlined from about 1925, allowing higher speeds while hunting with the ASDIC set, and in 1932 the streamlined dome became retractable in the latest ASDIC sets. When destroyer construction after the war restarted in 1924, it was quickly decided that the new *B* class destroyers would benefit from a new type of ASDIC set, the Type 119, which became the basis of destroyer ASDIC sets. ASDICs were also designed for, and fitted to, British submarines, to aid both attacks and evasion. The fact that by the mid-1930s the Royal Navy had a widely fitted and effective means of locating and attacking a submerged submarine was far more significant that its tactical use against submarines suggests. Indeed from 1927 onwards the Admiralty was engaged in a deliberate deception operation that praised the capabilities of ASDIC to try to dissuade potential enemies from investing in submarines on the basis that the submarine 'problem' had now been solved.[17]

Convoy and ASDIC were not the only parts of the solution to the anti-submarine problem. The experience of the war had shown that maritime airpower in all its forms had been a significant deterrent and impediment to submarine attacks. Unfortunately by the end of the war the Royal Navy did not control its own aircraft any more –

they were controlled by a new and not especially helpful service, the
Royal Air Force.

Not mastering new technology? The aeroplane

Unlike the submarine, the way the aeroplane was developed as a
maritime weapon was, thanks to the creation of an independent
Royal Air Force on 1 April 1918, almost completely outside the
control of the Royal Navy. Far more important than the bureaucratic control of air assets in terms of how the Navy thought about
using aircraft in a future war was the fact that almost all the former
Royal Naval Air Service personnel who had experience of maritime
air operations had transferred to the RAF. The Navy therefore not
only did not control the physical air assets but also did not control
the intellectual development either and would have to rebuild its
own expertise in maritime air warfare.

Despite its lack of in-house expertise, the Navy considered
the impact of airpower and naval aviation in a post-war questions committee between August 1919 and March 1920, which
while calling for the construction of aircraft carriers also argued
that the battleship was not obsolete. Running in parallel with the
Admiralty's investigations was an increasingly vigorous public argument over the future utility of battleships in the face of torpedo
attack from submarines, but especially from air attack with bombs
and air-launched torpedoes. In many respects it was a continuation
of the issue that had been raised by that happy disputant Admiral
Sir Percy Scott in the correspondence columns of *The Times* in the
summer of 1914, before the outbreak of war forestalled any detailed
discussion of the merits of Scott's claims. Appropriately it was Scott
who picked up the cudgels in December 1920 and returned to the
fray. He again questioned the role played by battleships in the face
of submarine and air warfare developments. It provoked a mass of
letters, both in support and also repudiating Scott's claims in no
uncertain terms. Both sides made use of the experience of World
War I in order to prove their arguments. Percy Scott gave back as
good as he got and, clearly enjoying himself immensely, peppered

The Times' correspondence columns with replies to his critics. It was even announced that the Admiralty had convened a committee to consider future battleship construction in the light of war experience. Finally in February 1921 *The Times* drew a line under the debate, pointing out in a leading article that although useful, the controversy had not reached any definitive conclusion.[18]

However, in March 1922, after the Washington Treaty had publicly committed Britain to naval parity not supremacy, the debate about the security of battleships from air attack was re-opened, only this time it rapidly took the form of an inter-service dispute between the Royal Navy and Royal Air Force over the relative merits of seapower and airpower, together with – of course – the question of who should get the scarce funds the Treasury was prepared to release for defence purposes. Both the Navy and army wanted their air forces back. Almost as soon as the war ended the Navy was questioning the support it was getting from the RAF. In December 1919 Hugh Trenchard, the commander of the RAF, pleaded (somewhat incoherently as usual – he struggled to make good arguments in person) with Beatty (the First Sea Lord) and Sir Henry Wilson (the head of the army) for a year's truce in the increasing bureaucratic warfare so that he could establish the RAF properly. Unfortunately Beatty, an enthusiast for airpower, agreed. If only he had known what he was letting the Navy in for.[19]

The efforts – reluctant on both sides – to find a workable compromise over the control of maritime airpower were given a new lease of life by the Trenchard–Keyes agreement, which set up the arrangement for the 'dual control' which persisted for most of the interwar period. The agreement set ratios for the number of naval aircrew and RAF aircrew used within the Fleet Air Arm (FAA). Essentially dual control meant that responsibility for naval aviation was shared between the Admiralty and the Air Ministry. The agreement – possibly because Roger Keyes, whilst undoubtedly brave, was not known for his intellect and was married to Trenchard's wife's sister – did not end the inter-service wrangling, which continued through the 1920s and 1930s. Points of contention at various times included the exact ratio of naval pilots to RAF pilots, the use of ratings as pilots, the refusal of the RAF to consider a dive-bomber and their attempts to sabotage any such dive-bomber design by ignoring all requests to develop a suitable bombsight. When the Navy went to war in 1939 its Blackburn Skua dive-bombers still lacked a proper bombsight. As regards the other aircraft, the Air Ministry believed that the Admiralty asked for the impossible, while the Navy felt that the RAF was not interested in its problems. The end result was that in terms of naval aircraft development the British were steadily falling behind the USA and the Japanese.[20]

Despite poor high-level relations, there was little sign of enmity between the RAF and the Navy on board the new aircraft carriers. By the late 1920s the Navy had six. Three of them were ripe for replacement: HMS *Argus*, HMS *Eagle* and HMS *Hermes*, which were only really experiments in aircraft carrier design. Only the large battlecruiser conversions, HMS *Furious*, HMS *Glorious* and HMS *Courageous*, were fast enough and carried enough aircraft to allow the Navy to try to work out how best to use these weapons in a future war. Having learnt much from its early experiments and its initial batch of aircraft carriers the Navy wanted a new carrier built from the mid-1920s onwards. But financial stringency (that self-perpetuating Ten Year Rule) and technical uncertainties ensured that the new and larger aircraft carrier kept being dropped from the construction programme until work finally started on it in 1935. One of the consequences of the small number of aircraft carried in the first generation of British aircraft carriers, coupled with the effects of 'dual control', was that the Navy developed a hankering for multi-role aircraft which could develop more force for the numbers than a number of single-role machines operating from the same ship. The result were aircraft like the Blackburn Skua fighter/ dive-bomber, the Fairy Swordfish torpedo bomber/spotter/reconnaissance aircraft and the World War II-era Barracuda torpedo/ dive-bomber/reconnaissance aeroplane.[21]

Table 4.2. The Royal Navy's first generation of aircraft carriers.

	Argus	Eagle	Hermes	Furious	Courageous	Glorious
Commissioned	1918	1924	1924	1925	1928	1930
Displacement (tons)	14,000	22,600	10,850	22,450	22,500	22,500
Speed (knots)	20	24	25	30	30	30
Aircraft	15	22	12	33	48	48

All the time there was continued dissatisfaction with dual control and in the late 1930s, as rearmament got seriously under way, the Navy made a concerted attempt to wrest back control of maritime aviation from the RAF. This time, much to the horror of the RAF, the politician tasked to investigate the control of maritime aviation, Thomas Inskip, came down firmly on the Admiralty's side. From 1937 the Admiralty would have control of the FAA. It was, however, only a partial victory for the Navy – the RAF's 'Coastal Area', the repository of all land-based aircraft and large flying boats that were dedicated to maritime operations, would remain with the RAF. The Navy's problems in assimilating the FAA, its shore-based infrastructure and in finding personnel were exacerbated by the expansion of the Navy as Britain sought to put right the deficiencies caused by the Ten Year Rule and the rearmament needed to face a new global threat.[22]

Rearmament

Rearmament was a politically difficult and sensitive topic for the British. Since 1922 they had put their faith in (naval) disarmament and the collective security offered by the League of Nations as the means to prevent a future war. Admitting that their peaceful aspirations had failed was a bitter pill to swallow. So, like all good politicians, the British government got round the problem by refusing to do anything, before finally accepting the situation.

The catalyst for rearmament was not, as might be expected, the rise of Hitler to power in Germany in 1933. Instead it was the

Japanese invasion of Manchuria in September 1931 that sparked the realization that Britain would have to rearm. In February and March 1932 the Japanese occupied Shanghai. In Britain the service chiefs asked for the Ten Year Rule to be lifted. However, disarmament was still at this stage high on the political agenda. Britain had just signed the London Naval Treaty, against the wishes of the Admiralty, and was pushing for a general disarmament conference in Geneva that would look at aircraft and armies, not just navies. However, coalition politics can be difficult beasts to manage. It was decided that British rearmament would therefore have to wait until after the Geneva Conference succeeded or failed.[23]

The breakdown of the Geneva Disarmament Conference came in October 1933 with Germany – now with the Nazi party at the helm – walking out of both the conference and the League of Nations; the Japanese had already stormed out of the League in March over Manchuria. Now Britain could be seen to rearm. The Defence Requirements Committee (DRC) was formed on 14 November that year. Between its formation and the end of 1935 the DRC produced three reports. The first, which was completed on 28 March 1934, was concerned with putting right the most obvious shortcomings of the armed forces. It asked for £70 million over the next five years (the total defence budget for 1934 was only £107.9 million), emphasized the need for spending on the Royal Navy over the other services and stated that Japan, not Germany, was the most pressing threat.

This did not sit well with the politicians. Neville Chamberlain, as Chancellor of the Exchequer, led the opposition to the report. The DRC plans were too expensive; Britain could not afford to prepare for war against both Japan *and* Germany – only Germany should be the issue. The DRC also proposed spending money on the wrong things. Chamberlain and his supporters wanted priority to go to the RAF *not* the Navy. This was due to public panics in the late 1920s and early 1930s about attacks from the air in a future war. Stanley Baldwin, the prime minister, just over a year earlier had coined the famous phrase 'the bomber will always get through'. Thus the politicians wanted a bomber force that would act as a conventional deterrent against Germany, despite the fact that strategic bombing was almost totally unproven in theory and in practice. Also, by making each of the armed services haggle with the Treasury over money, the government managed to avoid bringing the 'Deficiency Programme' into the gaze of the public and international observers until March 1935 when an explanatory defence white paper was published.[24]

Just before the March defence white paper was issued, the Cabinet discussed the possibility of a naval arms limitation treaty with Germany. The Germans were agreeable to the idea and both sides began talks in London on 4 June. Naval disarmament treaties would be used to help contain potential enemies and produce the type of navies the Royal Navy wanted to fight. The Anglo-German Naval Treaty of June 1935 may have approved a German fleet 35 per cent the size of the British and at the same time allowed Germany to own submarines, but it also did more. It effectively conned the Germans into giving up any interest in building a commerce-raiding fleet that could sorely try the Royal Navy in a future war; instead they were going to build a 'balanced fleet', the very type of fleet the Royal Navy would find easiest to counter in the event of war.[25]

The efforts to agree on a second naval treaty and indeed appeasement itself must be seen in a similar light. The proposals for battleship sizes at the Second London Naval Conference would have ensured that new warships would not be larger or more powerful than Britain's shrunken naval armaments industry could make. The development of appeasement after Italy's move into the German camp in 1935 also had a naval aspect. The addition of another likely enemy to the Royal Navy's growing list of potential adversaries around the globe worried the Admiralty and annoyed the First Sea Lord, Admiral Ernle Chatfield. Indeed the basic maritime strategic problem the British faced – too many enemies and too few ships as well as too little economic capacity to rearm – was perhaps the key driving force behind appeasement.[26]

By early 1935 it was clear that a reappraisal of Britain's strategic needs was needed. The DRC was asked to produce a new 'second' report, but this, completed in mid-1935, only asked the Cabinet for more guidance, something the politicians had been clearly trying to avoid. The third and final DRC report was approved by the Cabinet in February 1936 and, owing to the concerns the DRC had over the long-term intentions of Germany, included effectively a plan for the Royal Navy to be able to match German and Japanese naval power – a new 'two-power' standard. This new 'DRC standard' fleet was impressive, but it was felt that it would not be enough and that a 'new standard' fleet was needed to face three possible foes.[27]

Table 4.3. The naval rearmament plans.

	Battleships and battlecruisers	Aircraft carriers	Cruisers	Destroyer flotillas	Submarines
RN fleet in 1936	15	6	53	11	54
DRC 'standard' fleet	15	8	70	16	55
'New standard' fleet	20	15	100	22	82

In many respects, the debate about the level of naval spending was academic. There was not the economic capacity to build the 'new standard' fleet. The battleship-building holiday since 1922, the generally low levels of spending on the Navy after 1928 and the massive economic contraction in the depression of the 1930s had ensured that Britain's ability to quickly produce machines of the complexity of modern warships had been drastically reduced. Skilled labour, steel and other materials were in short supply too as money, materials and workers were thrown by the British at combating the airpower bogeyman.

Despite the problems and wrangles over rearmament, the materiel state of the Navy in August 1939 was much better than in 1932. Radar sets suitable for warships were close to production. Older battleships like HMS *Warspite* had received massive reconstructions, others more limited refits. Five new *King George V* class battleships

Fig. 4.4. HMS *King George V.*

had been laid down and two even larger *Lion* class battleships had been started. Seven new aircraft carriers were under construction or had entered service including five armoured fleet carriers, with more planned, and 19 new cruisers had been completed.

In September 1938 the Munich crisis threatened war but ended up promising 'peace in our time'. That month the eight Royal Naval Volunteer Reserve divisions were allowed to expand. In March 1939 Germany seized the rump of Czechoslovakia. During the spring of 1939 the Navy's intelligence analysis organization – the Operational Intelligence Centre (OIC) – was slowly refined and expanded and the Director of Naval Intelligence advised consular reporting officers and Lloyds agents what their preparations for war should look like. In July the naval reserves were called up and told to report for duty at the end of the month. In August Germany and the USSR signed a non-aggression pact (and secretly agreed to carve up Poland between them when Germany fabricated an excuse to invade). The Navy responded by mobilizing the OIC and preparing for war. The

Admiralty informed all commands what it thought the dispositions of the fleet would be if Japan intervened on the side of Germany following the outbreak of war and on 24 August, following discussions between the chiefs of staff, said that the situation with Germany was critical. Naval preparations for war would be complete by 1 September. That very morning Germany invaded Poland and the Admiralty sent a war-warning signal to all commands. At 11:17 on 3 September the Admiralty signalled all its ships and units: 'Total Germany'. World War II at sea had begun.

Chapter 5

World War II
Home Waters and the Arctic 1939–45

The war at sea until the fall of France

In September 1939 the Royal Navy went to war. The Admiralty had three broad priorities. The first was the defence of the waters surrounding Britain and northern Europe; second, the protection of supply lines through the Mediterranean, in particular the movement of oil tankers from the Persian Gulf to the United Kingdom; third, facing down any possible Japanese aggression in the Far East. These priorities exposed a problem that was to dog the Navy throughout the war – not enough ships, men or resources to fight a widening global war against three strong or extremely strong opponents. The Navy's peacetime rearmament plans would vastly increase its fighting potential as the ships now being built entered service, as would any new war-emergency construction plans, but it wasn't going to be enough to take on Germany, Italy and Japan at the same time. Fortunately in September 1939 the Navy only had to worry about beating the Germans while keeping a close watch on Italy and a weather eye on Japanese movements. The Navy's focus was therefore very clear – Germany, wherever her warships could be found – and the waters around the British Isles and the Atlantic in particular.

From the outset, the Home Fleet – Britain's main battlefleet – was engaged in waging the Battle of the Atlantic, that vital first role of the Navy. While Western Approaches Command was soon to become the headquarters most intimately involved in the battle, it was essentially an anti-submarine force. The German surface-raider threat could only be met by cruisers attached to various commands and stations around the world and reinforcements from the Home Fleet. While the convoy system swung into action the Home Fleet was also involved in shepherding to safety British merchant ships that were already at sea when war was declared. While carrying out anti-submarine patrols for this very reason, HMS *Ark Royal*, Britain's most modern aircraft carrier had been near missed by a U-boat's torpedoes on 14 September, and on the 17th HMS *Courageous* – one of only four large aircraft carriers available to the Royal Navy – was torpedoed and sunk with heavy loss of life. A worse humiliation was to follow in October when, during the night of the 14th/15th, *U-47* commanded by Günther Prien managed to penetrate the less than adequate defences of the Home Fleet's principal anchorage at Scapa Flow and torpedo the elderly *R* class battleship HMS *Royal Oak*. *U-47*'s first salvo of torpedoes only scored one hit which caused such minor damage to the bow that the *Royal Oak*'s crew thought it was an internal explosion in the paint store. Having calmly reloaded his bow torpedo tubes, Prien fired again and scored three hits which tore the ship's side apart in massive explosions. The *Royal Oak* capsized and sank, taking with her 833 crew.

The loss of the *Courageous* and *Royal Oak* were significant blows to the Navy, which had no real opportunity to inflict severe losses on the enemy. German surface raiders, however, soon gave the Royal Navy a chance to fight back. By the end of October 1939 the Admiralty knew of two raiders operating in the Atlantic. Together with the French navy, the British cast a net of hunting groups across the North and South Atlantic to find and destroy the German pocket battleships *Graf Spee* and *Deutschland*. The Allied effort to find the raiders was massive: four British battleships out of 12, all the aircraft carriers, two battlecruisers out of three, eight heavy and four light cruisers from a total of 54, while the French navy contributed two battlecruisers; their sole aircraft carrier and four cruisers were involved in the search or the enhanced protection of convoys.

The *Deutschland*, ordered to concentrate on independently routed merchant ships and to avoid enemy warships, achieved very little during her cruise through the North Atlantic. Only two merchant

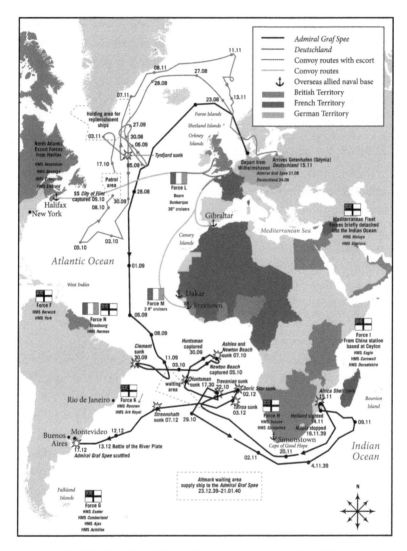

Fig. 5.1. British and French hunting groups, October 1939.

ships were sunk and a third captured during her cruise before she was ordered to return to Germany, arriving at Kiel on 15 November. The Admiralty's picture of German surface-raider attacks was complicated when in late November 1939 the German battlecruisers *Scharnhorst* and *Gneisenau* raided the British patrol lines between the

United Kingdom, Iceland and Greenland. Their object was to cause the British to fear that they had broken out into the North Atlantic. On 23 November they surprised the British armed merchant cruiser HMS *Rawalpindi*, armed with eight 6-inch guns, north of the Faeroes. At 16:04 the *Scharnhorst* opened fire at a range of around 8,000 yards; a couple of minutes later the *Rawalpindi* returned fire. It was no contest, but despite being hopelessly outgunned and outranged by the faster German battlecruisers, the *Rawalpindi* fought in the gathering dusk until she was crippled and ablaze. After less than ten minutes the battle was over and the *Rawalpindi*'s survivors were abandoning ship. The *Gneisenau* and *Scharnhorst* picked up survivors in the thickening darkness, until they feared that they had sighted another British ship and broke off contact in the darkness. Having avoided the Home Fleet, which, lacking an aircraft carrier and effective land-based reconnaissance support from the RAF, was somewhat limited in its ability to find the German ships, the *Gneisenau* and *Scharnhorst* returned to Wilhelmshaven on 27 November. Now only the *Graf Spee* was still at large.[1]

The *Graf Spee*, unlike the *Deutschland*, was having a successful cruise in the South Atlantic and Indian Ocean. After announcing herself by sinking the SS *Clement*, she sank another four ships on the Cape–Freetown route between 5 and 22 October. The *Graf Spee* then passed round the Cape of Good Hope and entered the Indian Ocean to cause as much disruption and confusion over her movements as possible, sinking an oil tanker off the East African coast on 15 November. She then turned round and headed back into the South Atlantic and the Cape–Freetown route, sinking her seventh and eighth victims on 2 and 3 December. The German pocket battleship then met her supply ship the *Altmark* in order to refuel. On 7 December 1940 the *Graf Spee* sank her ninth and final victim before heading south-west towards the River Plate estuary, an area dense with shipping. As she approached the River Plate on 13 December she was sighted by the heavy cruiser HMS *Exeter* and two light cruisers, HMS *Ajax* and HMNZS *Achilles*.

Commodore Henry Harwood, the commander of the British force, had suspected that the German warship would sooner or later turn up off the River Plate and had ordered his ships to concentrate there. His plan to deal with a pocket battleship was simple – attack at once, day or night with *Ajax* and *Achilles* and *Exeter*. Battle was joined at 06:14 and both sides' gunnery was accurate. The *Graf Speed* concentrated on HMS *Exeter*, inflicting heavy damage on her which disabled two of her three turrets, started fires and left her listing to starboard while her remaining turret continued to engage the enemy until she was forced to limp to the south. Despite being heavily damaged, the *Exeter* had repeatedly hit the German ship, but her 8-inch shells were not large enough to cause serious injury. Meanwhile, *Ajax* and *Achilles* were also engaging the *Graf Spee*. Like the *Exeter*, the gunnery of *Ajax* and *Achilles* was accurate, but again their 6-inch shells were too light to inflict critical damage. With the range down to 8,000 yards at 07:38 and still unable to inflict fatal damage in return for the hits they had received, it looked like the British cruisers might be destroyed. But the *Graf Spee* broke off the action and headed for the safety of a neutral port – Montevideo in Uruguay.

Using a mix of diplomacy and subterfuge the British managed to keep the *Graf Spee* in Montevideo while they rushed reinforcements to Harwood's battered force. The cruisers *Dorsetshire*, *Shropshire*, *Cumberland* and *Neptune*, the battlecruiser *Renown* and the aircraft carrier *Ark Royal* were converging on the Plate. Convinced that an overwhelming force awaited him, Captain Hans Langsdorff decided to scuttle his ship on the evening of 17 December rather than be interned or give the British a victory. Three days later, he shot himself. They might not have sunk the *Graf Spee* but it was still a massive propaganda victory for the British. A small force of cruisers, aggressively led, had fought a bigger and more powerful ship to a standstill – the Royal Navy had clearly recovered its Nelsonian verve and panache after the disappointments of World War I.

Closer to home, the Navy was intimately involved in the Allied attempts to blockade Germany, so that she would be denied vital raw materials and food. While little could be done against neutrals allowing goods to be moved into Germany, where they shared a land border, at sea this was a different matter and very quickly patrols of

Fig. 5.2. Above: HMS *Achilles*'s aft 6-inch gun turrets in action.
Below: Battle damage to HMS *Achilles*'s gun director.

submarines, cruisers and converted liners – armed merchant cruisers – were put in place to cordon off the entrances to the North Sea and hence to Germany. However, Norway was a problem, as large amounts of Swedish iron ore were shipped from Narvik and German ships could stay in neutral Norway's waters almost all the way to Germany and thus avoid the Allies.

By the early spring of 1940 the Allies had been considering laying minefields in Norwegian waters to force the German ships out into international waters. It was felt, however, that such action would lead the Germans to intervene in Norway. So the Allies decided that as well as laying mines, land forces would be needed to forestall German retaliation against Norway – Operation *Wilfred*. The Allies intended to put their plan into effect on 5 April, but it was then delayed until the 8th. Then on 7 April the Admiralty received indications that a major German operation was about to be launched. The British Naval Staff felt that an invasion of Norway was imminent; Churchill, the Navy's political head, and the First Sea Lord, Admiral Sir Dudley Pound, disagreed, thinking that a breakout into the Atlantic was the German intent. As a result the landing force was disembarked and the cruisers earmarked to transport the soldiers sent north to patrol the Greenland–Iceland–UK gaps but the minelaying went ahead as planned.

First blood at sea went to the Germans. The British destroyer HMS *Glowworm* encountered some destroyers and then the German heavy cruiser *Hipper*, which avoided the torpedoes the British ship fired at her. Heavily damaged by German shells, the *Glowworm* laid a smokescreen and, as the *Hipper* followed, managed to ram the German cruiser causing serious damage. The *Glowworm*'s captain, when the circumstances of her loss were discovered, was awarded the first Victoria Cross of World War II.

Events moved extremely quickly on 9 April. Denmark was overrun in a matter of hours and German forces were landed at Oslo, Bergen, Trondheim, Narvik, Kristiansand and Arendal. The Norwegians fought back as well as they could, sinking the heavy cruiser *Blücher* in Oslofjord, and damaging the light cruiser *Konigsberg*. Early on the 9th the battlecruiser HMS *Renown*, part of the Operation *Wilfred* force, managed to get in contact with the German battlecruisers *Scharnhorst* and *Gneisenau* and a brief running battle in dreadful conditions occurred before the Germans turned and ran, escaping in heavy rainsqualls. HMS *Truant*, a *T* class submarine, sank the light cruiser *Karlsruhe* off Kristiansand and the Cabinet now approved the use of unrestricted submarine warfare. It was also resolved that Allied land forces should be dispatched as soon as possible to support the Norwegians in their fight to throw out the Germans, but any such forces could not leave until 12 April at the earliest.

On 10 April, the Royal Navy went onto the attack. Fleet Air Arm Skua dive-bombers flying from the Orkneys sank the already damaged *Konigsberg* in Bergen harbour. At Narvik five British destroyers attacked, sinking two German destroyers, crippling three more and sinking six merchant ships and an ammunition ship; HMS *Hardy* and HMS *Hunter* were sunk while *Hotspur* was disabled. The force commander, Bernard Warburton-Lee, was killed and was awarded the second Victoria Cross of the war. That night, the British submarine *Spearfish* managed to put a torpedo into the pocket battleship *Lutzow* (formerly the *Deutschland*), wrecking her stern; for a time it looked as if she might sink, but the Germans managed to get her back to Kiel where it took a year to repair the damage.

British attempts to regain the initiative continued on 12 April; the Home Fleet's solitary aircraft carrier, HMS *Furious*, carried out an air strike on Narvik and Admiral William Whitworth, the commander of Operation *Wilfred*, was readying another attack on Narvik by surface ships, only this time in overwhelming force using the newly arrived battleship HMS *Warspite*. The second battle of Narvik (13 April) saw eight German destroyers and a U-boat sunk, leaving the German garrison isolated. However, there was no military force available to follow up the naval success – six days passed before ground troops were landed.

The Allied first landings in central Norway were on 17 April, but the effort to hold the area was futile – the British troops had not been trained to cope with the deep snow. On 28 April the decision was taken to abandon central Norway and concentrate on Narvik.

However, before the ground attack on Narvik could be mounted the British and French governments informed their commanders on 24/25 May that they were abandoning Norway. On 7 June the evacuation of the Allied forces from Narvik started; it finished on the 8th. Unfortunately after the evacuation the aircraft carrier *Glorious* and her two escorting destroyers were surprised by the *Scharnhorst* and *Gneisenau* on 8 June and all three British ships were sunk with exceptionally heavy loss of life. It was a terrible end to a sorry campaign which showed that much still needed to be learnt about amphibious operations, especially their command and control. Indeed the only silver lining was that while the Royal Navy had lost ships trying to prevent the German invasion, then land the army and finally evacuate it, the German navy's loses were far worse.

On 10 May the German army struck against France and the Low Countries. The Allies expected the Germans to carry out a repeat of the World War I Schlieffen Plan and attack though Belgium. The Germans, however, were planning for their main attack to go through the Ardennes and cut off the British and French forces as they advanced into Belgium; the German attack on Holland and Belgium was a diversion. Before Holland surrendered in the face of German air and ground attacks the Royal Navy had managed to get back to Britain the Dutch gold reserves, 26 merchant ships, 50 tugs and 600 barges and dredgers. The Navy was also able to carry out limited demolitions of some Dutch ports while attempts were made to block Zeebrugge and wreck Antwerp's port facilities.

By the evening of 13 May the French forces guarding the River Meuse at Sedan and Dinant were collapsing. Having broken through the main defences the German tanks were able to drive almost unopposed across northern France. A week later the Germans had reached the English Channel near Abbeville, cutting the British Expeditionary Force and the French 1st and 9th and Armies from their supplies, their reserves and their senior commanders. As the Germans neared the Channel coast it was realized that an evacuation of Allied forces trapped in northern France would be necessary and the task was given to Vice Admiral Bertram Ramsay, the chief of the Navy's Dover Command.[2]

The Allies' situation was deteriorating fast. On 23 May while the Navy was demolishing Boulogne harbour and evacuating the army garrison, there was a sharp fight between British destroyers and German tanks which had appeared on hills overlooking the harbour. Despite having to engage the Germans, three British destroyers successfully rescued about 3,000 soldiers, while another 1,600 or so were picked up that night by HMS *Windsor* and HMS *Vimeria*. At Calais, however, it was a different story. Through the 24 and 25 May the Navy kept the isolated garrison supplied – even landing army reinforcements – and stood ready to evacuate them when ordered. However, the army decided that the garrison must stay in place and fight until overrun by the Germans. On 27 May Calais fell. Now only Dunkirk remained as a possible evacuation route for hundreds of thousands of Allied troops.

Operation *Dynamo* – the evacuation of Allied troops trapped against the coast around Dunkirk – was launched at 19:00 on 26 May. It was hoped that 45,000 men from the BEF could be lifted in two days. In the end *Dynamo* lasted nine days and over 338,000 British, French and Belgian soldiers were evacuated. The lasting British myth about Dunkirk is that of the 'little ships' lifting soldiers off the beaches, of civilian involvement, the amateur, of the improvisation, of success – if not victory. The reality was rather different. The operation was successful because of four factors: relatively calm weather; the presence of British and French warships – mainly destroyers; personnel ships, which in peacetime had been cross-Channel passenger ferries or similar that had been taken up from trade and were manned by their peacetime merchant navy crews; and finally the use of the moles and breakwaters in Dunkirk's outer harbour to facilitate embarkation of large numbers of troops. Only on one day – 30 May – were more troops evacuated from the beaches than from the outer harbour. In all, 338,226 British and French troops (366,162 if those evacuated before the start of the operation are included) were brought back to Britain during the operation.[3]

Table 5.1. Operation *Dynamo*.

Date	Evacuated from the harbour	Evacuated from the beaches	Total
27 May			7,669 (nearly all from the harbour)
28 May	11,874	5,930	17,804
29 May	33,558	13,752	47,310
30 May	24,311	29,512	53,823
31 May	45,072	22,942	68,014
1 June	47,081	17,348	64,429
2 June	19,561	6,695	26,256
3 June	24,876	1,870	26,746
4 June	25,553	622	26,175

The Royal Navy suffered as it saved the British army from destruction. Six destroyers and five minesweepers were sunk; the anti-aircraft cruiser HMS *Calcutta*, 19 destroyers and seven more minesweepers were damaged. However, the end of Operation *Dynamo* did not mean the end of the evacuation of British forces from France – there were still 140,000 troops, together with large numbers of British civilians, outside German-held areas. The final evacuation of the remaining BEF units from Cherbourg, St Malo, Brest, St Nazaire and La Pallice lasted 11 days, from 15 to 25 June; well over 100,000 soldiers and British civilians were evacuated. The Channel Islands were also evacuated as it would have been impossible to defend them; the Germans occupied them on 30 June. 'For the first time since 1066 a portion of the British Isles passed under the yoke of a foreign invader.'[4]

Invasion scares and stalemate? 1940–42

The Battle of Britain – the Spitfire summer, the bravery of the 'Few', Britain alone and the RAF preventing a German invasion

– is perhaps one of the most cherished aspects of British national mythology along with Dunkirk and the Blitz. It is, however, a myth. Britain was not alone – the Commonwealth and Empire were standing shoulder to shoulder with Britain. The 'Few' were undoubtedly brave, but they did not stop an invasion. Behind the propaganda of August and September 1940 stood the Royal Navy, Britain's real defence against an invasion. If there was any one factor that caused the Germans to abandon any invasion plans – if indeed they were ever that serious about invasion – it was the fear of what British destroyers, and cruisers, let alone the battleships, would do to a German invasion force in the waters off south-east England.

The myth of the Battle of Britain is that Fighter Command defeated the Luftwaffe and thus prevented a seaborne invasion. Yet it seems that the Luftwaffe had in fact achieved air superiority over the coastal regions of south-east England by early September 1940, something that was considered an essential precursor to a successful invasion. By the end of September many of the vital sector stations covering the likely invasion area within Fighter Command's 11 Group had been severely damaged. Large formations of German aircraft were able to penetrate inland and widen their attacks. By September the Luftwaffe had gained at worst 'air parity' – the ability to control the air over friendly forces. However, given the wide-ranging attacks and the increasingly ineffective response by 11 Group, more realistically the Germans had achieved over south-east England a degree of local air superiority – the ability to carry out operations without prohibitive interference from the RAF. Only when the Germans attacked London – beyond the effective range of their own fighters – could the RAF mount serious opposition.[5]

Yet having apparently achieved local air superiority the German invasion did not come. Why? It is difficult to say with any certainty; it is unclear whether the Germans were really serious about an invasion – Operation *Sealion* – or whether they hoped to terrify Britain into capitulation with the threat of an all-out attack on British cities from the air. But the possibility that the Battle of Britain was only about giving credence to a threat to attack cities is unsatisfying. The normally disregarded role of the Royal Navy is a possible answer.

The relationship between the Royal Navy and the non-invasion of Britain is quite straightforward – the Germans had to invade by sea and were therefore at the mercy of the Royal Navy. The Germans knew this; indeed they had had first-hand experience of how dangerous a foe the Royal Navy was during their very recent invasion of Norway. Off Norway the Royal Navy had inflicted huge damage on the Kriegsmarine, and used Fleet Air Arm Skua dive-bombers to sink the light cruiser *Konigsberg*, while the Norwegians had destroyed the cruiser *Blücher*. At the same time, the *Gneisenau*, *Scharnhorst*, *Lutzow*, *Nurnberg* and *Leipzig* had been damaged and were still under repair. Even at Dunkirk, where the Royal Navy's freedom of movement was severely hampered by having to evacuate the BEF, the Luftwaffe sank just five of the 56 British destroyers that were deployed. The result was that by late August the Germans had just one heavy cruiser, five light cruisers and ten destroyers to defend an invasion force against a British force of eight cruisers, 36 destroyers with another 40 in reserve, plus the entire weight of the Home Fleet. Unlike the Kriegsmarine, the Royal Navy was still able to fight a demanding battle.[6]

The Germans had to find a solution to the British 'fleet in being'. The obvious answer was airpower, but Norway and Dunkirk had shown this to be an incomplete answer at best. More importantly, air superiority only lasted as long as good weather and daylight. Clouds, night or bad weather meant that there was little chance of ships being successfully attacked. The Luftwaffe in 1940 was not as accomplished at attacking warships as it was to become in 1941 in the Mediterranean. The inability of the Luftwaffe to protect the invasion force at night made it vulnerable to the Royal Navy's destroyers and cruisers. The Royal Navy knew this. Admiral Charles Forbes, the commander of the Home Fleet, considered that if an invasion occurred – which he discounted – it could be defeated at night within 24 hours of it being launched without bringing his battleships south from Scapa Flow. Even the government seemed to realize that an invasion was unlikely, dispatching large numbers of tanks, soldiers and fighter aircraft to the Middle East in August 1940.[7]

Propaganda, political expediency and myth-making does not, however, change the essential facts of 1940. Germany might have gained sufficient local air superiority to prevent the RAF interfering in Operation *Sealion* if it went ahead, but not the Royal Navy. It just was not possible for a German invasion fleet improvised from slow barges to get from embarkation ports – especially those sailing from the shelter of the Scheldt estuary – to England and back again in the hours of daylight. If the Germans had mounted Operation *Sealion* it is almost certain that British cruisers and destroyers would have inflicted devastating losses on the invasion force by night; the German navy was acutely aware of this.

The Battle of Britain is therefore the most important battle that the Royal Navy was never called on to fight. Seapower deters those who lack it and frightens those who neither understand nor have it. But the Kriegsmarine's heavy units which had been damaged during the Norway campaign would come back into action in the autumn and winter of 1940 and 1941, posing a renewed threat in the waters around the UK, the Atlantic and the Arctic for the Royal Navy and specifically the Home Fleet to deal with.

In October the pocket battleship *Admiral Scheer* sailed from Brünsbuttel and broke out into the Atlantic via the Denmark Strait. The German raider found the convoy HX 84 on 5 November and closed to attack it. The convoy's sole escort was the armed merchant cruiser HMS *Jervis Bay*, which on sighting the enemy at 16:50 immediately turned to attack the German ship in order to give the convoy time to scatter and escape in the approaching darkness. The *Jervis Bay*, armed with only 6-inch guns, was no match for the pocket battleship and by 17:20 she was ablaze from stem to stern. Only at 18:00, after the *Jervis Bay*'s crew started abandoning ship, did the *Scheer* stop firing at her and set off after the convoy. In the deepening gloom the *Scheer* only managed to sink five out of the 37 ships in the convoy; the rest escaped into the night. Despite great efforts by the Home Fleet to catch her if she tried to run for either Germany via the Denmark Strait or the French Biscay ports, the *Scheer* was not found. She remained at large until she passed back through the Denmark Strait in late

March 1941, arriving back at Kiel on 1 April, having sunk only 16 merchant ships.

The German heavy cruiser *Admiral Hipper* sortied out into the Atlantic at the end of November 1940, adding to the Admiralty's problems. However, the *Hipper* brushed up against the strong escort of a troop convoy on Christmas Day 1940 and was beaten off without loss. Having sunk only one merchant ship during her cruise, the *Hipper* arrived at Brest on 27 December, the first large German warship to make use of the French ports. After another short cruise in February 1941 when she surprised the unescorted SLS 64 and sank seven of the 16 ships in the convoy, *Hipper* headed back to Germany via the Denmark Strait. However, her place at Brest was soon filled by the battlecruisers *Scharnhorst* and *Gneisenau*. These two powerful ships had broken out into the Atlantic in early February 1941 as part of a coordinated operation with the *Hipper*, but they only narrowly escaped falling into the hands of the waiting Home Fleet on their first attempt to get into the Atlantic. The result, however, was successful – the Royal Navy was faced with two battlecruisers and a heavy cruiser loose in the North Atlantic, and a pocket battleship somewhere in the Central or South Atlantic. The Royal Navy's attempts to find these ships was limited by a lack of RAF long-range aerial reconnaissance, a shortage of aircraft carriers – at the end of 1940 the Home Fleet did not have one, the closest was *Ark Royal* with Force H at Gibraltar – and above all a shortage of modern cruisers and fast battleships. Only the German decision to observe the 300-mile Pan-American neutrality zone limited their freedom of action. Despite this the *Scharnhorst* and *Gneisenau* managed to sink or capture 115,622 tons of shipping. With the Home Fleet blocking the passages either side of Iceland, it was hoped that they would be caught, but instead the battlecruisers were making for France, not Germany. Yet they were sighted by an aircraft from Force H, but bad weather prevented an air strike being launched, allowing the two raiders to reach Brest on 22 March. Then in May 1941 it was the turn of Germany's newest and most powerful battleship – the *Bismarck*.[8]

The *Bismarck*, accompanied by the heavy cruiser *Prinz Eugen*, anchored in Bergen harbour mid-morning on 21 May; their departure from Kiel and passage out of the Baltic had been seen by the Swedes and passed informally to the Allies. Once in Bergen the ships were soon seen by a photo-reconnaissance Spitfire and the Admiralty's Operational Intelligence Centre warned that a commerce-raiding sortie was likely. The Home Fleet sailed in readiness to cover their patrolling cruisers in exits from the Norwegian waters into the Atlantic. The battlecruiser HMS *Hood* and the very new battleship HMS *Prince of Wales* were dispatched to support the cruisers *Norfolk* and *Suffolk* in the Denmark Strait, while the rest of the Home Fleet waited in Scapa Flow to watch the Faroes gaps. The next day a Fleet Air Arm reconnaissance plane managed to fly through terrible conditions to Bergen and found that the German ships had sailed. With this news the remaining ships of the Home Fleet were sent to sea in worsening weather which made air searches on 23 May impossible. The next news came just after 20:30 that day – HMS *Norfolk* had sighted the German ships in the Denmark Strait. With *Hood* and *Prince of Wales* closing quickly, battle was imminent.[9]

Hood and *Prince of Wales* sighted the German ships at 05:35 on 24 May, but Admiral Sir Lancelot Holland had not combined his forces with HMS *Norfolk* and *Suffolk*. Holland's ships opened fire at 05:52 when the range had fallen to 25,000 yards and two minutes later the German ships returned fire, quickly hitting the *Hood* and starting a fire amidships. At 06:00 the *Hood* was hit by the *Bismarck*'s fifth salvo and exploded – there were only three survivors. The ship that symbolized the prestige and superiority of the Royal Navy in the interwar period had been destroyed in less than ten minutes. The *Prince of Wales* tried to continue the action but was soon taking hits from the German ships, forcing her to turn away at 06:33. All now depended on *Norfolk* and *Suffolk* being able to continue to shadow the Germans until Admiral Sir John Tovey, commanding the Home Fleet, could intercept.[10]

Unfortunately the German force divided that evening, the *Prinz Eugen* successfully slipping away from the British shadowers to carry out attacks on merchant ships and convoys. However, she achieved nothing and arrived at Brest on 1 June. The *Bismarck*, on the other hand, was still very firmly in the British sights. Indeed that night at around midnight Swordfish torpedo bombers from HMS *Victorious* managed to locate and attack the *Bismarck*, but it seems that no hits were made. The British then lost touch with her.[11]

There then followed many nervous hours as the British tried to regain touch with the German battleship. Finally, at 10:30 on 26 May a Coastal Command Catalina flying boat sighted the *Bismarck* nearly 700 miles west of Brest. Unless the German ship could be slowed down Tovey and his battleships would be unable to catch up, and they were anyway very low on fuel. Fortunately Force H had been summoned from Gibraltar and HMS *Ark Royal* was close enough to launch an air attack with her Swordfish torpedo bombers. The first attack was a failure, managing to attack HMS *Sheffield* by mistake, although without doing any damage. The second attack did much better, scoring two torpedo hits, one on the port side amidships doing almost no damage. The second torpedo, however, hit the starboard side right aft, jamming the battleship's rudders. Without steering, all she could to was head into the prevailing wave direction – which was straight towards Tovey. At 08:43 on 27 May Tovey's two battleships – HMS *King George V* and HMS *Rodney* – sighted the *Bismarck* steaming slowly towards them.[12]

The British ships opened fire at 08:47 and by 10:15 the *Bismarck* had been pounded into a blazing wreck by repeated 16-inch and 14-inch shell hits at ever closer range – she had been unable to inflict any damage on the British in return; her last salvo was fired at 09:31. The British continued the pounding with the range down to 3,000 yards or less at times. At 10:36, having absorbed many hits, as well as three torpedoes, the *Bismarck* rolled over and sank. But her sinking did not mean the end of the German surface threat.[13]

With two battlecruisers and a heavy cruiser poised on the end of Britain's vital convoy routes, Brest became the centre of the Home Fleet's and the Admiralty's attention. British submarines patrolled outside the approaches to the port, hoping for a chance to torpedo the Germans if they tried to get back into the Atlantic, but a lack of aircraft carriers in home waters prevented any attempts to 'Taranto' the German ships; Coastal Command attacked with torpedo bombers – until the Germans put the ships in dry docks – and Bomber

Command was prevailed upon to launch air attacks which it did for the shortest period possible before going back to bombing the German countryside. Fortunately for the Royal Navy and the British, the Germans themselves decided to remove this dangerous threat to Britain's sea communications by shifting the ships at Brest to Germany via the English Channel and thence to Norway. The British plan to stop such a move, which relied heavily on the RAF, proved to be a dismal failure. The British had accurately predicted how the Germans would conduct the operation; the problem was that the British thought that the passage past Dover would set the timescale for the operation and that the Germans would pass Dover close to high tide. However, the Germans thought it more important to hide their departure and rely on surprise, speed and air cover to get them past Dover in daylight, irrespective of the time of high tide.[14]

At 19:30 on 11 February 1942 the *Scharnhorst*, *Gneisenau* and *Prinz Eugen* left Brest. The patrolling RAF aircraft suffered equipment failure and did not detect the German departure – nor did the RAF alert the Admiralty to the fact that there were holes in the net cast for the Germans. The first indication the Navy had that the Germans were forcing the Channel was at 10:25 when a radar station at Hastings reported a German convoy south-west of the straits. At 11:25 the Admiralty confirmed that these were the three German heavy ships. The limited forces at Dover and Harwich went into the attack as planned – five MTBs, six Swordfish aircraft and six destroyers – but scored no hits with their torpedoes and suffered heavy casualties – all six Swordfish were shot down. Meanwhile, snow was hampering the move of 28 RAF torpedo bombers to the area from the north of Britain; they could only attack after the Germans were well past Dover and again scored no hits, nor did the high-level bombers. Only as the German ships neared home did they suffer damage – from mines. The *Gneisenau* was slightly damaged, the *Scharnhorst* more seriously. It was a terrible blow to British prestige, but despite this it was a strategic defeat for the Germans – they had made the Royal Navy's task much easier by removing such a direct threat to the Atlantic convoys.

Waiting in the wings was the *Bismarck*'s sister ship, the *Tirpitz*. It was imperative that the Germans were deterred from using the *Tirpitz* against the Atlantic convoys. Fortunately there was only one dry dock big enough to hold her for repairs and maintenance – the Normandie Dock in St Nazaire. It was decided that a joint attack by commandoes and the Royal Navy could destroy the dock and prevent its use by the *Tirpitz* – the Navy had been used as a springboard for commando raids along the coast of occupied Europe since 1940. Such was the importance of the raid that the Navy was prepared to sacrifice a destroyer to ensure the destruction of the Normandie Dock gates. The attack went in during the early hours of 28 March 1942. The destroyer HMS *Campbeltown* had been altered to look like a German torpedo boat to help the force penetrate the five miles up the Loire estuary to St Nazaire; she had also been packed with three tons of explosives to destroy the dock gates. Three-quarters of a mile from the dock gates the Germans realized what was happening and opened fire on the *Campbeltown* and the motor launches carrying the commandoes, but to no avail. At 01:34, four minutes later than planned, the *Campbeltown* crunched into the dock gates and her embarked commandoes swarmed ashore. The motor launches too were landing their commandoes under a very heavy fire. Such was the strength of the German resistance that is proved impossible for the unarmoured motor launches to come back in to pick up the landing force and instead the commandoes attempted to escape over land but were all captured. As the naval force withdrew the losses continued to mount, but just before noon that morning HMS *Campbeltown* blew up, demolishing the dock gates and making it unusable. The raid was a success, but at heavy coast: out of 16 motor launches 12 were lost; out of 622 naval personnel and commandoes who took place in the raid only 228 returned to England, five more escaped overland to Spain, 169 were killed and 215 captured. The losses might have been heavy but the only dock the *Tirpitz* could use was put out of action and the *Tirpitz* never operated in the Atlantic. Instead she lurked in Norwegian fjords, a dark brooding presence for those embarking on the Arctic convoy route.[15]

The Arctic convoys 1941–45

On 22 June 1941 Germany invaded Russia. Churchill immediately committed Britain to providing military aid to the USSR, despite his well-known anti-communism. Finally, on 18 July, the Russians accepted – somewhat grudgingly – the British offer of aid. That aid could only be delivered either via an overland route through Persia which had limited capacity or by sea round the top of Norway and to the north Russian ports of Murmansk and Archangel – the Arctic convoys.

The political decision to run convoys to north Russia added greatly to the Royal Navy's problems and those of the Home Fleet in particular. The convoy route was hemmed in by polar ice to the north and Norway to the south and east. Furthermore, Norway provided ample anchorages and bases in its deep fjords for German warships and U-boats, as well as numerous airfields for the Luftwaffe. Arctic convoys could therefore expect to experience a range of attack far greater than the norm in the Atlantic, turning each convoy into a major naval operation. Worse still, during the summer months, near constant daylight deprived the convoys of any chance of hiding in darkness, while in winter the polar ice would force the convoys much closer to German bases in Norway. All the time there was the dreadful weather, the freezing water that would kill anyone within minutes of entering it, and the constant battle against the build-up of ice on ships which would threaten to sink them if ignored.

The first Arctic convoy – Operation *Dervish* – sailed in August from Iceland; it consisted of six merchant ships loaded with raw materials that the Russians desperately needed. The *Dervish* convoy had a close anti-submarine escort, in many respects similar in role to that of an Atlantic convoy, but here the similarity ended as over the horizon the Home Fleet's aircraft carrier HMS *Victorious* and two cruisers waited to pounce on any German surface ships that tried to intervene. The convoy was a success and all the merchant ships arrived safely in north Russia. The next convoy, PQ 1, was run at the end of September with 11 merchant ships, and at the same

Fig. 5.3. HMS *Jamaica*'s A turret and forecastle covered in ice.

time a return convoy, QP 1, sailed from Murmansk. In all, 12 PQ/QP convoys sailed before the end of 1941 and only one merchant ship out of 108 was lost to German action. This would not remain so during 1942.[16] From March 1942 the Germans started to react violently against the PQ/QP convoys; in particular the surface threat to the convoys was escalated. In February 1942 the Germans' 'Channel Dash' had brought the *Scharnhorst*, *Gneisenau* and *Prinz Eugen* back from Brest to strengthen naval forces in Norway. But the most important change was the German decision in early 1942 to base their new *Bismarck* class battleship, *Tirpitz*, in Norway where it could either try to break out into the Atlantic convoy routes or operate against the Arctic convoys. This made every Arctic convoy a major fleet operation for the Royal Navy. German reinforcements meant that the quiet passages of the early convoys were soon forgotten. In March PQ 13 lost five out of 19 ships to U-boats, aircraft and German destroyers operating from Norway. In May PQ 16 was heavily attacked. Then in July came the convoy that has become synonymous with disaster – PQ 17.

PQ 17 had sailed from Iceland on 27 June, the day after the returning convoy, QP 13, had left Archangel. Ice damage and a grounding as PQ 17 sorted itself out forced two merchant ships to drop out from the convoy, leaving 34 plodding towards Russia. The Germans found the convoy during the afternoon of 1 July, but sank nothing until 4 July, when three merchant ships were sunk and one damaged. The day before, the Admiralty discovered that the *Tirpitz* was not at her moorings but there was no certain information as to her whereabouts. The First Sea Lord and others at the Admiralty felt there was a strong possibility that the *Tirpitz* and possibly other German units were at sea. Naval intelligence disagreed, alluding to the absence of Enigma decrypts showing that the Germans had sailed, but this was not enough for the First Sea Lord. The convoy was ordered to scatter. Shorn of their protective escorts, as the merchantmen made their separate ways towards Russia they were exposed to the full weight of German U-boat and air attack. Only 11 merchantmen survived to reach Archangel. It was the worst convoy disaster of the war. The *Tirpitz* had returned to harbour without ever menacing the convoy. Only one more PQ convoy was run before Operation *Torch* absorbed the warships that were needed on the run to Murmansk and Archangel, forcing the suspension of the Arctic convoys.[17]

When the Arctic convoys resumed in December 1942 they received new code letters: JW for Russian-bound convoys and RA for homeward ones. Tovey also ensured that they were given a much stronger destroyer escort so that they could stand a chance of fighting off a German surface force rather than have the convoy scatter. The new arrangements were tested on 31 December 1942 when the German pocket battleship *Lutzow*, the heavy cruiser *Hipper* and six destroyers attempted to attack convoy JW 51B. The convoy had an escort of five *O* class fleet destroyers, one older destroyer plus other escorts with a covering force of two cruisers further off. In a brilliant example of convoy defence which earned the destroyer commander a Victoria Cross, the convoy's escorts fended off the German attacks until the British cruisers were able to close the scene and join the battle, forcing the Germans to retreat. In all, the British lost one old destroyer and a minesweeper, the Germans a modern destroyer; also the *Hipper* was damaged.[18]

In March the Admiralty decided that with the strength of German surface forces in Norway, it was impractical to run convoys during the Arctic summer – by the end of the month the *Scharnhorst* had joined the *Tirpitz*. The Royal Navy had tried in October 1942 to cripple the *Tirpitz* with 'chariots' – British versions of the Italian two-man 'human torpedoes', but the attack failed. In September 1943 they tried again, this time with midget submarines – X craft. The attack succeeded in crippling the *Tirpitz*, although the *Scharnhorst* was undamaged. When the *Tirpitz* was finally ready for sea trials, the Navy struck again, this time from the air. The Fleet Air Arm launched a well-executed attack – Operation *Tungsten* – in early April 1944. Forty Fairey Barracudas escorted by 79 fighters launched from HMS *Victorious*, HMS *Furious* and four escort carriers succeeded in hitting or near-missing the *Tirpitz* 16 times, leaving her crippled again. Improved German air defences frustrated subsequent FAA efforts to get another successful attack in, so the immobile *Tirpitz* was left for the RAF's Bomber Command, which finally sunk her on 12 November 1944.[19]

By the time the *Tirpitz* was sunk, the *Scharnhorst* had also met her end. In December 1943 the Germans attempted to intercept convoys JW 55B and RA 55A. On 26 December, in the darkness of the Arctic winter and the teeth of snowstorms and a raging gale, the *Scharnhorst* was detected and hunted by radar-equipped British cruisers and the battleship *Duke of York* – radar was even used to control the British ships' gunnery in the darkness. Ultra decrypts had given the British warning and allowed them to spring their trap. A running fight developed as the *Scharnhorst* tried to escape. Slowed by hits from the British cruisers as well as repeated hits by 14-inch shells from HMS *Duke of York*, the *Scharnhorst* was finished off with torpedoes fired by fleet destroyers summoned from their task of escorting RA 55A.[20]

In all, 40 convoys sailed from Iceland and the UK to Russia. From a total of 809 merchant ships, 65 (8 per cent) were sunk by enemy action or marine causes during the east-bound passage; 3,964,231 tons out of 16,366,747 tons of British, Canadian and US aid to Russia went by the Arctic route. These ships carried millions of tons of supplies: ammunition, raw materials, tanks, artillery, stream train, electronics, machinery, small arms and vehicles, all of which played an important part in stemming the German onslaught on Russia and enabled the Red Army to take the war to Germany. Across thousands of miles of steppe, forest, marsh and towns across Eastern Europe and Russia, wherever the Red Army was fighting, Allied – British – seapower was being felt in some small way, as it facilitated the liberation of Europe, from the east but also from the west.[21]

The liberation of Europe 1942–45

From the moment the evacuation of British forces had been completed in June 1940, the liberation of Europe was under consideration – which meant a seaborne invasion. However, the experience of Gallipoli in World War I and the debacle of Norway in 1940 had shown that amphibious assaults against modern weapons were not to be undertaken lightly. A great deal of planning and preparation would be needed; procedures would need to be worked out, command and control problems identified and resolved, equipment – both landing craft and for the landing force – would have to be designed, built and tested. While the Allies had had some successes with a variety of commando raids in Europe and the Mediterranean, as well as the attack on Madagascar in May 1942, these were not the size of landing that could hope to put ashore sufficient force or develop sufficient firepower to batter a way through the German coastal defences in France.

The first operation designed to see how difficult such a landing might be was the raid on Dieppe on 19 August 1942. The raid was a frontal assault on the fortified harbour. Elements of two Canadian infantry brigades and a Canadian tank regiment, plus supporting commando units, including a Royal Marines commando unit, were to overwhelm the German garrison, destroy everything of military value in the area and remain in possession of the town from low tide to the next high tide. An important consideration was whether it was possible to attack and capture a port intact so that follow-up

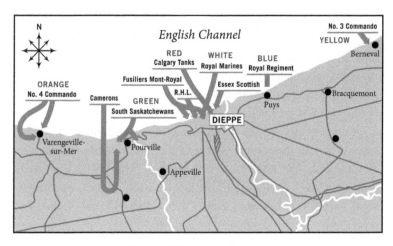

Fig. 5.4. The raid on Dieppe.

forces could be easily landed and fed into the battle – a vital consideration if the subsequent landings to liberate Europe were to be a success.[22]

The raid was a disaster. As the landing force approached by sea, part of it bumped into a German coastal convoy, which altered the defences as well as reducing the force landing on Yellow Beach to levels where it could not achieve its objective. On Blue Beach the infantry were pinned down as they landed. Without tanks or heavy naval gunfire support they could make no progress; the naval landing craft that attempted to evacuate the landing force suffered heavy losses. On Green Beach the South Saskatchewan Regiment made an unopposed landing but ran into German defensive positions as soon as it tried to move inland. In the centre the main assault on Red and White Beaches saw heavy casualties as the infantry tried to make headway against entrenched defenders. Even the presence of tanks did not help, as many were unable to get off the beach due to the height of the sea wall, and those that did were unable to get into the town to support the infantry as their paths were blocked by anti-tank obstacles. By 09:00, four hours after the landings started, it was clear that the main assault was a failure and evacuation was needed sooner than planned. But the German fire on the beaches and their approaches made the evacuation extremely difficult and only a few hundred troops could be taken off while the landing craft suffered heavy losses. By 12:40 it was all over and the land force had started to surrender. Out of a landing force of 6,088, 3,625 were killed, wounded or captured – just under 60 per cent. An invasion of Europe on these lines was clearly impossible.[23]

However, despite its failure the raid highlighted important lessons. It had demonstrated the difficulty of seizing a port by direct assault, the need for very heavy naval gunfire support (only eight destroyers were present off Dieppe), the need for permanent naval assault forces, headquarters ships, better close air support and specialized armoured vehicles to clear the beaches and immediate area of tank traps. All of these lessons were learnt. The invasion of Europe would be a very different affair to the raid on Dieppe.

Planning for the seaborne invasion of Europe initially coalesced around Anglo-American plans for Operations *Roundup* and *Sledgehammer* – ideas to invade in late 1942 in order to take the pressure off the Russians. It was realized that the plan was impractical, not least because of the experience of the Dieppe operation, and the planners' attention moved to the Mediterranean for Operation *Torch*. Serious planning restarted in spring 1943 and the outline plan was presented to the Combined Chiefs of Staff (the Anglo-American coordination committee) and the British and US political leadership at the Quebec Conference in August 1943. In October the complexities of the operation were becoming clear and it was decided that a separate naval commander would be needed; Admiral Bertram Ramsey was chosen for the job. Finally, in January 1944, the invasion plan was increased from three assault divisions to five in response to criticisms by the new land force commander General Bernard Montgomery. The naval plan – Operation *Neptune* – would have to do several things. First, it would need to land sufficient troops to overwhelm the defences. Second, it would need to provide gunfire support from warships to compensate for a lack of army artillery in the opening phases. Third, it would need to defend the embarked landing force and follow-up waves from German interference on, below or above the waves. Finally, it would have to ensure that sufficient reinforcements and supplies could be transported from the UK and USA and landed to build up the land force to a level where it could beat the German units that would be rushed to the area to contain the invasion.[24]

The invasion fleet was divided in two: the western task force consisting of Force U bound for Utah Beach and Force O heading for Omaha Beach, and the eastern task force with Forces G, J and S, which were heading for Gold, Juno and Sword Beaches respectively. Each of the five naval forces bound for the assault beaches were responsible not just for the protection of the landing force, but also provided the fire support for the assault. It was a massive undertaking. In all, there were 138 warships allocated for bombardment duties, including seven battleships, 23 cruisers and over 100 destroyers. In addition, another 226 ships acted as escorts for the ships carrying the assault and follow-up forces, and 287 minesweepers were used to clear the sea routes of German mines, while 4,125 landing ships and landing craft plus 864 merchant ships with their precious cargoes of men and equipment were shepherded to the landing zone. Further up and down the Channel, large naval forces stood ready to intercept any attempt by German U-boats and torpedo boats to attack the invasion convoys. It was quite simply the greatest naval operation ever mounted – and the majority of the ships and men were provided by the Royal Navy.[25]

Perhaps the most difficult task in the planning stage was not the organization of the assault but rather the organization of the reinforcements until the initial phase of the invasion had come to a conclusion towards the end of June. The raid on Dieppe had demonstrated that the cost of seizing a port would be prohibitive in terms of losses, so the Royal Navy developed during 1943 a portable harbour – the Mulberry. There was one for the British sector and one for the US, which would give the Allies port facilities at the beach itself rather than relying on capturing Cherbourg intact at an early stage of the operation. Additionally, the 'Pluto' scheme developed a means of quickly laying fuel pipes across the seabed to carry petrol from England to Normandy. Together they were a highly innovative approach to the logistical problems of liberating Europe.

Fig. 5.5. British troops come ashore from Royal Navy Landing
Craft Infantry (Large) during D-Day. In the distance
can be seen a Landing Craft Tank.

On 6 June 1944, after a delay of 24 hours due to poor weather,
the assault started. The moment that the first landing craft was due
to touch down on each beach varied: 06:30 at Utah and Omaha
Beaches, 07:25 at Gold Beach, 07:35 at Juno, and lastly 07:45 at
Sword, thanks to the need for the tide to cover offshore reefs. From
a naval point of view the landings were a complete success. By the
end of the day, all the assault divisions were ashore, the follow-up
forces were starting to be fed into the beachhead and over 75,000
men and their vehicles had been landed. Naval gunfire had been
highly effective in suppressing the German defences and then breaking up hostile probes and counterattacks, responding well to the
calls for assistance from the infantry. The casualties for the seaborne
landing force were also very low, around 3,000. The majority of
these occurred on Omaha Beach owing to a lack of specialized
assault armour as deployed on the British beaches, and poor weather

preventing the amphibious tanks from being launched as planned.[26]

With the landing force safely ashore and the beachhead expanding – if not as quickly as had been hoped – the naval effort moved towards building up the British, Canadian and American armies, as well as continuing to provide gunfire support until the front line moved beyond the range of the warships' guns. The construction of the Mulberry harbours at Gold and Omaha Beaches started on D-Day+1 and the harbours were in full swing by 9 June. Congestion caused by ships waiting to unload while the Mulberries were being built, especially bad in the American sector at Omaha Beach, was solved by the simple expedient of beaching the ships and unloading them directly onto the sand as the tide went out. In the first six days of the operation, 326,547 men, 54,186 vehicles and 104,428 tons of supplies were unloaded. Once the Mulberries came into operation the daily average of men, supplies and vehicles unloaded in Normandy between 15 and 18 June was 34,712 men, 24,974 tons of stores and 5,894 vehicles. Then, in the early hours of 19 June, a gale blew up that raged for three days. The American Mulberry harbour at Omaha Beach was destroyed and never rebuilt; the British one at Gold Beach was heavily damaged and repaired – possibly because the British were keener on the concept than the Americans. Despite this, in the week after the gale the daily average of vehicles landed was actually higher than before the storm. On 26 June the first of ship-to-shore fuel pipelines to unload tankers came into use. The end of June also saw the capture of Cherbourg. Unfortunately the Germans had comprehensively wrecked the port and a new task fell to the British and US navies – clearing captured harbours of obstacles and restoring the quays, cranes and docks to working order.

At sea the Royal Navy's 10th Destroyer Flotilla had intercepted and destroyed a raid by four German destroyers based in Cherbourg in the early hours of 9 June. Further out in the naval cordon around the invasion area the U-boats were suffering too at the hands of the Navy's anti-submarine forces – 12 were sunk in the Bay of Biscay or the English Channel during June. Such was the density of British anti-submarine forces that from the middle of June only U-boats fitted with snorkels could be used and even then they had a slim chance of survival. On 24 June the decision was made to wind up the Operation *Neptune* aspects of *Overlord*, and by the end of the month *Neptune* was over.[27]

But the Royal Navy's part in the liberation of Europe was not over – the Allied armies still needed supplies and these could only arrive by sea. The need to keep the Allied armies supplied and on the move became especially acute after the breakout from Normandy on 25 July. By the end of August the Allied armies were crossing the Seine; Paris was liberated on 25 August. On 3 September Brussels fell as the Allied armies charged forward and by the middle of the month the Allies were ranged along the Dutch frontier and then south-east of Luxemburg and into Alsace. There were not enough supplies to keep all the Allied armies moving, a problem that was exacerbated by General Eisenhower's broad-front policy that meant all Allied armies were supposed to be attacking all the time.

The key was Antwerp. Admiral Ramsey, on the day Brussels fell, had emphasized its importance and that it was useless unless the Scheldt estuary that led to the port was cleared of German gun batteries. The next day Antwerp was captured intact by the British 11th Armoured Division; but both banks of the Scheldt remained in German hands. While their guns commanded the approaches to the port, British minesweepers could not operate and the port would remain closed to Allied shipping. Allied generals like Eisenhower and Montgomery were focused on getting into Germany and across the Rhine – clearing the approaches to Antwerp was effectively forgotten and supplies still had to be dragged from the Normandy beachhead. It seems that Admiral Ramsey was not regularly included in the senior generals' strategic conferences and so the problems of opening Antwerp were not given due consideration. Only on 16 October did clearing the Scheldt estuary become a priority for the Allied armies.[28]

As British and Canadian units struggled across flooded and waterlogged countryside to clear the German defences, the Royal Navy was on hand with its landing craft to ferry units between islands and to bypass Nazi positions. By 31 October all that was left of the German defences was the island of Walcheren – but it

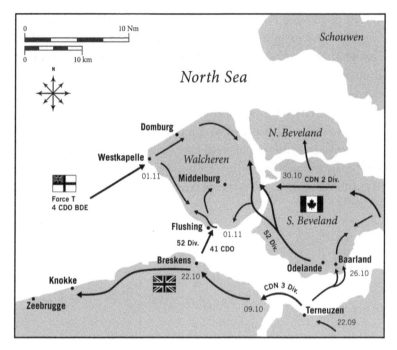

Fig. 5.6. The assault on Walcheren.

was an exceptionally difficult target. An amphibious assault was the answer. A two-pronged amphibious assault took place on 1 November, at the same time as the Canadians attacked the causeway that led to the island from the east. The eastern assault was led by 4 Commando (Royal Marines), with 52 Division as the follow up, all ferried across the Scheldt by landing craft to capture Flushing. The western assault faced a more heavily defended sector of the island and was supported by the battleship HMS *Warspite* – her last engagement of a career going back to Jutland – as well as monitors and a full supporting chorus of landing craft. The Navy put three battalions of Royal Marine Commandoes from 4 Special Service Brigade ashore, together with supporting armour. After very heavy fighting and many casualties, the last German position on Walcheren surrendered on 6 November, opening the way for shipping to use Antwerp. Within three weeks, the German minefields had been cleared and on 28 November the first supplies were landed at Antwerp, vastly reducing the Allies' logistics problems.[29]

With the supply situation restored, and the December German counterattack in the Ardennes defeated, the battle for Germany could begin. By March the Allied armies were at the Rhine. In the north, where the river was at its widest and the current strongest, the problems in mounting an assault crossing were severe. Again the Royal Navy was present, using landing craft to support the main British attack with amphibious LVT7 personnel carriers. Finally on 8 May, as the Royal Navy continued its unremitting war against U-boats and mines, Germany surrendered. The war in Europe was over.[30]

CHAPTER 6

World War II
The Battle of the Atlantic

At just after 19:30 on 3 September 1939 the Royal Navy's World War II – and the Battle for the Atlantic – started. The Donaldson Line's passenger ship, SS *Athenia*, en route for Canada with 1,418 passengers and crew aboard, was torpedoed without warning by the German submarine *U-30* about 250 miles north-west of Ireland. The sea was calm and the *Athenia* was slow to sink. Despite this, 112 lives were lost, including 28 Americans. World and especially neutral opinion was outraged and the Germans tried hard to deny that one of their submarines was responsible.

British intelligence estimates suggested that at the start of the war there were several U-boats stationed in the Atlantic waters. In fact by the second week of the war there were 21 at sea in the south-western and north-western approaches to Britain out of a total strength of 57. With the attack on the *Athenia* and other merchant vessels, the Admiralty understandably thought that the Germans intended to carry out an unrestricted submarine campaign – like the one in 1917–18 – from the outset. As a result, the Admiralty instigated convoys for all inboard and outbound merchant vessels on 7 September – the Battle of the Atlantic had begun. There was no 'phoney war' for the Navy.

The opening phase

The decision to start running convoys as soon as possible was all very well, but until the system could be swung into action, there was still a mass of shipping heading to and from Britain that needed to be protected. On any one day it was estimated that there could be up to 2,500 British flagged merchant vessels at sea. This mass of British shipping moving either towards or away from Britain were each given routes to follow by the Admiralty as a stop-gap measure, or were told to avoid the normal shipping lanes. Destroyers were formed into anti-submarine hunting groups to cover the move of British vessels though the south-western and north-western approaches to the United Kingdom – a move that found particular favour with the new political head of the Navy, Winston Churchill, who, as in World War I, constantly agitated for offensive action against the enemy.

The Navy, having recognized the usefulness of aircraft in anti-submarine operations, also used its aircraft carriers in the hunting groups. The RAF, too, were employed hunting submarines, but the RAF's dedicated maritime cooperation force, Coastal Command, had been starved of resources and so did not have many aircraft capable of flying far out into the Atlantic or indeed to patrol as far as the Norwegian coast. Much of the airborne anti-submarine effort in the opening days and weeks of the war therefore fell on the Royal Navy's aircraft carriers. The Navy had looked at building small 'trade protection' aircraft carriers as part of the rearmament plans, but there were insufficient resources and money to do this. Using fleet carriers for anti-submarine work was not a happy experience for the Navy. The almost new aircraft carrier HMS *Ark Royal* was near-missed by torpedoes from a U-boat on 14 September; her escorting destroyers pounced on the U-boat – *U-39* – and sank it. On 17 September HMS *Courageous* was sunk by a U-boat as she turned into the wind to operate her aircraft. In a sad repetition of the naval losses at the very start of World War I, it was found that not all of *Courageous*'s crew had been issued with lifejackets. Nearly half of her ship's company – 518 out of 1,260 – were drowned. The Navy only had four large 'fleet' aircraft carriers and three smaller ones at the start of the war; now a quarter of the large fast 'fleet' carrier force had been lost. The aircraft carriers were rapidly withdrawn from anti-submarine hunting groups.[1]

Fig. 6.1. HMS *Courageous* sinking after being torpedoed by *U-29*,
17 September 1939.

Despite the rapid introduction of convoys for ocean traffic
slower than 15 knots and for much of the coastal traffic, especially
along the British North Sea coast, and the use of hunting groups
to provide some protection for those ships already at sea when the
war started, the losses started to mount. In September, although no
ships in convoy were sunk, 199,896 tons of British, Allied or neutral
shipping was sunk by U-boats, mines, aircraft, warships and other
causes. By the end of December 1939, 816,729 tons of shipping
had been sunk since the start of the war. In the first half of 1940
another 1,647,508 tons of shipping was lost. Yet losses of convoyed
vessels remained very low compared to that of independently routed
merchant vessels.

Fortunately for the Royal Navy, the Germans did not have many
U-boats. In all, the maximum number of U-boats the Germans had
between September 1939 and the end of June 1940 fell, thanks
to the success of the Navy's anti-U-boat operations. The British
managed to sink 23 U-boats (another one was sunk by the Germans

accidentally). Better yet, of these 23 sunken U-boats, 16 were the larger types designed to work in the Atlantic. It seemed that the Navy's pre-war assessments of the submarine threat to British and Allied shipping was correct – significant in certain areas but containable thanks to convoy, destroyers and ASDICs – the British name for active sonar. Furthermore, the low numbers of U-boats and especially the larger 'Atlantic' types meant that the German submarines were not able to apply much pressure to the Allied shipping routes. They did not – yet – have the numbers needed to launch large 'wolf-pack' attacks while operating on the surface (not submerged) at night against convoys. The U-boat war might have been progressing the way the Royal Navy's pre-war thinking and plans expected it to, but it was not the only means of attack the Germans had in the Battle of the Atlantic.

Table. 6.1. Ships lost in convoy, while straggling from convoy or while independently routed, 3 September 1939–30 June 1940.

	Independents sunk by U-boat	Independents sunk by all other enemy action	Ships sunk while in convoy by U-boat	Ships sunk in convoy by all other enemy action	Stragglers from convoy sunk by U-boat	Stragglers from convoy sunk by all other enemy action
Sep 1939	39	10	0	0	1	0
Oct 1939	23	18	2	0	2	0
Nov 1939	15	27	2	4	1	0
Dec 1939	16	48	1	3	1	0
Jan 1940	26	33	3	3	1	2
Feb 1940	30	15	3	5	2	0
Mar 1940	15	18	0	5	0	0
Apr 1940	5	14	1	2	0	0
May 1940	8	12	2	0	0	0
Jun 1940	44	33	11	1	3	1

**Table 6.2. Losses of German 'Atlantic' submarines,
3 September 1939–30 June 1940.**[2]

U-boat type	Number in service	Number sunk	Percentage sunk
IA	2	0	0
VII	10	4	40
VIIB	11	6	54
IX	8	5	62
IXB	2	1	50
Total	33	16	48

What did concern the Admiralty were two very different threats. The first was the possibility that German warships and disguised merchant raiders would break out into the Atlantic and beyond to attack Allied shipping. The other threat was new and seemingly without a solution – the magnetic mine. Both had potential to cause disruption to shipping.

The surface-raider threat was solved thanks in part to the German's desire to avoid action with British warships limiting their freedom of action, but also to the success in finding and bringing to action the *Graf Spee* in December 1939. Having been harried by three British cruisers which had surprised her off the River Plate, the *Graf Spee* was forced to seek refuge in Montevideo where her captain scuttled her.

Solving the mine problem was, however, a very different issue to sweeping German warships from the Atlantic. Ordinary buoyant mines that were moored to the seabed and exploded when hit by a ship could be easily – if slowly – dealt with by the Royal Navy's minesweepers. The problem in the autumn 1939 was that the Germans were deploying a new mine that lay on the seabed and exploded as a ship passed overhead, either sinking the ship or causing massive damage. These new mines, laid by German U-boats, at night by destroyers dashing across the North Sea and by aircraft, could not be swept using conventional methods. Only by recovering a mine and dismantling it could the British devise a countermeasure. However, as the mines sat on the seabed rather than bobbing at

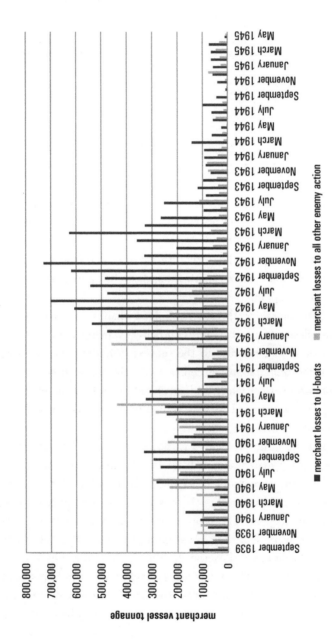

Fig. 6.2. British, Allied and neutral merchant ship losses by cause, September 1939–May 1945.[3]

a pre-set depth at the end of a mooring cable, British minesweepers had failed to recover one.

Luck smiled on the British when in November 1939 a German aircraft managed to drop two of the new mines on mudflats near Shoeburyness where at low tide they were spotted. A team of experts from HMS *Vernon*, the Navy's Torpedo and Mining School in Portsmouth, were sent to the site and set about defusing and disassembling the mines on 23 November. It was very much a trial-and-error process. Having discovered how the mine worked, countermeasures were quickly devised. Ships were fitted with electrical cables around their hulls to produce an electric current – and thus a magnetic field – to counter that of the ship's own magnetic signature, allowing these 'degaussed' ships to pass safely over the German magnetic mines. Equipment was developed to allow minesweepers to effectively sweep magnetic mines, and even some Coastal Command aircraft were fitted with huge electromagnets that allowed them to explode the mines when flying low over the water.

Yet the successes at sea against surface raiders, mines and U-boats between the autumn of 1939 and the spring of 1940 would soon be overturned by events on land, which would fundamentally change the Royal Navy's war. The German army launched its long-expected attack in the west and Italy entered the war on the Axis side.

From the fall of France to Pearl Harbor

The shockingly successful German attacks, first on Denmark and Norway and then on the Low Countries and France, transformed the Battle of the Atlantic. Britain's geographical position barring the German navy's access to the Atlantic, which had so limited the Germans in World War I, had been outflanked to the north and the south. Now Germany controlled the Atlantic seaboard of Europe from the North Cape of Norway to the French border with Spain.

While the rest of the German armed forces may have been surprised by the speed and completeness of their success in the west, the German U-boat arm acted extremely quickly to exploit the situation. France surrendered on 22 June. The next day on the orders of Karl Dönitz, the head of the German U-boat arm, a special train carrying key personnel, spares and weapons was dispatched to the French Biscay ports. The first U-boat – *U-30* – entered Lorient for refuelling and rearming on 7 July. Now U-boats would not have to make the long and risky trip round the north of the British Isles to reach the Atlantic, allowing shorter transit times to the shipping lanes and longer time on patrol as far as 25°W.[4]

The expansion of the German U-boat arm, which had been ordered in late 1939 and early 1940, was also starting to take effect. Slowly – too slowly for Dönitz's liking – the size of the U-boat fleet was increasing. With more U-boats the Germans could change their tactics. Now they intended to launch their attacks on convoys at night, en masse, with the U-boats running on the surface. This would mean that the U-boats would be difficult to detect on the surface with sonar, or by lookouts, while a mass attack would ensure that the convoy's escort was overwhelmed. Meanwhile, independently routed shipping, rather than convoys, remained the chief casualties of the battle.

For the Royal Navy the fall of France had two immediate effects. First, all shipping –in convoy or not – was now routed via the northwestern approaches to Britain and the Channel was effectively closed to large amounts of shipping. This meant that new bases had to be established in Northern Ireland, Scotland and north-west England to support the Navy and Coastal Command. Iceland was seized to prevent the Germans making use of it following the fall of Denmark. It also meant that west coast ports like Liverpool and Glasgow became major convoy assembly areas. Second, the fall of France meant that an invasion of Britain seemed a possibility and many of the destroyers used as convoy escorts were redeployed to watch for and fight off a German invasion armada.

The end result was that Allied shipping losses mounted in the summer and early autumn 1940: 585,496 tons in June, 386,913 tons in July, 397,229 tons in August, 448,612 tons in September and 442,985 tons in October, with the U-boats playing an increas-

Fig. 6.3. The workhorses of the Battle of the Atlantic 1940–43: the *Flower*
class corvette HMS *Charlock* showing the modifications that helped deal with
the dreadful weather in the North Atlantic. The forecastle has been extended
back as far as the funnel, the gun has been raised up on a bandstand to stop
waves washing over it, the mast has been stepped behind the bridge and a
radar has been fitted at the rear of the bridge.

ing role. June also saw the first merchant shipping losses whilst in
convoy (not those ships that had become separated from the convoys
and were 'stragglers') since March 1940 and the highest convoy
losses of the war to date. But these losses were not in vain; it focused
British attention on the need to ensure the 'safe and timely arrival'
of every convoy. In the remorseless logic of the battle, the only way
the British could win was to ensure that their merchant ships got
where they were needed, when they were needed, irrespective of
whether any U-boats were destroyed in the process.

SC 2 (a slow convoy from Sydney, Nova Scotia, to the UK) felt
the weight of a U-boat pack attack between 6 and 10 September
1940. Four U-boats tailed the convoy, attacking it at night on 6/7
and 8/9 September, despite RAF Coastal Command Sunderland
flying boats entering the fray during the day on 7 September, forcing the U-boats to dive but not stopping their attack that night.

Towards the end of the month HX 72 (a fast convoy from Halifax, Nova Scotia, to the UK) was hit, losing 11 ships including stragglers from the convoy. Then in October it was SC 7's turn: 17 ships were sunk out of 34. The U-boat wolf-pack was making its presence felt on the convoy routes. In an effort to increase the numbers of destroyers available to the Royal Navy, British bases were swapped for 50 worn-out World War I-vintage US destroyers in September 1940. But these took time to refit. Only nine were in service by the end of the year and only 30 by May 1941. More significantly the War Emergency Programme of convoy escorts was starting to bear fruit; *Flower* class corvettes entered service from April 1940 onwards. But U-boats were only part of the problem. In November 1940 convoy HX 84 was forced to scatter in the face of an attack by the German pocket battleship *Admiral Scheer*. The convoy's escort, the armed merchant cruiser HMS *Jervis Bay*, immediately turned to attack the vastly superior German ship and was destroyed for its heroic stand allowing the ships of the convoy to escape into the approaching dusk, earning its commanding officer, Captain Edward Fegen, a posthumous Victoria Cross.[5]

Table 6.3. Numbers of convoys arriving/departing the UK and the percentage losing one or more merchant ships, June 1940–December 1941.

Month	Number of convoys arriving or departing the UK	Number losing one or more merchant ships	Percentage
June 1940	60	6	10
July 1940	49	8	17
August 1940	48	10	21
September 1940	48	10	21
October 1940	48	6	13
November 1940	35	7	20
December 1940	36	3	8
January 1941	34	3	9

February 1941	33	6	18
March 1941	29	8	28
April 1941	31	4	13
May 1941	31	9	29
June 1941	31	1	3
July 1941	30	4	13
August 1941	40	3	8
September 1941	30	5	17
October 1941	33	5	15
November 1941	29	4	14
December 1941	28	2	7

Nor did the New Year 1941 bring any respite for the British. The numbers of convoys attacked and losing ships whilst still in formation – as opposed to those ships that had dropped out of the convoy for one reason or another – and the tonnage sunk by U-boats was starting to increase after a lull in January and February. Worse still, German aircraft were starting to cause heavy losses of merchant ships as they approached the North Channel. The impact of all these losses was that British imports were falling. In May 1940 Ministry of Food imports totalled 2,035,000 tons; in November 1940 only 954,000 tons were imported. The import of essential war materials was also affected by the increasing shipping losses and the amount of shipping immobile while it was awaiting repair in British yards. From a monthly high of 2,161,000 tons in August 1940 it had fallen to 1,202,000 tons in February 1941.[6]

The deteriorating situation caused Winston Churchill to issue his 'Battle of the Atlantic declaration' on 6 March 1941. This call to arms was aimed at government as a whole rather than just the Royal Navy. Churchill called for RAF bombing attacks on U-boat bases and construction yards and the German battlecruisers that were in the French port of Brest (which was done half-heartedly – no U-boat bases in France were attacked). The slow turnaround of shipping was addressed, as were the delays in ship repairs. The Ministry of Transport and the Ministry of Labour were told to sort out the mass of shipping waiting to be unloaded and the congestion within the transport network. Above all, the directive also established a high-level Cabinet committee – the Battle of the Atlantic Committee – to oversee the British *national*, not just naval, effort towards winning the battle.

The Battle of the Atlantic was, in every sense, a battle of dry statistics. But if the pulse of the battle could only be seen in the neat columns of imports reaching Britain, of shipping sunk or constructed and of U-boats sunk, there was blood aplenty to be found in the detritus of the battle: the debris littering the ocean, the oil spreading over the sea and the survivors in open boats or bobbing in lifejackets, clinging on to the hope that they would be found and picked up before the Atlantic claimed them.

Yet things were not as bad as some feared in March 1941. In an attack on convoy OB 293 on 7/8 March 1941, Günther Prien, the man who sank the battleship *Royal Oak* in Scapa Flow, and one of Germany's most renowned U-boat 'aces', was killed. His submarine, *U-47*, was spotted at night while it was on the surface closing for an attack on the convoy by HMS *Wolverine*. A five-hour chase ensued, and at 05:19 on 8 March *U-47* was forced to crash dive to avoid being rammed. The *Wolverine* charged straight in and showered *U-47* with depth-charges – an orange glow under the water lasting ten seconds marked the destruction of the German submarine.[7]

The next week, during a U-boat pack attack on convoy HX 122, *U-100*, commanded by the 'ace' Joachim Schepke, was caught on the surface by HMS *Vanoc*. Unseen by *U-100* the *Vanoc* closed at speed and rammed *U-100* level with her conning tower, pinning Schepke in the U-boat's mangled superstructure as it rolled over and sank, leaving a few of the crew struggling in the water. As the *Vanoc* was exploring the extent of the damage to her bow – it was slight – HMS *Walker* gained an ASDIC contact nearby and drove in to attack. After the spray from the depth-charges subsided the *Vanoc* was able to signal the *Walker* that a submarine had surfaced astern of her. There now followed, in the words of HMS *Vanoc*'s captain, Commander Deneys, 'some confusion' as the *Vanoc* hurriedly tried to get under way without mowing down the survivors that were

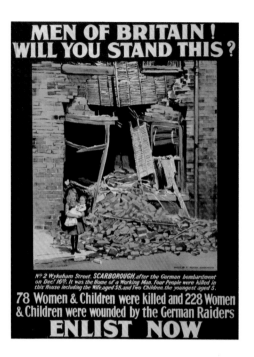

Plate 1. British propaganda posters following the Scarborough raid.

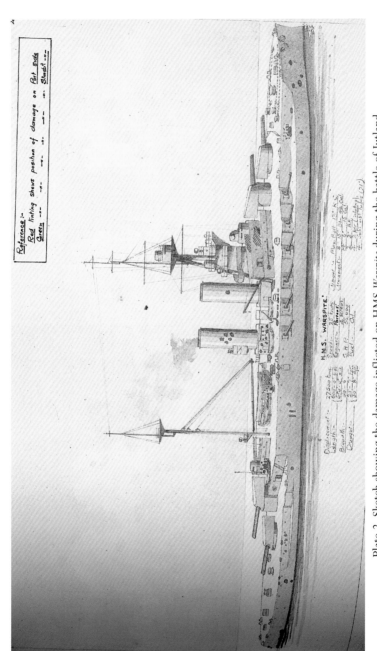

Plate 2. Sketch showing the damage inflicted on HMS *Warspite* during the battle of Jutland.

Plate 3. The attack on Taranto, 11 November 1940. Painting by D. Cobb.

Plate 4. A Fleet Air Arm Buccaneer launching from the flightdeck of a carrier.

Plate 5. A Polaris missile being launched.

Plate 6. Fleet Air Arm Lynx helicopter.

Plate 7. HMS *Illustrious* with Fleet Air Arm Sea Harriers
and RAF Harrier GR7s.

Plate 8. Royal Navy 'Junglie' Sea Kings in Bosnia.

near her propellers and both ships tried to avoid hitting each other as they manoeuvred into position to attack the surfaced U-boat. *Vanoc* managed to get her guns to bear first and opened fire, while the *Walker* closed the U-boat which appeared to be trying to signal its surrender. Before the *Walker* could get a boat over to try to take the submarine as a prize, she sank, leaving her survivors struggling in the water. The last man to be picked up was *U-99*'s commander, Otto Kretschmer, a leading U-boat ace. All in all, March saw Dönitz lose five U-boats, which, even if they had not included three of the top aces, would have been a blow.[8]

The reason why HMS *Vanoc* was able to spot *U-100* in the darkness of a North Atlantic March night was down to the deployment of new equipment – radar. The Navy had originally invested in radar to give sufficient warning of an approaching enemy air raid. However, it was very quickly realized that it would also be useful for fighting at night and in low visibility. The first surface search radar small enough to be fitted in destroyers and other escort craft was the 1.5m wavelength Type 286 and this started appearing from the summer of 1940 onwards. It proved invaluable in helping escorts find their convoys and for detecting straggling merchant ships in bad weather or at night. It was the early version of the Type 286, where the ship had to be turned to change the direction the fixed radar aerial was looking, which *Vanoc* used to such effect on 17 March. However, the 286, owing to its 1.5m wavelength, had difficulty detecting an object as small as a trimmed-down U-boat running on the surface; the best ranges achieved were at about the 1.5 miles mark. A better radar was needed and this came in the form of the Type 271, a 10cm wavelength set which was more than capable of seeing a U-boat on the surface out to a few miles. The prototype 10cm set had been tested in November 1940 and was then rushed into production. It was a godsend for the convoy escorts and started to appear in the North Atlantic convoy routes in the summer of 1941. More importantly, following the savaging of HX 126 before its anti-submarine escort had reached it, the Royal Navy and the Royal Canadian Navy introduced a complete transatlantic escort system for the convoys. Only the minor panic caused by the brief appearance of the German

Fig. 6.4. An example of the CVE: HMS *Trumpeter*, a *Ruler* class escort carrier. These were small ships and often bad weather made flying operations very difficult. In March 1943 convoy HX 228 had the maiden use of a CVE on the North Atlantic convoy routes. The weather was so bad that her aircraft could make no contribution to the battle raging around the convoy.

battleship *Bismarck* (see Chapter 5) near the convoy routes threatened the by now well-established routine of the convoy cycle.[9]

The other significant threat the Navy faced in autumn/winter 1940 and especially spring 1941 was German air attack. The losses due to air attack in the north-western approaches were so bad that finding a solution even featured in Churchill's 'Battle of the Atlantic declaration'. What the Navy needed were aircraft carriers to protect its convoys, but it had too few 'fleet' carriers to spare for such risky tasks. Nor had it been able to build 'trade protection' carriers during rearmament before the war; there was not enough money available to do everything. However, since January 1941 the Admiralty had been involved in producing the first of these trade protection or 'escort carriers' (CVEs) in the shape of the converted merchant ship HMS *Audacity*. Unfortunately, converting or building new ships was a time-consuming process. The immediate solution was to go back to an idea from the very start of naval aviation and use aircraft that could be launched from a ship but have to either ditch alongside the mother ship or head for an airbase on land when their task was done – the single aircraft Catapult Aircraft Merchantman (CAM ship) and the larger multi-aircraft Fighter Catapult Ships like HMS *Springbank*. With the German attack on the Balkans in May 1941 and then Russia in June 1941, much of the German Luftwaffe moved away from Western Europe and losses due to air attack fell.[10]

Sinking by U-boats also plummeted in the late spring and early summer of 1941. It was baffling for the Germans, as it seemed that suddenly there were no convoys. How the British had suddenly found a way to emasculate the U-boats became one of the most precious secrets of the entire war. It was down to signals intelligence: the British had broken the 'unbreakable' German naval codes.

The Admiralty and its Naval Intelligence Division under Rear Admiral John Godfrey were fully alive to the ways in which intelligence could be used both strategically and tactically. Indeed it was the desire to use intelligence in time to influence daily events that caused the Admiralty to set up the Operational Intelligence Centre (OIC) which in time became the hub of the Admiralty's control of the entire naval war. For the Battle of the Atlantic there was a special focus. The Submarine Tracking Room had the job of trying to keep tabs on where all the German U-boats were – even while they were at sea. To do this it needed information and happily the German wolf-pack tactics involved a lot of signalling between the U-boats at sea and Dönitz's headquarters. The Germans used the 'Enigma' machine to encypher messages, which they believed to be unbreakable. Thus the OIC had a mass of messages it could not read. However, direction finding allowed the OIC and its subordinate Submarine Tracking Room to work out where U-boats were even if they did not know what the U-boats were saying to each other. As more direction-finding stations were set up in Iceland and Canada, so the location information every time a U-boat sent a radio message got better and better, to the point where the Admiralty could try to manoeuvre convoys around the U-boats' patrol lines. Traffic analysis could tell much about the unit making the signal without the need to read the messages. Short messages might be weather or sighting reports, longer ones could mean that a U-boat was getting ready to return to base. The man who had to make sense of all this in 1941 was a barrister who had volunteered to help the Navy in any capacity at the outbreak of the war, Rodger Winn. Winn rapidly developed an uncanny ability to understand U-boat operations and predict what Dönitz might do next. But the holy grail of the intelligence war was breaking the codes and cyphers that protected radio messages.[11]

The German naval Enigma machine had more combinations than its Luftwaffe and Wehrmacht equivalents – a choice of any three from eight rotors rather than any three from five. This made the naval Enigma settings much harder to calculate and without each day's settings the messages sent in that 24-hour period could not be read. The Navy needed to capture an Enigma machine with its current setting to give it a toehold in breaking the codes. Thanks to commando raids, the capture of German weather ships lurking in the more remote areas of the North Atlantic, and above all the capture of *U-110* in May 1941, meant that the British code-breaking centre, Bletchley Park (or 'BP'), using electro-mechanical computers – 'Bombes' – had been able to read on and off the German naval Enigma *Heimisch* (or home waters) code, which was used by U-boats in the Atlantic, from February to June 1941 but just not fast enough to be used operationally. Finally the *Heimisch* code – the Allies called Enigma decrypts 'Ultra' – was effectively mastered from July onwards and was read concurrently with the Germans – a massive achievement and one that lasted to the end of the war with at most a 72-hour delay.[12]

However, Ultra generally and the reading of the German Home Waters Enigma was not a panacea for all the problems the Royal Navy faced. Not only was the German Enigma code for foreign waters never broken but Ultra material had to be very carefully handled to ensure that the Germans received no indication that their codes had been cracked. Sometimes this meant that the British had to ignore information because to act on it would have given away the Ultra secret. The strategic as well as tactical information was too precious to risk for a quick minor victory. Nor did Ultra prevent several convoys in the autumn and early winter of 1941, such as SC

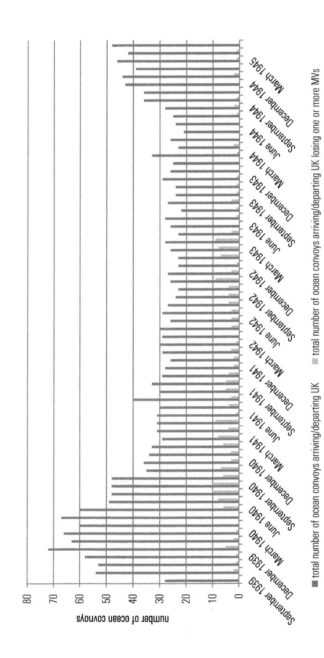

Fig. 6.5. The monthly total of convoys arriving or departing from Britain.

42, being savaged by well-handled U-boat packs when the action was moving faster than Bletchley Park could decrypt the signals about it. Yet over all, the advantage seemed to be with the British and Canadian navies, not the U-boats. Then on 7 December 1941 the war changed – permanently.

The defeat of the wolf-packs

The attack on Pearl Harbor, which brought Japan, Britain and the USA into conflict in the Far East, and especially Hitler's declaration of war on America on 11 December, helped tip the Battle of the Atlantic in the U-boats' favour. Not only had the war widened to include a significant naval opponent – Japan – which would require resources, ships and men that the Royal Navy could ill spare, but it opened up a new area of operations on the east coast of the USA away from the well-drilled convoys and their escorts.

Five U-boats – all that the German navy was prepared to send, despite Dönitz's pleas for more – were quickly redeployed to the US east coast and there found a mass of unprotected and unconvoyed shipping. In mid-January they were joined by more U-boats and their experiences became known as their second 'Happy Time'.

The British (and Canadians) were far from happy. They were putting a great deal of effort into convoying merchant ships safely across the Atlantic, but once the ships passed into American waters the US authorities took no meaningful steps to protect them. The Americans did not even order coastal cities and towns to enforce a blackout until mid-April, which allowed merchant ships to be silhouetted by the shore lights and made them easy targets of U-boats loitering off shore. The carnage spread south-west along the US eastern seaboard and into the Caribbean. Nor could Ultra help: the wolf-packs were not in use on the US eastern seaboard – there was no need for them and that meant no radio signals. Worse still for Bletchley Park and the OIC, Dönitz decided to redesign the Enigma machines his U-boats were using by adding a fourth rotor in February 1942, vastly increasing the possible combinations that had to be broken and requiring BP to develop new 'Bombes'. The resulting Ultra blackout in the Atlantic would last until December 1942.[13]

The Americans tried everything except listen to the accumulated anti-U-boat experience of the British and Canadians, and they would not try convoy. So while the loss rate of convoyed ships in the Atlantic fell from 1.5 per cent between July and December 1941 to 0.5 per cent between January and 31 July 1942, the losses of independent – non-convoyed – ships rocketed upwards from 26 per cent to a disastrous 89 per cent, most of which was occurring in American waters. After numerous British protests about the losses in waters under the nominal protection of the USN, and mostly because everything else had been tried and failed, the Americans finally started adopting convoy in June 1942.[14]

With the introduction of convoy progressively along the US eastern seaboard and into the Caribbean, the rich pickings of merchant shipping dried up. Dönitz's U-boats retuned to the main arena, the North Atlantic convoy routes, during the summer of 1942. They were vastly assisted by the fact that in February 1942 the German naval intelligence section's code breakers, B-Dienst, succeeded in breaking the British Naval Cypher No. 3, which was used for all Allied North Atlantic convoy messages.[15]

Yet the Admiralty faced another battle during the spring, summer and autumn of 1942. The wolf-packs might have returned to the North Atlantic but the British had internal issues to be resolved – the RAF and Royal Navy were at war with each other in the corridors of Whitehall.

This 'Battle of the Air' was an argument over resources. On one side there was the Royal Navy and the RAF's Coastal Command. On the other were the Air Ministry, the Air Staff and Bomber Command. The issue was the supply of aircraft by the Air Ministry for both the Royal Navy and Coastal Command – the reason these aircraft were needed was to attack U-boats. The Navy had long recognized the usefulness of aircraft in anti-submarine warfare and once the Battle of the Atlantic was under way the Navy had wanted to supply air cover using small escort carriers. Unfortunately this was not a quick fix, so as a short-term solution the Navy wanted more support from Coastal Command. Coastal Command, however, was the most neglected of the RAF's commands and had suffered from a number of failed rearmament plans for its long-range flying boats. Using long-range bombers converted into anti-submarine aircraft was a solution to this problem, but this brought Coastal Command into conflict with the Air Ministry, Air Staff and Bomber Command who wanted to bomb Germany, not ensure the safety of raw materials that would keep their aircraft flying.

Coastal Command was also a victim of its own success and the entry of the USA into the war. So effective was Coastal Command's efforts at inhibiting U-boats activities in 1941 (even if they were not sinking them) that the U-boats moved further out into the Atlantic where the flying boats and converted bombers lacked the range to operate. What was needed were very long-range aircraft (VLR). Only these VLR aircraft had the range and endurance to operate in the 'air gap' that existed in the mid-Atlantic beyond the range of normal aircraft operating from Canada, Iceland and the UK. In September 1941 Coastal Command received seven VLR Liberator aircraft under Lend-Lease and divided the solitary squadron (120 Squadron RAF) equipped with them between Northern Ireland and Iceland. However, all subsequent deliveries of US long-range and VLR Liberators went to RAF bomber squadrons in the Middle East or to the civil airline, BOAC. The only aircraft Coastal Command was getting were Lend-Lease aircraft from America and only then because the American bomber types had proved to be useless for Britain's night-bombing offensive. Then when the USA entered the war in December 1941 the Americans needed to expand their own air forces and the Lend-Lease supply of bombers dwindled.[16]

The Admiralty and Coastal Command made repeated requests for more VLR aircraft to help in the Battle of the Atlantic, but they were constantly rebuffed by the Air Staff and the bomber barons in the RAF. The arguments became increasingly bitter as 1942 drew on. The new commander in chief of Bomber Command, Air Marshal Sir Arthur Harris, even wrote to Churchill to tell him that Coastal Command was achieving 'nothing essential to our survival or to the defeat of the enemy' and that it was 'merely an obstacle to victory'.[17]

In order to try to disarm the bitter dispute over allocation of aircraft, the Anti-U-boat Committee was formed in November 1942. It rapidly came to the conclusion that the Admiralty's request for only 40 more VLR aircraft, at a time when Bomber Command was losing nearly that number a night, was entirely reasonable, especially as the RAF's latest plan to expand Bomber Command had been declared impossible to achieve. However, the aircraft would have to be supplied by the Americans, not come from Bomber Command. Happily the Casablanca Conference in January 1943 to decide joint Allied grand strategy made the supply of VLR aircraft for the North Atlantic a high priority. The first new aircraft started arriving in February 1943.[18]

VLR aircraft were not the only new weapons and techniques that were entering the U-boat war. An aircraft's ability to hunt U-boats was also improved by the introduction of the Leigh Light, a high-powered searchlight that could be used to illuminate at night a submarine on the surface in the final stages of an attack when a radar target became hidden by false echoes. It was used with great effect by Coastal Command, especially in their 'Bay Offensive' – the attempt to make a virtue of necessity by attacking U-boats as they transited across the Bay of Biscay in order to get to the convoy routes – an area that was within the range of the medium-range aircraft that made up the bulk of the anti-submarine aircraft in service.

The convoy escorts also saw new equipment reaching them throughout 1942. Hedgehog was a spigot mortar that fired 24 contact-fused weapons ahead of an escort which allowed the hunting warship to remain in sonar contact with a submerged U-boat. Conversely, an attack with depth-charges that were dropped off the stern and sides of a ship meant that as the ship passed over the submerged U-boat contact was lost, giving a good submariner a chance to slip outside the lethal range of the depth-charges. Things were getting harder for the U-boats if they stayed on the surface too. By mid-1942 most escorts were fitted with the superior Type 271 radar, and a significant minority were also fitted with a shipborne version of the high-frequency detection finding equipment

(HF/DF) which had been used to great effect by the OIC to deduce which convoys were under threat of an attack. These ship-borne HF/DF sets gave the escort commander a valuable way of assessing the number and rough position of U-boats manoeuvring to get into position for an attack. Escorts (or aircraft if they were present) could be directed down the HF/DF bearing to force U-boats to submerge and lose contact with the convoy. More and better ships were also coming into service, reducing the reliance on the slow and small *Flower* class corvettes. The increasing numbers of escorts also allowed the British to form 'support groups' in September 1942. These long-awaited groups were tasked with going to the aid of a threatened convoy and its escort, not only to reinforce it but also to give it the resources to hunt U-boats to destruction rather than having to break off the hunt in order to get back to the convoy to ensure its safe and timely arrival at its destination. The convoy was now becoming not just a defensive arrangement but also one where the Allies could mount local offensives against the U-boats.[19]

No sooner had the first support groups been formed than they had to be broken up to provide the escorts for the Allies' first major combined offensive – Operation *Torch*, the invasion of French North Africa. While the invasion convoys suffered almost no losses to U-boats, the drain of resources from the North Atlantic helped make November 1942 a dreadful month for shipping losses: 807,754 tons in all areas, 508,707 in the North Atlantic. Only the dreadful weather in December 1942 and January and February 1943 kept the U-boats at bay. In March 1943 there was a series of massive battles around the convoys SC 121, SC 122, HX 228 and HX 229. These saw significant losses to the U-boats, despite the efforts of the Royal Navy, Coastal Command and the Royal Canadian Air Force. In all, 77 merchant ships were sunk while in convoy during March 1943. Between 6 and 11 March SC 121 lost 13 either in convoy or straggling out of 57 ships; HX 228 got off more lightly between 10 and 13 March with only four merchant ships and one of the escorts, HMS *Harvester*, sunk out of 60. Both convoys suffered from terrible storms that made station keeping and attacking U-boats when detected difficult, but the surface escorts managed to sink two U-boats. The

38 merchant ships of HX 229 suffered next both from storms and then the U-boats themselves, with 12 ships being sunk on the night of 16/17 and to 18 March. SC 122 with 51 merchant ships was badly scattered by storms, too, and from 17 to 19 March the U-boats sank nine ships that were straggling or still in the convoy. Only one U-boat was sunk in exchange for the losses in HX 229 and SC 122.[20]

Despite the severity of these losses, they did not threaten to cut Britain's supply lines. The losses in March were bad, but not the worst. As the Admiralty's own assessment pointed out, this did not mean the value of convoy was diminished, as the total percentage of ships lost was roughly constant. Where there was a crisis – and one that had been bubbling away in the background for a while – was in the global shipping shortage that the Allies faced. But this shortage was not caused by ships being sunk, although this clearly did not help. In fact since July 1942 (with the exception of November 1942) the Allies had been building more ships each month than the Germans had been sinking. The shortage of shipping was caused, quite simply, by the Allies mismanaging what shipping they had and neglecting to allow for the amount of ships needed for their plans to attack Germany and Japan to succeed. The American military were particularly bad at shipping management, especially in the Pacific where merchant ships were often used as warehouses rather than being unloaded, preventing them being used for new tasks. Crisis or not, one thing was clear at the end of March 1943: with the increasing numbers of U-boats at sea in the North Atlantic and the Germans reading the Allied signals to and from the convoys, evasion was no longer an option. The convoys would have to be fought through to their destinations in Britain and the New World.[21]

April saw several large pack attacks on convoys, but Bletchley Park's successful attack on the four-rotor U-boat Enigma machines – 'Shark' – was bearing fruit. There were several convoys, such as HX 230, HX 231, ON 176 and ONS 4, which, thanks to the OIC, Bletchley Park, the newly reformed support groups, aircraft, both land-based – especially the increasing numbers of VLR aircraft – and from HMS *Biter*, the Royal Navy's first CVE to be used on the North Atlantic convoy routes, and the USS *Bogue*, a USN CVE, were able to fight off determined attacks for very few losses, if any. Ultra decrypts also showed that the U-boat crews were getting increasingly wary of air attack. The result was that the U-boats only managed to sink 56 merchant ships (327,943 tons).[22]

The numbers of German U-boats were such at the start of May that the OIC assessed that all routes across the Atlantic were now blocked. There were two wolf-packs of 15 and 17 vessels loitering along the western edge of the air gap, another pack of 13 south of Cape Farewell, Greenland, and a final pack of 13 across the Gibraltar route to the west of the Bay of Biscay. Into this mass of U-boats steamed ONS 5. For once the weather worked in the Allies' favour and the massive storm that engulfed ONS 5 ensured that the U-boats lost contact before an attack could be mounted. However, on 4 May the U-boats regained contact after three days of searching. Fortunately, the first of two support groups had already arrived to reinforce the convoy escort and the warships started an arduous running battle with the U-boats which lasted for three days. During the battle the U-boats managed to sink 12 merchant ships from the convoy, but lost seven of their own to aircraft and warships.[23]

The next convoys in the Germans' sights were HX 237 and SC 129. The OIC tried unsuccessfully to steer both round the massive concentrations of U-boats, but the Germans' ability to read the convoy codes allowed them to match the OIC move for move. HX 237's escorts, which included the CVE HMS *Biter*, managed to sink three U-boats for the loss of only three merchant ships. HX 237 also saw the first use by the Allies of an air-dropped homing torpedo, the 'Mark 24 mine'. It destroyed *U-266*. SC 129 also put up an impressive fight, sinking two U-boats in exchange for two merchant ships sunk. The U-boats could not sustain this level of losses and worse was to follow. Air and surface escorts protecting SC 130 managed to sink three U-boats for no loss during a battle that lasted from 18 to 20 May. It was the same with the attack on HX 239 between 21 and 23 May where no merchant ships were sunk, but one U-boat was. On 24 May Dönitz ordered the U-boats away from the North Atlantic into areas that might be less well defended. In all, 41 U-boats were sunk in May 1943, over twice

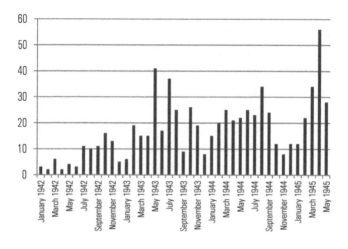

Fig. 6.6. U-boats sunk (all causes), 1 January 1942–9 May 1945.

the number of the previous worst month of losses. They had been defeated.[24]

The closing struggles

The Germans may have suffered a defeat, but they were carrying on with the fight. In September 1943 the wolf-packs returned to the North Atlantic convoy routes, this time armed with homing torpedoes. But the Royal Navy and the RCN were ready and waiting; six merchant ships were sunk from ONS 18 and ON 202, as well as three escorts, in exchange for three U-boats in a four-day battle. The German success was short-lived. The countermeasure to the German acoustic homing torpedo was already in development, thanks to an earlier intelligence scare than such weapons were about to enter service. More ominously the low U-boat losses in September quickly rose again. By mid-November Dönitz again had to admit defeat and withdraw from the convoy routes to go and search in less dangerous areas. The days of wolf-pack attacks were ending.[25]

Over the winter of 1943–44 many convoys made the Atlantic

crossing without any attempts by the U-boats to stop them. From January at least one CVE or MAC ship (a smaller version that retained its cargo-carrying ability while flying the Merchant Navy ensign) could be sailed with every convoy. The air support during the day over the convoys, and day and night across the U-boat transit routes from their bases, forced the U-boats to remain submerged during the day and only operate on the surface at night to charge their batteries. As a result the time to get across the Bay of Biscay and out into the Atlantic was lengthening; the U-boat operating areas were steadily moving to the east and into the coastal waters of Britain.

The Allies deployed better weapons too. The Squid anti-submarine mortar was first used in January 1944; it exploited the information from more advanced sonars like the Type 147 which had entered service in the autumn of 1943. Better radars meant that air and surface units could spot the snorkel masts used by U-boats in 1944–45 to recharge batteries while they were dived. Sonarbuoys were introduced in December 1943 which allowed aircraft to listen for the sound of a submerged U-boat, increasing the usefulness of the Allies' homing torpedoes. Magnetic Anomaly Detectors to indicate the presence of a submerged U-boat were also used successfully by aircraft in February 1944. Life was getting very difficult for the U-boats and as their losses mounted the Allied merchant ship losses fell.[26]

That the Royal Navy was now an excellent anti-submarine force was beyond any doubt. Commanders like Peter Gretton or 'Johnnie' Walker – whose 2nd Escort Group destroyed six U-boats between 31 January and 19 February 1944 – were past masters at sinking U-boats. Walker, however, would not survive the war; he died of a stroke having refused any rest during three years of war.[27]

Nor could the Germans achieve any appreciable successes for the mass of shipping that was launched across the English Channel in June 1944. Protecting the Allied invasion fleets was a layered anti-U-boat defence of ships and aircraft. Yet despite loss after loss, the U-boats still kept trying to attack. The greatest technical challenge was yet to come. The Germans finally started receiving new designs of U-boats – the Type XXI and Type XXIII – which were very fast underwater, indeed faster than some of the Allied escort vessels, thus threatening to undermine the hard-won Allied anti-submarine superiority. But they arrived too late. The first of the Type XXI ocean-going U-boats only became operational on 30 April 1945 while the Type XXIII, which was operational from January, only carried two torpedoes, limiting its ability to be a serious threat in coastal waters. The delay in the German construction plans was due in no small part to the Allied strategic air forces' attacks on the German transport system during the winter of 1944–45 (against the wishes of Bomber Command). These attacks slowed the rate of production of the submarines by delaying the movement of the pre-fabricated components.

With the German unconditional surrender on 7 May 1945, the Admiralty signalled that all U-boats were to surface at noon on 8 May and make for designated British ports; over 150 did so, but 221 scuttled themselves at sea or in harbour rather than surrender. As the U-boats made their way on the surface in accordance with the Admiralty's order, they flew the Royal Navy's white ensign above their own flag. The Battle of the Atlantic was over.[28]

CHAPTER 7

The Mediterranean and the Far East 1940–45

At 16:00 on 9 July 1940 HMS *Warspite* hit the Italian battleship *Giulio Cesare* with a 15-inch shell at the unprecedented range of 26,200 yards – over 13 miles. Receiving damage at such an extreme range unnerved the Italian admiral and he ordered his ships to turn away and break off the action. By 16:48 the battle of Calabria, fought some 90 miles south of the toe of Italy and the first significant clash between the Royal Navy's Mediterranean Fleet under Admiral Sir Andrew 'ABC' Cunningham and the Italian Regia Marina, was over. Only the Italian air force – the Regia Aeronautica – continued the battle, ineffectively bombing both sides in a display of even-handedness that would have cheered the British as much as it depressed the Italian crews.

The battle had come about because both Italy and Britain needed to pass supplies through the Mediterranean. The British needed to send them along the Mediterranean's long east–west axis in order to supply Malta, which had been evacuated as a naval base before the start of the war owing to its proximity to Italian airbases, and to British forces in Egypt and the Middle East. If Britain could continue to use the Mediterranean its shipping could avoid a much longer and time-consuming ocean voyage round the Cape of Good Hope to the Middle East via the Suez Canal. The Italians were therefore keen to prevent the British from being able to operate in the Mediterranean. On the other hand, the Italians needed to get supplies from Italy to their Imperial possessions in North Africa, something the British were determined to prevent. Importantly, in early July both the British and Italian fleets were at sea covering convoys because they had prior knowledge of each other's plans. The British had been reading the Italian naval codes since 1937. Italy, through its agents in Egypt and its own signals intelligence operations, also had knowledge that the Mediterranean Fleet was at sea.

But this was not the first major clash of the war in the Mediterranean. The first clash between battlefleets had occurred nearly a week earlier at the western end of the Mediterranean on 3 July. There, at the naval base in Mers El Kébir, near the port of Oran in North Africa, the British attacked not the Italians, who had invaded France on 10 June, but their erstwhile ally France in a display of quite breathtaking ruthlessness. In a matter of minutes a British naval force had blown up one French battleship and badly damaged another as well as damaging other minor vessels.

The cause of this violent attack on an ally was the British desire to ensure that with the surrender of France on 24 June after the German Army's Blitzkrieg, no French warship that was outside of metropolitan France would fall into enemy hands. If the Germans got hold of the French navy, it would change not just the balance of naval power in the Mediterranean but also in the North Sea and English Channel, where the German navy was still reeling from the losses it had suffered at the hands of the British fleet during the Norway campaign. At Alexandria Cunningham, ignoring pressure from Whitehall and Churchill, persuaded the French ships there to demilitarize themselves. But the large French force at its North Africa base near Oran was a different matter. There Admiral James Somerville, commanding the British naval force off the port, ordered the French to either join the British and take up arms against Germany, sail for a West Indian port and once there demilitarize their ships, sail with reduced crews to a British port, or scuttle all their ships. Unsurprisingly the French refused, so Somerville, acting on the orders of the British War Cabinet, sank the French force. It was an act that more than any other demonstrated Britain's resolve to fight whatever the cost.

The French capitulation, despite the action to destroy the French ships at Oran, did disturb the British strategy for the Mediterranean. The Allied plan was for the British to take care of the eastern basin of the Mediterranean with their fleet at Alexandria, while the French Mediterranean Fleet at Toulon and Oran would look after the western basin. With the French surrender this plan was in tatters and the Admiralty had to find a naval force to contest any Italian moves to command the western end of the Mediterranean. The result was the formation of Force H, a small force centred on an aircraft carrier and a battlecruiser or faster battleship, plus supporting cruisers and destroyers, based at Gibraltar. From Gibraltar Force H commanded by Somerville could act independently in the western Mediterranean, cooperate with the main British Mediterranean Fleet under Cunningham, operate in the Atlantic against any German warships that broke out to try to raid the convoy routes, or support the Home Fleet. It was the best solution to a bad strategic problem in the summer of 1940 – too many enemies and too few ships to fight them with.

The Mediterranean 1940–41

Having dealt with the problem of the French fleet – in Cunningham's case by negotiated disarmament or in Somerville's by sinking it – the Royal Navy could turn its attention to its new enemy – the Italian navy and air force. The threat of air raids had ensured that Malta had been evacuated as a fleet base before the outbreak of hostilities and instead was only a forward operating base for light forces and submarines. On the other hand, Malta was potentially an important asset if it could be defended from air attack, as it sat astride British lines of communication between Gibraltar and the Suez Canal and also commanded Italian communications between the mainland and its Libyan empire.

Table 7.1. Composition of British, French and Italian
Mediterranean fleets, June 1940.[1]

	Battle-ships	Battle cruisers	Aircraft carriers	Cruisers 8in.	Cruisers 6in.	Destroy-ers	Subs	Escort vessels
Britain	5	0	1	0	9	31	12	5
France	3	2	1	7	7	44	46	22
Italy	5	0	0	7	12	111	107	10

However, if the Royal Navy was to take the offensive against the Italians, Cunningham needed reinforcements in addition to the presence of Force H at Gibraltar. Cunningham's problems were also exacerbated in July when the British ability to read the Italian codes started to dry up, which may have contributed to a lull within the Mediterranean between July and October 1940. It was clearly a frustrating time for the Mediterranean Fleet; short of ships, it made 16 sweeps into the eastern and central Mediterranean but only sighted Italian warships on three occasions. Worse, the Royal Navy and RAF only managed to intercept about 2 per cent of the 690,000 tons of shipping the Italians used to keep their Libyan forces supplied between June and December.

While Force H and the Mediterranean Fleet may not have found the Italian Fleet over the summer and autumn of 1940, it did not mean that the British were idle. Various Italian ports were bombarded by warships or attacked by Fleet Air Arm aircraft: Tobruk on 5 July by aircraft from HMS *Eagle*, Bardia on 6 July, 17 and 24 August, and Cagliari on 8 July by FAA aircraft from Force H and again on 2 and 31 August. More importantly, as part of Operation *Hats*, not only was Malta resupplied but valuable reinforcements were passed through the Mediterranean to Cunningham's fleet. By the end of *Hats* Cunningham had received an armoured fleet carrier, HMS *Illustrious*, the battleship HMS *Valiant*, the heavy cruiser HMS *York* and the anti-aircraft cruisers HMS *Coventry* and *Calcutta*, while HMS *Ajax* arrived via the Suez Canal in place of HMS *Neptune*. Soon after *Hats* another heavy cruiser, HMS *Kent*, joined Cunningham's fleet.

With these reinforcements came much better equipment. HMS
Valiant, unlike her sister HMS *Malaya*, already with Force H, had
received a major reconstruction in the late 1930s and had been
fitted with radar sets for air warning and gun ranging, as was HMS
Ajax. The anti-aircraft cruiser *Coventry* carried air search radars
and HMS *Illustrious* too was fitted with the new radar sets. The
arrival of an additional aircraft carrier was especially important as
the ship came with an air group of 19 badly needed Fulmar fighters (a distinct improvement on the few Sea Gladiators available to
the Mediterranean Fleet) and 18 Swordfish torpedo bombers. The
Illustrious was also fully conversant with the concepts of 'fighter
direction' using information from radar sets, a technique pioneered
by *Ark Royal* in the Norwegian campaign.[2]

Having two aircraft carriers with the Mediterranean Fleet and
another one based at Gibraltar with Force H not only increased
the Navy's reconnaissance and air-defence capabilities in the
Mediterranean theatre but also its strike capability. Cunningham
was keen to make use of his new ships. Rear Admiral Sir Lumley
Lyster, who had arrived with HMS *Illustrious* to command the
Mediterranean Fleet's aircraft carrier squadron, brought up the
possibility of an air attack at night on the Italian Fleet's main base
at Taranto using Swordfish torpedo bombers launched from HMS
Illustrious and HMS *Eagle*. Cunningham, unsurprisingly, was enthusiastic about this aggressive idea for getting at an enemy who had been
eluding him. It was Cunningham's intention to celebrate Trafalgar
Day on 21 October by sinking as much of the Italian Fleet as possible. Unfortunately a fire in *Illustrious*'s hangar meant the operation
had to be delayed until mid-November.

On 28 October, however, Italy invaded Greece; the result was
that the next day the Royal Navy started transporting army and RAF
personnel and equipment to Crete, where a major base was planned
in the Suda area, as well as to mainland Greece. The result was that
the attack on Taranto – Operation *Judgement* – was dovetailed with
a series of fleet operations to cover convoys to and from Greece and
the Aegean. Indeed between 4 and 14 November no fewer than ten
operations were mounted by the Royal Navy in the Mediterranean.

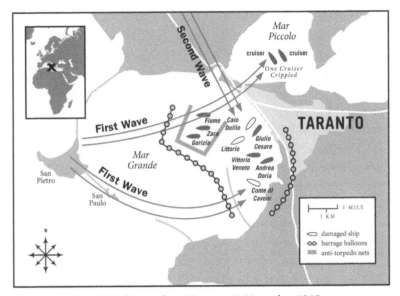

Fig. 7.1. The attack on Taranto, 11 November 1940.

It had been intended that both HMS *Eagle* and HMS *Illustrious* would be used for the attack, but it transpired that *Eagle* was having severe problems with her aircraft fuelling system, so only *Illustrious* was available to make the attack, although aircraft and experienced aircrews were transferred to the *Illustrious* to augment the strike force. The attack was launched on 11 November in two waves, each comprising torpedo-carrying Swordfish biplanes, as well as others armed with flames to illuminate the Italian ships in the harbour – the aircraft dropping flares were also to bomb ships in the inner harbour as well as port installations to keep Italian attention focused away from the low-level approach of the torpedo bombers. The attack was an outstanding success considering the size of the strike force and its less than modern Swordfish aircraft. Three battleships were hit: the *Conte di Cavour* was so badly damaged by a single torpedo hit that she never went to sea again, the *Littorio* suffered three torpedo strikes and was out of action for four months, while the *Caio Diulio* was out of action for six months. Additionally, the cruiser *Trento* and some destroyers as well as the oil storage depot received bombs hits, not all of which exploded. It was the single most devastating air attack on a force that any navy had yet experienced.

At the other end of the Mediterranean Force H was also making its presence felt. On 27 November it clashed off Cape Spartivento with an Italian force that had sailed from Naples and consisting of the battleships *Vittorio Vento* and *Giulio Cesare*, seven heavy cruisers and 16 destroyers. Force H was engaged in covering a convoy carrying supplies to Egypt, and Somerville successfully drove off the superior Italian force, which retreated at speeds greater than most of Force H could muster in pursuit. Somerville sensibly called off the chase in order to ensure the safety of the convoy. Thanks to Taranto, and the aggressiveness of the Mediterranean Fleet and Force H, the British had a clear moral ascendancy over the Italians by the end of 1940. Unfortunately, the Germans were about to make their presence felt in the Mediterranean.

With only an hour's warning, thanks to a signal intercepted by HMS *Warspite*, on 10 January German dive-bombers screamed down on a surprised Mediterranean Fleet. At the time of the attack the fleet was involved in Operation *Excess* – covering the passage of a convoy from Gibraltar to Malta and Greece. Despite very heavy anti-aircraft fire, the German bombers from the Luftwaffe's Fliegerkorps X, including a squadron specializing in anti-shipping work, pressed home their attacks. In less than ten minutes Cunningham's only modern aircraft carrier, HMS *Illustrious*, was hit by six 1,000lb bombs and crippled. Worse, after limping to Malta for hasty repairs, she was hit again by more bombs from German aircraft flying from their new bases in Sicily. Eventually she made her way to the USA for a long refit and repairs. The next day HMS *Gloucester* was badly damaged by a bomb dropped by a German dive-bomber while HMS *Southampton*, blazing furiously after two or three bomb hits, had to be abandoned and sunk by the British.

The Royal Navy's war in the Mediterranean was getting harder.

Even German aircraft cannot be in two places at once, however, and at the other end of the Mediterranean Force H carried out an audacious, if not downright impudent, raid on Genoa, La Spezia and Leghorn on Italy's north-west coast on 9 February. It was, as the

British press gleefully pointed out, a Drake-like exploit that humili-
ated Italian naval and air forces.

With the Germans now threatening the Balkans and Greece,
another task was added to the Royal Navy's portfolio of burdens on
4 March 1941 — the transportation, protection and ongoing support
of a British expeditionary force in Greece. Towards the end of the
month, intelligence was suggesting that a major Italian operation,
probably against one of the convoys heading to Greece, was in the
offing. On 27 March an RAF reconnaissance aircraft spotted three
Italian cruisers south of Sicily and heading for Crete. Cunningham
ordered his fleet to sail after nightfall.

The next morning Cunningham's new aircraft carrier, HMS
Formidable, launched an air search which found Italian cruisers to the
north-west. At 08:00 Cunningham's cruiser force, which was some
way ahead of the battleships, reported that enemy cruisers were in
sight to the north. The British cruisers then tried to lead the Italians
onto Cunningham's battlefleet, during which the British cruisers
were shocked to suddenly find themselves under fire from the Italian
battleship *Vittorio Vento*, an event that hastened their moves towards
Cunningham. Meanwhile, Cunningham ordered HMS *Formidable*
to launch air strikes which succeeded in slowing the *Vittorio Vento*.
The air attack persuaded the Italians to retreat, but unfortunately
the damage to their battleship was not enough to allow Cunningham
to catch up before dusk. Cunningham decided to try to attack the
Italians at night and ordered in his destroyers. While the destroyers were off hunting the Italians, HMS *Valiant*'s radar detected a
stopped ship nine miles away to the south-west. The battlefleet went
to action stations and closed what was hoped to be an Italian battleship. By 22:20 the fleet had closed to under four and a half miles,
but then just a few minutes later a destroyer on the opposite side
of the fleet reported six more ships, the largest two of which were
recognized as *Zara* class cruisers. When the range was less than two
miles to this new and still unsuspecting Italian force, the British
battleships opened fire. At point-blank range the 15-inch broadsides
of HMS *Warspite*, *Valiant* and *Barham* did terrible damage in only a
few minutes. Both the *Zara* and the *Fiume* sank in flames and two

Italian destroyers were sunk in the melee. Separately, Cunningham's destroyers sank the stopped ship, which turned out to be the cruiser *Pola*. While Cunningham did not manage to catch the *Vittorio Vento* as he hoped, the battle of Matapan was a crushing victory.[3]

On land, however, the Germans went on to the offensive. First in North Africa, Rommel's combined German and Italian forces attacked the British 8th Army on 31 March. By the end of April Rommel's forces had chased the British out of Libya to the Egyptian border, leaving the garrison at Tobruk under siege and reliant on the Royal Navy for supplies – a siege that would last for 242 days. Churchill insisted that the Mediterranean Fleet disrupt the main Axis supply port of Tripoli. On 21 April Cunningham's battleships and their escorts appeared off Tripoli and bombarded it, causing much damage and without being attacked on their way back to Alexandria.

A week after Rommel started his offensive, German forces attacked Yugoslavia and Greece simultaneously. After just over 15 days of fighting, the Allied forces were facing destruction and the decision to evacuate the British expeditionary force was taken, while the Mediterranean Fleet was still returning from its bombardment of Tripoli. From 24 April the Royal Navy started picking up the survivors of the British and Commonwealth forces from beaches on Greece's southern coast. As the Germans had almost total air supremacy, the naval losses were heavy: 26 warships and transports were sunk rescuing 50,732 soldiers.

Such was the operational tempo in the Mediterranean that as soon as the evacuation of Crete was completed both Force H and the Mediterranean Fleet had to mount another of their interlocking operations to pass a convoy of tanks for the 8th Army through the Mediterranean under the noses of the Luftwaffe and the Italians. Fortunately cloud cover shielded the ships involved in Operation *Tiger* and only one transport ship was lost to a mine.

Then the Germans turned on Crete.

The Navy's role in the defence of Crete was straightforward: stop German units reinforcing their airborne landings by sea and keep the British and Imperial forces fighting on Crete supplied. The execution of these duties, however, was extremely difficult. There was effectively no fighter protection for naval forces in the vicinity of Crete and to achieve both its aims, the Royal Navy would have to operate under the very noses of German airbases in newly occupied Greece. The Navy managed to intercept the seaborne German reinforcements on 21 and 22 May and neither German convoy reached Crete. However, German air attacks on the British ships were incessant. Between 21 May and 23 May, two cruisers (*Fiji* and *Gloucester*) and four destroyers were sunk. Unfortunately the situation on Crete deteriorated during 21 May, despite the success of the Navy in preventing German reinforcements from reaching the island by sea. With Maleme airfield in their hands, the Germans were able to reinforce at will by air, despite the blockade the Royal Navy had placed around the island.

The decision to evacuate was taken on 27 May, following the final collapse of British and Imperial forces around Suda-Maleme. In all, over 16,000 troops were evacuated to Egypt, but the naval cost was extremely heavy. The Mediterranean Fleet's only aircraft carrier was badly damaged and repairs took six months; three battleships had been damaged – the *Warspite* was out of action for seven months, *Barham* just two while the *Valiant* was never out of action. Three cruisers were sunk, *Fiji*, *Gloucester*, and *Calcutta*, while another six were damaged and likely to be under repair for up to 25 weeks; six destroyers were sunk and seven more damaged. Worse still, most of the repairs were beyond the capability of facilities in Egypt, ensuring that ships had to be sent vast distances for permanent repairs, lengthening the time they would be unavailable.

The losses suffered by the Mediterranean Fleet during the battle for Crete represented a significant reduction in Cunningham's fighting strength. The impact was almost immediate and long lasting through the summer of 1941. The Mediterranean Fleet was effectively immobilized for long periods for want of destroyers and cruisers to locate an enemy force and shield the fleet. The capability gap caused by the damage to *Formidable* meant that the battlefleet was constrained to operating at night or under the rather limited range of land-based fighters. The air cover situation was made worse by the German occupation of Crete and Greece and the eviction of the British army from Libya, allowing the Axis to establish airbases on either side of the eastern Mediterranean.[4]

Malta, however, was still available as a base for aircraft and submarines, and, from Trafalgar Day 1941, surface ships. This was when Force K – the Home Fleet cruisers *Aurora* and *Penelope* plus two destroyers from Force H – arrived at the island. The Admiralty had permitted unrestricted submarine warfare within 30 miles of the Italian or Italian-held coast from the outset. The results were impressive: between June 1940 and December 1941 352 Axis ships of over 800,000 tons were sunk. However, British losses, especially in submarines, were high: in the six months from June 1940 the Navy lost nine submarines in the Mediterranean; in 1941 another eight failed to return from patrol. However, the real crimp on German and Italian land forces in Libya was not due to the Royal Navy but more mundane factors. The North African ports such as Tripoli and Benghazi (Tobruk remained in British hands during 1941) simply did not have the capacity to deal with the large volumes of supplies a modern army needed.[5]

As 1941 drew towards its close, the Navy's losses in the Mediterranean continued to mount, but now it was capital ships that were being lost, not just cruisers, destroyers and submarines. On 13 November Force H was returning to Gibraltar after yet another sortie flying in fighters to Malta when HMS *Ark Royal* was hit by a single torpedo fired by *U-81*. Eventually, after hours of work trying to save her, she capsized and sank. Then it was the Mediterranean Fleet's turn: on 24 November HMS *Barham* was hit by a salvo of three torpedoes fired by another German submarine, *U-331*, and as she capsized her magazines exploded. This was followed by a reinforced Force K blundering into a minefield in mid-December while looking for an Italian convoy; HMS *Neptune* sank after hitting four mines – there was just one survivor – while both the *Penelope* and *Aurora* were damaged, the latter badly, and the destroyer HMS *Khandahar* was also sunk. The final blow of the year came on 19 December when Italian 'human torpedoes' penetrated the defences at Alexandria and placed limpet mines on HMS *Valiant* and *Queen*

Elizabeth; both were badly damaged and knocked out of action.

Would 1942 be any better? Not for months.

The Mediterranean, 1942–44

The year 1942 opened with the Mediterranean Fleet in woeful condition without an aircraft carrier or a single operational battleship. Nor were any reinforcements likely to improve Cunningham's lot. Thanks to the fast deteriorating situation in the Far East, the Admiralty had informed Cunningham that all reinforcements would be heading for the Eastern Fleet, not his command. Meanwhile, Malta's position was deteriorating under the siege that the Germans and Italians had thrown round the island. By February fuel was running short and Cunningham attempted to run three fast merchant ships to Malta and take back the empty shipping already there. Unfortunately the attempt was smashed by Axis airpower; while the four empty ships reached Alexandria safely, the Malta-bound ships were heavily bombed – two had to be sunk, as they were so badly damaged, while the third managed to reach Tobruk. In March another attempt was made to get supplies through, but the operation – *MG1* – was unsuccessful. Rear Admiral Philip Vian, commanding the cruisers which were the heaviest ships available to escort the convoy, carried out a textbook defence of the convoy, holding off superior Italian surface ships, including a modern battleship, twice during 22 March, once in the early afternoon and then during the dog watches. However, the delays this imposed on the convoy meant that the merchant ships were unable to reach Malta before dawn broke on 23 March. Axis aircraft mercilessly attacked the ships as they straggled towards Malta, and while the surviving ships were being unloaded. Only 5,000 tons out of 26,000 tons of supplies reached the island.[6]

This was, however, Cunningham's last battle as commander of the Mediterranean Fleet. On 1 April 1942 he was relieved by Admiral Sir Henry Harwood, the victor of the battle of the River Plate. Cunningham left for Washington to head up the British delegation there – probably the only British naval officer with the professional standing and temperament to stand up to American's irascible and somewhat anti-British head of the US Navy, Admiral Ernie King.

The British naval position in May 1942 was so weak and such were the demands on the fleet as a whole, that it was decided that no convoy could be run from Gibraltar to relieve Malta. However, the aerial pounding the island was receiving made reinforcing the air defences absolutely imperative if Malta was to survive. As no British aircraft carrier was available in April, the USS *Wasp* was borrowed from the USA and used to launch 47 Spitfires to fly on to the island, only for the aircraft to be rapidly destroyed in the days after they reached their destination. The operation was repeated in early May but this time the USS *Wasp* was joined by the elderly British carrier HMS *Eagle*; the two ships launched 64 Spitfires, 61 of which reached Malta on 9 May. The next day these new aircraft were successful in action defending Malta and starting to turn back the Axis tide in the central Mediterranean. HMS *Eagle* made three more runs to fly in Spitfires, once more in May and twice in June, adding another 55 fighters to the island's arsenal.

Fighters were, however, only part of Malta's needs. Some materials could and were sent in by submarine or by one of the Navy's fast minelayers such as HMS *Welshman*, but only in small amounts. What was needed was to get another convoy through. It was decided to run convoys from Gibraltar (Operation *Harpoon*) and Alexandria (Operation *Vigorous*), timed to arrive at Malta on consecutive days. The *Harpoon* convoy of six merchant ships ran through determined air, mine and surface attacks, losing four cargo ships sunk and several warships damaged. However, the two merchant ships that did reach Malta on 14 June – the day the 8th Army started its pell-mell retreat from Gazala following its defeat by Rommel's Afrika Korps – landed about two months' worth of supplies. Unfortunately the *Vigorous* convoy from Alexandria also ran into extremely heavy air attacks and was threatened by an overwhelming surface force. The result was that, having run short of ammunition, the convoy was forced to return to Alexandria. The failure of the two operations was very much down to the Royal

Navy's weakness in major units at this time. Only the obsolete and small aircraft carriers *Argus* and *Eagle* could be spared for the *Harpoon* convoy, while none were available for the *Vigorous* convoy; only one battleship, the unmodernized *Malaya* was available to cover the *Harpoon* convoy and none for the *Vigorous* convoy. Airpower and submarines, which the British tried to use as a substitute for surface ships to meet the Italian naval threat, clearly were not as effective as hoped, although the submarine *P-35* sank the Italian heavy cruiser *Trento* after it had been hit by an airstrike. Another convoy would soon be needed to resupply Malta.[7]

In August 1942 a new attempt to break Malta's siege was made, this time from Gibraltar only and with massive surface support. The 14 merchant ships of Operation *Pedestal* were escorted by two battleships, three aircraft carriers, six cruisers and 34 destroyers, plus corvettes and minesweepers. Additionally, the aircraft carrier *Furious* was loaded with Spitfires which were to be flown to Malta, and eight submarines were on patrol to try to intercept any moves by the Italian fleet. On 10 August the convoy passed Gibraltar and the enhanced escort formed round it. The next day *Furious* was launching her Spitfires for Malta when, without warning, HMS *Eagle* was hit by four torpedoes fired from *U-73*, which had slipped past the escorts undetected. The four torpedo hits caused immense damage to the old ship and, having heeled sharply to port, she capsized and sank in about eight minutes. The loss of the *Eagle* meant a 25 per cent reduction in the convoy's fighter protection until it came within the range of aircraft operating from Malta. At dusk, the first air attacks occurred but did not cause any damage. The next day, 12 August, the convoy had to deal with massed air and submarine attacks. By the end of the day the aircraft carrier HMS *Indomitable* had been damaged and the destroyer HMS *Foresight* disabled, but only one of the merchant ships had been damaged and subsequently sank. However, the weight of attacks had disorganized the convoy as night fell.[8]

Soon after the capital ships and their escorts turned back towards Gibraltar, leaving the convoy and its close escort to pass through the narrows between Sicily and North Africa, a series of explosions

Fig. 7.2. Operation *Pedestal*. HMS *Eagle* can be
seen sinking on the horizon.

damaged the cruisers *Nigeria* and *Cairo* and the tanker *Ohio*. Then
came another air attack which sank the merchant ships *Empire Hope*
and *Clan Ferguson*, while the *Brisbane Star*, which was damaged in
the same attack, eventually reached Malta. Then the cruiser *Kenya*
was torpedoed but was able to keep up with the convoy despite the
damage. The Axis attacks on the convoy continued throughout the
night. At 00:40 enemy motor torpedo boats – E-boats – attacked
the convoy from both sides until after 05:00. HMS *Manchester*, a
Town class light cruiser, was hit twice and had to be scuttled, while
four more of the merchant ships (all stragglers) were hit and sunk,
with one more damaged but still able to keep up with the convoy.
With daylight on 13 August came more air attacks. The merchant
ship *Waimarama* was bombed and sunk in a massive explosion;
later the *Ohio* was repeatedly damaged and disabled, as was the
Dorset, while the already torpedo-damaged *Rochester Castle* was hit
by a bomb but continued under way. At 18:00 the three surviving
merchant ships still able to move sailed into the Grand Harbour,
Malta. The next day the *Brisbane Star* reached the harbour, followed
on the 15th by the *Ohio*, which was towed into port, Five ships out
of 14 reached Malta; an aircraft carrier, two cruisers and a destroyer

were sunk, and two aircraft carriers and two cruisers damaged in order to get the merchant ships through to the beleaguered island. But it was enough to keep Malta going until Allied fortunes in the Mediterranean changed in the late autumn.[9]

In July, while the Navy was still wrestling with the problem of keeping Malta supplied, the Allies decided that as an invasion of Europe in 1942 was impractical, efforts should be made to launch a combined attack on North Africa – Operation *Torch*. The planners looked at an invasion across five sites: at Casablanca in French Morocco, plus Oran, Algiers, Philippeville and Bone in Algeria to allow a rapid advance into Tunisia before the Axis could react. But there were not enough ships to support five separate landings, so the final plan only included assaults on Casablanca, Oran and Algiers, with Admiral Cunningham returning to his old Mediterranean stamping ground as the overall commander of the naval task forces.

On 8 November, the assaults went in. At Casablanca – a USN responsibility – there was resistance from Vichy French forces, but it was eventually overcome by the US army. In the centre, around Oran, unexpected shoals caused problems for the landing craft, but stubborn resistance from the defending Vichy French was overwhelmed by the next day. In Algiers the assault troops were openly welcomed by the French and resistance was slight. The Allies' first joint amphibious operation, despite the huge risks and the problems encountered in the planning and execution of the invasion, was a success, but unfortunately the land force was slow to exploit the collapse of the Vichy forces and capture Tunisia, as the Germans had got there ahead of them. Months of heavy fighting ensued as the Allies slowly pushed back the Germans until on 13 May the surviving German forces in Tunisia surrendered.[10]

Before the Germans had been thrown out of North Africa, the Allies had been considering what the next step in the Mediterranean should be. Sicily was the obvious target, and to facilitate it a most unusual and audacious deception campaign was mounted: Operation *Mincemeat* – 'the man who never was'. This operation saw the Naval Intelligence Division obtain a dead body, dress it in a Royal Marines uniform, create a cover identity for it, place misleading documents

on it indicating that Sardinia and Greece were the targets for invasion not Sicily, and then have a submarine place the body with
all the supporting 'evidence' in the sea off Spain where it drifted
ashore. The Spanish gave the Germans the documents to copy
before returning them to the British naval attaché. The Germans
swallowed the story and the deception, moving troops and materiel
away from Sicily.[11]

In naval terms the assaults on Sicily went well; the assault on
Italy was another matter. The landing force at Salerno was not well
handled by the military commanders and the narrowness of the
beachhead meant that there was a great deal of congestion in getting
supplies, men and equipment ashore while the Germans reacted
most violently. The invasion force was heavily attacked from the
air and the Fleet Air Arm was hard pushed to contain the worst
of the German raids. More significantly the Royal Navy was at the
receiving end of a new weapon, the German radio-controlled glider
bombs, one of which disabled HMS *Warspite* on 16 September and
which were very difficult to defend against while the Allied air
defence was so weak. However, days before, *Warspite* had led the
Italian fleet into captivity following the Italian capitulation after the
invasion of their mainland. On 11 September Admiral Cunningham
signalled the Admiralty: 'Be pleased to inform their Lordships that
the Italian battlefleet now lies at anchor under the guns of fortress
Malta.'[12]

The surrender of Italy did not bring the war in the Mediterranean
to an end. The British were anxious to take advantage of the Italian
surrender to grab islands in the Aegean which had been garrisoned
by Italy – the Americans were less interested, seeing it as yet another
British effort to avoid invading France. Again the main weight fell on
the Royal Navy, and between 10 and 14 September 1943 the islands
of Kos and Leros were seized. However, the Germans had complete
air superiority and were determined to eject the British from the
region. By mid-October it was all over; it was in many respects a
repeat of 1941 – an unmitigated and avoidable disaster.

In central Italy the Allied advance had stalled at Monte Cassino –
the Gustav Line – and an amphibious assault to unhinge the German

position was planned. On 22 January 1944 a joint Anglo-US naval task force attacked either side of the town of Anzio. Within a week 68,886 men plus hundreds of tanks, guns and thousands of tons of supplies had been landed by the Allied navies. Again, German air attacks were damaging and ships were lost to German radio-controlled glider bombs; the cruiser HMS *Spartan* was hit and capsized. Ashore, the Allied ground forces were again badly handled and were stopped dead by the German defences. Rather than being a means of unhinging the German front, Anzio became a besieged enclave, supplied by sea, for months, until reinforced Allied troops were able to go on the offensive *after* the Gustav Line had been broken in mid-May 1944.[13]

The next major act of the war in the Mediterranean was the invasion of southern France in August 1944. This time the Royal Navy was very much the junior partner to the US Navy and the operation on 15 August was very much an American affair. However, the Royal Navy still remained active along both coasts of Italy, giving support where needed and running supplies. In September 1944 the Germans started evacuating Greece and the Aegean and into the vacuum stepped the Royal Navy – a return that did not have the accompaniment of Stuka dive-bombers as in 1941 and 1943. On land the Allies continued their slog up Italy until the unconditional surrender of German forces in the region on 2 May. The war in the Mediterranean might now be over, but already – and for months previously – the main weight of the Navy had shifted to the Far East and the war against Japan.[14]

The Far East, 1941–45

Japan had been Britain's supposed naval enemy for much of the interwar period and its aggression in Manchuria had persuaded the British government to end its dalliance with disarmament in the early 1930s. But such was the situation that Britain faced in 1939 and 1940 that no ships were available to send to the Far East – quite simply there were more pressing matters for the Royal Navy and its Dominion naval partners to face in the Atlantic and Mediterranean.

However, Japan did not join the fighting against Britain in 1939 or 1940. But this does not mean that the area was peaceful. As early as 1939, German surface raiders had operated in the Indian Ocean against Allied merchant vessels, and were hunted by British and Commonwealth cruisers. The *Graf Spee* was the first to penetrate the Indian Ocean in November 1939 and was followed by the *Admiral Scheer* in February 1940, but between them they only sank three ships in the area. However, the Germans also dispatched a number of disguised merchant raiders – converted merchant ships with their armament hidden away from prying eyes – to the Central and South Atlantic, Antarctic and Southern Oceans, Indian Ocean and the Pacific. Between the start of 1940 and the end of 1941 four disguised merchant raiders operated in the Indian Ocean – the *Atlantis*, *Orion*, *Pinguin* and *Kormoran* – with the *Komet* together with the *Atlantis* and *Orion* in the Pacific. In total these five raiders sank 77 merchant ships and whalers – some 451,225 tons of shipping. The Navy's patrolling cruisers had some successes: HMS *Cornwall* found and destroyed the *Pinguin* on 8 May 1941 off the Horn of Africa, the Italian disguised raider *Ramb I* was sunk by HMNZS *Leander* on 27 February in the Arabian Sea, and HMS *Devonshire* caught and sank the *Atlantis* in the Atlantic on 22 November 1941.[15]

However, a disaster had already occurred when on 19 November 1941 the Australian cruiser HMAS *Sydney* found and tried to stop the *Kormoran*, which was pretending to be a Dutch steamer, off the west coast of Australia. For reasons that have never been explained, the *Sydney* closed to within a mile, parallel to the *Kormoran*'s course. Realizing there was no chance of bluffing its way out of trouble, at 16:35 the *Kormoran* unleashed a devastating surprise close-range gun and torpedo attack. The *Sydney* opened fire at almost the same moment as the Germans, and both ships suffered mortal damage in around ten minutes of fighting; the ships then drifted apart blazing furiously. By nightfall they were out of sight of each other. The *Sydney* was never seen again and all 645 of her crew perished; the *Kormoran* scuttled herself after her engines failed as a result of battle damage and 318 out of the 399 personnel on board were either picked up by Allied ships or reached Australia in lifeboats.

Patrolling cruisers to deal with German surface raiders were not, however, the answer to the problem with Japan. Fundamentally the British naval problem from 1939 to 1941 was how to deter Japan from entering the war rather than getting ready to fight her. Unfortunately deterrence was not just a naval problem but a political one. It was Churchill and his Foreign Secretary, Anthony Eden, who forced the Admiralty to dispatch the new battleship HMS *Prince of Wales* and the veteran battlecruiser HMS *Repulse* – Force Z – in October 1941 to Singapore to act as the deterrent force they felt was needed, against the wishes of the Admiralty who instead wanted to establish a balanced fleet by March 1942. Force Z arrived in Singapore on 2 December 1941, the day after the Japanese had decided on war. Deterrence had failed.[16]

In the early hours of 8 December – about the same time as the attack on Pearl Harbor was going in – Japanese aircraft bombed Singapore. Perhaps appropriately, the Navy's first shots in this new war were from its anti-aircraft guns. With the outbreak of fighting, the commander of Force Z, Admiral Sir Tom Phillips, took command of all HM ships in the Far East area at 08:00 on 8 December. Even before the Japanese had attacked Pearl Harbor, they had started their seaborne landing in northern Malaya. At 00:25 on 8 December – some 80 minutes before the attack on Pearl Harbor – the Japanese attempted to land at Kota Bharu. Despite being initially held by the defenders, by dawn they were ashore and establishing themselves after very heavy fighting. About this time landings were also occurring on the Siamese coast at Singora, Tepa and Patani to little or no opposition.

As the Japanese were already ashore, it was imperative that their forces were attacked while they were still vulnerable – before they had completed unloading troops, supplies and equipment. At 17:35 on 8 December Admiral Phillips sailed with all the ships he had available to attack the Japanese forces at Singora and Kota Bharu, as it was felt that these areas were probably outside the range of Japanese anti-shipping aircraft in southern French Indochina. It was a very small force – the modern battleship *Prince of Wales*, the battlecruiser HMS *Repulse* and four destroyers of various types and antiquity.

Unfortunately, despite the cloudy weather and rain that shielded the ships from Japanese air observation, Force Z was sighted by the Japanese submarine *I-65* at 13:40 on 9 December. Then at 17:40 Japanese reconnaissance aircraft were sighted and it was clear that any chance of surprising the Japanese landing force had been lost – Force Z turned around. At 23:35 that day a report was received that the Japanese were landing at Kuantan, over 150 miles further south than the then southernmost landing at Kota Bharu. As this was even further from the Japanese airfields in Indochina, and close to the return track to Singapore, Phillips decided to investigate, but he did not ask for RAF fighter cover or inform anyone at Singapore of his change of plan. By 08:45 on 10 December reconnaissance by *Prince of Wales*'s Walrus aircraft and the destroyer HMS *Express* proved the report false. At 10:26 a land-based Japanese aircraft found Force Z.[17]

The Japanese had 85 bombers already in the air waiting for information on Force Z and at 11:00 they saw the British ships ahead of them. They launched a devastating and highly disciplined attack that saw first the *Prince of Wales* hit and mortally damaged by a single torpedo hit on her stern at 11:44, and then HMS *Repulse* hit by a single torpedo amidships, which she shrugged off. Both ships kept up the fight. However, the slowly sinking but still moving *Prince of Wales* was hit again by three more torpedoes at 12:23. In the same mass attack *Repulse* was unable to dodge all the torpedoes aimed at her and was hit by up to four more torpedoes just after 12:25; she capsized and sank at 12:33. At 13:10 the order was given to abandon HMS *Prince of Wales* as she listed steeply to port; then at 13:20 she turned turtle and sank. Force Z had been destroyed and with it the Royal Navy's main strike force in the Far East.[18]

By 31 January British and Imperial land forces had retreated to Singapore Island and the causeway linking it to the mainland was demolished. On 15 February 1942 Britain experienced its worst ever defeat when the British army and Allied forces surrendered at Singapore. An American–British–Dutch–Australian (ABDA) command had been established in early January and its naval component consisted of a number of cruisers from all four states and supporting destroyers – the Royal Navy's contribution was HMS *Exeter* as well as some destroyers. As the Japanese invaded Borneo and the Dutch East Indies, the ABDA naval strike force tried to intervene.

At the battle of Java Sea on 27 February the ABDA force tried to sink an invasion convoy heading for Java. The ABDA force had severe problems due to the lack of common tactics and procedures between the different nationalities in the naval force. HMS *Exeter* was hit in the boiler room by an 8-inch shell from one of the Japanese cruisers and forced to pull out of the battle, while the British destroyer *Electra* and the Dutch *Kortenaer* had been sunk by torpedoes. The ABDA force tried to get at the Japanese force again after dark, but HMS *Jupiter* was sunk by a mine (probably a mislaid Dutch one) and the Dutch cruisers *Java* and *De Ruyter* were torpedoed and lost. The surviving cruisers, HMAS *Perth* and the USS *Houston* broke off the action, but the next night blundered into a Japanese force off Batavia that was in the act of landing, and in a vicious close-range battle both ships were destroyed. On 1 March HMS *Exeter*, hastily patched up and heading for repairs in Trincomalee, was caught and sunk by a force of four Japanese cruisers and three destroyers in the Java Sea. The naval defence of the Dutch East Indies was now gone; Java fell on 9 March. All the Admiralty could do was to try to save what ships and soldiers could be got past the Japanese, who were rapidly spreading through the area. The closest British bases from which the war could be fought were now Trincomalee in Ceylon and Fremantle in Western Australia.[19]

The battering the Royal Navy had received in the Far East was not yet over. Although the Admiralty had been attempting to rebuild the Eastern Fleet at Ceylon, many of the ships sent to the Indian Ocean were obsolescent or, in the case of the aircraft carriers, with inexperienced and weak air groups. It was enough to make the commander of this poisoned chalice, Admiral James Somerville, despair. Then the Japanese took steps to keep the British off balance. Admiral Chūichi Nagumo, who commanded the Japanese aircraft carriers in the attack on Pearl Harbor, took four of his fast carriers and four fast battleships and struck at the Royal Navy at Ceylon. Trincomalee was bombed and at sea the cruisers *Cornwall* and *Dorsetshire* were lost as well as the obsolescent carrier *Hermes* to air strikes. Somerville's

handling of his ships – keeping the four very vulnerable unmodernized World War I-era *R* class battleships out of the way, while trying
to get close enough to launch air strikes of his own from his two
modern armoured fleet carriers – prevented things from being
much worse. However, the Admiralty ordered the Eastern Fleet to
shift its main base from Ceylon to Kenya, 3,000 miles to the west.[20]

From the early summer of 1942 until 1944 the Royal Navy
was on the defensive in the Indian Ocean, with distance from the
enemy, not the quality or quantity of its ships, the most important
factor in its safety. It had enough ships to deny the Indian Ocean to
the Japanese and to safeguard it as a vital supply route to and from
the Middle East and Australia, but little else. Nor did they have a
fleet train like the United States Navy that would allow them to
remain at sea without having to return to refuel. Instead a secret
refuelling base had to be built in the Maldives. Only the Navy's
submarines could take the fight to the enemy, but Japanese shipping
was not plentiful in the Bay of Bengal, although the light cruiser
Kuma was sunk and the *Kitagami* damaged in January 1944. The only
real offensive the British could mount at sea was at the start of May
1942 when the Vichy French island of Madagascar was successfully
invaded and captured, to forestall any possible Japanese moves.

**Table 7.2. Royal Navy (including Imperial forces) strength
in the Far East and Indian Ocean, 1941–45.**[21]

	Dec 1941	Dec 1942	Dec 1943	Dec 1944	Aug 1945
Battleships and battle-cruisers	2	4	2	5	5
Aircraft carriers	1	2	0	4	9
Cruisers	21	20	18	17	22
Destroyers	13	20	20	33	59
Submarines	1	7	14	38	47

Armed merchant cruisers	12	13	3	0	0
Escort carriers	0	0	1	5	22
Fleet support	0	0	0	5	
Amphibious ships	0	0	2	10	3

With the winding up of the naval campaign in the Mediterranean, as well as the sinking of the *Scharnhorst* and the crippling of the *Tirpitz* in northern waters, the Admiralty could now send modern warships to the Eastern Fleet in early 1944. Just as importantly, more modern aircraft were reaching the carrier air groups – Barracuda torpedo/dive-bombers and Firefly strike fighter/reconnaissance aircraft, as well as Lend-Lease American naval aircraft such as the Hellcat and Corsair fighters and Avenger torpedo/dive-bombers. These additional resources allowed a rejuvenated Eastern Fleet under Somerville to start attacking Japanese bases and economic facilities in Sumatra and Java. In April 1944 the island of Sabang off Sumatra was attacked by British aircraft carriers and bombarded by the Eastern Fleet's battleships. Then in May the Eastern Fleet launched successful air strikes against an oil refinery at Surabaya in Java; both this and the April operation were strengthened by the presence of the carrier USS *Saratoga*. July saw Sabang struck for the second time. All in all, eight such attacks on Japanese possessions along the Malay barrier were mounted between March and October 1944.[22]

More significantly, it was accepted, grudgingly by Churchill, and in the face of outright opposition from the highest echelons of the US Navy who did not wish to share the coming battle with anyone, that the Royal Navy would send a British Pacific Fleet to fight alongside the US Navy in the assaults to clear away the final obstacles to an invasion of the Japanese home islands.

On 22 November Admiral Sir Bruce Fraser hoisted his flag as the Commander in Chief British Pacific Fleet (BPF) and much of the resources of the Eastern Fleet were transferred across to his command. Such was Fraser's seniority that he outranked the US naval commanders. To avoid awkward command issues, he decided, once in the Pacific, to direct the fleet from onshore, while day-to-day command at sea was carried out by his deputy, Vice Admiral Sir Bernard Rawlings. Fraser had actually been in command of the Eastern Fleet since August 1944 – Somerville had been sent to Washington to take on Admiral Ernie King who was the professional head of the US Navy and the chief cause of US opposition to the BPF. King is often characterized as anti-British, but this is perhaps unfair. He was certainly irascible and bullying but, above all, pro-US Navy rather than anti-British. With intense British pressure, however, King's opposition to the BPF was overcome. The Royal Navy would share in the forthcoming victory over Japan.

In March 1945 the British Pacific Fleet joined the US Navy's Central Pacific command. On its way from Ceylon to first Australia and then to the Admiralty Islands chain the BPF carried out two massive raids on the oil refinery at Palembang, Sumatra. The BFP's first operation was as part of US Admiral Raymond Spruance's 5th Fleet. Operating as Task Force 57, the BPF was as part of the Okinawa invasion force – Operation *Iceberg*. Task Force 57 was given the task of suppressing Japanese airfields on Sakashima Gunto, an island group between Okinawa and Formosa, thus preventing the Japanese from moving aircraft to the invasion site from bases further west. From 26 March until 20 April the BPF attacked the Japanese airfields and fended off retaliatory strikes before withdrawing to refit and replace lost aircraft. It is a telling comment on the combat power of the BPF that it was replaced not by a task group from the US fast carrier task force, TF 58, but the escort carriers of the US 5th Fleet's Carrier Support Group. On 4 May TF 57 was back on station and launching attacks against airfields for the next three weeks, until on 25 May the BPF again withdrew to Manus to refit. The BPF returned to the fray on 16 July, this time as TF 37 attached to Admiral William Halsey's 3rd Fleet, which was ranging up and down the Japanese coast at will. At this stage of the campaign, not only was the BPF launching aircraft against the Japanese mainland but was also engaging in shore bombardments using its battleship *King George V* and its cruiser force.[23]

Away to the south-west, the Eastern Fleet's successor, the East Indies Fleet commanded by Vice Admiral Sir Arthur Power, was also carrying the fight to the Japanese. The year 1945 began well when five destroyers found and sank the Japanese heavy cruiser *Haguro* in the Malacca Straits in a brilliantly executed torpedo attack that scored eight hits on the Japanese ship, which went down in a matter of minutes. X-craft midget submarines were used to cut the submarine telegraph cables from Saigon to Singapore and Hong Kong (*XE4*) and then the one from Hong Kong to Singapore (*XE5*). X-craft were also deployed against Japanese ships immobilized by a lack of fuel in Singapore harbour. On 31 July two X-craft penetrated the harbour and laid limpet mines on the heavy cruiser *Takao*. The mines blew the *Takao*'s bottom out and she sank upright in the shallow water. The commander of *XE3*, Lieutenant Ian Fraser, and his diver, Leading Seaman James Magennis, were both awarded the Victoria Cross. The Royal Navy's submarines had also scored a major coup the previous month when HMS *Trenchant* successfully hit the heavy cruiser *Ashigawa* in the Banka Straits. Hit by five torpedoes – demonstrating the value of the *T* class submarine's heavy bow salvo, the *Ashigawa* sank in about 30 minutes.[24]

On 15 August, following the triple hammer blows of the nuclear bombs dropped on Hiroshima and Nagasaki, the destruction of the Japanese 'Kwantung' Army in Korea and Manchuria by the Russian army after the USSR entered the war on 9 August, and the often overlooked near starvation of the Japanese thanks to the Allied submarine campaign, the Japanese surrendered unconditionally. At sea the BPF's logistics situation, always fragile thanks to its small *ad hoc* fleet train, was critical. It was decided that only a small squadron could be supported in Japanese waters and thus be present at the formal surrender. In the end only the battleships *Duke of York* (with Admiral Fraser) and *King George V*, the aircraft carrier *Indefatigable*, the cruisers HMS *Newfoundland* and HMNZS *Gambia* plus ten destroyers (two of them Australian) remained off Japan and were allotted berths in Tokyo Bay to witness the ceremony. On 2 September the Japanese formally surrendered to the representatives of the Allied powers on the USS *Missouri*; Admiral Sir Bruce Fraser signed on behalf of Great Britain. The Royal Navy's World War II was over.

CHAPTER 8

The Cold War 1945–64

Peace found Great Britain with the largest and most powerful navy it had ever possessed, with almost 9,000 vessels and, in 1944, a personnel strength of almost 800,000, not including almost 74,000 from the WRNS. Yet now it was only the second largest in the world and a third of the size of that of the United States. Despite this the Royal Navy had been crucial in creating the conditions for victory in all theatres of the war. Victory in the Battle of the Atlantic against the Kriegsmarine had ensured the successful execution of D-Day and the liberation of Western Europe. Success in the Mediterranean against the Italian navy and the German Luftwaffe had protected the vital oil supplies in the Middle East and allowed the liberation of North Africa and southern Europe. The Royal Navy's deterrent posture in the Indian Ocean had ensured the flow of oil from the Middle East, and even in the largest war theatre of all, the Pacific, dominated by the United States Navy, Britain had played an immensely important role, especially in 1945, which culminated in the largest fleet it had ever deployed – the British Pacific Fleet.[1]

However, Britain was not just the keeper of a huge and global naval instrument – it was also effectively bankrupt. The immediate post-war world was not going to see the adulation or plaudits that should have been heaped upon the Navy. Having been the defender of the nation for centuries and the steadfast protector of its empire, the Royal Navy now found itself in turbulent and mystifying times. This was not a new situation, as the Navy had ridden out tumultuous times before, but what was different in 1945 was the scale and intensity of the challenges that faced the Senior Service. The end of the war had heralded not just one new epoch in the form of the atomic age, which seemed to be mesmerizing many of the political and military leaders in both Washington and London, and naturally in Moscow as well, but many new eras that would come to shape the size and capabilities of the Royal Navy in the decades to come.[2]

The end of the war had seen a host of new technological ages begin, with developments in jet aircraft, helicopters, missiles, radar and other sensor technology, all of which continue to the present day. Of equal significance was that the strategic political environment had drastically altered. Britain had finished the war no longer as leader of the anti-Axis Grand Alliance as it had been earlier in the conflict nor as one of the newly termed superpowers, but found itself quite obviously behind the political, military and economic might of both the United States and the Soviet Union. Politically the world would be increasingly shaped by the two new giants; economically it would be controlled by the United States. Great Britain was still the largest Imperial power the world had ever seen but it did not have the economic wherewithal nor arguably the political leadership to ensure that this remained the case. And its closest ally, America, would ensure that this was so, at least in the short term. Having generously initiated the Lend-Lease system when Britain could no longer afford to pay for supplies, the United States abruptly ended it at war's end. This forced Britain to pay for supplies, return Lend-Lease materials and raised questions over the ability to maintain American-supplied equipment. Thus the Royal Navy in the immediate aftermath of the war found itself facing a dire economic situation, an unknown political system and vast technological challenges, including atomic weapons. All of these had to be addressed if there was any chance of retaining a modicum of utility and viability in the future.[3]

Money and atoms

Perhaps the two most pressing problems in 1945 were the dual issues of money and the atomic bomb. Finances had always been a problem but with the nation effectively bankrupt there was naturally a desire to cut the defence budget. By the war's end approximately 50 per cent of Britain's gross domestic product was being spent on the war effort, a figure that was completely unsustainable. Each of the armed services needed to make huge reductions to free up not just money but manpower; towards the end of the war, for example, the Navy had reached its largest ever strength of just under one million. Many of the best and brightest of Britain's younger generation were to be found in the Royal Navy owing to the technological demand made upon it during the war and the requirements placed upon personnel. These would need to be released back into the workforce and help in post-war reconstruction and new civilian production. Recognition existed in Britain that the Royal Navy's position as the world's premier naval service had now lapsed and that the United States, at a strength of three million, had become the dominant global naval force. This gave heart to those calling for a reduction in the Royal Navy, as America could now assume its share of global responsibilities and perhaps many of Britain's pre-war policing roles. Policing the empire and projecting global power appeared to suggest long-term, huge forward-deployed forces. When there were massive economies to be made, and in a world with apparently little threat, this was an area of the Royal Navy that could easily be reduced. As a result a massive and at times hasty demobilization of manpower, ships and naval air squadrons began and arguably remained unchecked until 1950. The Navy's strength of almost 9,000 vessels at the end of the war had just over a year later become a force of some 800 major warships and auxiliaries with a personnel total of 492,800. The following year the Navy's total strength was due to decline to 192,665, becoming the smallest of the three services.[4]

The Harwood Committee, which sat from November 1948 to February 1949, was perhaps the first considered attempt to structure British defence for the next ten years in terms of size, manpower, equipment and technology, as it was felt that the main Soviet threat would have fully emerged by then. Research and development were seen as the key rather than maintaining large standing forces. The committee aimed to limit total defence forces to no more than

600,000, though with a recognition of the Navy's premier role in the defence of Britain's interests, especially in the Atlantic. That said, the Navy was given the smallest budget of the services, with a naval estimate of only £166 million. These limited funds were to maintain a carrier and small ship force with the battleships being phased out of service. The construction of existing ships was stretched out and personnel levels were to be cut to around 100,000 – a far cry from the nearly 200,000 initially wanted by the Navy in the aftermath of the war. In future the Royal Navy would concentrate its efforts in the Atlantic and Mediterranean, the latter a historically important area of operations and seeing the largest British naval forces for much of the post-war period. The Far East would be an American responsibility with the Persian Gulf a joint zone of operations and the Indian Ocean a Commonwealth problem. Unfortunately for the committee many of their findings were overtaken by events in Korea in the summer of 1950.[5]

The other issue was the atomic bomb. Its creation through the Manhattan Project heralded a new age of uncertainty for existing military forces. The atomic issue clouded and influenced many into believing that all wars, certainly those that challenged Western interests, would result in the use of American atomic weapons. The lessons resulting from the destruction of Hiroshima and Nagasaki in early August 1945 were arguably not well learnt. But that did not stop advocates of the new weapon – in the main, air force officers, technocrats and politicians seeking a cheaper defence budget – from suggesting that all wars would become atomic ones. The bombings of Japan seemed to suggest that one bomb from one aircraft could destroy an entire city with all of its attendant infrastructure, industry, military and communications sites and of course its population. Land-based air forces in particular, who would have an initial monopoly on the carriage of such large weapons, were in the vanguard of espousing such views and it naturally had an adverse impact on proven doctrine, on the other services, on their funding and on their political profile within government. The shrinking post-war budgets would now have to contend with the development and production of atomic bombs; moreover, it would also have to create the equally and at times more expensive planes from which they would be dropped. Due to the size of the early bombs, large aircraft, increasingly built and well equipped with all the technological developments of the day, would be needed, and for Britain after 1945 this would be a massive undertaking. But for air forces it seemed that finally their belief in strategic bombing had been proven correct. The airpower prophets of the interwar years had preached about the destruction of an enemy's war-making capacity rather than having the war-fighting capacities of navies and armies battling for years at great cost in lives and funds. Theorists suggested atomic warfare was a quick and far cheaper option than maintaining vast armies, navies and tactical air forces. The Royal Navy and the United States Navy – the two largest navies in the world – found it difficult to combat the dangerous preconceived conclusions of many and of air force propaganda that all wars would be atomic. The events of the 1950s would begin to throw doubt upon this air force view of future warfare, but by then the rise of the Soviet Union in its own right as an atomic and later nuclear power, together with the move towards nuclear deterrence between East and West, would continue to give the land-based air forces of both America and Great Britain a pre-eminence over maritime power until this situation began reversing in the 1960s.[6]

A dangerous and busy peace

Despite the impact of air force propaganda the Royal Navy was fairing somewhat better than its American counterpart. There was obviously no immediate threat to continental America and by 1946 the United States' only large non-American hemisphere colony, the Philippines, had become independent, leaving just territories in their backyard that needed limited protection. Even the advent of the Cold War left little solace for their navy, as the Soviet threat was centred primarily on its armies and air forces which pointed towards Europe, the Red Navy being seen at the time in a negative light by its leadership. The Royal Navy, on the other hand, could at least find some contentment in the fact that Britain's empire and Commonwealth would require policing and protection, a role that would persist for some time at varying levels and occasionally require considerable effort. In the first years of peace, however, the Royal Navy found itself amazingly busy with many deployments, particularly in the Mediterranean and Asia.

Before World War II had even ended, Britain's navy found itself involved in a series of regional, ideological and colonial struggles. Civil war had erupted in Greece in 1944 and British units already in the country as the Germans withdrew found themselves dragged into the struggle between monarchist forces backed by the West and a large communist uprising. The Royal Navy deployed in support of British ground forces, providing transportation and logistical assets but also aerial support with naval aircraft. Britain's involvement drew to an end by late 1946, during which time the Balkans had been the backdrop to one of a number of crises proving that size, prestige and power could be negated by simple means. In October 1946 the destroyers HMS *Saumarez* and *Volage* fell foul of mines laid in the Corfu Channel by Albania, supposedly aided by Yugoslavia. In May 1946 British cruisers had been fired on while in international waters, so the Navy decided to demonstrate the international rights of passage in October with the two destroyers escorting two cruisers. Unfortunately both destroyers were mined with the loss of 44 personnel but *Volage* managed to tow the *Saumarez* to safety under the protection of aircraft from the carrier HMS *Ocean*. In November the Royal Navy swept the Corfu Channel. It was a large undertaking, involving 11 minesweepers, two cruisers, three destroyers and two frigates, all under the air umbrella of HMS *Ocean*, which cleared 22 mines and allowed free international passage once again. The Corfu Incident was a timely reminder of the limits that can be placed upon naval action by renegade powers, but at least the right of free passage had been maintained.[7]

At the same time, British forces were heavily involved in security operations in the eastern Mediterranean with the policing of Palestine from 1945 to 1948. The Navy's role deepened with the imposition of a blockade, placating the Arab population but denying European Jews fleeing the Holocaust and the destruction of their homes a chance to emigrate to a new 'homeland'. This resulted in a large-scale and domestically unpopular operation, not to mention one that was hugely unpopular in the international system. The deployment included the carrier HMS *Triumph* which used her aircraft to identify Jewish refugee ships which were then boarded by parties from British destroyers. By May 1948 when British involvement drew to a close and the Palestinian/Israeli question was passed to the United Nations the Navy had stopped 47 ships carrying over 60,000 refugees, interning their captives mostly in Cyprus. It had been a large operation and one the Royal Navy had been heavily and successfully involved in, but it had received much criticism for its blockade.[8]

Besides the Mediterranean the Navy found itself deeply committed in Asia in the immediate post-war period, a deployment that lasted up to the late 1960s. The now victorious British Pacific Fleet and Indian Ocean forces found themselves not demobilizing immediately as many had hoped but deployed on active duty for both humanitarian and war-fighting purposes. The liberation and transportation of the many thousands of prisoners of war who had been held by the Japanese in horrific conditions, most from the fall of Malaya and Singapore in early 1942, was of pressing importance. However, many were incarcerated throughout South East Asia and some even in Japan. Unfortunately Asia had become unstable with Western-backed and trained anti-Japanese forces beginning to raise arms against their previous colonial masters. Britain and the Royal Navy found itself in a series of fresh shooting wars before the end of 1945. In Indochina British units who were there to liberate French forces and accept the Japanese surrender soon found themselves fighting American-backed and trained communist-dominated nationalist anti-Japanese forces, the Viet Minh. Ultimately a successful and quite bizarre coalition that comprised British, French and rearmed Japanese troops was created, a prelude to the complexions of that region which would persist into the twenty-first century. Indeed British naval units were back off the coast of Indochina in the summer of 1954, led by the carrier HMS *Warrior*, covering the withdrawal of British personnel following the collapse of the French colonial administration. Twenty-one years later they would return once more to cover the evacuation of British personnel following the overthrow of the American-backed government in South Vietnam, but in 1945 all this lay in the future. By the summer of 1946 the uprising had been effectively quelled, allowing the Japanese and British forces to withdraw. But there was no respite for the Navy as simultaneously in the Dutch East Indies British units fought independently and alongside Dutch troops to liberate British prisoners and in an attempt to stifle independence, a struggle that lasted until late 1946 for Britain and December 1949 for the Dutch.[9]

But for Britain and the Royal Navy the largest conflict was the beginning of the Malayan Emergency. In 1947 the Malayan colonial administration found itself under threat from an insurgency led by the Malayan Communist party, which had been the British-trained Malayan Peoples' Anti-Japanese Army during the war. The struggle in Malaya would last for over ten years and see large-scale naval deployments in support of the civil authorities involving carrier operations, land-based naval air operations including the Navy's deployment of Britain's first helicopter squadrons for troop transport, naval gunfire support, the employment of the Royal Marines as well as crucial blockade and transportation missions. The blockade role saw all manner of naval assets employed, including mine-warfare vessels acting as impromptu offshore patrol units, all of which closed down the waters off Malaya, successfully isolating the insurgents.[10]

Indeed 1947 proved very eventful, as the Royal Navy found itself stretched in the Mediterranean, involved on a number of fronts in South East Asia and playing a prominent role in the independence of India and Pakistan, including the training of their navies and the transfer of ships to them. Later it performed a similar role in the independence of Ceylon, which eventually became Sri Lanka. If this was not enough, the Navy found itself embroiled in the long and bloody civil war in China which had raged intermittently for decades but was drawing to a conclusion by October 1949. In China the inherent flexibility of maritime power meant that the Navy was very much Britain's military presence and enforcer of foreign policy, not just off the coastline but within the country as well, on the vast rivers that penetrated into the mainland. This only ended with the Yangtse Incident, when HMS *Amethyst* was held 'captive' by communist forces from April to the end of July 1949, finally escaping and receiving a hero's welcome upon her return to the fleet. Besides China becoming communist in 1949, the year also became the turning point in East–West relations. The Berlin blockade came to an end, the Washington Treaty was signed, which soon established the North Atlantic Treaty Organization (NATO), and the explosion of the Soviet Union's first atomic bomb finally heralded the Cold War, with significant implications for the Royal Navy.[11]

The Cold War

The rise of the Cold War created both opportunities and drawbacks for the Royal Navy. A known and aggressive threat was now challenging British and Western interests, although it was a small but developing naval threat. Earlier grandiose Soviet naval expansion programmes had collapsed by 1949 in the face of various problems, but a substantial submarine-building programme and the rump of a cruiser programme remained. Both were being built with commerce-raiding and sea-denial missions in mind, much like the German navy in World War II. These were obviously a threat to British interests and needed dealing with. Initially the Admiralty argued that only battleships were powerful enough to do so, but in an age of austerity it was unlikely that large numbers (if any) of the ships that had dominated warfare at sea from the age of sail to the outbreak of World War II would be retained in the long term. Large numbers of aircraft carriers together with new and powerful anti-shipping aircraft on board was a flexible alternative, but money and procurement issues together with split opinions within the naval hierarchy meant that this was not practical in the short term. Moreover, the rise of the Soviet Union and its atomic capability thrust a dagger directly at Europe, raising questions concerning naval survival. The possibility that a navy could survive an atomic attack had been shown as early as 1946 by the United States Navy during the first of the various Bikini Atoll atomic tests, but critics of naval power wanted to know what was the point of survival if the world had been destroyed. The Royal Navy countered with arguments based on deterrence and the theory that conventional forces should be used for all missions short of atomic exchange, where they had major roles to play. This thinking would be augmented in the early 1950s with the development of future war theories known as the Broken Backed War. The Navy argued that after an initial intensive period of war, mostly atomic, the warring sides would settle down, recuperate and prepare for a new set of hostilities. Conventional forces would be needed to support the first phase and become essential for the second.[12]

However, much of this discussion fell on deaf ears as the British atomic programme, begun in secret in January 1947, continued apace, as did the four different aircraft programmes that had been initiated to carry the new weapons. The Royal Navy by 1950 was facing, after five years of hectic and intense global operations, a situation in which it was being sidelined in favour of atomic weapons for strategic defence, deterrence and war fighting while conventional land-based forces defended Germany against the vast Soviet military machine (while naturally keeping an eye on developments within Germany). The arguments between those who supported a global maritime/air posture versus those who favoured a European continental commitment increasingly saw the latter proponents winning the political and funding battle. That was until the summer of 1950, when across the other side of the world a conflict broke out that demonstrated that not all wars would be atomic and that a series of limited conventional struggles between East and West played out in the shadow of the nuclear age might be more likely and survivable.

The Korean conflict

The Korean War began in June 1950 when 90,000 well-trained and equipped communist North Koreans launched an invasion of the capitalist, Western-focused South. Better motivated and organized than their southern brethren, they quickly routed a demoralized force that had been reinforced by American troops taken from occupation duties in Japan. The southern capital, Seoul, was captured and airfields overrun. Finally the South stabilized a position around the port of Pusan on the south-eastern tip facing Japan. The bulk of Korea was now communist and the successes of the East in the late 1940s appeared to be continuing into 1950. Initially the West responded diplomatically, mobilizing the United Nations Security Council (UNSC) and getting the authorization to use armed force to repel the North Korean invasion.[13]

The second response was to dispatch military forces to act against the North Korean invaders. The naval response saw the arrival of two carriers, the USS *Valley Forge* and HMS *Triumph* arriving off Korea by the end of the first week of the conflict. The carriers were crucial in providing air support to the now United Nations forces in the Pusan perimeter as the airfields of South Korea were in enemy hands and the American air force jet aircraft based in Japan had too little range to provide useful and adequate air support to the ground forces. HMS *Triumph* was carrying out her first air strikes against North Korean targets by 3 July. Following closely on the heels of the first carriers were further United States' ships, some of which carried land-based World War II fighters – for example, American Mustangs that could only reach Korea on the back of naval vessels but at least could use the rough and ready forward operating strips at Pusan. HMS *Triumph* was replaced by HMS *Theseus* on 5 October, by which time the *Triumph*'s air group was down to 11 aircraft. The *Theseus* brought more capable Sea Furies and Firefly Vs, providing greater striking power for the United Nations.

So began a constant rolling deployment of British aircraft carriers that would last the entirety of the war, with the aircraft flying nearly 23,000 sorties, a seventh of the total carrier sortie total. The carriers could project power throughout Korea, being able to sit on either side of the peninsula and move up and down the coastline, constantly being able to deploy firepower when and where needed. British ships operated off the west coast of Korea, with British admirals permanently in charge of controlling the international naval force that operated there, with the United States Navy operating off

the east coast. Even when the South had been liberated and stabilized, British, American and Australian carriers remained on station
because of their flexibility and ability to respond far quicker than
land-based aircraft operating from the South. Eventually a third of
all missions flown and a third of all ordnance dropped were by naval
aircraft. And for Britain the dispatch of the carriers was the key
naval and airpower deployment, with five carriers (including one
Australian) and an aircraft repair ship which also briefly acted as a
carrier deployed to the theatre.[14]

The Navy's Fleet Air Arm (FAA) provided all of Britain's combat
air elements during the Korean War. No RAF combat aircraft were
deployed there (bar some Hong Kong-based Sunderland flying boats)
owing to the service not wanting to send forces, officially, for fear
of weakening the western defences in Germany. Royal Navy carriers dropped 15,200 bombs and fired 57,600 rockets and 3,300,000
rounds of aircraft ammunition from their 20mm cannons. Royal
Navy ships steamed 2,100,550 miles during the war, carrying out
essential duties throughout the campaign, even transporting the
first British army units into theatre on the back of the cruiser HMS
Ceylon and the carrier/repair ship HMS *Unicorn*. The vital logistical
line remained throughout the war. The Navy also provided constant
naval gunfire support to forces ashore, with the cruisers HMS
Kenya and *Jamaica* even supporting the 'all American affair' landings at Inchon in September 1950, with Fireflies from HMS *Triumph*
providing direction for their guns. British naval units of all types
were highly regarded by their American allies; the British even
briefly commanded all naval forces on one occasion.[15]

For the first armed test between East and West it might be
surprising that atomic weapons were not employed. Their use was
considered more than once, but they were never sanctioned for a
number of reasons. A limited American stockpile required caution,
as the United States could ill afford to use them if they might be
needed in Europe or elsewhere. Additionally, America did not
want to escalate the war beyond Korea or antagonize the communist world for fear of Soviet retaliation, especially against Europe.
Korea's topography was also a hindrance. But the principal reason

Fig. 8.1. The bridge of HMS *Belfast* during a bombardment of
communist positions during the Korean War.

was a lack of targets that warranted the use of atomic weapons.
There simply wasn't anything in theatre that could not be attacked
by conventional means. There were instances when naval aircraft
had simply run out of targets. On more than one occasion FAA Sea
Furies and Fireflies attacked ox-drawn carts as legitimate targets for
lack of anything else.[16]

Naval power proved itself vital in Korea. The years since World
War II had witnessed a physical decline in naval assets as well as
doubts about the viability of naval power. Many considered that
amphibious operations were a thing of the past and therefore there
was little reason for aircraft carriers and very little credence was
given to the use of naval gun support. Without amphibious operations, mine warfare became less important and the need for strategic sealift to move ground forces also now seemed irrelevant.
It appeared that the whole structure of modern naval power
was collapsing. Korea placed a break on this thinking and on the
downward spiral of profile and funding. Washington dramatically

increased its naval spending and expanded its force structure, while the British government increased defence spending from just over 8 per cent of GDP in 1950 to 15 per cent by 1953. Korea came none too soon for the Western navies. Neither armies nor air forces could physically reach Korea without naval power, as the distances were too great. Only ships could reach the Korean peninsula. And it was naval power (admittedly mostly American) that liberated the South following the amphibious assault at Inchon in September 1950, naturally supported by carriers. Naval power saved the United Nations forces – over 100,000 troops – by withdrawing them from Hungnam in the face of the Chinese army that had intervened in October 1950. They were then re-inserted into the South to stabilize the front, which in conjunction with naval support stopped the South from being overrun once more. Troops and equipment were able to reach South Korea through a huge and constant strategic sealift effort and then to operate continually off the coastline. This was due to American and British naval forces achieving sea control, with British cruisers and escorts taking a lead in dispatching the North Korean navy early in the conflict. But the destruction of their navy did not stop North Korea from trying to deny Korean waters to the United Nations in the South as they deployed innumerable mines, which focused naval thinking on the growing mine threat from the Soviet Union and its satellites.

Post-Korean problems and developments

The Korean War had allayed much of the thinking regarding the limited utility of navies in the atomic age, but it did not end the pressure on the Royal Navy. The war had seen a number of developments that would influence the 1950s. The first major one was the continuing naval struggle with new technology, best epitomized by jet aircraft at sea; the second major development was government recognition that funding was increasingly unaffordable for British defence.

The war in Korea had also demonstrated the continued crucial importance of carrier power, its flexibility and strategic mobility far outstripping that of its land-based rivals. However, Korea had also shown that sea-based naval airpower appeared, technologically speaking, to be lagging behind that of land-based air forces, especially with regard to jets. The first ever jet to land on a carrier was British, a Sea Vampire, landing on HMS *Ocean* as early as December 1945. But after prolonged testing, technical issues and financial constraints the Royal Navy would have to wait until 1952 until its first frontline squadron of jet aircraft – Supermarine Attackers – was declared operational and a further two years before naval jet squadrons regularly deployed on British carriers. The considerable testing, evaluation and experimental work by the FAA would prove of use; however, the rather conservative approach by the Admiralty together with limited funding and RAF dominance in the air industry meant that the early strides by the FAA were soon lost. British aircraft in Korea had shown themselves to be inferior to Soviet-supplied Mig-15s, ironically powered by Rolls-Royce Nene engines, copies of which had been passed to both the Soviets and the Americans after World War II. The piston engine FAA aircraft, Sea Furies and Firefly Vs, had proven themselves excellent platforms for ground attack but were no match in air-to-air combat with the Migs, but neither were American naval aircraft, which were a mixture of piston and jet-engine machines. America's naval aircraft deficiencies could be rectified through the huge increase in defence spending attributable to the Korean War, but in Britain it was a different story. More capable aircraft were coming into service such as the Seahawk jet fighter ground attack aircraft and the Sea Venom all-weather jet fighter, but these were still inferior in performance to the Mig-15.[17]

Newer and larger aircraft were due to enter service from the late 1950s. The new aircraft raised serious questions about the viability of the existing aircraft carriers of the day in terms of safe operations and the size of the embarked air group. Britain's carrier force during the Korean War was provided primarily by light fleet carriers of the *Colossus* class, designed and laid down in World War II to carry approximately three dozen piston-engine aircraft. The much heavier and far faster jet aircraft raised questions about their suitability.

Fig. 8.2. HMS *Eagle* in the early 1950s with Sea Furies, a Firebrand and Sea Hornet ranged on deck. Right aft can be seen one of the Fleet Air Arm's new jet aircraft, a Supermarine Attacker.

Even the larger carriers of the *Centaur* class entering service at the time of the Korean War and the yet larger carriers of the *Audacious* class appeared unsuitable for operating jet aircraft, and even if they could be made to they would not be carrying many of them. Luckily a number of British innovations in the early 1950s allowed the Royal Navy to modify the existing ships – and those still in build – to successfully operate the new jets. Most notably the creation of the angled deck for safer landings, the steam catapult replacing the hydraulic variant and the deck-mirrored landing system all allowed the launching and safe recovery of the increasingly heavier and faster machines – 1950s breakthroughs that continue to be used in the twenty-first century. More importantly these developments enabled the Royal Navy to keep their smaller carriers operational and at the cutting edge of carrier development throughout the 1950s and into the following decade without having – initially anyway – to pursue the construction of supercarriers as the Americans had begun undertaking during the Korean War. But as the carrier jet evolved in the 1950s from aircraft that were only marginally bigger and faster than their World War II piston-engine brethren to machines that were four or five times heavier by 1960, it was recognized that newer and larger carrier platforms would be needed to maintain the viability of Britain's key power projection asset.[18]

Besides sparking a drive to maintain a cornerstone in naval capability with carrier technology, Korea also sparked a defence discussion about the future structure and role of all three of the armed services. By 1952 the British government had decided that the spiralling defence bills resulting from Korean War rearmament, together with the research and development costs accruing from atomic, jet and missile programmes, were increasingly unaffordable. Consequently the chiefs of staff were instructed to look for alternatives. Following a 'closed door' session at the Royal Navy Staff College, Greenwich, the result was the Global Strategy Paper. Although it was never implemented, its findings and legacy influenced defence decisions in the immediate aftermath of Korea. Ironically the Global Strategy Paper favoured an atomic approach to British defence in the future despite the experience of Korea. Atomic weapons were seen as cheaper alternatives to large conventional forces, a way that Britain could maintain relatively large physical military power while also maintaining high levels of prestige in the international community. Unfortunately for the writers of the paper, atomic weapons and their delivery systems did not provide the hoped-for savings and few major economies would be made. Moreover, resistance from the services at the time of Korea meant that little would realistically come of the paper. Undeterred, however, a new process began in 1953 – the Radical Review – which aimed to build upon the earlier work and save money while retaining defensive capability. The Royal Navy and the FAA in particular were targeted as areas that could be trimmed. In fact the FAA came under attack as superfluous to future war. The Admiralty naturally resisted, arguing that not all wars would be nuclear, and even if there were a nuclear exchange the limited numbers available and small size of them would not be enough to bring Britain to its knees. There would therefore be a period of 'Broken Backed' warfare where conventional forces would need to fight on after nuclear attack, a notion supported by many. By 1955 the Navy had fought off the worst elements of the Radical Review and appeared to have safeguarded its air arm, with the annual defence statement including references to the Navy's future war arguments. However, in many ways the damage had been done through a series of salami-slicing exercises imposed upon defence in an attempt to decrease the budget. Rather than ending a major capability, the decisions implemented post Korea saw a reduction across the board impacting on everything – bar the atomic programme. The result was a loss of capability in all areas rather than the removal of one entire role or commitment. Orders were cut and delivery dates extended. Procurement and strategy decisions were deferred. Consequently, by the time the Royal Navy was asked to mount its next major effort, it found itself unable to respond soon enough to avoid the disaster that became Operation *Musketeer* – the attack on the Suez Canal Zone in the autumn of 1956.[19]

Operation *Musketeer*

Following the seizure of the International Suez Canal Company by the Egyptian leader Gamal Abdel Nasser in July 1956, Britain's prime minister, Anthony Eden, ordered the retaking of the Canal Zone. The loss to Britain and France of the prestigious Suez Canal was too much to bear; moreover, it set an unwelcome precedent that other countries might follow. Nasser was regarded with great suspicion, especially by the French, concerning his growing interference in Western-sphere Arab nations. The retaking of the canal, together with hopefully Nasser's removal, would resolve a number of issues for the British and French governments. Unfortunately the post-Korean salami-slicing process had reduced the immediate deployablility of all British forces. French units were in similar shape following their withdrawal from Indochina in 1954. Only one British carrier, HMS *Eagle*, was operational in the Mediterranean in the summer of 1956. It was far too small a force to attempt to neutralize Egypt's armed forces and cover an amphibious assault against the Canal Zone, especially as the Egyptian government had been in receipt of large quantities of weapons from the Eastern bloc, including Mig-15s and their larger and more capable stablemates, the Mig-17s.[20]

Three months would go by before sufficient British and French forces, operating under strained command relations, would be ready to launch the intervention. The scale-down after Korea had seen amphibious forces sold off, little investment in the Royal Fleet Auxiliary (RFA) and the modernization of the FAA crawl forward at a snail's pace. The other services were no better off. The Royal Marines carrying out the amphibious assault were to be joined by the army's Parachute Regiment, which had had few opportunities for airborne assault since World War II. In the summer of 1956 the troops that were to lead the invasion, the Royal Marines and the Parachute Regiment, were fighting terrorists in Cyprus. The RAF provided nearly 100 bombers and an equal number of fighters, including the new Valiant atomic bomber, but time was needed to increase the capabilities of the airbases on Malta and Cyprus before these aircraft could be used in theatre. Even then the RAF only managed to fly half the daily sortie rate of the carrier-based aircraft – 1.4 sorties per day compared to the 2.8 of the FAA. Worse yet, the land-based air forces were also flying aircraft that were inferior to those of the Egyptians.

Through the mobilization of reserves, the buying back of equipment sold earlier and raiding scrap heaps, Britain deployed the largest task force since World War II, alongside the French navy, with seven aircraft carriers at its heart, three British strike carriers (*Eagle*, *Albion* and *Bulwark*), two French strike carriers (*Arromanches* and *La Fayette*) and two British light fleet carriers (*Ocean* and *Theseus*) employed for the first time in war as helicopter assault ships. France even deployed a battleship. Following the pre-arranged Israeli invasion of Egypt in October and the intervention by British and French assets in the name of the 'international community' Egypt witnessed a week-long aerial bombardment of targets by land-based and carrier aircraft. This was followed by airborne and amphibious

Fig. 8.3. HMS *Theseus* en route to Suez with Royal Marine
Commandoes, their vehicles and helicopters embarked.

assaults to seize the Canal Zone. However, the operation was halted
by Britain and France following immense global diplomatic and
financial pressure resulting in major political embarrassment for the
British government.[21]

The military side of Operation *Musketeer* was mixed. Often
regarded as the only success in the crisis, it would be fairer to
portray it as highlighting both strengths and weaknesses. Naval
power had once again shown itself as flexible and mobile, being
able to operate in the eastern Mediterranean with immunity from
attack, though there were concerns during the operation. Despite
the problems it faced the Royal Navy managed to deploy a fleet of
five carriers, three cruisers, 13 destroyers, six frigates, 17 landing
vessels, five headquarters or maintenance vessels, 15 minesweepers
and 24 vessels of the RFA, together with 13 FAA squadrons. The
Navy's first use of jet aircraft in combat had proved highly successful, and its use of the 'cab rank' structure of maintaining aircraft
in a near permanently airborne status provided ground forces
with quick responding power that was far more flexible than the
land-based assets of the RAF and the French air force. The British

Fig. 8.4. The helicopter and seaborne
assault takes place at Port Said.

aircraft carriers employed angled decks and steam catapults (the
latter on board HMS *Eagle*) for the first time in combat and proved
their worth in operating large numbers of aircraft and attaining high
sortie rates, with over 1,600 carrier sorties launched. Another first
was the use of helicopters from HMS *Ocean* and *Theseus* to launch 45
Commando, Royal Marines, in the world's first deployment of ship-
based air assault in an amphibious operation.[22]

However, there were also weaknesses. Principal among them
was speed. It had taken three months to mobilize and assemble the
forces needed, during which time world public opinion had shifted
from being either pro-British or at least neutral to openly hostile to
Britain and France. Operationally the shortages in equipment had
an impact and there was a recognition that there were too few helicopters of sufficient carrying capacity. The Navy's first use of jet
aircraft had proved successful but partly because the Egyptian air
force had mostly refrained from fighting, either fleeing the country
or remaining on the ground – where much of it was destroyed. Had
the Egyptian's capable aircraft, notably the Mig-15s and Mig-17s,

engaged British aircraft things might have been very different. The amphibious shipping, landing craft and RFA vessels also needed desperate replacement, with the latter dating back to before World War II.

The Sandys Review

One result of Suez was the change in prime minister, with Harold Macmillan replacing Anthony Eden. More significantly Duncan Sandys, former Minister of Supply, became the new Defence Secretary. He was tasked with a review of Britain's capabilities and a reduction in their cost. Additionally, he was to ensure that another *Musketeer*-style scenario would not end in failure again. As Minister of Supply, Sandys had been a vocal advocate of nuclear weapons and increasingly missile technology as its future delivery system. He had also espoused the end of manned aviation, certainly in the context of NATO's defence against the Soviet Union's growing missile defences. During the Radical Review he had also been a major critic of traditional naval power, particularly aircraft carriers. However, even he was forced to admit that Britain's atomic status, obtained in 1952, and soon-to-be-gained thermo-nuclear status had not deterred Nasser's designs on the canal. There were obviously limitations to the nuclear age. Consequently he conceded that when dealing with non-atomic powers outside of Europe, such as Egypt, conventional forces, critically including aircraft carriers, had proved essential.[23]

The 1957 Sandys Review has often been portrayed as placing the bulk of cuts following the restructuring of defence spending on the Royal Navy, with the loss of the reserve fleet, auxiliaries, shore establishments and few new ship orders. However, in reality the Navy actually fared much better. The lessons of Suez would be learnt and implemented over the ten years following the disaster. Naval airpower continued its modernization at an increased rate and by 1960 the Navy would have larger numbers of more capable carriers in service than ten years earlier; soon the FAA would be equipped with aircraft that were superior to their land-based counterparts. Work also continued on the design of future carriers to replace, in the 1970s, the wartime-built ships, which eventually became the *CVA-01* class. HMS *Albion* and *Bulwark* were converted into larger helicopter assault ships with much more capable Wessex helicopters than their Suez equivalents. In the early 1960s new amphibious ships would be designed and ordered, in the form of HMS *Fearless* and *Intrepid*, and the *Sir* class landing ship logistic vessels. Moreover, the RFA would be completely rebuilt throughout the decade allowing for worldwide support of the fleet. Simultaneously work would continue on introducing new classes of surface ship, including the eight *County* class destroyers, the first Royal Navy vessels to be armed with the new Sea Slug guided anti-aircraft missiles, with other missiles encompassing many roles under development. The Sea Slug, though taking nearly 15 years to enter service, heralded another new age for the Navy and initiated a programme of indigenous anti-aircraft missiles that continues today. The Sea Cat short-range missile soon began replacing gun emplacements on board Navy vessels at the start of the decade and by the end of the 1960s the Sea Dart medium-range missile would enter service, only retiring in 2013.[24]

The submarine service would see its first nuclear-powered submarine, HMS *Dreadnought*, commissioned in 1962. Fifteen years after the explosion of the world's first atomic bombs the Navy had successfully harnessed the power of the atom for attack and power purposes. FAA Supermarine Scimitars had become Britain's first naval aircraft to be able to carry nuclear weapons and a much more potent platform in the form of the NA39 Blackburn Buccaneer was nearing operational status. Additionally, American F-4 Phantoms, also nuclear capable, were ordered, giving the Royal Navy in the 1960s the most capable fighter bomber in the Western world. The Buccaneer, however, had been conceived as early as 1951 as a nuclear carrier-based bomber, an excellent example of naval forethought at the time of Korea, and it would allow British aircraft carriers to act in a NATO nuclear strike role. Since 1955 the Navy had also been showing interest in the American Polaris submarine-launched ballistic missile programme as an alternative to RAF land-based projects. In 1962 this would successfully come to fruition following the collapse of the RAF's missile procurement. In the meantime it had pushed ahead with a series of nuclear-powered attack submarines, HMS *Dreadnought* being the first, giving the submarine service an unlimited global underwater reach, though reliant on American reactor technology. The *Dreadnought* was followed by five larger, improved and British nuclear-powered attack submarines of the *Valiant* class – the start of a continuous nuclear building programme lasting into the twenty-first century.[25]

There were also other anti-submarine warfare improvements, with large numbers of new frigates and aviation assets, both carrier-based fixed-wing Gannet aircraft and new helicopters for operations from escort ships, such as Wessex for the *County* Class and Wasp for the new *Leander* and *Tribal* class frigates. Both helicopter types were capable of carrying anti-shipping missiles as well as torpedoes and depth-charges. Developments continued in other areas, particularly with regard to ship-based radar and sonar equipment. All these innovations were aimed at the growing Soviet navy but were also capable of supporting a worldwide deployment of naval power.[26]

The 1957 review and the Navy's planning before and after Suez had allowed for the creation of flexible forces that would be crucial in pursuing British foreign policy east of Suez. West of Suez, essentially NATO's area of operations, would increasingly be defended by new nuclear weapons programmes based on missile technology, with Polaris missiles on Royal Navy submarines, ultimately following a series of cancellations for land-based delivery systems. The European continental commitment was also reduced by cutting the British Army of the Rhine by almost a third and halving the size of the RAF in Germany. Conscription ended for all services, and smaller professional regular forces would be the future.[27]

The move to an all-professional force was welcomed by many, as it promised to continue the slow process of improvements being experienced by naval personnel in the late 1950s. Living conditions had changed very little in the ten years after World War II. In fact sailors of the Edwardian era would have felt at home on the mess decks of post-war British ships. The failure to develop the living conditions of the men after the war was compounded by the relative improvements in life ashore for civilians which widened the gap of inequalities between civilian and serviceman, particularly by the time of the Sandys Review. Moreover, naval personnel were quick to notice that the other services provided more facilities than the Navy. Pay had remained fairly static and deployments were long, often three years – a tradition that dated back to the Victorian era of Imperial policing. There was often little chance of sailors being accompanied by their spouses, unlike in the other services. Back in Britain it was little better with small, if any, support for naval families.

National Servicemen on short-term engagement began to make their unhappiness clear. Discipline occasionally faltered, and re-enlistment, which was crucial to maintaining a large core of experienced personnel, drastically declined. Investment in the Navy seemed increasingly wasteful. The end of National Service saw large reductions in personnel strength and a move to an all-professional force. For the Royal Navy it meant its personnel numbers shrank from 121,000 to under 100,000 by the end of 1961. This forced the Admiralty to improve retention and recruitment, as well as pay and pensions, discipline, accommodation, food and welfare, in order to maintain numbers and effectiveness. However, much more work was needed, and this would continue into the 1970s.[28]

East of Suez

In the 1960s, as the other services shrank, it appeared that the Royal Navy and the Royal Marines were expanding; certainly their roles and capabilities gave more than that impression to the other services and in reality it was true: in 1962 the army and RAF manpower levels shrank while that of the Royal Navy increased by 1,000. The Navy would increasingly be based overseas, almost a throwback to a pre-World War II business-as-usual policy. The east of Suez forces would effectively be 'naval fire brigades' increasingly based in Aden and Singapore that would respond as needed to future crises; indeed the crises had begun to erupt as early as 1958.[29]

A key component of the 'fire brigades' were the Royal Marines who had become far more than just naval infantry in their deployments in the post-war world. Described as 'shock troops' by the world's press at the time of Suez, the Marines had deployed in all major British operations from Malaya and Korea to Suez and would be at the forefront of forthcoming deployments in the 1960s. Ironically in the immediate post-war world their future had been uncertain but they were retained, partly for morale and discipline purposes but also to avoid the drastic decision of totally losing a capability were they to be disbanded or amalgamated into the army. Indeed the army had chosen to disband their commando units, thinking amphibious operations unlikely in the nuclear age, while the Navy at least retained the core of an amphibious force. It was a wise decision, as the next two decades and far beyond were to show. By the time of Suez the Navy had decided on the key capability of projecting power from the sea and the Royal Marines were central to this task. Their numbers would continue to increase into the 1960s, as would the availability of dedicated shipping, including the commando carriers *Albion* and *Bulwark*, until decisions later in the decade, beyond the Navy's control, began a contraction.[30]

Two years after Suez, however, Britain found itself operating alongside America with an intervention in the Middle East in support of the governments of the Lebanon and Jordan, where the Royal Navy deployed a carrier force in conjunction with the Americans, stifling Egyptian-backed anti-government forces. In 1961 a more pressing crisis occurred when the newly independent Kuwait seemed to be on the brink of being overrun by Iraq. Royal Marines from 42 Commando on board HMS *Bulwark* provided the first ground forces on 1 July, and were joined by 45 Commando flown from Aden later that day. The carrier HMS *Victorious* arrived in the northern Persian Gulf on 9 July, providing an all-weather air umbrella over Kuwait, until she was replaced by HMS *Centaur* at the end of the month. RAF and army units were also moved into Kuwait, with tanks, vehicles and other equipment coming mostly by sea. Significantly the radar-equipped Sea Vixens on board *Victorious* were far more capable than the Hunters of the RAF, plus the powerful radar on board was essential for aircraft control for all services.

Additionally, some of the non-naval forces were not acclimatized and therefore militarily ineffective. Despite RAF and army failings, the Kuwait deployment, Operation *Vantage*, was a resounding success for the Royal Navy and was followed by a series of operations supporting newly independent governments in East Africa, the Arabian peninsula and South East Asia.[31]

In December 1962, 42 Commando operating from HMS *Bulwark*, with HMS *Hermes* providing cover, helped stabilize Brunei from an armed insurrection. Then from the spring of 1963 until 1966 British and Commonwealth forces were involved in the Indonesian Confrontation when they were employed to repulse Indonesian attempts to absorb Eastern Malaysia (part of the island of Borneo). The Navy's involvement was large. All five strike carriers were deployed in a deterrent role at various stages of the Confrontation, together with five FAA helicopter squadrons that operated from land bases for troop support alongside the Royal Marines. Additionally, large numbers of escort vessels and minor warships were employed for interdiction and blockade purposes. Overall the Navy intercepted 90 per cent of all Indonesian incursions. Simultaneously, the Navy had to respond to crises in East Africa following mutinies in newly independent Kenya, Uganda and Tanganyika (the most serious) in 1964. The revolt by parts of the Tanganyika army in January saw HMS *Centaur* intervening with 45 Commando as well as her more normal strike group and embarked RAF helicopters.[32]

During these operations two major developments had taken place which were to have major ramifications for the Navy and British defence as a whole. The first was the decision to buy the American Polaris submarine-launched intercontinental ballistic missile system; the second was the coming to power in 1964 of the Labour party under Harold Wilson. Following the collapse of the RAF nuclear deterrent programmes by 1962 and the staunch support Britain had given the United States during the October Cuban Missile Crisis – including the mobilization of the Navy's nuclear-armed aircraft carriers – it was decided that America would be approached for its Polaris system, which had entered service with the US Navy in 1960. In the December state meeting between John F. Kennedy and

Harold Macmillan, America agreed to supply five Polaris systems to Britain to be placed on British-built boats and armed with British-built warheads. This option was far superior to maintaining the V-bombers which had been costing some 10 per cent of the annual budget and would have needed replacing in the 1970s even if they had been fitted with a new stop-gap deterrent. The cost of the Polaris programme was estimated at over £300 million for the system, warheads and submarines; it ran on time and on budget, entering service in 1968.[33]

The decision to pass the nuclear mantle to the Navy would result in it providing the centrepiece of Britain's nuclear deterrent and the major contribution to NATO, as well as providing the bulk of the capability in the non-nuclear, non-NATO east of Suez role, with the enhanced amphibious capability supported by the new *CVA-01* class aircraft carrier. The government was increasingly

Fig. 8.5. The new British strategic nuclear deterrent of the late 1960s onwards – the nuclear-powered submarine armed with intercontinental ballistic missiles. Here the first Polaris strategic missile from HMS *Resolution* is launched.

– by design or accident – pursuing a maritime-orientated security policy. This brought the Royal Navy into direct competition with the RAF, something they had successfully avoided in the late 1950s despite the increasing possibility that Polaris would replace the RAF nuclear programmes. The RAF's main rationale for existence – strategic bombing – had now been lost and their services east of Suez curtailed as airbases were denied them as former colonies became independent. Accordingly the RAF strove to regain ground and challenge the future dominance of the Navy.[34]

It was an amazing situation. Air forces, the RAF in particular, had paid lip service to conventional warfare and the tactical use of airpower during their near monopolistic control of nuclear weapons from the end of World War II through the 1950s and into the 1960s. The air force, which had directed the bulk of its procurement effort towards acquiring large long-range bombers for delivering nuclear weapons, suddenly became in the 1960s immense proponents of heavily modernized tactical – land-based of course – airpower. This move was at the very moment that their deterrent monopoly was challenged by carrier-based nuclear bombers and more importantly the deployment of ballistic missile-carrying nuclear-powered submarines. From the early 1960s the RAF started to produce an enormous amount of literature discussing the benefits of what became known as the 'island basing' strategy of land-based aircraft versus the Navy's carrier force. It was nothing more than an RAF attempt to maintain its role and its funding, which from World War II until the 1960s constituted the single largest segment of the British defence budget.[35]

The Royal Navy may have been able to ride out the challenge of the RAF to its tactical airpower and east of Suez roles if it had not been affected by a number of factors that were developing by the mid-1960s. Key amongst them was the coming to power of Harold Wilson's Labour party in 1964, which brought a new set of political, economic and technological challenges with which the Navy would have to deal.

CHAPTER 9

The Cold War 1964–89

The coming to power of Harold Wilson's Labour party in 1964 marked yet another watershed for the Royal Navy. By the end of the 1960s, following the various challenges and evolving political objectives set by the new administration, the service would be radically changed. The twin-track defence policy – of east of Suez and west of Suez – that had been initiated by Duncan Sandys following the Suez Crisis would become single track, centred on threats and operations in support of European security within the confines of Europe and its immediate vicinity. The Navy, which had been progressively building its global power projection capabilities centred on modernizing, new-build aircraft carriers, amphibious forces and strategic sealift, would from 1966 see this capability curtailed and very shortly thereafter mostly ended.[1]

As it entered the 1970s the Navy would increasingly be seen as a European player with its forces embedded within the defence of the North Atlantic against the growing menace of the Soviet fleet. Its system of global basing would disappear as Britain's defence forces as a whole shrank to fit the new political and economic agenda of the day. Aden would be evacuated in 1967 and the last Arabian base in 1971, the Navy being told that it would never return. (Nine years later it did return with the Armilla Patrol and in the twenty-first century established a full-time presence and base in Bahrain.) Singapore, Simonstown in South Africa and the Indian Ocean would be vacated too. Only Hong Kong would survive with a permanent British naval presence throughout the 1970s and into the 1980s, but this at a remarkably reduced level. The changes towards a

Eurocentric deployment initiated in the 1960s would continue into the 1980s, finally arrested only by the immensely successful demonstrations of naval power throughout the decade with deployments in support of Britain's interests in the Persian Gulf (the Armilla Patrol 1980–90), the Falklands conflict of 1982, the eastern Mediterranean (the Lebanon 1982–84) and finally the Gulf War of 1990.

Wilson comes to power

When Labour came to power in October 1964, 13 years after Clement Attlee had lost office to Winston Churchill, the Royal Navy could justifiably have felt confident in its future. The list of new-build vessels and intended construction was impressive. They included at least one (out of three hoped for) *CVA-01* class attack carriers, anti-submarine warfare command cruisers and new Type 82 guided missile destroyers of the *Bristol* class carrying the newest of Britain's guided missiles, the Sea Dart air-defence weapon. Four *Resolution* class Polaris armed nuclear submarines with new nuclear-powered attack submarines were also under construction. The amphibious fleet was well on its way to expansion with the building of HMS *Fearless* and *Intrepid* and the RFA was beginning a complete modernization process that would see 28 new-build vessels joining the auxiliary service. Overseas naval bases had been heavily updated and the deployment of the Navy in support of British interests from these had continued apace since the late 1950s and in fact showed no sign of slacking in the new decade. All of which was heavily supported by America, which saw the Royal Navy's contribution to global stability as being of far greater importance than Britain's European contribution.[2] Naval nerves concerning the more extreme wing of the Labour party and their desire to cut defence spending, which would have diminished the role of the Navy and put paid to Polaris, were steadied by statements by Wilson and his new Defence Secretary, Denis Healey. They intended that Britain would fulfil its global roles and commitments, including the acquisition of Polaris. However, as developments showed, they intended that this would be achieved in somewhat different and hopefully cheaper ways than their predecessors. What this actually meant to Britain's defence services began to be realized in 1965 with a swathe of cuts imposed upon procurement. Britain's economy had begun to falter following Harold Macmillan's days of 'never having it so good' and pressure was being exerted on the defence budget. This was especially so as a large number of 'big ticket' procurement programmes were beginning to increase in size and cost and a series of significant deployments such as the confrontation in Indonesia were beginning to deepen.[3]

The Healey cuts

In 1965 naval procurement remained very much intact, including that of aircraft carrier and nuclear-powered submarine programmes. Acquisitions for the RAF, however, did not. Three key air force programmes, the TSR2, P-1154 and HS681, were cancelled in favour of what were seen as cheaper but less capable platforms. The British Aircraft Corporation's TSR2 (tactical strike and reconnaissance) aircraft was cancelled in April 1965 in favour of the American F-111. The Hawker Siddley P-1154, a supersonic short take-off and vertical landing (STOVL) aircraft, was terminated in favour of the sub-sonic P-1127 in February 1965. Similarly the HS681 strategic short take-off and landing (STOL) jet aircraft was replaced by the smaller, shorter-range American C-130 Hercules. Other programmes and platforms were also affected. The result was to have a profound effect on the already worsening relations between the RAF and the Navy as the air force felt deep cuts whilst seeing an apparent resurgent naval capability.[4]

The decision to replace the RAF V-bombers with Navy Polaris submarines in December 1962, arguably undermining the main rationale for an independent air force – strategic bombardment – can be seen as the catalyst for the worsening relations between the Navy and the RAF. After the decision to buy Polaris, the RAF focused on the TSR2, which besides its primary roles of conventional strike and reconnaissance also had a sizeable nuclear strike capability for European defence. However, its cancellation in the spring of 1965 suggested an end to long-range manned bombers in the RAF. The RAF were already aware of their vulnerability and from 1962 started work on using the TSR2 fleet for the east of Suez role, which brought it into direct competition with the Navy's strike carriers. The Royal Navy in its turn was aware of this challenge and began working against the TSR2 (and the proposed naval variant of the P1154, which was a potential threat to the large strike carriers), the lynchpin of the future RAF strategy, whilst attempting to ensure the survival of the CVA-01 programme. At the forefront of this movement had been the Chief of the Defence Staff, Lord Louis Mountbatten, and the First Sea Lord, Casper John. By the spring of 1965 amid much controversy – then and now – the air force's aircraft were cancelled on the grounds of cost overruns and delays; the F-111 was to be purchased instead. A home-grown alternative proposed by the Defence Secretary and the Navy was the Blackburn Buccaneer, already successfully in service and about to be improved by the new Mark 2 variant. But being a naval aircraft it was consistently dismissed by the RAF, until, with no option left, it was forced on them later in the decade.[5]

Either way the damage was done. The Royal Navy's deterrent programme remained on track, although only four missile-carrying submarines would be acquired as opposed to the eight to 12 that were initially thought necessary for a global deterrent in the early 1960s and the five initially intended by 1964. Long lead items for the fifth were ordered but nothing came of these. The carrier programme remained intact, although for now only one carrier was definitely in the government's procurement schedule for service from 1975. All of the other major naval programmes also survived the 1965 bloodbath, unlike the RAF's. Consequently the RAF re-doubled its island-basing strategy to provide itself with a prestigious role that would result in funding and a renewed profile, otherwise it faced a situation of existing solely to support the Navy east of Suez and the army west of Suez. This was an unacceptable situation for the RAF hierarchy which saw itself as the premier service during the 1950s when it had been responsible for the nuclear deterrent, Britain's ultimate guarantee of defence.[6]

Following the termination of the TSR2 programme the RAF attempted to ensure the survival of its replacement, the F-111, and within an ever worsening economic situation this became even more essential. Ultimately it targeted the cancellation of the CVA-01 and was certainly partly responsible for its demise in 1966. The RAF argued that it could provide airpower east of Suez and for the roles required of the Navy. Figures provided stated the RAF's F-111 option to be some 75 per cent cheaper than the CVA-01. For a government that wished to maintain roles and commitments but at a significantly lower cost, it came as a natural conclusion that the CVA-01, a project bedevilled by Treasury interference, was cancelled.[7]

The RAF had mounted a far more organized set of arguments than the Royal Navy. Mountbatten and Caspar John had both now retired and the supporters of a modernized and balanced navy were far fewer on the ground. There were many other contributing factors, together with some that have entered folklore, which became prominent in the cancellation. The role of Denis Healey was one. The Defence Secretary openly favoured the RAF arguments and the way they argued, perhaps because, according to some, he felt more socially comfortable around air force officers than their naval counterparts. This was aided by the overall weakness of the naval case due to the poor presentation and substance of their argument for the retention of carriers. Essentially the Navy failed to articulate the many and varied roles of carrier aviation. The government of the day believed carriers in the 1960s to be useful primarily for supporting amphibious operations. However, they also realized the need to support a lesser but perhaps more immediately pressing role, that of covering the withdrawal from empire and peacekeeping. Such views were as nonsensical then as they are today: the carriers' role in a myriad of different missions was overlooked by government and arguably the Navy itself. Carriers seemed to be regarded, somewhat bizarrely by a number of naval personnel, as essential for peacetime operations such as evacuation yet their significance in wartime was becoming less prominent. There were also very real divisions within the Navy which contributed to the decision to cancel the new British supercarrier. Significant echelons within the service were convinced that the future of the Navy lay solely in waging the Cold War and that the primary platform for this struggle was the nuclear-powered attack submarine. It was felt by some that in order to ensure sufficient funding for submarines, the Navy procurement budget should not be diluted by construction of large surface ships such as carriers or by their more expensive attendant air groups.[8]

Other political pressures were also building, most noticeably within the Labour party where many were increasingly moving against what they saw as global interference bordering on neo-colonialism, with the potential for more dangerous proxy actions on behalf of America, such as the Vietnam War. Another faction in the Labour party were aware that Britain needed to show a more Eurocentric defence posture if it were to stand any chance of accession into the European Community, where Britain was accused by its main critic, France, of being too global in outlook and not a true European player. The conclusion of both factions was an ending of global capabilities and therefore the roles and platforms that enabled them. Consequently a divided navy attempting to argue the case for a balanced force against a determined and united Treasury and an air force tacitly, or more likely strongly, supported by the Defence Secretary combined with a hostile ruling political party ended the CVA-01 programme in the 1966 defence statement together with its attendant escorting destroyers, the Type 82 (though the first, HMS *Bristol*, was completed but initially only to act as a radar test bed).[9]

Instead the defence statement confirmed the order for the American F-111 to operate globally from bases east of Suez, many of which perversely did not exist, while those that did required expensive investment to become operational, totally undermining the cost argument of the RAF. However, the decision allowed the government to be seen as maintaining its global role even if the maths did not make sense. Besides cancelling the CVA-01 it also ended the careers of the Navy minister Christopher Mayhew and First Sea Lord Richard Luce, both of whom resigned. However, one bright note concerned the escorting anti-submarine warfare cruisers, which survived due to their importance in protecting the future capital ship of the fleet, the nuclear submarine. The existing carriers and the bulk of amphibious shipping would also survive, at least until they reached the end of their natural lives during the 1970s, providing Britain with a residual if dwindling balanced fleet capability.

The end of east of Suez

However, this victory – of sorts – was short lived for both the Navy and air force, for by 1967 the economic situation had deteriorated to an unacceptable point and continued deteriorating throughout the year and resulted in two further defence statements. The second statement at the start of 1968 announced the end of Britain's carriers, the F-111 procurement and the east of Suez role.[10]

Healey had decided that defence could no longer be structured around two poles, the east and west of Suez strategy created by Duncan Sandys. Politically, economically and seemingly strategically British defence was best situated in Europe. This belief had a tremendous impact on British defence forces and the Royal Navy in particular. The path it created for the Navy would continue until the end of the Cold War. In the short term it meant the ending of the carrier force. HMS *Victorious*, following a minor fire in 1967, was discarded in 1968. *Centaur*, in reserve since 1966 awaiting conversion to a commando carrier, would never enter service again. *Eagle* and *Albion* would be placed in reserve in 1972, again never to re-enter service, whilst *Hermes* would transition from a strike carrier into an anti-submarine/commando carrier supporting the *Bulwark* in the 1970s. Only *Ark Royal* would enter the 1970s with anything like a future and that was supposed to end mid-way through the decade, though ultimately it would almost see the decade through before being retired and scrapped.[11]

In the medium term the Navy would re-orientate itself from a globally deployable force, much of it based east of Suez with substantial infrastructure throughout Arabia and South East Asia, into a European-based force pursuing an Atlantic-centric posture dominated by anti-submarine operations against the growing Soviet fleet.

Fig. 9.1. HMS *Albion* with her commandoes embarking on Wessex helicopters. The combination of a commando carrier with one of the new LPDs, HMS *Fearless* and HMS *Intrepid*, together with the RFA providing afloat support to the task group made for an immensely flexible foreign policy instrument for the British government during the late 1960s and 1970s.

This increasingly submarine- and small-surface-ship-orientated force effectively became known as the Eastlant Navy from the middle of the 1970s. In the longer term it meant the demise of Britain as a balanced and global player. Should Britain ever countenance an overseas operation, Healey believed that it would be alongside an ally. Ironically it would be a substantial ally that did possess a balanced capability, namely America. Britain had become as guilty as the rest of Europe during the Cold War in deciding to ride on the back of America's military might.

Yet even with the substantial and long-term cancellation of the CVA-01 and the illogical and arguably unwarranted and precipitate rundown of the remaining carrier force, the tempo of operations for the Royal Navy maintained itself throughout the remainder of the 1960s and into the 1970s. As early as 1965 the Navy found itself in one of the potentially weirdest yet most heavily tasked missions of the post-war period with the imposition of the Beira Patrol against

Fig. 9.2. HMS *Chichester*, a Type 12 frigate, was one of many Royal Navy vessels involved in enforcing the Beira blockade between 1966 and 1975 in response to Rhodesia's mostly white minority government's unilateral declaration of independence on 11 November 1965.

landlocked Rhodesia. Following the unilateral declaration of independence by the white minority Smith regime in Rhodesia, Britain's last major African colony, pressure was brought on the Wilson government to respond. With direct military intervention ruled out, an embargo was imposed and the Royal Navy tasked to enforce it, deploying to the Indian Ocean where it attempted to disrupt and stop cargo bound for Rhodesia via the Portuguese-controlled Mozambique port of Beira. This deployment was terminated in 1975 owing to the large numbers of escort vessels required, as well as the number of larger ships, including carriers, used to carry out diplomatic conferences between the British and Rhodesian governments. The failure of the mission lay in the attempt to blockade a landlocked country when its neighbours allowed the transit of goods from their ports, including importantly South Africa.[12]

In the meantime the Royal Navy had ended its deployments in support of the confrontation in Indonesia in 1966, but this was followed in 1967 by the sending of the largest task force since Suez to oversee the withdrawal of British forces from Aden during its hurried transition to independence. The next year saw the commissioning of the first *Resolution* class Polaris missile-armed nuclear submarines, with their first deployment in 1969, transferring to the Navy Britain's nuclear umbrella from the RAF but also giving it the same old problem, namely the credibility of the deterrent. Almost as soon as Polaris entered service the system was regarded as less than credible against the growing ballistic missile defences of the Soviet Union. So began a modernization process that evolved through the Antelope and Super Antelope programmes before finalizing as the Chevaline Project. This process remained highly secret and was not announced to parliament until Margaret Thatcher's Conservative government took office in 1979. Costing three times the initial price of Polaris, at over £1 billion, and having remained hidden from all and yet funded from within the core defence budget, it came as a tremendous shock to many but confirmed the Royal Navy's status in terms of nuclear programmes.[13]

The 1970s and the Eastlant Navy

By the early 1970s as the four submarines of the *Resolution* class entered service the Navy's position as the holder of the nuclear guarantee was unassailable even though the RAF retained a size-able nuclear bomber force. Together with the Polaris boats nuclear-powered attack submarines would start to enter service with the *Swiftsure* and *Trafalgar* classes throughout the next two decades. However, the Navy's conventional force structure was arguably not so healthy. The carrier rundown had been mirrored with a loss in amphibious ships and auxiliaries which would continue throughout the 1970s and into the next decade, though some would be kept in service owing to a number of developments in the 1970s such as the continuing Beira Patrol, intervention in support of British Honduras and the Caribbean and covering the American withdrawal from Vietnam. However, in the medium term the Navy's global presence was shrinking, with all naval bases east of Suez gone by the end of the 1970s (bar Hong Kong) in favour of the Atlantic defence posture. NATO was now the primary security mission for all British defence forces and was expected to remain so for the remainder of the century.

If the Navy and the British government thought that this was going to give a semblance of stability in terms of funding and roles they were proven wrong. The political and economic challenges that had shaped the Navy since 1945 were going to continue through-out the next few decades. Four years of Conservative government from 1970 and 1974 had attempted to reverse some of the decisions made by the previous Labour administration. But Britain's economic position worsened, badly affected by the 1973 oil crisis which saw the West punished by the oil-producing Middle East for tacitly and sometimes openly supporting Israel. This led directly to a new Labour government and a new defence review delivered by the Defence Secretary, Roy Mason. Unable to cut major commit-ments outside of the European NATO theatre, as they were already quickly dwindling, British defence priorities were reorganized along what became known as the 'Four and a Half Pillars'.[14]

On the face of it the Navy benefited from their creation, but in reality it began to suffer at the hands of another series of salami-slicing cuts. The Four and a Half Pillars would, officially anyway, remain British defence policy until after the end of the Cold War. The four primary pillars were: the nuclear deterrent, conventional defence of the homeland, commitment to land-based NATO defence in Germany, and commitment to NATO's maritime defence in the Atlantic. The remaining half a pillar was Britain's defence of residual overseas territories and interests. The Navy provided the primary contributions to two of the primary pillars and key support to the remaining ones. Additionally, it would at times provide the only contribution to the overseas support role. Yet this was not reflected in the decisions taken in the 1974–75 review nor the next in 1981. Although the roles seemed logical, the result of the review was a decision to cut defence spending by £4.5 billion over the next ten years. With no external commitments to provide significant savings, the end result was a rundown of front-line units, support, logistics, training and fuel. There was also a series of early retirements, procurements curtailed and others extended. The Labour government, however, was keen that the economic situation was not worsened by too drastic a cut in procurement and the resulting negative impact on an already fragile industrial base. Consequently much of the new-build projects managed to survive including the *Invincible* class anti-submarine cruisers, Type 42 destroyers, a smaller cheaper variant of the Type 82, Type 21 and Type 22 frigate programmes. The latter was a sophisticated anti-submarine frigate but was also fitted with Sea Wolf, the world's first ship-based missile system designed to destroy missiles as well as aircraft, which was hailed as the most modern anti-submarine surface ship in the world. Moreover, there was even room for innovation with continued experimentation with hovercraft and the acquisition of new technology, as the orders for the Sea Harrier in 1975, the Navy's first hydrofoil and investment in new lightweight and heavyweight torpedoes, anti-shipping and anti-aircraft missiles and helicopters showed.

The NATO Eurocentric roles did not stop wider deployments in support of British interests either. The Royal Navy found itself responding to the threat from Guatemala towards British Honduras (now Belize) in 1974 with the dispatch of HMS *Ark Royal*, the withdrawal from Vietnam in 1975 and the sending of a deterrent force to the Falklands to forestall Argentine moves against the islands in 1977. Closer to home the Navy undertook what was the third and final Cod War against Iceland from 1975 to 1976. The issue surrounded Britain's fishing rights in what Iceland claimed were her waters. The first 'war' had been waged in the late 1950s, but after ten years of peace a new dispute broke out. Briefly resolved tensions resurfaced again in 1975 with Iceland claiming a 200-mile economic exclusion zone. The Navy responded to aggressive Icelandic gunboat activity against British trawlers by deploying large numbers of vessels. Ultimately, with many nations also moving towards a similar territorial zone and with periodic Icelandic threats to remove NATO bases from its territory if its wishes were not allowed, Britain was forced to accede to Iceland's demands. Their demand interestingly became the accepted economic exclusion zone for

Fig. 9.3. HMS *Falmouth*, a *Rothesay* class frigate, being rammed by the Icelandic gunboat *Tyr*, 6 May 1976.

the world's maritime community enshrined in the United Nations Convention of the Law of the Sea III. The 'war' might have been lost but the experience was essential for lessons learnt in protecting British economic interests, including new vessels for the Fishery Protection Squadron, Britain's oldest standing naval force.[15]

At the same time, and in an attempt to retain a modicum of balanced capability, the Navy managed to establish a new European role for its amphibious shipping when Royal Marines, alongside their Dutch counterparts, became the reserve force to support Norway on NATO's northern flank against possible Soviet aggression. This required the retention of much of the flexible amphibious units together with annual training, which continues in various guises to the present. In fact the demands on the Royal Marines were high as they also became required to provide protection for the Polaris submarines based at *Neptune* in Faslane and for Britain's growing North Sea oil and gas installations. On top of this, Marines would start deploying to Northern Ireland to help police the ongoing 'Troubles' that had erupted earlier in the decade. This saw a permanent naval presence of patrol vessels employed to intercept terrorist arms shipments (part of the Northern Ireland Patrol Squadron) operating offshore and on the locks and rivers of the province. Additionally, there were more than periodic deployments of FAA helicopters to support the security services. These deployments would continue well into the twenty-first century when the Northern Ireland Patrol Squadron was finally disbanded as a result of the Good Friday peace accords. However, it would come at a cost with not just the loss of serving personnel in Northern Ireland but bomb attacks against others, most notably the murder of Lord Louis Mountbatten on his boat in August 1979 and the bombing of the Royal Marine Band barracks at Deal on 22 September 1989 killing 11 bandsmen.[16]

The notion of retaining a balanced capability for the Royal Navy was achieved with the orders for Sea Harriers for the new *Invincible* class anti-submarine command cruisers. It was recognized that the modernizing escort force of the Navy was vulnerable to the growing capabilities of the Soviet naval air force. Their Bear and Badger

Fig. 9.4. A Fleet Air Arm Sea Harrier shadowing a Soviet naval
air force long-range patrol and strike Tupolev 'Bear'.

bombers with anti-shipping cruise missiles of ranges of 200 miles
neutralized the missile defences of the new Type 42 destroyers. A
vestige of layered air defence was needed and the Sea Harrier fitted
the bill. Initially the Navy wanted 50 Sea Harriers but after a veto
from the Treasury only 25 were ordered following the intercession
of the prime minister in 1975; more were to follow. Earlier experimentation with Harriers had progressed well during the 1960s and
early 1970s involving dozens of ships from numerous navies, including ironically Argentina. In British service they would be used
primarily for air defence of the anti-submarine forces of the Royal
Navy operating in the eastern Atlantic but they would eventually be
called upon for far more.

Changes in roles and equipment in the 1970s were mirrored by
personnel changes, perhaps most significantly with respect to the
Women's Royal Naval Service (WRNS). A 1974 survey suggested
that the WRNS ought to be integrated into the mainstream Royal

Navy. The service had been established during World War I and re-established at the start of World War II. During the war the WRNS had initially fulfilled various secretarial and domestic duties but this would widen to encompass far more important roles such as the manning of harbour vessels for personnel movement. A number would also serve at sea but more often than not in merchant ships as signal officers. One of the greatest benefits of the WRNS was their forming permanent staff within establishments, as opposed to their more transient male counterparts, thus providing considerable stability. Post-war a corps of 3,000 permanent WRNS were kept to continue the administrative tasks and support roles in Royal Navy establishments globally.

However, the WRNS had been trained separately and this remained the case in the post-war world, training at a newly established unit, HMS *Dauntless*. The result was that their career progression was severely limited. In 1976 the movement to integrate began following a report in 1974, a process that has continued ever since, with WRNS officer training moving to Britannia Royal Naval College, Dartmouth, from Greenwich. Six years later in 1981 rating training changed as well as HMS *Dauntless* was closed and WRNS ratings joined their male counterparts at HMS *Raleigh*. However, both officers and ratings were still trained separately, the former in the famous Talbot Division. However, pressures to integrate, not least to counter falling male recruitment, saw the decision to integrate training completely and open up much of the front-line Navy to women. This had been resisted in the past officially for financial reasons, as the need to alter ships' accommodation seemed prohibitively expensive, but unofficially there were many concerns regarding fraternization and the lowering of male efficiency. However, in 1990 the decision to properly integrate the WRNS was made resulting in Dartmouth's first mixed cohort joining and training together. Later in the same year WRNS officers and ratings joined their first ship, the frigate HMS *Brilliant*, and for the first time 'officially' went to sea, even though at least one hydrographic WRNS officer had served in the South Atlantic during the Falklands conflict in 1982. Effectively no post was barred with the exception of submariner and even this has now changed as female submariners begin to train in 2013.[17]

Conditions changed even on board ship. With the introduction of the new *County* class destroyers between 1962 and 1970, living conditions for sailors entered a new age. The ships were capacious compared to previous vessels, well lit and hammock free. The sleeping icon of many generations had finally been banished on new Navy vessels in favour of folding bunks. Decks were well lit, food improved and was now served in electric galleys with ratings eating en masse, a process that had begun with carrier crews earlier but was now mirrored by the smaller ships of the fleet. These developments were well received, but of course the end of some traditions such as the daily rum ration in August 1970 did not go down so well. It was even debated in parliament. It was recognized, however, that the daily consumption of rum did not fit well with the Navy entering a technological age where the wits of the operators of modern equipment needed to be sharp. However, the loss of rum was replaced by senior rates being allowed to run their own bars within their messes. This was seen as both a prestigious move, bringing them on to a par with officers' wardrooms, and as more practical and controllable.

There were changes in the different specializations that made up the officer corps and the senior and junior ratings of the Navy during the 1970s too. The service was getting more technologically advanced, with missiles forming the main armament of ships like the *County* class, the Type 21, 22, 42 and 82 frigates and destroyers that were designed or entered service in the 1970s. Gas turbines were replacing steam turbines and boilers. As a result the training needs of specialists throughout their careers changed. Following on from the creation of a single officer corps with the 'General List' and 'Supplementary List' in the late 1950s, the 1970s saw revisions and changes to the specializations within which officers were employed. The old executive branch officer specializations of gunnery, torpedoes, signals, navigation, and anti-submarine warfare were replaced by the 'Principal Warfare Officer' who was trained to conduct all-arms battles, although there was still room for some specialization. Similarly the executive branch ratings specializations were revised, with gunnery being the most notable casualty, becoming the 'Missile Branch'. The training for these new 'warfare' officers and ratings was moved to a new facility, the School of Maritime Operations at HMS *Dryad* near Portsmouth – the old branch schools like HMS *Mercury*, HMS *Vernon* and HMS *Excellent* were wound down and closed. There were also significant changes in the engineering and electrical branches. The 1970s saw the creation of the Weapons Engineering Branch for both officers and ratings from the old Electrical Branch. At the same time the Mechanical Engineers took responsibility for electrical power generation. By the end of the decade, up to 2,600 ratings had voluntarily transferred across from the Electrical/Weapons Engineering Branch to the new electrical sub-specialization division of the Mechanical Engineering Branch.

Many of the changes that took place during the 1970s had been intended to streamline training and reduce costs. Yet in 1977 at a summit of NATO ministers it was agreed that as a result of the whole-scale degrading of Western defence over the last decade all member states were to increase their defence budgets by 3 per cent in real terms, above their national inflation figures, for a period of ten years. The previous years of cuts from the 1960s had taken a toll on Western defence, particularly the alliance's naval capability. The Soviet navy had spent two decades expanding and modernizing under the able Admiral Sergey Gorshkov. Since the early 1970s it now possessed the second largest navy in the world, overtaking the Royal Navy. Moreover, it enabled the Soviet Union to command a large global presence, often deploying from former Royal Navy bases, such as Aden. The Western alliance needed to rebuild its force levels, yet ultimately only two nations within NATO, Turkey and Britain, managed to fulfil this commitment in the allotted timescale. This fulfilment of the commitment ought to have thrown the Navy a financial lifeline, but this was not be, as a new oil crisis following on from the Iran–Iraq War of 1979 threw the economic aspirations of the new Conservative government under Mrs Thatcher, elected in the same year, into turmoil. The new government was determined not to cut the NATO commitment – and it would not be cut – but at the same time, it would not be able to procure everything the services were asking for in order to fulfil the Four Pillars created earlier in the decade.[18]

Key amongst these was the nuclear deterrent. The Callaghan government of the late 1970s had deferred a decision on the replacement of the *Resolution* class submarines and their Polaris missiles to the next parliament. As mentioned earlier Polaris had been updated continually throughout the 1970s. Indeed, as soon as it entered service it was regarded as being incapable of penetrating the Soviet anti-ballistic missile defences around Moscow. Thus through the programmes known as Antelope, Super-Antelope and finally Chevaline the Polaris missiles were fitted with manoeuvrable re-entry warheads, penetration aids and decoys. The cost was three times that of the initial Polaris programme and surprisingly it came from within the core defence budget unbeknown to parliament until announced by Francis Pym, the new Conservative Defence Secretary. Even this, however, was a stop-gap measure. Thus the new Thatcher administration inherited the decision to replace Britain's nuclear deterrent and in 1980 her government chose the American system Trident I, or C4 as it was also known, which was then being adopted by the US Navy. The following year, as the Americans moved to Trident II (or D5), Britain matched its decision, effectively 'ring fencing' the nuclear programme. The benefits were immediate for the Royal Navy as it once again was seen as the provider of Britain's nuclear deterrent, the key platform during the renewed Cold War that had worsened following the Soviet invasion of Afghanistan in December 1979 (although the RAF and FAA would also retain freefall nuclear weapons until the 1990s). Options other than submarine-launched ballistic missiles were looked at but none provided a credible, capable deterrent, and all were ultimately regarded as more costly than the Trident option. However, the drawbacks for the service were equally large, as the new programme would effectively be paid for by the Royal Navy, and without a large increase in its vote in the defence budget it could well cripple naval procurement, creating divisions within the Navy and a political furore seeing a repeat of what had happened in the 1960s.[19]

Nott and *The Way Forward*

In the meantime the Navy's key role in securing British interests overseas was once again demonstrated with the Iran–Iraq War. Saddam Hussein's attack against Iran's Ayatollah Khomeini prompted a return to the Persian Gulf of the Royal Navy, with the creation of the Armilla Patrol in 1980 for the protection of British-flagged and friendly tankers. Tankers of any nationality increasingly became targets of the warring nations as each attempted to stem the flow of oil and therefore the income of their opponent. Usually three escort ships and an RFA were in theatre at any one time and would remain so long after the war ended.[20]

However, 1981 not only saw the first full year of the Armilla Patrol and the move towards the Trident D5 choice (which was made public in March 1982) but also witnessed what many senior naval officers saw as the darkest day in terms of defence decisions since the cancellation of CVA-01. Rightly or wrongly the 1981 review of Defence Secretary John Nott is viewed by many as a turning point in post-war British and naval history. The second oil crisis brought about by the Iran–Iraq War precipitated another financial crisis which inflicted further economic woe upon an already fragile British economy. However, the Thatcher government was determined to stand by its NATO commitment of a 3 per cent increase in real defence funding. Yet there was no way it could also fulfil what was becoming an enormous shopping list of expenditures to modernize the British forces as well as trying to rectify the salami-slicing cuts in pay and conditions, as military wages failed to keep up with inflation, experienced by the military following the implementation of Roy Mason's review during the 1970s. Accordingly, John Nott was moved to the Ministry of Defence in January 1981 as part of a reshuffle by Mrs Thatcher which saw also Francis Pym, the previous Defence Secretary, become Leader of the House of Commons. Nott's remit was to re-adjust defence spending, not to cut it, and ensure that Britain was able to fulfil its commitments.

In theory nothing was sacrosanct, although Trident was ring fenced. In reality Nott used Mason's Pillars from the 1970s and simply asked the services to lay out their case in terms of their functions and what was required to achieve them. The army and air force articulated their cases well, aided by the European dimension of the continental commitment which seemed impervious to deep cuts, with only peripheral tinkering taking place. Additionally, it was considered cheaper to leave forces and their dependants in Germany than bring them home, even though their military contribution to the alliance could be regarded as limited. But the Navy, it seemed once again, was unable to provide a coherent defence of the importance of naval power nor a balanced fleet concept. They apparently addressed the key requirement of anti-submarine warfare against the growing Soviet submarine force whilst paying little attention to the more balanced nature of naval power. The reality, however, was somewhat different: the First Sea Lord, Sir Henry Leach, had a number of meetings directly with the prime minister where he laid out the essential flexible nature of seapower in support of Britain's wider foreign policy aims. His arguments, however, fell on deaf ears. Nott's primary concern was Trident and the funds it would absorb, the lion's share of defence spending for some time. This, the primary defence role, would benefit the Navy; therefore they could afford to be cut elsewhere. The government strove to ensure that the cuts to be imposed on the Navy were not seen as the price of Trident. This process failed. Nott's position was aided by his misapprehension that surface ships were vulnerable and expensive, with submarines playing the most important role in protecting Britain's and Europe's supply routes across the Atlantic. The resulting Nott review of June 1981, *The Way Forward*, saw the decision to remove a considerable number of ships, both Royal Navy and Fleet Auxiliary, from the active list, losing for Britain its most flexible foreign policy instrument.[21]

The carriers would be reduced to two vessels of the *Invincible* class, the first being sold to Australia with the remainder nominally being in service one at a time, though this was not guaranteed. In theory they would be used to lead a task force on overseas deployments, but again this was not guaranteed as Nott's review also stated that the task force might be led by a destroyer. The amphibious shipping was to be reduced to nothing by 1984 and the escort force cut from 59 to 50 initially, with a further eight transferring to reserve. Reductions, however, would have continued apace and by 1985 would have included all the 1960s and 1970s vintage *Bristol*, *County*, *Leander* and *Rothesay* class ships. Moreover, the new Type 42 destroyers would retire in the 1990s and would not be replaced, leaving another significant void in capabilities. Orders for Type 42 destroyers and Type 22 frigates would be curtailed and the new less expensive Type 23 frigate or an even cheaper option would be pursued. This meant an escort force half the level that Nott had inherited – 36 escorts by 1991 – and that was due to reduce even further during the 1990s. New investment in ship defence systems would end and there would be cuts to the Sea Harriers. Procurement of British submarine-launched torpedoes would also end in favour of the cheaper American variant. As a result of the large surface reductions there would be less need for the auxiliary services and their vessels would likewise be cut. By 1991 it was anticipated that the RFA would number just six ships, from the figure of 23 at the time of Nott. Additionally, the South Atlantic patrol vessel HMS *Endurance* would be scrapped following her deployment in 1982. With the large fleet rundown, some 30 naval establishments would also close, including Chatham and Gibraltar, with Portsmouth also being scaled down.[22]

The only positive outcomes of the review would be an increase in mine-warfare vessels, when funds permitted, and a growth in the submarine service, on top of the orders for the new Trident submarines. The nuclear-powered submarine was now seen as the capital ship of the Royal Navy. One other announcement was that, for now at least, the Royal Marines would survive as part of the Navy. The naval establishment was horrified but only Keith Speed, the Navy Minister and a former naval officer, would lose his position, sacked when he refused to resign following his public condemnation of the Nott review, leading to the naval quip at the time of 'less Nott, more Speed'.

More importantly another era had come to an end. The position of First Lord of the Admiralty had been scrapped with the creation of the Ministry of Defence on 1 April 1964, but with a Navy Minister taking over the portfolio. Keith Speed's vocal condemnation of the Nott review, which had resulted in his sacking in 1981, was now followed by a re-organization of the defence ministers. No longer would the three services be represented by an individual minister. Instead the existing three ministers were replaced by a minister for the armed forces, procurement, pay, pensions and so forth – a situation which remains to the present.[23]

Britain's closet ally was greatly concerned. Caspar Weinberger, the US Defence Secretary, declared as much in discussions prior to the announcement, wanting assurances from Britain. He naturally liked the promises dealing with expenditure increases but was blunt about the cuts to the Royal Navy, as they flew in the face of American naval increases and attempts to re-energize Western naval power following decades of cuts. Fundamentally Weinberger and his Naval Secretary, John Lehman, saw the Royal Navy as Britain's most useful contribution to the alliance and stated that the shortfall created by the loss of so many British ships could not be covered by the US Navy. The American press was also highly critical of the decisions, painting Britain as simply one more European ally free riding on the back of American defence expenditure. And in many ways it was right. However, the Nott review was not going to stand and within a year it had been overtaken by international events that saw its central decisions reversed. Key amongst these was the Falklands conflict of 1982.[24]

The Falklands conflict

On 2 April Argentine forces invaded the Falkland Islands and followed this by seizing South Georgia, South Shetland, South Orkneys and South Thule (the latter three never having been claimed by Argentina). The military dictatorship in Argentina had planned to invade the Falklands in early 1983 in an attempt to stop 150 continuous years of British control and give themselves a much needed popularity boost, which having murdered some 30,000 of its own people was desperately required. Additionally, the seizure could well provide a much needed economic windfall from suspected deposits of hydrocarbons throughout the South Atlantic and Antarctica. An invasion plan had been drawn up by the Argentine navy in the early 1970s and provided the blueprint for the operation in the 1980s. However, the navy, the junior partner in the Argentine dictatorship, possibly seeking a higher status within government, pre-empted the plan by orchestrating a crisis over South Georgia at the end of March 1982. They were spurred on by the Nott review, which was rightly interpreted as the end of Britain's ability to intervene. The public retirement of HMS *Endurance* (without replacement) was of great concern to the British Foreign and Commonwealth Office, but their fears had been overridden by Nott, who, along with most others, did not anticipate an Argentine invasion. However, *Endurance*, still in the South Atlantic, was dispatched to South Georgia to remove the Argentine scrap-metal dealers and more importantly marines that had landed there and precipitated the crisis. Consequently Argentina's navy was able to coerce the dictatorship into earlier action to invade the Falklands and remove the British presence rather than undergo the embarrassment of Argentine forces being removed forcibly by the British, which naturally would have been catastrophic for an already unpopular dictatorship. Neither the Argentine navy nor the country's military leaders expected Britain to respond. In fact in 1982 hardly anyone expected Britain to respond.[25]

However, Britain *did* respond and Argentina's invasion of the Falkland Islands on 2 April 1982 once again demonstrated the incredibly versatile nature of naval power. When an emergency meeting was held by Mrs Thatcher to discuss the options available she was informed by Nott and the chiefs of the army and air force that little could be done because of the distances involved. The army could not operate without air support and the RAF could not provide it. Luckily Sir Henry Leach was also present at the meeting and argued that it was essential that Britain should act. He questioned what hopes Britain might have of deterring or dealing with the Soviet war machine if it was unable to oust Argentina from British sovereign territory. What message would it send out to the wider world about

British capabilities and its ability to defend its interests or those of its friends if it couldn't deal with an Argentine invasion? Moreover, Leach promised that in just three days a task force could be assembled and dispatched to the South Atlantic to begin the process of retaking the Falklands. Thatcher, acutely aware that the three-month build-up to Suez in 1956 had cost the operation any chance of success, accepted Leach's offer, not least because it displayed a level of martial spirit that was lacking in the rest of the room. On 5 April, just three days after the invasion, a task force began sailing from British and overseas naval bases. Of course it was partly a publicity stunt: ships were stored and loaded hastily and incorrectly in front of the world's press; once en route, however, equipment was moved from one ship to another to ensure the correct unloading once in theatre. But the message was clear and well sent: Britain was determined to regain control of her territory.[26]

Although Operation *Corporate*, as the mission to retake the islands was called, was a tri-service effort, naval power was the key. The force, including the carriers HMS *Hermes* and *Invincible* and the amphibious units and fleet auxiliaries that had been either sold or were due to decommission prior to the conflict, proved vital to the operation. The 8,000-mile logistical line could only be furnished through seapower. Over 95 per cent of the equipment used in the conflict travelled in ships, either naval, fleet auxiliaries or ships taken up from trade. By the end of the campaign over 100 of the latter would have been employed as troop transports, tankers and auxiliary helicopter carriers. The exclusion zone created around the Falklands, designed at first to stop the movement of Argentine supplies and later to ensure that non-combatants did not wander into the war zone, was initially enforced by nuclear-powered attack submarines and later Sea Harriers and missile-armed Lynx helicopters. The result was a crippling of Argentine logistical lines and a failure to extend the major runway on the islands.[27]

South Georgia was retaken on 25 April via an assault from the sea, giving Britain its first victory in the campaign. Argentina lost any chance of gaining air control in the conflict on 1 May when it lost ten aircraft on the first day of hostilities over the Falklands and the

Fig. 9.5. The ferry *Norland* in San Carlos waters with
HMS *Antelope* sinking in the background.

Argentine air force told its fighter pilots not to engage Royal Navy
Sea Harriers. By the end of 2 May Argentina had lost sea control
when its heavy cruiser, the *Belgrano*, was sunk by HMS *Conqueror*,
forcing the rest of its navy back into Argentine waters, leaving the
scene set for Argentina to wage an airborne sea-denial campaign
against the Task Force now operating in greater numbers around the
islands. But at immense range, with no air cover and suffering innumerable logistical and command and control problems the bravely
flown Argentine aircraft suffered at the hands of Sea Harriers, ships'
missiles and guns (and special forces raids) which broke the attack
and resulted in over 100 aircraft and helicopters being lost during
the campaign. The Task Force commanders needed to whittle down
the Argentine air strength as a prelude to the amphibious campaign.

By 21 May the Task Force felt comfortable enough to launch the
amphibious assault at San Carlos waters which would culminate in
the surrender of the Argentine garrison at Port Stanley on 14 June.
However, it would come at a cost: HMS *Sheffield* was lost to an Exocet
missile on the 4 May and HMS *Ardent* and *Antelope* were lost to bomb

attacks. The worst day was 25 May when HMS *Coventry* and MV *Atlantic Conveyor* were both lost to Argentine air attacks. Many of the escort vessels were deliberately placed in front of the amphibious and civilian ships taken up from trade. These ships were 'high-value units' whose loss could have major complications for the land campaign. When the *Atlantic Conveyor* was sunk along with her cargo of Chinook and Wessex helicopters, the British forces lost the means to turn their landing force into an 'air portable' force, with the consequence that ground forces had to 'yomp' their way across the Falklands rather than being carried into battle. Throughout the ground campaign the Royal Navy would provide a constant stream of support from naval gunfire, to movement and to air attack. Royal Marines fought both on the ground and in the air, and the overall ground command-ers were Royal Marines (Brigadier Julian Thompson, RM, latterly replaced by Major General Jeremy Moore, RM). The Royal Navy also deployed almost 150 helicopters and 28 Sea Harriers to the conflict zone. Operational alongside them were ten RAF Harriers and one Chinook helicopter and a squadron of the Army Air Corps.[28]

The retaking of the Falklands came at a price, however, with 255 British deaths and the loss of six ships and over 30 aircraft and heli-copters; 12 more ships were damaged. But these figures were far smaller than either the Navy or the government had expected and were certainly smaller than they would have been willing to accept before a withdrawal was ever contemplated. Ships had been lost as a result of human error and technical deficiencies, and in the after-math of the conflict the government implemented not just a review but also saw to it that lessons were learnt. The essence of the Nott review was overturned and a balanced fleet was retained. By 1985 the Navy briefly possessed four aircraft carriers. Replacements for Sea Harriers lost in the war were ordered, as were extra numbers on top. The Sea Harrier underwent a modernization programme that by the 1990s had turned it into Europe's most capable fighter with new Blue Vixen radar and American AMRAAM missiles. The Fleet Air Arm was the first service outside the USA to have this capability. Airborne early warning for the fleet, lost in the 1970s, was resurrected during the campaign with Searchwaterradar-modified Sea King helicopters, although arriving too late to see service in the conflict. The amphibious force was retained and naturally the Royal Marines' standing was enhanced, with extra helicopters ordered for them as well. The escort force was now to remain around 50 for the remainder of the decade. Ships lost in the Falklands would be replaced and others modernized, with improvements in missiles, extra guns, improved construction and damage-control training. The design of the Type 23 frigate began to show evidence of lessons learnt, as it was transformed from an ocean-going tug that trailed a towed array sonar to find Soviet submarines into a multi-purpose frigate capable of engaging sub-surface, surface and aerial targets. Four new Type 22 frigates were now equipped with the standard 4.5-inch gun and a Goalkeeper close-in weapons system, overturning the earlier 'all-missile' armed ships designed in the 1970s. Critically the Royal Fleet Auxiliary also survived. During the campaign it had made a Herculean effort in terms of logistical support and was rewarded in the post-conflict period with the bulk of its pre-Nott numbers remaining intact. Moreover, the landing ship *Galahad*, lost in the conflict, was replaced by a new, larger version. Finally, the South Atlantic patrol ship HMS *Endurance* was also retained in service and eventually replaced. The publication of the *Lessons of the Falklands Conflict* in December 1982 was a recognition that if Britain wanted to protect and promote its interests beyond its borders (and certainly outside Europe) then the primary method was the maintenance of a balanced and capable navy.[29]

Back to the future

Of course this still left the government with a large financial problem. An enormous amount of expenditure was now earmarked for post-conflict lessons and the savings that were designed to accrue from cuts to the Navy were effectively reversed. How were the books to be balanced? This would be the task of the new Defence Secretary, Michael Heseltine, who was appointed in January 1983 to replace Nott. The latter had offered his resignation at the time of the Falklands crisis, as had the Foreign Secretary, Lord Carrington.

Although the latter's was accepted Nott's was not. However, the 1983 Cabinet reshuffle allowed Mrs Thatcher to replace him with Heseltine, who during his tenure oversaw large-scale privatization and more familiar salami-slicing that resulted in over £3 billion of savings, thus allowing the post-Falklands regeneration to continue. Although certain decisions such as the decrease in manpower levels and the closing of Chatham could not be reversed, it can be argued that the Royal Navy found itself at the end of the 1980s in a far more robust position than it had begun the decade. Modernization of all aspects of the Navy had taken place, from airpower, to escort vessels, submarines and mine warfare. The *Vanguard* class Trident boats were under construction and four new conventional submarines of the *Upholder* class were about to come into service, with more planned. New improved Type 42, Type 22 and Type 23 destroyers and frigates were in build. Arguably the most advanced mine-warfare vessels in the world, the *Brecon* and *Sandown* classes, were also under construction. Plans were being made for new amphibious ships, and the Fleet Auxiliary had received new tankers and was building two new support ships, whilst a civilian veteran of the Falklands crisis, the *Contender Bezant*, was acquired as the new aviation training ship, RFA *Argus*, dramatically improving this capability and giving the naval service a very large and flexible asset. And behind closed doors replacements for the *Invincible* class were being considered, even though the last of these, HMS *Ark Royal*, had only entered service in 1985.

After the Falklands the Royal Navy continued to demonstrate its flexibility with the ongoing support of the security services in Northern Ireland and the increasingly significant Armilla Patrol which was being seen by some as a renewal of the east of Suez strategy – navy escorts were not just in the Persian Gulf but found themselves visiting East Africa and Singapore, much like in the 1960s. There was the provision of a deterrent posture with regard to Argentina in the South Atlantic as well as commitments to Hong Kong, the Caribbean and NATO standing forces.

Moreover, new crises appeared which needed naval forces. Among these, the intervention in Lebanon from 1982 to 1984 stands out. American, British, French and Italian forces were deployed as peacekeepers to separate the warring factions following Israel's intervention in Lebanon in 1982. Although regarded by many as a failure, the small British force fared well. It was supported in Beirut from the sea with Royal Navy escorts and interestingly RFA *Reliant*. This was another Falklands veteran that was on short-term lease to provide yet another flightdeck using an American containerized helicopter support system. In this way she was able to support Royal Navy Sea Kings and RAF Chinooks, although replaced later in the decade by the far larger RFA *Argus*. Disaster relief and humanitarian intervention continued throughout the 1980s, including the evacuation of civilians from Aden in 1986, including Russians, and the aid given by Royal Navy and RFA vessels to Montserrat following the island's volcanic eruption.

By the end of the decade the Royal Navy could feel justifiably proud of its achievements, especially when placed in the context of the Nott review of 1981. It had survived that episode and more importantly organized and spearheaded the liberation of the Falklands the following year. Its force structure and order of battle was essentially the same as it had been in 1981 and in some respects larger. More importantly in terms of technology and capabilities, it was far in advance of where it had been at the start of the decade. It was playing a much more global role than either it or the politicians at the time of Nott could have foreseen and its profile was far higher. This was partly a reflection of Western naval power as a whole, which had undergone an American-led resurgence during the decade. However, the end of 1989 was also about to usher in a new period of transformation brought about once again by unforeseen political and residual economic challenges that would shake not just the Western alliance but the whole global political system down to its foundations.

CHAPTER 10

The End of the Cold War to the War on Terror 1989–2001

By the autumn of 1989 economic pressures were once again beginning to affect the defence budget. The ten-year NATO period of real defence expenditure increases had stopped in 1987 and the procurement budget looked likely to spiral out of control once more. All three services had presented considerable future spending plans and tried to maintain their current force levels into the 1990s. The Royal Navy had dipped below the 50-escort level but its nuclear-powered submarine, mine-warfare and aviation complements had increased in size. The carrier and amphibious forces had remained static and work was progressing very slowly on possible replacements. Keeping the Navy's order of battle into the 1990s would be unachievable without significant increases in the defence budget. However, of greater immediate significance were developments in Germany and Eastern Europe. Mikhail Gorbachev, the Soviet leader, had informed the Warsaw Pact that he was no longer going to enforce the Brezhnev Doctrine. This doctrine allowed the Soviet Union to intervene in the internal affairs of a fellow communist state that was deemed to be undergoing a counter-revolution; that is, any Eastern European country that appeared to be breaking away from Moscow's control would be stopped. This was no longer the situation and the Eastern Bloc was effectively handed its own destiny.[1]

On the back of this, borders opened and the free movement of citizens in Eastern Europe dramatically increased. On the night of 10 November 1989, following immense pressure, the Berlin Wall was opened to allow even easier access. This heralded the beginning of the end of the Cold War, although cracks had already begun to appear. Western politicians and defence leaders alike were presented with a major opportunity. Dominated by the thought of war in Europe, the policies of the Western alliance had resulted in defence forces that were unbalanced and inherently land-centric. This situation could be addressed through what US President George H.W. Bush termed the 'new world order'. This would have to be achieved rapidly, as the ending of the Cold War actually released more tensions than it eradicated, and soon the globe descended into a new world disorder. The static European-orientated forces would not be able to cope with the forthcoming pressures. Unfortunately Western governments took the opportunity to cut defence spending and forces rather than re-orientate them towards a new flexible military posture. In this respect Britain was no different to its allies.

Options for change?

The British statement on defence estimates for 1990 announced to parliament in the spring did not take the developments of the previous winter into account, as many initially and incorrectly believed that there would be no fundamental change to the status quo in Europe for some time. This, however, had been rectified in the summer of 1990 when the Defence Secretary, Tom King, unveiled his Options for Change paper. This was not a review in the traditional sense but the beginning of a series of re-adjustments to Britain's defence posture. Supposedly evolutionary rather than revolutionary, the stance of the 1990 paper was sound, talking of the creation of flexible forces to address the uncertainty of the new strategic situation. However, the reality was far different. The defence forces were simply cut by 25 per cent in terms of manpower and standing military equipment. This was certainly true of the Royal Navy: manpower was to drop to 60,000 by the middle of the decade from 62,600 in 1990. The surface escorts, submarines and mine-warfare assets were all reduced, as were manpower levels, with around 42 escorts to be maintained along with 16 submarines. The new *Upholder* class conventional submarines were capped at the first four rather than the 19 intended earlier in the decade, while the Navy's five early nuclear-powered submarines of the *Valiant* and *Churchill* classes were slated for premature retirement to achieve the new target. They would begin to be joined by *Swiftsure* submarines. However, the carriers, amphibious forces and Royal Marines remained intact.[2]

The 1990 decisions were compounded by worse news in the following years as the Options for Change process continued. In 1991 further cuts were imposed upon the services as the government attempted to fulfil the widely quoted, though never achieved, defence dividend, including another reduction of 5,000 in manpower. More cuts would be announced in 1993. Perhaps most dramatically the new *Upholder* class would be retired. The last commissioned of the four boats had yet to achieve a full year's service when notice of their retirement was given. The Navy had offered them up as unpalatable cuts in the face of ongoing Treasury demands, thereby losing a major capability. At the time, there were thoughts that elements within the hierarchy of the submarine service wished to become an all-nuclear navy, mirroring developments in the US Navy. Further cuts were experienced within the surface fleet, which was now to possess less than 42 escorts, with a reduction in mine-warfare vessels as well. However, the carrier force together with their air groups once again remained intact.[3]

By 1994 the next round of Treasury-inspired cuts were being discussed, this time under the direction of the new Defence Secretary, Malcolm Rifkind. However, he seemed more robust and fought a rearguard action, demanding that any savings produced in the budget would be ploughed back into procurement and front-line forces. Rifkind's Frontline First Review of 1994 was a timely decision as it allowed for £1.5 billion that was released via cuts in recruitment, training, logistics and infrastructure to be ploughed back into procurement. By 1996 manpower levels had dropped to below 50,000. However, the process was critical for the Royal Navy as it allowed for the continued acquisition of the new Merlin anti-submarine helicopters and significantly it funded the new helicopter platform HMS *Ocean* which had been authorized in 1993. The latter was finally a replacement for HMS *Bulwark*, retired as far back as 1981. More importantly it would become one of the most flexible and heavily employed assets of the Royal Navy for the next two decades. However, as with earlier defence reviews, the decisions taken at the start of the 1990s did not create stability and long-term planning for the services, as they were overtaken by international events erupting across Europe, Africa and the Middle East.[4]

A shield, a storm and a sabre

A month on from the publication of *Options for Change* George H.W. Bush's new international situation had become the new world disorder that some had feared when Saddam Hussein invaded and occupied neighbouring Kuwait. Iraq, a nominal ally of the West, had now become an arch enemy. The Western response was swift with Bush and Thatcher presenting a united front against the flouting of international law. The American response was Operation *Desert Shield* which was designed to protect Saudi Arabia from a potential Iraqi incursion. The loss of Iraqi, Kuwaiti and potentially Saudi oil would have been too much for the international system to bear. Initially at the heart of *Desert Shield* was a naval force as the Americans manoeuvred vast naval power into the region. Britain's Persian Gulf force, the Armilla Patrol, spearheaded Britain's response, which would become Operation *Granby*. Mrs Thatcher's first thought, remembering the Falklands, was to dispatch HMS *Invincible* until Alan Clark, one of her defence ministers, pointed out its military capability when compared to a vastly larger American carrier. Later during the crisis HMS *Ark Royal* and a task group was dispatched to the Mediterranean, releasing US assets, especially those that were monitoring Libya, which was suspected of sympathizing with Iraq. More importantly significant British naval power would be sent to the Persian Gulf to aid in the liberation of Kuwait. These vessels would become part of the international maritime coalition that comprised over 165 ships from 14 nations.[5]

Initially naval forces were to provide an embargo force in the eastern Mediterranean, Red Sea and Persian Gulf in fulfilment of UN resolutions that called for the blockade of Iraq. During the last three months of 1990 the embargo operations saw over 2,000 ships challenged, the majority by British warships. Naval forces were then to provide protection for Saudi Arabia and for the critical movement of equipment into Saudi territory for the land component of *Desert Shield*. For Britain alone this meant 144 voyages by chartered merchant ships and RFAs (and airlift) that moved over 400,000 tons of equipment including nearly 17,000 vehicles. Once again ships accounted for 95 per cent of all equipment moved by the coalition. Then the naval forces were to prepare for combat and the next stage of the campaign, *Desert Storm*. By December 1990, a month before the opening of hostilities, the Royal Navy and RFA presence in the Persian Gulf comprised 16 ships. By February this had increased to 26 vessels and one submarine. It was the second largest force after that of the US Navy. Many of the assets were mine-warfare vessels, an essential requirement as countless mines had been laid during the Iran–Iraq War and even more with the Iraqi invasion of Kuwait. American plans called for the use of battleships for naval gunfire support against Iraqi targets in Kuwait as well as demonstrating a large amphibious feint against those same targets. For both of these to be successful a clear path was needed to Kuwaiti territorial waters and for this the Royal Navy mine-clearance assets were crucial.[6]

Desert Storm began with a barrage of air strikes. The air campaign began on the night of 16 January when over 1,400 sorties were launched, 600 from the flightdecks of American carriers even though naval aircraft provided only 30 per cent of the air assets in the theatre. Additionally, 104 Tomahawk land attack missiles were fired in the first 24 hours. Aircraft sortie rates would continue with an average of 1,200 a day for the next five weeks before the ground campaign was launched. By late January and early February Royal Navy Lynxes operating from HMS *Cardiff* and *Gloucester* in the northern Persian Gulf fired 26 Sea Skua missiles that destroyed ten Iraqi vessels, almost a third of their navy. The remainder of the Iraqi navy was mostly dispatched by American carrier-based aircraft launching far longer-range and heavier Harpoon anti-shipping missiles. The way was clear for the mine-clearance operation that would see 41 miles of waters cleared, allowing American battleships and the amphibious groups to manoeuvre off the Kuwaiti coastline. Some 270 mines were neutralized, mostly by five *Hunt* class minesweepers: HMS *Atherstone*, HMS *Cattistock*, HMS *Dulverton*, HMS *Hurworth* and HMS *Ledbury*. Three more would be dispatched later. One can only wonder what it must have been like to operate in the 700-ton *Hunt* class British minesweepers in Gulf temperatures and in mine-infested waters while American 1-ton shells were fired over their positions into a vast and hostile Iraqi army. Royal Navy escorts were also tasked with support and protection of American ships. During one of these missions HMS *Gloucester* became the first ship in history to shoot down a missile with a ship-based missile when her Sea Dart system destroyed an Iraqi-launched Silkworm anti-shipping weapon that was heading towards USS *Missouri* on 25 February. This dramatically demonstrated that the updates following the Falklands War to the Sea Dart's radar and software had made a marked difference to its capabilities.[7]

Logistics and the supply chain were also heavily dominated by maritime issues. It was impossible to move the army's armoured division other than by sea, and during the *Desert Shield* and *Desert Storm* campaigns the naval component maintained its efforts. Two Sea King Junglie squadrons, 845 and 848, were attached to the British armoured division for its offensive into Iraq for *Desert Sabre* (the land campaign), whilst 846 operated in the Gulf ferrying supplies between the hard-worked RFAs and Royal Navy vessels. RFAs carried out 167 replenishments in order to allow the Navy vessels to remain on station. RFA *Galahad* also acted as a support ship, together with HMS *Hecla* and *Herald*, to the minesweeping force during part of the campaign, as the previous dedicated mine-warfare vessel, HMS *Abdiel*, had been scrapped and not replaced in 1988. Interestingly the *Abdiel* had successfully acted as the mine-warfare headquarters ship in the Persian Gulf, clearing mines from

Fig. 10.1. The Type 42 destroyer HMS *Gloucester*, seen here on her return
from the Persian Gulf, achieved a first in 1991 when she fired two
Sea Darts at an Iraqi Silkworm missile and shot it down.

the Iran–Iraq War as late as 1987.[8]

Naval power had once again proved essential in this campaign and it resulted in the successful liberation of Kuwait at the end of February. As with previous wars, navies had helped create the conditions for victory on land by achieving dominance at sea. The movement of the coalition forces was predominantly via the sea. Iraq was blockaded by sea, helping to undermine its economy and demonstrating considerable resolve on the part of the coalition and international community as a whole. United States naval power contributed greatly to the air campaign that eroded Iraq's ability to fight. The waters in the northern Persian Gulf were dominated by British and American naval units. In the last week of the war 19 of the Royal Navy's 26 ships were operating in the north, having helped destroy the enemy's naval force and neutralizing much of the mine threat. The Royal Navy and the US Navy were the only forces to operate in the northern part of the Gulf until after the end of hostilities, and in the last days of the war the nine northern-most coalition ships were all British. Naval air assets and fleet auxiliaries had also provided support throughout the whole region during the campaign, ashore as well as over the Gulf. Additionally, two Royal Navy submarines, HMS *Opossum* and *Otus*, were camouflaged to operate in the shallow Persian waters, enabling them to support the insertion of special forces into Iraqi-held territory.[9]

However, the liberation of Kuwait would not be the end of British naval operations in the Persian Gulf. After the war the mine-warfare vessels remained on station to continue their clearance work. Additionally, naval bomb disposal teams, including American and Australian as well as British, were involved in making safe a series of offshore oil platforms that had been booby-trapped by withdrawing Iraqi forces. This helped avoid an even larger environmental disaster than was already happening following the blowing up of numerous land-based oil wells by Saddam Hussein's retreating army.

Moreover, a more important direct deployment was made following the expected post-war break-up of Iraq. Western-inspired rebellions by Shia Muslims in the south and Kurds in the north against the Iraqi government failed, creating a mass exodus of refugees, especially in the mountainous north. The result was that the international community imposed no-fly zones over the rebellious areas in an attempt to stop Saddam Hussein's forces from crushing the uprising. In the north this was extended to include the creation of an effective umbrella region for the Kurds that was protected by forces from over a dozen nations. This included the deployment of Royal Marines from 40 and 45 Commandoes and their 'Junglie' Sea Kings of 845 and 846 Squadrons. They had been transported to Turkey by RFA *Argus* and given extra logistical support by RFA *Resource*, also based in Turkey, for the operation which became known as *Haven*. The humanitarian mission succeeded and provided a buffer zone between Kurds and Iraqi government forces. The deployment of the Royal Marines and their actions on the ground during Operation *Haven* were regarded as a great success but unfortunately attempts to create a similar situation in the next major crises in Yugoslavia and Somalia did not have the same results.[10]

Interestingly if America, as the dominant naval power in the

Fig. 10.2. Royal Navy mine-warfare vessels such as HMS *Hurworth*, seen
here leaving Portsmouth, were crucial in allowing the coalition
vessels to operate off the coastline of Kuwait. They were
some of the first vessels sent and the last to leave.

region in the last quarter of the century, had acted in the summer
of 1990 as Britain and the Royal Navy had acted in 1961 during
Operation *Vantage* and sent naval forces to create an umbrella around
Kuwait, the war may not have happened at all. Unfortunately the
deterrent and poise effect of naval power was not used to its full-
est effect by the American government, and the diplomatic messages
sent were confused. However, the actions led by the American and
British navies during the crisis certainly showed many of the benefits
of maritime power. Certainly the lesson of pre-emptive deployment
was learnt and pursued throughout the 1990s with respect to Iraq.
Saddam Hussein's constant failure to fully implement a series of UN
resolutions and continual interference with officials of the international body prompted a reaction. Accordingly the United States and
Britain responded with punitive raids against targets in Iraq. Naval
forces played a prominent role within these and the deployments
began to escalate by the late 1990s. Operation *Bolton* in November

1997 saw the dispatch of HMS *Invincible* and a combined carrier air group of Navy FA2 Sea Harriers as well as RAF Harrier GR7s in an attempt to bolster forces in the Gulf and send coercive messages to Iraq's government. They carried out patrols over the southern no-fly zone as well as training alongside their American counterparts. By March the force in the Persian Gulf had been joined by HMS *Illustrious* in order to apply extra pressure and relieve the *Invincible*. By April both *Illustrious* and her sister had left the Gulf. However, by January the following year HMS *Invincible* was back, this time as part of Operation *Bolton II* carrying out more air patrols following Iraqi actions. After two months of operations the carrier group left at the start of April 1999, but the Armilla Patrol remained, together with mine-warfare vessels. However, operations would not just continue but escalate in the early years of the new century with the successful maritime-dominated interventions in Afghanistan and Iraq in 2001 and 2003 respectively, the latter finally removing Saddam Hussein.[11]

The Balkans

After the liberation of Kuwait in 1991 the new world order contin-ued to collapse with the breakdown of failed states, most notably Yugoslavia and Somalia. During the international intervention in East Africa the Navy played only a small role, but in the former Yugoslavia its impact and that of international naval power as a whole was critical, if late, in ending the bloodiest European conflict since World War II. Yugoslavia, a creation of the treaties that ended World War I, collapsed into chaos as a number of its constituent states announced their independence during 1991 and 1992. Serbia, the largest state within Yugoslavia, refused to accept this and, in conjunction with the Serb-dominated Federal Army, attempted to forestall attempts at independence. The result was war. Western European countries, not wishing to intervene directly on the ground but at least to be seen as imposing some order on the chaos, sent naval forces to the Adriatic to initially monitor the situation and then implement a UN arms embargo on the warring factions. The Royal Navy was to become heavily involved in what became known as

Operation *Sharpguard*. This operation was designed not just to monitor the situation but to intercept arms supplies and other contraband heading to the war zone. During the course of an increasingly large international operation 37,000 ships were challenged, with 3,900 boarded.

As the situation on the ground deteriorated and civilian casualties mounted, humanitarian aid and peacekeepers were needed and delivered via the UNHCR and its Protection Force. With little will on the part of the warring groups to seek peace, the peacekeepers, initially with little firepower, found themselves increasingly frustrated and useless. What firepower that could be made readily available more often than not came from the sea. In January 1993 HMS *Ark Royal* had been sent into the Adriatic carrying Sea Harriers and (unusually) 'Junglie' Sea Kings. In her task group was RFA *Argus* carrying troops and equipment to support the British forces already committed to the UN force. Royal Marine 'Junglies' would be deployed for the duration of the crisis and provided not just troop transport but considerable emergency aid to the international forces deployed and to the local population. As usual, the bulk of the equipment, as in so many wars before, was transported via the sea. The *Ark Royal* was replaced by HMS *Invincible* in August 1993 and so began a near constant cycle of British carrier operations throughout the crisis, naturally supported by RFAs and escorts – deployments that also ran concurrently with actions in the Persian Gulf.[12]

Attempts to enforce a degree of sanity upon the worsening situation saw the creation of no-fly zones over Bosnia and safe zones on the ground, much as in post-war Iraq. However, implementation of these was sporadic, especially as collateral damage had to be avoided, which imposed strictly limited rules of engagement. Operation *Deny Flight*, as it was known, saw the need for increasing numbers of aircraft. The benefits of carrier-based aircraft employed from their moveable bases, which overcame the weaknesses affecting land-based assets operating from Italy and elsewhere, were quickly seen. Weather became less of a problem and reaction times to requests from international forces on the ground were far quicker for the mobile sea-based aircraft. Neither were the aircraft affected by the land bases' operating schedules, which saw a decrease in weekend flying during the crisis. Sea Harriers flying from *Invincible* class carriers became increasingly important and prominent. *Deny Flight* also saw the first deployment of the Sea Harrier FA2 in 1995, much modified since the time of the Falklands. In fact Sea Harriers flew a constant stream of combat air patrol, close air support and reconnaissance missions throughout the crisis. Their ability to maintain a swing capability was much appreciated by commanders. The aircraft also carried on-board cameras as well as air-to-air and air-to-ground weapons.[13]

Finally the NATO Secretary General, Manfred Wörner, recognizing the West's impotence and following a series of atrocities in Bosnia, managed to create sufficient support for NATO to take an active lead in bringing the war to an end by launching a series of air strikes against Serb targets in 1995. This together with a series of coordinated and successful offensives by anti-Serb forces on the ground led to a cessation of hostilities and finally the Dayton Peace Accords. NATO's air campaign, Operation *Deliberate Force*, was the first time that the organization had carried out offensive action. Carrier-based aircraft once again proved their worth. The eight Sea Harriers on board HMS *Invincible* flew over 150 sorties during the three-week campaign and were joined by aircraft from US, French and eventually Spanish carriers and from NATO airbases in Italy. More importantly the strengths and flexibility of sea-based naval airpower were once again demonstrated as they had been in the Persian Gulf, gradually persuading the politicians of the day of the need for larger, more capable carriers. Additionally, the years of Adriatic and Gulf deployments in the 1990s also witnessed the first combined Royal Navy and RAF air groups, paving the way for further and closer integration later in the decade.[14]

The 1990s also saw another large-scale deployment, but in this instance one of a more ceremonial nature when the Royal Navy covered the end of British rule over Hong Kong in July 1997. A task force including the royal yacht *Britannia* on her last major overseas visit before decommissioning at the end of the year was dispatched to Hong Kong. It saw the official handover of the colony to Chinese communist control and ended another era as the last British naval base outside Europe closed. It left behind just a handful of personnel in Singapore and some 50 or so on Diego Garcia in the Indian Ocean (policing some 5,000 American servicemen). The last of the three Hong Kong patrol vessels of the *Peacock* class, out of the original five built especially for service in the colony, were transferred to the Filipino navy.

The 1990s also witnessed a number of other notable closures for the Royal Navy which brought to an end a series of national and international presences. Of historical note was the closure of HMS *Malabar*, the last Royal Navy presence in Bermuda in 1995. Closer to home the Royal Naval Engineering College, Manadon, in Plymouth was closed and its functions transferred to civilian universities. The Royal Naval Staff College, Greenwich, was also closed, with its responsibilities transferring to the temporary Joint Services Staff College at Bracknell before relocating to purpose-built facilities at Watchfield near Swindon.

The Strategic Defence Review

The year of withdrawal from Hong Kong coincided with the new Labour government coming to power. One of its key priorities was to establish a firm and long-term basis for the defence and foreign affairs portfolios which had been seen as problem areas for the Labour party since the 1970s. Consequently the new government launched the Strategic Defence Review in the summer of 1997, arguably the most comprehensive and longest defence review in British history. Over the course of a year the Defence Secretary, George Robertson (later Secretary General of NATO), led a review that came to be regarded as more open and inclusive of interested parties than ever before. No matter who had won the 1997 election a review was expected to deal with the constant challenges brought about by the end of the Cold War. Not least, the years between Malcolm Rifkind's Frontline First Review of 1994 and the release of the Strategic Defence Review in July 1998 had seen a recognizable shift within Britain's strategic defence thinking.

The Eurocentric policies of the Cold War years were beginning to dissipate and the Ministry of Defence had begun to create joint-service rapid-reaction forces and a move to tri-service command structures, especially true under Rifkind's successor, Michael Portillo. Additionally, the Royal Navy had become increasingly proactive in the run-up to the next major review – a marked difference to previous years. The Navy was responsible for a series of publications that reflected the shift in thinking as well as highlighting savings in the future. These publications, such as *The Fundamentals of British Maritime Doctrine* (BR 1806) published in 1994, would successfully influence the forthcoming review, as would the creation of the Maritime Contribution to Joint Operations in 1998 (though this had been formulated and released earlier as Maritime Manoeuvre). The Joint Operations publication was the precursor to the joint expeditionary nature of the forthcoming Strategic Defence Review and was a reflection of recent experience. By the middle of the 1990s the Navy had realized that operations since the end of the Cold War (and in fact since the Falklands) were outside the European home-base at the end of extended sea-based supply lines, seeing power projected ashore but only following the achievement of sea and air control. In anticipation of future operations and recognizing limitations to existing platforms, they also realized that newer, larger and more flexible power-projection assets would be needed for the new century. But as in the past that would bring the Navy into direct conflict with the other services for the limited funds available. In order to avoid the problems of the 1960s onwards the Navy articulated a case for joint and expeditionary equipment that could be employed for all the services. For instance, future carriers were sold as joint aviation assets to remove the single-service stigma. It seemed rational and sensible and avoided the duplication of the past in terms of wasted time and expenditure.

Consequently the Strategic Defence Review published in July 1998 was far more supportive of the Royal Navy in terms of rhetoric and in the actual decisions made than any review since World War II. As in previous reviews nothing was officially sacrosanct, though in reality both the *Vanguard* class Trident missile submarines in build for the Navy and the RAF's Eurofighter programme were ring-fenced. However, unlike previous reviews expeditionary warfare and striking from the sea were at its heart. Naturally the Navy would endure a loss of personnel, as would all services. Surface escorts also saw further reductions (now down to 32) as did the numbers of submarines, but far more positively the Defence Review intended to expand certain areas. The three existing *Invincible* class carriers were to be replaced with two new, larger carriers, dubbed CVF, from 2012 onwards. These would displace more than three times the size of the carriers they would replace. Replacements were also agreed for the Sea Harrier. The Royal Navy had already become an interested partner in the American JAST aircraft demonstrator programme. This would soon be subsumed into the Joint Strike Fighter project. At the time, a competition existed between three American consortiums to provide the US military with cheap fifth-generation aircraft to replace earlier platforms, but critically including a short take-off and vertical variant. This was a natural choice to replace the Sea Harrier and one the Treasury was willing to accept given that the bulk of the costs were being borne by America. It was also favoured because, being a small aircraft, it could fit on board existing *Invincible*-size ships.[15]

With expeditionary warfare being at the heart of the review it was decided that HMS *Ocean* would be joined by two new Landing Platform Dock ships, HMS *Albion* and *Bulwark*, which would replace the 1960s vintage *Fearless* and *Intrepid* and at a tonnage that was half as large as the older vessels. The RFA would see four new *Bay* class Landing Ship Docks replace their *Sir* class Landing Ship Logistic vessels, the *Bay* class being twice the size of the ships they replaced. Additionally, Robertson confirmed the previous administration's intention to increase the size of government-controlled transport vessels, as six Ro-Ro vessels, the *Point* class, would be bought and employed to transport British military equipment around the world. Britain would have more government-owned strategic sealift capability at the start of the twenty-first century than it had possessed since World War II. The lessons of the conflict of the previous decades were gradually being learnt and implemented.

The escort force was proving more of a problem. Plans for its rejuvenation with the replacement of the Type 42 destroyers with the Franco-Italian-British Horizon frigate programme had encountered trouble. The project had never really experienced calm waters from its inception. During the 1980s NATO had proposed a common frigate programme for its naval forces, the NFR90 or NATO Frigate Requirement 1990. Unfortunately the various participating nations differed on requirements and Britain became the first country to leave, rapidly followed by others until it collapsed. In its place countries either developed national programmes or collaborated with partner nations. One such consortium was the Horizon Project for a new frigate with powerful radars and a state-of-the-art missile system – a programme that was increasingly seen as being very far over the horizon. Eventually in the new millennium the government dispensed with the international consortium and pursued a national programme, the Type 45 destroyers of the *Daring* class that would finally enter service from the end of the first decade. However, delays resulted as a consequence of spiralling costs and only six ships would be delivered out of the 12 intended to replace the increasingly worn-out Type 42s. That said, the Sampson radar system, the Aster 15 short-range and Aster 30 medium-range air defence missiles (latterly retitled Sea Vixen) on board were a quantum leap on the 1960s Sea Darts of the Type 42s in terms of speed, engagement range and kill capability.[16]

The submarine service also benefited, not just with the whole *Vanguard* programme being confirmed but also with the decision concerning the new *Astute* class of nuclear-powered attack submarines. These were designed to replace the *Swiftsure* class of nuclear boats that were built during the 1970s. Their design had evolved from an earlier programme known as the *W* class but remained stillborn as a result of the Options for Change process at the start of the decade. The *Astute* class was also an innovation for British nuclear submarines, as they were almost twice the size of existing hunter-killer submarines, displacing nearly 7,500 tons and fitted with a reactor core that was designed to last its entire life. This would avoid the costly and time-consuming refuelling that the rest of the nuclear submarine fleet had to undergo.

Besides achieving considerable success in gaining official approval for expeditionary warfare and new assets, the Navy's promotion of joint operations with its sister services also achieved considerable recognition. The Strategic Defence Review continued the movement towards a series of joint commands and structures but at an accelerated speed. Key amongst these were developments in aviation. Two new joint command structures were created, Joint Force 2000 and Joint Helicopter Command. Within the former was also the creation of Joint Force Harrier. Joint Force 2000 saw the Navy assuming the responsibility for all Britain's military-owned maritime flying assets including RAF Nimrod maritime patrol and Sea King search-and-rescue helicopters. The Royal Navy's senior aviator, Admiral Iain Henderson, Flag Officer Naval Aviation, became Flag Officer Maritime Aviation and the commanding officer of No. 3 Group which controlled the RAF's maritime assets. For the first time since World War II, when it had operational command of Coastal Command, the Royal Navy controlled all of Britain's maritime aviation assets. Henderson was aware of problems with joint air-command structures in the past, particularly the failed years of the interwar period, and was determined not to see them repeated. However, the new command structure would be short lived, as early in the new century Henderson's successor was out-manoeuvred by the RAF when for reasons of 'economy' it reconfigured its command structure, moving the Nimrods and Sea Kings to its other two groups, and regained direct control of its air assets once again. The inter-service rivalry of the 1960s was still very much alive and would remain so.[17]

However, the sub-command of Joint Force 2000, the Joint Harrier Force, lasted longer than its parent body but had also expired by 2010 with the demise of Britain's Harrier force. Joint Force Harrier was created on the back of the successful Royal Navy and RAF carrier deployments during the interventions in the Adriatic and Persian Gulf. It was also an attempt to streamline the Harrier community. It was initially seen by members of the Fleet Air Arm as a takeover of naval fixed-wing assets. Simultaneously it was seen by the RAF as a pre-emptive raid by the Navy to acquire all the Harriers. Either way, it would prove to be a sounding board for the future as decisions would soon be made on which American Joint Strike Fighter, or Joint Carrier Borne Aircraft as Britain initially called the aircraft, would be acquired (the latter name would evolve into Joint Combat Aircraft, losing some of its natural naval connotations). The Lockheed Martin option and its F-35 family was chosen. The short take-off and vertical-landing F-35B was chosen in 2004 to fulfil Britain's requirement and as a replacement for the Sea Harriers and RAF Harriers. Ironically at that point many were favouring the conventional carrier take-off and landing variant for increased versatility, greater range and lower lifetime costs. Additionally, sceptics of Joint Force Harrier were somewhat confirmed in their thoughts when the decision to retire the Sea Harrier in favour of an all RAF Harrier, but joint flown and controlled, force was announced. The loss of the air defence function of the fleet was grave but was seen as a temporary acceptable risk prior to the F-35 coming into service in the next decade. Moreover, the *Invincible* class carriers were now viewed as attack carriers and had been converted to operate as such – not bad for a ship designed in the 1960s to hunt Soviet submarines and only carry nine anti-submarine Sea King helicopters.[18]

The other joint administrative structure proved to be much more resilient. Joint Helicopter Command was created to oversee all battlefield support helicopters including the Navy's Commando Helicopter Force of Sea King 'Junglies' and Lynxes as well as the RAF's Chinook, Puma and Merlin forces. The Navy's 'grey' ship-based Sea King, Lynx and Merlin helicopters were retained under its direct control.[19]

The end of the century

In the meantime the renewed interest in projecting power overseas in pursuit of security by prime minister Tony Blair's government was quickly demonstrated by a series of rapid interventions close on the heels of the deployments in the Persian Gulf. Military forces would be deployed to crises in Kosovo, East Timor and Sierra Leone. The

Royal Navy had prominent roles in all three.

Following renewed Serbian tensions in the Balkans over the future of the autonomous region of Kosovo, NATO forces launched Operation *Allied Force*, initially an aerial campaign, commencing on 24 March 1999, to ensure that the crisis did not spiral into a Bosnia-style situation for lack of determined international effort. HMS *Invincible* sailed to the Ionian Sea on 10 April, on her way home after taking part in Operation *Bolton II* in the Persian Gulf. This was a clear demonstration of the flexibility of nationally owned and controlled sea-going airbases. Her Sea Harriers would fly over 300 hours of combat air patrols until May when the carrier left the area. Perhaps more importantly the opening stages of the air campaign had begun with Tomahawk Land Attack Missiles being launched from NATO submarines, including HMS *Splendid*. This was the first time that a British submarine had launched these missiles in an operation. The Tomahawks, the American missile that had come to prominence during the liberation of Kuwait, had been purchased off the shelf for the Royal Navy after that war. It gave Britain its longest-ranged (unrefuelled) conventional precision strike weapon, and made the Navy only the second service in the world to have this capability. It would be successfully employed on a growing number of occasions in the following decade. The Royal Navy also provided Type 23 frigates to provide escorts to a French carrier also operating in theatre, and, following the cessation of hostilities in June, the Navy mine-warfare assets HMS *Atherstone* and *Sandown* remained in theatre to clear jettisoned bombs not dropped on Serbian targets.[20]

Three months later and the Type 42 HMS *Glasgow* responded to take part in an Australian-led international effort to provide stabilization forces to East Timor. Indonesian forces were withdrawing but tensions erupted in the small former Portuguese colony as it moved towards independence. Royal Marine and Gurkha forces were also dispatched during the successful transition from Indonesian control. However, it was Operation *Palliser*, the intervention in Sierra Leone in May 2000, which demonstrates excellently the Navy's concept of the Maritime Contribution to Joint Operations. The Royal Navy had been used by the government throughout the 1990s to implement

British foreign policy, support what was left of a failed state and help the UN there. But this was normally with the presence of an escort vessel. By 2000 the situation had become dire. Close on the heels of Kosovo, Tony Blair felt that another humanitarian intervention was necessary. An initial requirement to evacuate British nationals from Sierra Leone expanded into a carrier-led task force which enabled a stabilization mission to take place. British forces sent to hold the airport soon found themselves being supported by HMS *Illustrious* and 13 Sea Harriers and Harrier GR7s plus an entire amphibious-ready group led by HMS *Ocean* including 42 Commando and helicopters from the Joint Helicopter Command sent to relieve the initial troops. This show of force in the classic style of the 1960s interventions stabilized the situation on the ground and Sierra Leone as a whole. It was a very considerable demonstration of naval power, which besides the *Illustrious* and *Ocean* comprised HMS *Chatham* and *Argyll* and RFAs *Fort George*, *Sir Bedivere*, *Percivale* and *Tristram*. However, the amphibious forces did return in November to demonstrate British intentions to resolve the situation, carrying out an amphibious assault in the process.[21]

It left few in doubt of the capability of naval power. The *Illustrious* Task Group and the amphibious-ready group were both re-tasked onto station from prior commitments, with *Illustrious* travelling 2,500 miles in five days. This versatility and flexibility displayed throughout the twentieth century would be needed even more in the first decade of the new century and in fact no sooner than 2001 following the terrorist attacks against New York and Washington in September.

The Royal Navy 2001 to Today

The Royal Navy at the start of the twenty-first century once again found itself with mixed fortunes. It was proving essential to the British government in executing a new and confident foreign policy under Tony Blair, as it was the main military instrument in the crises that had erupted since the end of the Cold War. Yet simultaneously the Navy's political footprint and public support base were far smaller than at any time in a century. It was no longer part of the regular consciousness of the British public, press and parliament. Yet the demands placed upon the Navy had not shrunk over the course of the twentieth century and in its last decade its commitments had in fact begun to increase. Yet in terms of manpower (41,500 by 2002) and fighting vessels it was comparable to that of the period after the Napoleonic Wars, even though the service was still expected to operate and support British foreign policy on a truly global scale. At the start of the new century the Royal Navy found itself supporting a series of commitments to British and Western security, some of which had lasted over half a century, but it was soon to take on new tasks such as the global war on terrorism and the fight against piracy. Worse for the Navy was that these new operations, such as the one in Afghanistan, were increasingly seen as land battles where naval forces seemed to play little part. Consequently the profile and public standing of the Navy has suffered, with the average Briton seeing all ground forces in the theatres of war as belonging to the army and everything that flies belonging to the RAF. Nothing could be further from the truth, as naval air squadrons, Royal Marines, logisticians, medical and intelligence personnel have all provided immense support to the campaigns. On a number of occasions the naval services have provided over half of all forces deployed at any one time in Afghanistan.[1]

2003, the Gulf again

The Navy's involvement in the Persian Gulf had been continuous since the Iran–Iraq War but the scale of its activities reached new heights in 2003. The war in the spring of that year was seen as a much more maritime-dominated effort than the 1991 liberation of Kuwait. This was partly aided by the fact that the majority of journalists reporting the war were embedded with naval units. Saddam Hussein had resisted international pressure for over a decade, finally pushing the American and British governments to act. However, the initial intent to invade Iraq collapsed as the original Anglo-American plan to launch the bulk of the effort into Iraq from southern Turkey was vetoed by the Turkish parliament. As a consequence the US Navy and the Royal Navy increased the scope of what had only been a holding action in the Persian Gulf to secure the southern oil installations. The lack of major host-nation support, as a result of Saudi Arabia also refusing access to its territory, compounded the problem of basing but increased the significance and flexibility of naval power.[2]

For the Royal Navy, Operation *Iraqi Freedom*, as the Americans called the 2003 intervention (Operation *Telic* for Britain), saw a full brigade-size amphibious assault against the Al Faw peninsula to secure the port of Umm Qasr. It would be a contested assault, a situation that most thought unlikely at the start of the century. Supporting this action would be a far larger naval force than had been present in 1991. The Royal Navy provided an amphibious task group, a mine countermeasures group and an afloat support group. Three nuclear-powered submarines would also see employment in the Gulf. HMS *Ark Royal* and HMS *Ocean* both acted in the helicopter assault role. Eight escort vessels were deployed for operations, and four RFA *Sir* class landing ships supported the amphibious assault and the minesweeping force, the latter being comprised of eight *Hunt* and *Sandown* mine-warfare vessels together with HMS *Roebuck*, a hydrographic survey vessel. There were 11 more RFAs providing the afloat support capability, including RFA *Argus* with its primary casualty reception role heavily emphasized. Another was RFA *Crusader*, a chartered Ro-Ro strategic lift vessel. She operated alongside four more government-owned Ro-Ro vessels of the *Point* class manned by sponsored reservists. Completing the naval force were six chartered merchant ships.[3]

Alongside the Royal Navy were the US and Royal Australian Navies and between them they successfully executed the assault into Iraqi territory, beginning the end of the regime. Further forces were dispatched from Kuwait. American carriers provided the larger part of combat aircraft and firepower for the coalition but the Royal Navy still contributed three escorts on the gunline using their 4.5-inch guns against land targets. Moreover, the submarines HMS *Splendid* and *Turbulent* launched Tomahawk missiles against targets inland. Overhead the Fleet Air Arm provided air mobility, anti-tank weaponry, reconnaissance and command and control capabilities through the deployment of seven squadrons, which saw the first combat use of Merlins, ASaC7 Sea Kings and HMA8 Lynxes. The Lynxes and Gazelles of 847 Squadron were particularly important supporting the Royal Marines ashore. The use of naval power had been a clear vindication of the Maritime Contribution to Joint Operations concept. However, although the war was won, the peace was lost, as the vacuum created in the aftermath was filled by extremists and led to the outbreak of various insurgencies.[4]

Maritime security

Neither did the end of the war see an end to hostilities on the world's seas. The wars in Afghanistan and Iraq had fuelled terrorist attacks at sea as well as from sea, moving the war on terror onto the world's oceans. This was compounded by the rise of global piracy, particularly prevalent off the east and west coasts of Africa, which has cost the global economy billions of pounds as various measures have been employed to contain the threat. Attempting to counter Somali piracy has resulted in three standing naval forces being created by the European Union, NATO and the wider international community, with the Royal Navy playing a role in them as well as operating Merlins from land bases together with others alongside ASaC Sea Kings from RFAs in the Indian Ocean. These operations, however, have contained but not eradicated piracy. Moreover, the exploitation of the sea by organized crime also escalated at the start off the new century, increasing demands even further. The Navy was tasked with countering all these developments and remains central to them today.

Counter-drug operations in the Caribbean have also been of great importance and have placed another heavy burden on the Navy, not just through the deployment of escort vessels that normally enter the nation's tabloid headlines but also RFAs that have played a critical but less public role. Tens of millions of pounds have been intercepted per year and sometimes hundreds of millions are caught, seriously interrupting the illicit trade. The presence of the Navy in the West Indies dates back hundreds of years but since the 1980s and Mrs Thatcher its role in the interception of narcotics has been particularly important. The presence of British ships, be they warships or fleet auxiliaries, with their communications facilities, fast boats and helicopters, has aided greatly in interrupting the flow of illegal drugs. Cooperation between the Royal Navy, the US Coastguard and the American Drug Enforcement Agency has been considerable. This can partly be explained by the fact that most Caribbean nations welcome the extra firepower that the outside intervention forces can provide. There is also a far smaller chance of drug cartels influencing foreign navies than some Caribbean law enforcement bodies. The naval presence will naturally continue in the West Indies, not just to stave off criminal activity but also to provide assistance to British dependent territories, often in the form of disaster relief, especially during the hurricane season.[5]

More reviews

These activities and more occurred during a decade of great political and economic turmoil. The war on terror began to unravel the Strategic Defence Review of 1998, which besides the usual rationalization and economies was also motivated by achieving a reinvigorated joint expeditionary edge for Britain's armed forces. Much of this was brought about by the long-term land commitments in the Middle East since 2001 and the subsequent return to Afghanistan in 2005, which although expeditionary in nature were not what were expected or anticipated in 1998. Certainly they cannot be held up as the joint (and hoped-for) naval-dominated operations espoused by the Strategic Defence Review and the Royal Navy at the end of the twentieth century; instead they have become increasingly land centric in orientation and perception, if not in reality. Worse still were the cuts imposed on the Navy in order to free up funds for the wars themselves, most notably in Afghanistan since 2001. These have seen surface ships, from hydrographic vessels such as HMS *Roebuck* to aircraft carriers such as HMS *Ark Royal*, being retired prematurely to pay for the deployments. Additionally, critical platforms such as the Sea Harrier in 2006 and the Harrier GR9/9A fleet in 2010 have retired, together with deep cuts in the numbers of escorts, mine-warfare vessels and fleet auxiliaries. Personnel levels have likewise continued to fall, declining to 30,000 by 2015. The final large-scale cuts to release money for the war in Afghanistan came with the Strategic Defence and Security Review of October 2010.[6]

The shift in strategic posture began earlier with reviews in 2002 and 2004 attempting to keep the 1998 Strategic Defence Review on track but seeing the course for the rest of the decade laid down; Iraq and Afghanistan were paramount. Any medium- or long-term plans and procurement would have to wait, especially for funding. Politically the Royal Navy has also had to face constant internal political challenges from a series of British prime ministers. Tony Blair, a supporter and employer of naval power, was replaced by Gordon Brown who understood the industrial arguments but not the strategic employment benefits of navies. Labour was then replaced by the Conservative-dominated coalition government, with the resulting defence review of David Cameron's administration appearing to sympathize with the arguments of the RAF rather than those of the Navy in 2010.[7]

Procurement has also provided challenges. The 1998 review had laid out long-term procurement up to 2015 with the year-long review being properly funded for future expenditure. Unfortunately two major wars and a number of procurement cost overruns began to derail the 1998 plans. British involvement in Afghanistan had cost over £17 billion alone by the start of 2012. Naval procurement programmes also caused concerns. The *Queen Elizabeth* carriers doubled from the initial £2.3 billion to over £5 billion. *Astute* class submarines suffered serious delays and increases in cost, with American technical help eventually required to bring the programme back on track. while the Type 45 destroyer programme, although not going above its intended budget, resulted in only six ships being built as opposed to the 12 initially envisaged. However, these seem insignificant when compared with other procurement projects such as the RAF's Eurofighter Typhoon, which became an ever widening abyss that had easily surpassed £20 billion in research, development and production costs by 2010 and is expected to cost over £37 billion for the lifetime of the programme and will only result in just over 100 aircraft entering British service. Delays and cost overruns also seriously affected the Nimrod update, with some £4 billion being expended for eventually nine aircraft (none of which entered service), and the Future Strategic Tanker programme which will see £13 billion being spent for just 14 aircraft.[8]

The 2010 general election provided a platform to carry out a more far-reaching defence assessment and this came in the form of the Strategic Defence and Security Review of October 2010. Unlike the 1998 review, which had taken a year to formulate, the new review only took some three months, which naturally brought some criticism. Most critics, however, waited for the findings. At the time, the review detailed cuts for all three services but provided the least comfort to the Royal Navy, for although the RAF lost aircraft and squadrons they were mostly maritime in flavour and not what was regarded as their core role of land-based attack operations. This supported contentions that the RAF and the outgoing Chief of the Defence Staff sacrificed the inherently flexible Harrier community to safeguard their Tornado force. Cuts to the Royal Navy included the early retirement of the last four Type 22 frigates (with the escort force dropping to 19 vessels), the carrier HMS *Ark Royal*, the whole of the recently updated Joint Harrier fleet, three fleet auxiliaries (with the sale of another) and the end of the Nimrod programme. Britain was going to take another assessed risk that it did not need fixed-wing capability at sea until the future carriers and their Joint Strike Fighters entered service from the middle of the decade. The gap left by Nimrod would be filled by utilizing existing air assets such as the already stretched Navy Merlins.[9]

Libya and the future

But as is often the case the findings of the 2010 review were not borne out by events, as the Arab Spring in North Africa showed. Less than six months later Britain found itself co-leading with France another coalition effort to initially protect Libyan refugees and then isolate and neutralize the Libyan government of Colonel Muammar Gaddafi. This soon became a NATO-orchestrated mission known as Operation *Unified Protector*. Whilst French, American Marine Corps and Italian firepower predominantly came from the flightdecks of carriers – the two latter nations employing Harriers – Britain was forced to employ costly, time-consuming and slow-responding land-based aircraft on missions to support the coalition's objectives. Over 3,000 sorties were flown by the RAF that resulted in 600 targets being attacked, whereas French naval aircraft from their carrier *Charles de Gaulle* flew over 1,500 sorties resulting in 785 ground-attack missions.

More successfully, and again demonstrating the flexibility of naval power, the Royal Navy carried out humanitarian and evacuation actions, mine clearance, embargo and blockade duties, key naval gunfire support work, further Tomahawk strikes, ground surveillance and target direction with ASaC 7 Sea Kings. The naval task force also employed five AAC Apaches from HMS *Ocean*, which in their 22 sorties managed to destroy 100 targets – one-sixth of the RAF's total for a fraction of the effort.[10]

The Royal Navy's acquisition programme after Libya has remained mostly on track with the aim of seeing the first future carrier, HMS *Queen Elizabeth*, operational by the end of the decade. There will also be a totally rejuvenated Fleet Air Arm compared with that of 2010, new escort vessels of the Type 26 class with new land-attack missiles, smaller modular warships that should replace existing mine warfare, offshore patrol and hydrographic vessels as well as new RFA vessels such as the four *Tide* class 37,000-ton support tankers ordered in 2012. The Type 45 destroyers should also be on course for Britain's first ballistic missile defence capability. And the submarine service will have received its seven *Astute* class submarines as well, finalizing the designs of the successor to the *Vanguard* class. Thus should the plans of the second decade of this century become reality; the Royal Navy of the third decade will be more powerful and capable of global deployments in a way not seen in anyone's lifetime to date, being at the forefront of both Britain's offensive and defensive weapons systems.[11]

The Royal Navy started the twenty-first century in a very different shape to that at the start of the twentieth century – far, far smaller in terms of manpower and ships, with just a handful of overseas bases and a political and public profile probably smaller than for centuries. Yet the naval service in the intervening 100 years had grown to unbelievable sizes, reaching almost a million personnel before returning to a strength more akin to the age of sail. It had successfully implemented a myriad of roles and commitments, fought the greatest wars in history and time and again helped to create the conditions for victory in all of them. It had successfully fought under, on and over the world's waters as well as on lands around the world, as well as being a key player in Britain's global commitments, especially the Western alliance. Levels of technology had surpassed comprehension and the ability to influence the world's land mass and the world's populations had achieved new heights. In the twenty-first century the Royal Navy has the ability to reach with conventional weapons the bulk of the world and with nuclear weapons the whole of it in a way that it could not have envisaged in the age of the dreadnought.

More importantly a number of key roles for Britain's security are performed purely by naval power – anti-piracy, countering maritime terrorism, fishery and economic resource protection and anti-drug interdiction being some, arguably below the threshold of war. In wartime, naval power has at times been either the dominant or the only military force able to be employed by Britain. This could well be a situation that continues into the future. In fact governments on both sides of the Atlantic have made clear in the second decade of this century that land-based wars will now be avoided. The flexibility that naval power brings will allow nations to have a global footprint without enduring physical land-based commitments. Neither should the economic drivers of the international system be overlooked. The process of globalization that began hundreds of years ago on the back of wooden sailing ships continues into the twenty-first century. Global trade is seaborne, British trade is seaborne, Britain's trade is global. Therefore there will always be a requirement to keep the global highway stable, and today Britain's only asset to accomplish this is, as it has been for centuries, the Royal Navy.

Notes

Introduction

1. P. Kennedy, *The Rise and Fall of British Naval Mastery* (London, 1991), p. 243; A.J. Marder, *The Anatomy of British Sea Power* (New York, 1972), p. 281; R.K. Massie, *Dreadnought* (London, 1993), p. vii; E. Weyl, 'The progress of foreign navies', in T.A. Brassey (ed.), *The Naval Annual 1898* (Portsmouth, 1898), p. 19.

2. T.A. Brassey, 'The progress of the British navy', in T.A. Brassey (ed.), *The Naval Annual 1898*, pp. 12, 16; W. Laird Clowes, 'The Great Naval Review', *Illustrated London News*, 3 July 1897, p. 10; Marder, *British Sea Power*, p. 281; Massie, *Dreadnought*, p. vii; *Saturday Review*, 19 June 1897, p. 379; *Saturday Review*, 3 July 1897, p. 5.

3. Brassey, 'The progress of the British navy', p. 12; Marder, *British Sea Power*, p. 281; Massie, *Dreadnought*, p. vii.

Chapter 1. The Last Years of Pax Britannica

1. *Standard*, 18 December 1899, p. 4.

2. A. Belby, *The Victorian Naval Brigades* (Dunbeath, 2006), pp. 127–62; A. Belby, 'Ex Africa semper aliquid novi: The Second Boer War 1899–1901', in P. Hore (ed.), *Seapower Ashore* (London, 2001), pp. 181–207; R. Brooks, *The Long Arm of Empire* (London, 1999), pp. 214–36. See also C. Burne, *With the Naval Brigade in Natal* (London, 1902); T. Jeans (ed.), *Naval Brigades in the South African War* (London, 1901).

3. *The Times*, 29 November 1899, p. 15.

4. R. Mackay, *Fisher of Kilverstone* (London, 1973), pp. 225–30, 233–6.

5. C.C.P. Fitzgerald, 'Training of seamen in the Royal Navy', *National Review*, vol. 35 (1900), pp. 625–34; J. Corbett, 'Education in the Navy (I)', *The Monthly Review* (March 1900), pp. 34–49; J. Corbett, 'Education in the Navy (II)', *The Monthly Review* (April 1900), pp. 43–57; J. Corbett, 'Education in the Navy (III)', *The Monthly Review* (September 1900), pp. 42–54; see also J. Corbett, 'Lord Selborne's Memorandum',

The Monthly Review (February 1903), pp. 28–41; J. Corbett, 'Lord Selborne's Memorandum (III)', *The Monthly Review* (March 1903), pp. 40–53; J. Corbett, 'Lord Selborne's Critics', *The Monthly Review* (July 1903), pp. 64–75.

6. R.L. Davidson, *The Challenges of Command* (Farnham, 2011), pp. 103–4; H.W. Dickenson, *Educating the Royal Navy* (Abingdon, 2007), pp. 171–6, 195–8; Marder, *The Anatomy of British Sea Power*, pp. 420–1; Mackay, *Fisher*, pp. 274–83.

7. Davidson, *The Challenges of Command*, pp. 12–13, 63–4, 103–4; G. Penn, *Snotty: The Story of the Midshipman* (London, 1957), pp. 121–9; G. Penn, *HMS Thunderer* (Emsworth, 1984), pp. 61–3.

8. A. Carew, *The Lower Deck of the Royal Navy 1900–1939* (Manchester, 1981), pp. 47–53; E. Grove, *The Royal Navy Since 1815* (Basingstoke, 2005), p. 105; A.J. Marder, *From the Dreadnought to Scapa Flow*, vol. 1 (London, 1961), pp. 267–8.

9. D. Redford, *The Submarine: A Cultural History from the Great War to Nuclear Combat* (London, 2010), pp. 77–88; D. Redford, 'Naval Culture and the Fleet Submarine', in D. Leggett and R. Dunn (eds), *Re-inventing the Ship: Science, Technology and the Maritime World 1800–1918* (Farnham, 2012), pp. 157–72.

10. A. Blond, *Technology and Tradition: Wireless Telegraphy and the Royal Navy 1895–1920* (unpublished PhD thesis, University of Lancaster, 1993), p. 68.

11. Blond, *Technology and Tradition*, p. 66; N. Lambert, 'Transformation and Technology in the Fisher Era: The Impact of the Communications Revolution', *Journal of Strategic Studies*, vol. 27 (2004), p. 282; N. Lambert, 'Strategic Command and Control for Manoeuvre Warfare: Creation of the Royal Navy's "War Room" System, 1905–1915', *Journal of Military History*, vol. 69 (2005), pp. 373–4, 378–9.

12. E. Grove, 'Seamen or Airmen? The Early Days of British Naval Flying', in T. Benbow (ed.), *British Naval Aviation: The First 100 Years* (Farnham, 2012), pp. 7–26.

13. The highly involved subject of long-range gunnery is brilliantly explored in J. Brooks, *Dreadnought Gunnery and the Battle of Jutland* (London, 2005). In contrast to the argument put forward by Brooks, there is the previously unchallenged argument regarding the superiority of the Pollen system put forward by J. Sumida, *In Defence of Naval Supremacy* (Boston, MA, 1989).

14. J. Rüger, 'The symbolic value of the *Dreadnought*', in R. Blyth, A. Lambert and J. Rüger (eds), *The Dreadnought and the Edwardian Age* (Farnham, 2011), pp. 9–18.

15. A. Lambert, 'The power of a name: tradition, technology and transfor-

mation', in R. Blyth, A. Lambert and J. Rüger (eds), *The Dreadnought and the Edwardian Age*, pp. 19–22, 26–8. For an examination as to how this was paid for see M. Daunton, '"The Greatest and Richest Sacrifice Ever Made on the Altar of Militarism": The Finance of Naval Expansion, c. 1890–1914', in R. Blyth, A. Lambert and J. Rüger (eds), *The Dreadnought and the Edwardian Age*, pp. 31–50.

16. D. Boyce, *The Crisis of British Power: The Imperial and Naval Papers of the Second Earl of Selborne, 1895–1910* (London, 1990), pp. 136, 144, 144–6, 154–5; F. Coetzee, *For Party or Country: Nationalism and the Dilemmas of Popular Conservatism in Edwardian England* (Oxford, 1990), pp. 42–3; H. Herwig, *'Luxury' Fleet. The Imperial German Navy 1888–1918* (Amherst, NY, 1987), pp. 34–9, 42–3; Marder, *The Anatomy of British Seapower*, pp. 456–67; Massie, *Dreadnought*, pp. 184–5; Mackay, *Fisher*, pp. 236–7; cf. N. Lambert, *Sir John Fisher's Naval Revolution* (Columbia, SC, 1999), pp. 177–82.

17. H. Ion, 'Towards a naval alliance' in P.P. O'Brien (ed.), *The Anglo-Japanese Alliance, 1902–1922* (London, 2004), pp. 39, 41; K. Neilson, 'The Anglo-Japanese alliance and British strategic foreign policy alliance', in P.P. O'Brien (ed.), *The Anglo-Japanese Alliance, 1902–1922*, pp. 50–4; I. Nish, *The Anglo Japanese Alliance* (London, 1966), pp. 174–7, 213–18.

18. A. Morris, *The Scaremongers: The Advocacy of War and Rearmament 1896–1914* (London, 1984), pp. 101–2.

19. Morris, *The Scaremongers*, pp. 135–47; Lambert, *Sir John Fisher's Naval Revolution*, pp. 56–7.

20. C. Bridge, *Sea Power and Other Studies* (London, 1910), p. 84.

21. M. Seligmann, 'A prelude to the reforms of Admiral Sir John Fisher: the creation of the Home Fleet, 1902–3', *Historical Research*, vol. 83 (2010), pp. 506–19.

22. Lambert, *Sir John Fisher's Naval Revolution*, pp. 99, 101–15; Redford, *The Submarine*, pp. 94–103.

23. Cited in P. Kennedy, 'The Relevance of the Prewar British and American Strategies of the First World War and its Aftermath', in J.B. Hattendorf and R.S. Jordan (eds), *Maritime Strategy and the Balance of Power* (Basingstoke, 1989), p. 168; see also G. Till, 'Corbett and the emergence of a British school?', in G. Till (ed.), *The Development of British Naval Thinking* (London, 2006), pp. 73–82.

24. M. Seligmann, *The Royal Navy and the German Naval Threat 1901–1914* (Oxford, 2012), pp. 46–64.

25. J. Brooks, '*Dreadnought*: Blunder, or Stroke of Genius?', *Journal of Strategic Studies*, vol. 14 (2007), p. 163; Lambert, *Sir John Fisher's Naval Revolution*, pp. 92–4; Seligmann, *The Royal Navy and the German Threat*, pp. 65–70; Sumida, *In Defence of Naval Supremacy*, pp. 51–61; J. Sumida, 'Sir

John Fisher and the *Dreadnought*: The sources of naval mythology', *Journal of Military History*, vol. 59 (1995), pp. 625.

26.   O.D. Skelton, *Life and Letters of Sir Wilfred Laurier* (Toronto, 1921; abridged ed., 1965), II, p. 114; quoted in A Offer, *First World War: An Agrarian Interpretation* (Oxford, 1991), pp. 205–6.

27.   N. Lambert, 'Economy or Empire? The fleet unit concept and the quest for collective security in the Pacific, 1909–14', in N. Neilson and G. Kennedy (eds), *Far Flung Lines: Studies in Imperial Defence in Honour of Donald Mackenzie Schurman* (London, 1997), pp. 55–76.

28.   J. Corbett, *Principles of Maritime Strategy* (New York, 2004), p. 90.

Chapter 2. Waiting for the Next Trafalgar

1.   TNA, ADM 116/1372, Letter from *Tatler*, 16 July 1914; NMRN, *List of Ships in Commission*, 1909 to 1914; J. Corbett, *Naval Operations*, vol. I (London, 1920), pp. 11–18; Marder, *From the Dreadnought to Scapa Flow*, vol. 1, pp. 287–8. The Home Fleets had been created by the First Lord of the Admiralty, Winston Churchill, and the then First Sea Lord, Admiral Sir Francis Bridgeman, in mid-1912 and comprised the old Home Fleet, strengthened by the ships of the former Atlantic Fleet.

2.   N. Lambert, *Planning Armageddon: British Economic Warfare and the First World War* (Cambridge, MA, 2012), pp. 211–12.

3.   A. Temple Patterson (ed.), *The Jellicoe Papers*, vol. 1 (London, 1966), pp. 43–4. See also the letter from Jellicoe to Hamilton, dated 7 August 1914, in Temple Patterson, *The Jellicoe Papers*, vol. 1, p. 48.

4.   NMRN, CB 1585, Naval Staff Monographs (Historical), monograph 6, p. 2; Temple Patterson, *The Jellicoe Papers*, vol. 1, pp. 43–5.

5.   NMRN, CB 1585, Naval Staff Monographs (Historical), monograph 6, pp. 4–20.

6.   This point is made most forcefully in Lambert, *Planning Armageddon*, chapter 5, especially pp. 199–210. See also D. Stevenson, 'War by Timetable? The Railway Race before 1914', *Past & Present*, no. 162 (February 1999), p. 192.

7.   Lambert, *Planning Armageddon*, pp. 270–8; E. Osborne, *Britain's Economic Blockade of Germany 1914–1919* (London, 2004), pp. 58–82; see also G. Kennedy, 'Intelligence and the Blockade, 1914–1917: A Study in Administration, Friction and Command', *Intelligence and National Security*, vol. 22 (2007), pp. 699–721; G. Kennedy, 'Strategy and Power: The Royal Navy and the Foreign Office and the Blockade, 1914–1917', *Defence Studies*, vol. 8 (2008), pp. 190–206; G. Kennedy, 'The North Atlantic Triangle and the blockade, 1914–1915', *Journal of Transatlantic Studies*, vol. 6 (2008), pp. 22–33.

8. Osborne, *Britain's Economic Blockade of Germany*, pp. 84, 99, 100, 104.

9. NMRN, CB 1585, Naval Staff Monographs (Historical), monograph 11, pp. 108–48; Grove, *The Royal Navy Since 1815*, p. 109; B. Ranft (ed.), *The Beatty Papers*, vol. 1 (Aldershot, 1989), pp. 108–11; S.W. Roskill, *Admiral of the Fleet Earl Beatty. The Last Naval Hero: An Intimate Biography* (London, 1980), pp. 82–5.

10. NMRN, CB 1585, Naval Staff Monographs (Historical), monograph 8, pp. 170–4; P. Beesly, *Room 40: British Naval Intelligence 1914–1918* (London, 1982), p. 49.

11. NMRN, CB 1585, Naval Staff Monographs (Historical), monograph 8, pp. 182–3; Beesly, *Room 40*, p. 49.

12. NMRN, CB 1585, Naval Staff Monographs (Historical), monograph 8, pp. 179–88; J. Corbett, *Naval Operations*, vol. II (London, 1929), pp. 22–43; R. Hough, *The Great War at Sea 1914–1918* (Edinburgh, 2000), pp. 125–7; Marder, *From the Dreadnought to Scapa Flow*, vol. 2, pp. 134–42; Roskill, *Beatty*, pp. 102–5.

13. NMM Beatty Papers, BTY 4/6/7, HMS *Lion*'s report of proceedings, 27 January 1915; NMRN, CB 1585, Naval Staff Monographs (Historical), monograph 12, pp. 210–17; Corbett, *Naval Operations*, vol. II, pp. 84–99; Hough, *The Great War at Sea*, pp. 130–43; Marder, *From the Dreadnought to Scapa Flow*, vol. 2, pp. 156–68; Ranft (ed.), *Beatty Papers*, vol. 1, pp.201–5; Roskill, *Beatty*, pp. 108–15.

14. Marder, *From the Dreadnought to Scapa Flow*, vol. 2, pp. 79–81, 369.

15. *Ibid.*, pp. 73–4.

16. TNA, ADM 116/1436, Engineer Rear Admiral's 112/14 to CinC Nore, 28 September 1914; TNA, ADM 116/1436, NS20026/14, 24 November 1914; TNA, ADM 116/1436, Commodore (T)'s 706/855, 6 December 1914; TNA, ADM 116/1436, N22687/14, 19 December 1914; TNA, ADM 116/1436, NS826/1915, 28 December 1914.

17. W. Hackmann, *Seek and Strike* (London, 1984), pp. 11–17, 21–4, 45–52.

18. Corbett, *Naval Operations*, vol. I, p. 205; I. Gardiner, *The Flatpack Bombers: The Royal Navy and the Zeppelin Menace* (Barnsley, 2009), pp. 37, 38–40, 42–5, 47–50; E. Grove, 'Air Force, Fleet Air Arm – or Armoured Corps', in T. Benbow (ed.), *British Naval Aviation: The First 100 Years* (Farnham, 2011), pp. 29–30.

19. Grove, 'Air Force, Fleet Air Arm', pp. 30–1.

20. J. Nathan, *Soldiers, Statecraft, and History: Coercive Diplomacy and International Order* (Westport, CT, 2002), p. 66.

21. Hough, *The Great War at Sea*, pp. 99–102; Marder, *From the Dreadnought to Scapa Flow*, vol. 2, pp. 85–7.

22. T. Curran, 'Who was Responsible for the Dardanelles Naval Fiasco?', *Australian Journal of Politics and History*, vol. 57 (2011), pp. 17–33.

23. Marder, *From the Dreadnought to Scapa Flow*, vol. 2, pp. 275–86.

24. NMRN, OU 6337(40), Review of German Cruiser Warfare 1914–1918, pp. 1–13.

25. Marder, *From the Dreadnought to Scapa Flow*, vol. 2, p. 103.

26. Corbett, *Naval Operations*, vol. I, pp. 355–71; Marder, *From the Dreadnought to Scapa Flow*, vol. 2, pp. 112–18.

27. Corbett, *Naval Operations*, vol. I, pp. 431–54; Marder, *From the Dreadnought to Scapa Flow*, vol. 2, pp. 121–4.

28. NMRN, OU 6337(40), Review of German Cruiser Warfare 1914–1918, pp. 1–3.

29. NHB, *Statistical Review of the War Against Merchant Shipping* (Admiralty, 1918), p. 22.

30. Figures from NHB, *Statistical Review of the War Against Merchant Shipping* (Admiralty, 1918), pp. 16, 22.

31. D. Redford, *The Submarine*, pp. 103–11.

Chapter 3. A Second Trafalgar?

1. This account of the battle is based on the information in the excellent examination of the battle by A. Gordon, *The Rules of the Game: Jutland and British Naval Command* (London, 2000). For an analysis of the problems of long-range gunnery see the superb Brooks, *Dreadnought Gunnery and the Battle of Jutland*.

2. Figures from J. Campbell, *Jutland: An Analysis of the Fighting* (London, 1986), pp. 338–41.

3. Marder, *From the Dreadnought to Scapa Flow*, vol. 5, pp. 130–1.

4. Carew, *The Lower Deck of the Royal Navy 1900–39*, pp. 72–82, 88–99.

5. U. Mason, *The Wrens 1917–77* (Reading, 1977), pp. 13–34; U. Mason, *Britannia's Daughters: The Story of the WRNS* (London, 1992), pp. 1–31.

6. H. Newbolt, *Naval Operations*, vol. IV (London, 1928), pp. 91–8. For the submarine campaign in the Baltic see M. Wilson, *Baltic Assignment: British Submariners in Russia: 1914–1919* (London, 1985).

7. TNA, ADM 186/603, CB 1554, The Economic Blockade, p. 21.

8. BL Add Mss 48992, Jellicoe to Balfour, 29 October 1916, pp. 61–74; Temple Patterson (ed.), *The Jellicoe Papers*, vol. 2, pp. 89, 92; Grove, *The Royal Navy Since 1815*, pp. 128–9.

9. Figures from NHB, *Statistical Review of the War Against Merchant Shipping*, p. 22.

10. R. Bacon, *The Dover Patrol*, vol. II (London, n.d.), pp. 351–6; G. Bond, *The Evans of the Broke Story* (London, 1961), pp. 8–17; Marder, *From the Dreadnought to Scapa Flow*, vol. 4, pp. 107–8; Newbolt, *Naval Operations*, vol. IV, pp. 376–8; G. Till, 'Passchendaele: The Maritime Dimension',

in P. Liddle (ed.), *Passchendaele in Perspective: The Third Battle of Ypres* (London, 1997), p. 85.

11. Marder, *From the Dreadnought to Scapa Flow*, vol. 4, pp. 323–49; S.W. Roskill, 'The Dismissal of Admiral Jellicoe', *Journal of Contemporary History*, vol. 1 (1966), pp. 69–93.

12. A. Wiest, 'The Planned Amphibious Assault', in Liddle (ed.), *Passchendaele in Perspective*, pp. 210–11.

13. J. Edmonds, *Military Operations 1916*, vol. 2 (London, 1938), pp. 485–91; D. Jerrold, *The Royal Naval Division* (London, 1923), pp. 188–207; C. Page, 'The Royal Naval Division, 1914–19', in P. Hoare (ed.), *Seapower Ashore* (London, 2001), pp. 221–3.

14. TNA, ADM 116/1339, Tanks (Landships) Inception and Evolution; TNA, CAB 42/4/1, CID 225B, Admiralty Landships, 4 October 1915; Grove, 'Air Force, Fleet Air Arm – or Armoured Corps?, p. 36; P. Wright, *Tank* (London, 2000), pp. 26–30,

15. Jerrold, *The Royal Naval Division*, pp. 227–41; C. Page, *Command in the Royal Naval Division* (Staplehurst, 1999), pp. 115–24; Page, 'The Royal Naval Division, 1914–19', pp. 224–8.

16. Figures from War Office, *Statistics of the Military Efforts of the British Empire During the Great War* (London, 1922), pp. 258–71.

17. *Ibid.*, p. 271; Page, 'The Royal Naval Division, 1914–19', pp. 233–6.

18. C. Goulter, 'The Royal Naval Air Service: A Very Modern Air Service', in S. Cox and P. Gray (eds), *Air Power History: Turning Points from Kitty Hawk to Kosovo* (London, 2002), p. 52.

19. Figures from War Office, *Statistics of the Military Efforts of the British Empire During the Great War*, pp. 60–1.

20. CB 3304(1A), *The Defeat of the Enemy Attack on Shipping 1939–1945*, pp. 6–10; Goulter, 'The Royal Naval Air Service', pp. 54–5; W. Hackmann, *Seek and Strike* (London, 1984), p. 70; A. Price, *Aircraft versus Submarine* (London, 1973), pp. 20–1; J. Terraine, *Business in Great Waters. The U-boat Wars, 1916–1945* (London, 1989), pp. 74–8.

21. Goulter, 'The Royal Naval Air Service', pp. 58–61; Grove, 'Air Force, Fleet Air Arm – or Armoured Corps', pp. 40–1, 43.

22. Grove, 'Air Force, Fleet Air Arm – or Armoured Corps', pp. 46–7, 51.

23. *Ibid.*, pp. 50–2.

24. *Ibid.*, pp. 50–1; Marder, *From the Dreadnought to Scapa Flow*, vol. 5, p. 141–2.

Chapter 4. Disarmament and Rearmament: The Interwar Period

1. NMRN, RNM 2001/48/5, Letter from Roger Talbot to his mother, 22 November 1918; Roskill, *Earl Beatty, the Last Naval Hero*, p. 279; 'The Graphic' Souvenir of the Germany Navy's Surrender (London, 1918), p. 4.
2. S.W. Roskill, *Naval Policy Between the Wars*, vol. 1 (London, 1968), p. 72.
3. *Ibid.*, pp. 124–5; Carew, *The Lower Deck of the Royal Navy*, pp. 143–9.
4. Figures from B. Mitchell, *British Historical Statistics* (Cambridge, 2011), pp. 591, 594. Figures for 1938 and 1939 do not show the value of Defence Loans.
5. C. Bell, *The Royal Navy, Seapower and Strategy Between the Wars* (London, 2000), p. 22; O. Babji, 'The Royal Navy and the Defence of the British Empire', in K. Neilson and G. Kennedy (eds), *Far Flung Lines* (London, 1997), pp. 173–6; Bell, *The Royal Navy, Seapower and Strategy*, pp. 22, 24.
6. A. Agar, *Baltic Episode* (London, 1963), pp. 80–97; G. Bennett, *Cowan's War* (London, 1964), pp. 33–6, 124–7; Roskill, *Naval Policy*, vol. 1, pp. 144–50.
7. TNA, CAB 23/15, War Cabinet Minute 616A, 15 August 1919.
8. Roskill, *Naval Policy*, vol. 1, p. 71.
9. *Morning Post*, 12 November 1921, p. 4.
10. D. Redford, 'Collective Security and Internal Dissent: The Navy League's Attempts to Develop a New Policy towards British Naval Power between 1919 and the 1922 Washington Naval Treaty', *History*, vol. 96 (2011), pp. 48–67; *Scotsman*, 18 March 1921, p. 4; *Daily Telegraph*, 16 December 1921, p. 10.
11. Bell, *The Royal Navy, Seapower and Strategy*, p. 25; J. Maiolo, *Cry Havoc: The Arms Race and the Second World War 1931–1941* (London, 2010), p. 106.
12. Roskill, *Naval Policy*, vol. 1, p. 533.
13. G. Till, 'Airpower and the battleship', in B. Ranft (ed.), *Technical Change and British Naval Policy 1860–1939* (London, 1977), pp. 110–13; J. Moretz, *The Royal Navy and the Capital Ship in the Interwar Period* (London, 2002), pp. 41–6; Roskill, *Naval Policy*, vol. 1, pp. 221, 223–5.
14. P. Ackermann, *Encyclopaedia of British Submarines 1901–1955* (Penzance, 2002), pp. 199–205, 305–8; Redford, *The Submarine*, pp. 77–88, 117–18; Redford, 'Naval Culture and the Fleet Submarine, 1910–1917', pp. 168–72.
15. TNA, ADM 1/8703/158, No. 955/S.100, Letter from RA (S) to Admiralty, 3 December 1926; Minute by Director of the Tactical Division, Naval Staff, 8 April 1925; TNA, ADM 1/8703/158, No. 955/S.100, Letter from RA (S) to Admiralty, 3 December 1926. See also Redford, *The Submarine*, pp. 118–21.

16. TNA, ADM 1/8694/2, Admiralty Board Minute 2142, 21 December 1925; TNA, ADM 167/72, Memoranda 2138, 3 December 1925; Ackermann, *Encyclopaedia of British Submarines*, pp. 362–3.

17. J. Maiolo, 'Deception and Intelligence Failure: Anglo-German Preparations for U-boat Warfare in the 1930s', *Journal of Strategic Studies*, vol. 22 (1999), pp. 56, 57–62.

18. TNA, ADM 1/8586, Final report of the Post-War Questions Committee, 27 March 1920; see also Roskill, *Naval Policy*, vol. 1, pp. 113–17; *The Times*, 5 June 1914; see also Lambert, *Sir John Fisher's Naval Revolution*, chapter 9 especially pp. 302–3; *The Times*, 6 November 1920, p. 9; *The Times*, 6 December 1920, p. 13; *The Times*, 7 December 1920, p. 13; *The Times*, 8 December 1920, p. 13; *The Times*, 9 December 1920, p. 13; *The Times*, 10 December 1920, p. 11; *The Times*, 11 December 1920, p. 11; *The Times*, 13 December 1920, p. 13; *The Times*, 14 December 1920, p. 13; *The Times*, 15 December 1920, p. 13; *The Times*, 16 December 1920, p. 13; *The Times*, 20 December 1920, p. 11; *The Times*, 21 December 1920, p. 11; *The Times*, 22 December 1920, p. 11; *The Times*, 23 December 1920, p. 11; *The Times*, 24 December 1920, p. 11; A. Hurd, '"Great Ships Or – ?" A Footnote to the *Times* Correspondence', *Fortnightly Review*, vol. 109 (1921), pp. 240–54; Anon, 'Great Ships or – ?', *The Times*, 4 February 1921, p. 11. Interestingly Roskill in his survey of the interwar period, *Naval Policy Between the Wars*, makes no mention of the public debate in the winter of 1920–21 regarding the obsolescence or not of the battleship.

19. Grove, *The Royal Navy Since 1815*, pp. 155–7; Roskill, *Naval Policy*, vol. 1, pp. 234–68, 356–99; G. Till, *Air Power and the Royal Navy* (London, 1979), pp. 32–9.

20. Grove, *The Royal Navy Since 1815*, pp. 173–4; D. Hobbs, 'Naval Aviation 1930–2000', in R. Harding (ed.), *The Royal Navy, 1930–2000: Innovation and Defence* (London, 2005), pp. 76; Roskill, *Naval Policy*, vol. 1, pp. 393–8; Till, *Air Power and the Royal Navy*, p. 100.

21. N. Friedman, *British Carrier Aviation: The Evolution of the Ships and Their Aircraft* (London, 1988), p. 169; Hobbs, 'Naval Aviation 1930–2000', pp. 75–6; Till, *Air Power and the Royal Navy*, pp. 65–7, 100–3.

22. Grove, *The Royal Navy Since 1815*, pp. 174–6; Roskill, *Naval Policy*, vol. 2 (London, 1976), pp. 392–413; G. Till, 'Competing Vision: The Admiralty, the Air Ministry and the Role of Air Power', in T. Benbow (ed.), *British Naval Aviation: The First 100 Years* (Farnham, 2011), pp. 66–7; Till, *Air Power and the Royal Navy*, pp. 51–7.

23. Babji, 'The Royal Navy and the Defence of the British Empire', pp. 180–1; Bell, *The Royal Navy, Seapower and Strategy*, p. 99; N. Gibbs, *Grand Strategy: Rearmament Policy*, vol. 1 (London, 1976), pp. 80–1; G.A.H.

Gordon, *British Seapower and Procurement between the Wars* (Annapolis, 1988), p. 107; Kennedy, *The Rise and Fall of British Naval Mastery*, p. 337; J. Maiolo, *The Royal Navy and Nazi Germany* (Basingstoke, 1998), p. 13.

24.   Babji, 'The Royal Navy and the Defence of the British Empire', pp. 184–5; Bell, *The Royal Navy, Seapower and Strategy*, pp. 99–103; Gordon, *British Seapower and Procurement between the Wars*, p. 124–6; Mitchell, *British Historical Statistics*, p. 591; G. Peden, *Arms, Economics and British Strategy: From Dreadnoughts to Hydrogen Bombs* (Cambridge, 2007), pp. 102–3, 108–17; P. Williamson, *Stanley Baldwin* (Cambridge, 1999), pp. 47, 305–6.

25.   Bell, *The Royal Navy, Seapower and Strategy*, pp. 103–6; Maiolo, *The Royal Navy and Nazi Germany*, pp. 67–70; Redford, *The Submarine*, pp. 131–5; see also W. Rahn, 'German Naval Strategy and Armament 1919–1939', in P. O'Brien (ed.), *Technology and Naval Combat in the Twentieth Century and Beyond* (London, 2001), pp. 119, 121–3.

26.   Bell, *The Royal Navy, Seapower and Strategy*, pp. 117, 120; Gordon, *British Seapower and Procurement between the Wars*, p. 156–7; Grove, *The Royal Navy Since 1815*, pp. 170–1; Maiolo, *The Royal Navy and Nazi Germany*, pp. 142–7; Roskill, *Naval Policy*, vol. 2, p. 358.

27.   TNA, ADM 1/9081, Board Memo on a new standard of naval strength, 26 April 1937; TNA, CAB 16/112, DRC 37. Spending on the Royal Navy in 1935 was £56.6 million (Mitchell, *British Historical Statistics*, p. 591); Roskill, *Naval Policy*, vol. 2, pp. 358–9.

Chapter 5. World War II: Home Waters and the Arctic 1939–45

1.   NHB, CB3301(1), Naval Staff History, *Home Waters and the Atlantic*, vol. 1 (1954) p. 42; TNA, ADM 1/19900, Sinking of the *Rawalpindi*.

2.   C. Barnet, *Engage the Enemy More Closely* (London, 1991), pp. 140–1; S. W. Roskill, *The War at Sea*, vol. 1 (London, 1954), pp. 207–11.

3.   Roskill, *The War at Sea*, vol. 1, pp. 224–7; see also A. Calder, *The Myth of the Blitz* (London, 1992), pp. 26–8; M. Smith, *Britain and 1940: History, Myth and Popular Memory* (London, 2000), pp. 44–5; BBC news, 'Ceremony marks 70th anniversary of Dunkirk evacuation', http://news.bbc.co.uk/1/hi/uk/10188650.stm (accessed 8 July 2010).

4.   NMRN, BR 1736 (48)(2), Naval Staff History, *Home Waters and the Atlantic*, vol. 2 (1961), p. 127.

5.   H.R. Allen, *Who Won the Battle of Britain?* (St Albans, 1974), pp. 173–5; A. Cumming, *The Royal Navy and the Battle of Britain* (Annapolis, 2010), p. 75; A. Cumming, 'The warship as the ultimate guarantor of Britain's freedom in 1940', *Historical Research*, vol. 83 (2010), pp. 166–7, J. Ray, *The Battle of Britain: New Perspectives* (London 1996), pp. 80–2.

Even the official history was unable to disguise the decline of the air defence system in late August and early September; see B. Collier *The Defence of the United Kingdom* (London, 1995), pp. 203–17. For the definition of air superiority see http://www.raf.mod.uk/rafcms/mediafiles/374F7380_1143_EC82_2E436D317C547F5B.pdf (accessed 21 February 2013).

6.   K. Larew, 'The Royal Navy in the Battle of Britain', *The Historian*, vol. 54 (1992), pp. 243–5; J. Levy, *The Royal Navy's Home Fleet in World War II* (Basingstoke, 2003), chapters 4 and 5.

7.   Cumming, 'The warship as the ultimate guarantor of Britain's freedom in 1940', pp. 185–6; Cumming, *The Royal Navy and the Battle of Britain*, pp. 118, 119; Levy, *The Royal Navy's Home Fleet*, chapter 5; J.R.M. Butler, *Grand Strategy*, vol. II (London, 1957), p. 308.

8.   Levy, *The Royal Navy's Home Fleet*, pp. 78–81.

9.   NMRN, BR 1736(3/50), The Chase and Sinking of the *Bismarck*, pp. 3–7.

10. NMRN, BR 1736(3/50), pp. 7–9; Levy, *The Royal Navy's Home Fleet*, pp. 90–3.

11. NMRN, BR 1736(3/50), pp. 9–20; Levy, *The Royal Navy's Home Fleet*, pp. 96–8.

12. NMRN, BR 1736(3/50), pp. 20–4.

13. NMRN, BR 1736(3/50), pp. 32–5; Barnett, *Engage the Enemy More Closely*, p. 312–14.

14. NHB, BR 1736(7)(48), The Passage of the *Scharnhorst*, *Gneisenau* and *Prinz Eugen* through the England Channel, 12 February 1942, pp. 1–5; D. Redford, 'Inter and Intra-Service Rivalries and the Battle of the Atlantic', *Journal of Strategic Studies*, vol. 32 (2009), pp. 913–16, 923–4. In August 1941 the Butt Report, which analysed over 600 photographs taken at the moment bombers released their bombs, concluded that only one in five Bomber Command aircraft were dropping their bombs within five miles of a target in Germany, falling to one in ten if the target was in the Ruhr. The Air Staff and Bomber Command refused to accept the findings of this independent report. Post-war analysis suggests that not less than 49 per cent of British bombs dropped on south-west Germany between May 1940 and May 1941 fell on open countryside: see R. Davis, *Bombing the European Axis Powers* (Maxwell, Al, 2006) pp. 29–30; D. Richards, *The Royal Air Force 1939–1945*, vol. 1 (London, 1953), p. 239; C. Webster and N. Frankland, *The Strategic Air Offensive Against Germany 1939–1945*, vol. 1 (London, 1961), pp. 178–80.

15. NHB, BR1736(34)(48), The Attack on St Nazaire.

16. B. Ruegg and A. Hague, *Convoys to Russia* (Kendal, 1993), pp. 20–5, 84; A. Hague, *The Allied Convoy System 1939–1945* (St Catherines, Ontario,

2000), pp. 187–91; R. Woodman, *Arctic Convoys* (London, 1995), pp. 33–51.

17. Woodman, *Arctic Convoys*, pp. 213–57.
18. D. Pope, *73 North: The Battle of the Barents Sea 1942* (London, 1988).
19. J.D. Brown (ed. D. Hobbs), *Carrier Operations in World War II* (Barnsley, 2009), pp. 23–8.
20. Barnett, *Engage the Enemy More Closely*, p. 739–44.
21. *Ibid.*, p. 748; Hague, *The Allied Convoy System*, pp. 188–91; Woodman, *Arctic Convoys*, pp. 441–5.
22. Roskill, *The War at Sea*, vol. 2, pp. 240–4; NHB, BR1736(26), Raid on Dieppe (Naval Operations), pp. 1–8.
23. NHB, BR1736(26), Raid on Dieppe (Naval Operations), pp. 15–16, 19, 20–30, 33–9, 50.
24. NMRN, BR1736(42)(1), Operation *Neptune*: Landings in Normandy, June 1944, pp. 14–17; J. Ehrman, *Grand Strategy*, vol. V (London,1956), pp. 279–86, 332–5; M. Howard, *Grand Strategy*, vol. IV (London, 1972) pp. 191–275.
25. See NMRN, BR1736(42)(1), Operation *Neptune*.
26. NMRN, BR1736(42)(1), Battle Summary no. 39, Operation *Neptune*, pp. 90–107; Ehrman, *Grand Strategy*, vol. V, pp. 337–43; Roskill, *The War at Sea*, vol. 3, part 2 (London, 1994), pp. 36–53.
27. Barnett, *Engage the Enemy More Closely*, pp. 829, 835.
28. *Ibid.*, pp. 845–9; R. Neillands, *The Battle for the Rhine 1944. Arnhem and the Ardennes: The Campaign in Europe* (London, 2005), pp. 77–85, 155–7; Roskill, *The War at Sea*, vol. 3, part 2, pp. 145–6.
29. NMRN, BR1736(37), The Campaign in North-West Europe, June 1944–May 1945, pp. 47–54; Barnett, *Engage the Enemy More Closely,* pp. 850–1; Neillands, *The Battle for the Rhine 1944*, pp. 167–73; Roskill, *The War at Sea*, vol. 3, part 2, pp. 147–54.
30. NMRN, BR1736(37), The Campaign in North-West Europe, June 1944–May 1945, pp. 68–9.

Chapter 6. World War II: The Battle of the Atlantic

1. TNA, ADM 156/95, Loss of HMS *Courageous*, Board of Enquiry, 4 October 1939, p. 4, recommendation 26.
2. Figures from G. Hessler, *The U-Boat War in the Atlantic 1939–1945* (London, 1989), p. 48; CB 33049 (1A), *Defeat of the Enemy Attack on Shipping*, Appendix II; U-boat histories downloaded from http://www.uboat.net:8080/boats/listing.html (accessed November 2012).
3. Roskill, *The War at Sea*, vol. 1, p. 615.
4. Hessler, *The U-Boat War*, p. 48; Terraine, *Business in Great Waters*, p. 256.

5. Barnett, *Engage the Enemy More Closely*, p. 183.

6. K. Smith, *Conflict over Convoys: Anglo-American Logistics Diplomacy in the Second World War* (Cambridge, 2002), pp. 249–50.

7. Terraine, *Business in Great Waters*, p. 314; Barnett, *Engage the Enemy More Closely*, pp. 262, 262.

8. TNA, ADM 1/11065, Reports of Proceedings HMS *Vanoc* and HMS *Walker* for HX122 and the Sinking of *U-100*; Terraine, *Business in Great Waters*, pp. 315–16.

9. D. Howse, *Radar at Sea: The Royal Navy in World War 2* (London, 1993), pp. 57–8, 79, 84–8, 100; see also Terraine, *Business in Great Waters*, pp. 315–16, which states that *Vanoc* had a Type 271.

10. Barnett, *Engage the Enemy More Closely*, pp. 275–6; Friedman, *British Carrier Aviation*, pp. 177–9; Redford, 'Inter and Intra-Service Rivalries in the Battle of the Atlantic', pp. 907–8.

11. W. Gardner, *Decoding History* (London, 1999), pp. 120–45.

12. P. Beesly, *Very Special Intelligence* (London, 2000), pp. 70–2, 94–6; F. Hinsley, *British Intelligence in the Second World War*, vol. II (London, 1981), pp. 170–9; J. Winton, *Ultra at Sea* (London, 1988), pp. 94–6; see also Terraine, *Business in Great Waters*, pp. 325–6, which implies that 'Hydra' and *Heimisch* are different codes when they are the same thing. Hydra was the name given to the code after 1943.

13. Hinsley, *British Intelligence*, vol. II, p. 179; Terraine, *Business in Great Waters*, pp. 424–5.

14. CB 33049 (1A), *Defeat of the Enemy Attack on Shipping*, p. 302.

15. Hinsley, *British Intelligence*, vol. II, pp. 177–9.

16. Barnett, *Engage the Enemy More Closely*, pp. 458–76; R. Goette, 'Britain and the Delay in Closing the Mid-Atlantic "Air Gap" during the Battle of the Atlantic', *The Northern Mariner* (2005), pp. 19–41; Redford, 'Inter and Intra-Service Rivalries', pp. 906–12.

17. TNA AIR 8/405, Harris to Churchill, 17 June 1942; Redford, 'Inter and Intra-Service Rivalries', pp. 899–928.

18. Redford, 'Inter and Intra-Service Rivalries', pp. 899–928.

19. J. Rowher, *The Critical Convoy Battles of March 1943* (London, 1977), pp. 36–7.

20. Barnett, *Engage the Enemy More Closely*, pp. 597–600; Roskill, *The War At Sea* vol. 2, p. 486; Rowher, *The Critical Convoy Battles of March 1943*, pp. 210–13; Terraine, *Business in Great Waters*, pp. 558–69.

21. TNA, ADM 199/2060, Monthly Anti-Submarine Report, March 1943, 15 April 1943, p. 3; TNA CAB 86/3, AU (43) 97, 31 March 1943, tables 1 and 2; D. Redford, 'The March 1943 Crisis in the Battle of the Atlantic: Myth and Reality', *History* (2007), p. 67. The global shipping shortage is covered in the excellent C. Behrens, *Merchant Shipping and*

the Demands of War (London, 1955) and equally good Smith, *Conflict over Convoys*.

22. Barnett, *Engage the Enemy More Closely*, pp. 602–3; D. Syrett, *The Defeat of the German U-Boats* (Columbia, SC, 1994), pp. 25–62; Terraine, *Business in Great Waters*, pp. 588–93.

23. Barnett, *Engage the Enemy More Closely*, pp. 606–9; Syrett, *The Defeat of the German U-Boats*, pp. 63–95; Terraine, *Business in Great Waters*, p. 594.

24. Price, *Aircraft versus Submarine*, pp. 105–10, 138; D. Syrett, 'The Safe and Timely Arrival of SC130, 15–25 May 1943', *American Neptune* (1990), pp. 219–27; Syrett, *The Defeat of the German U-Boats*, pp. 96–144.

25. Syrett, *The Defeat of the German U-Boats*, pp. 181–229.

26. Price, *Aircraft versus Submarine*, pp. 105–10, 138.

27. A. Burn, *The Fighting Captain* (Barnsley, 1993), pp. 124–38, 171–2; Terraine, *Business in Great Waters*, p. 624.

28. Barnett, *Engage the Enemy More Closely*, p. 858.

Chapter 7. The Mediterranean and the Far East 1940–45

1. CB 3302(1), Naval Staff History, *The Mediterranean*, vol. 1, p. 22.

2. Howse, *Radar at Sea*, p. 63.

3. NMRN, BR1736(35), Battle Summary 44, The Battle of Cape Matapan.

4. M. Simpson (ed.), *The Cunningham Papers*, vol. 1 (Aldershot, 1999), pp. 451–2, 454.

5. BR 1736 (52)(2), Naval Staff History, *Submarines*, vol. II, p. 277; Barnett, *Engage the Enemy More Closely*, p. 220; Roskill, *The War at Sea*, vol. 1, p. 307; M. Van Creveld, *Supplying War: Logistics from Wallenstein to Patton*, 2nd ed. (Cambridge, 2004), pp. 184–92, 199–200; Grove, *The Royal Navy Since 1815*, p. 195; R. Hammond, *The British Anti-Shipping Campaign in the Mediterranean 1940–1944: Comparing Methods of Attack* (unpublished PhD thesis, University of Exeter, 2011), pp. 51–2.

6. NMRN, BR1736(11), Battle Summaries 18 & 32, Selected Convoys (Mediterranean), 1941–1942, pp. 34–53.

7. NMRN, BR 1736(11), Selected Convoys (Mediterranean), pp. 55–79.

8. *Ibid.*, pp. 87–90.

9. *Ibid.*, pp. 90–7, 133–4.

10. NMRN, BR1736(31), Operation *Torch*: Invasion of North Africa.

11. E. Montagu, *The Man Who Never Was* (London, 1968).

12. BR 1736(27), The Invasion of Sicily: 'Operation *Husky*'; Barnett, *Engage the Enemy More Closely*, pp. 627–56.

13. Barnett, *Engage the Enemy More Closely*, pp. 686–90.

14. NMRN, BR1736(36), Battle Summary 43, The Invasion of the South of France.

15. NMRN, CB 3303(1) Naval Staff History, War with Japan, vol. 1, pp. 33–4; E. Grove (ed.), *Defeat of the Enemy Attack on Shipping* (Aldershot, 1997), table 27.

16. Barnett, *Engage the Enemy More Closely*, pp. 394–406; C. Bell, 'The "Singapore Strategy" and the deterrence of Japan: Winston Churchill, the Admiralty and the Dispatch of Force Z', *English Historical Review*, vol. 116 (2001), pp. 604–34.

17. NMRN, BR 1736(8)/1955, Loss of HM Ships *Prince of Wales* and *Repulse*, pp. 9–12; BR 1736(50)(2), Naval Staff History, War with Japan, vol. 2, p. 48.

18. NMRN, BR 1736(8)/1955, Loss of HM Ships *Prince of Wales* and *Repulse*, pp. 12–17. The number of torpedoes that hit the *Prince of Wales* appears to have been overestimated; the torpedo that delivered the fatal blow is also disputed. Subsequent surveys of the wreck have shown that the first torpedo hit was the fatal one and that there appears to have been four torpedo hits in total. See http://www.rina.org.uk/hres/Death%20 of%20a%20Battleship%20-%202012%20update.pdf (accessed 9 January 2013).

19. BR 1736(50)(2), Naval Staff History, War with Japan, vol. 2, pp. 94–9.

20. *Ibid.*, pp. 127–8; Barnett, *Engage the Enemy More Closely*, p. 863.

21. Figures from NHB 'Pink Lists' for December 1941, 1942, 1943, 1944 and August 1945 include all warships listed as operating or refitting in/ around the Indian Ocean and the Far East, that is, at various times, the China Fleet, East Indies Command, Eastern Fleet, RAN, RNZN, British Pacific Fleet, as well as attached Allied 'Free' navies.

22. Barnett, *Engage the Enemy*, pp. 871–3; Grove, *The Royal Navy Since 1815*, pp. 209–10.

23. NMRN, BR 1737(50)(6), Naval Staff History, War with Japan, vol. 6, pp. 196–203; Barnett, *Engage the Enemy More Closely*, pp. 890–2; D. Hobbs, *The British Pacific Fleet* (Barnsley, 2011), pp. 126–58, 175–99, 252–93.

24. NMRN, BR 1737(50)(6), Naval Staff History, War with Japan, vol. 6, pp. 38–42; NMRN BR 1736(52)(3), Naval Staff History, Submarines, vol. 3, pp. 11–17; Barnett, *Engage the Enemy More Closely*, pp. 893–4 ; W. Jameson, *Submariners VC* (Penzance, 2004), pp. 188–204.

Chapter 8. The Cold War 1945–64

1. Hobbs, *The British Pacific Fleet*, pp. 377–89, D. Wettern, *The Decline of British Seapower* (London, 1982), pp. 1–14; D. Brown, *The British Pacific and East Indies Fleets: The Forgotten Fleets' 50th Anniversary* (Liverpool, 1995), pp. 112–17; J. Winton, *The Forgotten Fleet: The Story of The British*

Pacific Fleet (Wadhurst, 1995), pp. 389–403; R. Chesnau (ed.), *Conway's All the World's Fighting Ships: 1922–1946* (London, 1980), pp. 4–5.

2.　L. Freedman, *The Evolution of Nuclear Strategy* (London, 1989), pp. 22–33; B. Brodie, *Strategy in the Missile Age* (Princeton, 1965), pp. 150–2.

3.　E. Grove, 'The Royal Navy, 1945–1990', in P.P. O'Brien (ed.), *Technology and Naval Combat in the Twentieth Century and Beyond* (London, 2001), pp. 185–99; E Grove, 'The Royal Navy and the Guided Missile', in R. Harding (ed.), *The Royal Navy, 1930–2000: Innovation and Defence* (Abingdon, 2005), pp. 193–212; N. Friedman, *The Postwar Naval Revolution* (London: 1986), pp. 9–14; Wettern, *The Decline of British Seapower*, pp. 1–27.

4.　E. Grove, *Vanguard to Trident: British Naval Policy Since World War II* (London, 1987), pp. 1–38; Wettern, *The Decline of British Seapower*, pp. 1–2.

5.　J.R. Hill, 'British Naval Planning Post 1945', in N.A.M. Rodger (ed.), *Naval Power in the Twentieth Century* (London, 1990), pp. 216; Grove, *Vanguard to Trident*, pp. 47–51.

6.　J. Slessor, *Strategy for the West* (London: 1954); V. Orange, *Slessor, Bomber Champion: The Life of Marshall of the RAF Sir John Slessor* (London, 2006); L. Freedman, 'The First Two Generations of Strategists', in, P. Paret (ed.), *Makers of Modern Strategy: From Machiavelli to the Nuclear Age* (Oxford, 1986), pp. 735–38; G.L. Dyndal, *Trenchard and Slessor: On the Supremacy of Air Power over Sea Power* (Trondheim, 2007), p. 63; G. Till, 'Naval Power', in C. McInnes and G.D. Sheffield (eds), *Warfare in the Twentieth Century: Theory and Practice* (London, 1988), pp. 101–3.

7.　Grove, *Vanguard to Trident*, pp. 154–5.

8.　N. Stewart, *The Royal Navy and the Palestine Patrol* (London, 2002); V. Flintham, *High Stakes: Britain's Air Arms in Action, 1945–1990* (Barnsley, 2009), pp. 30–6; M. Dewar, *Brush Fire Wars: Minor Campaigns of the British Army Since 1945* (London, 1990), pp. 17–26.

9.　Flintham, *High Stakes*, pp. 22–9.

10.　Grove, *Vanguard to Trident*, pp. 150–2; Flintham, *High Stakes*, pp. 101–26.

11.　M.H. Murfett, *Hostage on the Yangtze: Britain, China and the Amethyst Crisis of 1949* (Annapolis, 1991).

12.　R.W. Love Jr, *History of the US Navy*, vol. 2 (Harrisburg, 1992), pp. 286–7; J.T. Greenwood, 'The Emergence of the Postwar Strategic Air Force, 1945–1953', in A.F. Hurley and R.C. Ehrhart (eds), *Air Power and Warfare: Proceedings of the Eighth Military History Symposium* (Washington DC, 1979), pp. 215–44; Grove, *Vanguard to Trident*, pp. 84–5; R. Moore, *The Royal Navy and Nuclear Weapons* (London, 2001), 64–93; P.

Towle, 'Blackett and Nuclear Strategy', in P. Hore (ed.), *Patrick Blackett: Sailor, Scientist, Socialist* (London, 2003), pp. 201–16.

13. H.S. Truman, *Memoirs: Years of Trial and Hope, 1946–1952* (New York, 1965), pp. 378–87.

14. J.R.P. Lansdown, *With the Carriers in Korea: The Fleet Air Arm Story, 1950–1953* (Worcester, 1992).

15. D. Hobbs, 'British Commonwealth Carrier Operations in the Korean War', *Air Power Review*, vol. 7 (2004), pp. 68–9; G. Thomas, *Furies and Fireflies Over Korea* (London, 2004), p. 22.

16. T. Delpech, *Nuclear Deterrence in the 21st Century: Lessons from the Cold War for a New Era of Strategic Piracy* (Santa Monica, 2012), pp. 70–3; Thomas, *Furies and Fireflies*, p. 141; B. Cull and D. Newton, *With the Yanks in Korea*, vol. 1 (London, 2000), pp. 258–98.

17. L. Marriott, *Jets at Sea: Naval Aviation in Transition, 1945–1955* (Barnsley, 2008), pp. 1–29; O. Thetford, *British Naval Aircraft Since 1912* (London, 1991), pp. 21–6.

18. Friedman, *British Carrier Aviation*, pp. 268–86; L. Marriott, *Jets at Sea*, pp. 120–6.

19. J. Baylis and A. MacMillan, 'The Global Strategy Paper of 1952', *Journal of Strategic Studies*, vol. 16 (1993), pp. 200–6; Grove, *Vanguard to Trident*, p. 115; Brodie, *Strategy in the Missile Age*, pp. 168–72; T. Benbow, 'British Naval Aviation and the Radical Review, 1953–55', in T. Benbow (ed.), *British Naval Aviation: The First 100 Years* (Farnham, 2011), pp. 125–50.

20. G. Carter, *Crises Do Happen: The Royal Navy and Operation Musketeer, Suez 1956* (Falmouth, 2006), pp. 96–8; I. Spellar, 'Limited War and Crisis Management: Naval Aviation in Action from the Korean War to the Falklands Conflict', in T. Benbow (ed.), *British Naval Aviation: The First 100 Years* (Farnham, 2011), pp. 151–76.

21. I. Ballantyne, *Strike from the Sea: The Royal Navy and US Navy at War in the Middle East, 1949–2003* (Barnsley, 2004), pp. 22–7; M.H. Coles, 'Suez 1956: A Successful Naval Operation Compromised by Inept Political Leadership', *Naval War College Review*, vol. 59 (2006), p. 114.

22. I. Spellar, 'The Suez Crisis', in T. Lovering (ed.), *Amphibious Assault: Manoeuvre from the Sea* (Woodbridge, 2007), pp. 421–36; Carter, *Crises Do Happen*, pp. 96–8.

23. Command Paper 124, *Defence Outline of Future Policy* (London, 1957); W. Rees, 'The 1957 Sandys White Paper: New Priorities in British Defence Policy?' *Journal of Strategic Studies*, vol. 12 (1989), pp. 215–29; Wettern, *Decline of British Seapower*, pp. 135–48.

24. S.R. Twigge, *The Early Development of Guided Weapons in the United Kingdom, 1940–1960* (Reading, 1993), pp. 28–30, 161–6; Grove, 'The

Royal Navy and the Guided Missile', pp. 193–212.

25.   K. Young, 'The Royal Navy's Polaris Lobby, 1955–62', *Journal of Strategic Studies*, vol. 25 (2002), pp. 56–86. Grove, *Vanguard to Trident*, pp. 218–44; Wettern, *Decline of British Seapower*, pp. 212–28; J.E. Moore (ed.), *The Impact of Polaris: The Origins of Britain's Seaborne Nuclear Deterrent* (Huddersfield, 1999), pp. 30–3; K. Darling, *Blackburn Buccaneer* (Marlborough, 2006), pp. 16–21; Thetford, *British Naval Aircraft Since 1912*, pp. 64–5, 256–7.

26.   R. Willams, *Fly Navy: Aircraft of the Fleet Air Arm Since 1945* (Shrewsbury, 1989), pp. 120–6, 128–31; Thetford, *British Naval Aircraft Since 1912*, pp. 361–9.

27.   M. Dockrill, *British Defence Since 1945* (Oxford, 1988), pp. 65–81; Grove, *Vanguard to Trident*, pp. 245–79.

28.   D. Phillipson, *Roll on the Rodney: Life on the Lower Deck of Royal Navy Warships after the Second World War* (Stroud, 1999), pp. 133–5; C.H. Bailey (ed.), *Social Change in the Royal Navy, 1924–70: The Life and Times of Admiral Sir Frank Twiss* (Stroud, 1996), pp. 201–9; J. Wells, *The Royal Navy: An Illustrated Social History, 1870–1982* (Stroud, 1994), p. 228.

29.   Command Paper 1639, Statement on the Defence 1962, *The Next Five Years* (London: 1962), Annex One.

30.   J.D. Ladd, *By Sea By Land: The Authorised History of the Royal Marine Commandos* (London, 1998), pp. 260–343; J. Thompson, *The Royal Marines: From Sea Soldiers to a Special Force* (London, 2000), pp. 417–88; I. Spellar, 'The Seaborne/Airborne Concept: Littoral Manoeuvre in the 1960s?', *Journal of Strategic Studies*, vol. 29 (2006), pp. 53–82.

31.   Naval Historical Branch, N/NHB/9/65, BR 1736(55), Naval Staff History: *Middle East Operations: Jordan/Lebanon 1958, Kuwait 1961*; D. Lee, *Flight from the Middle East* (London, 1980), pp. 179–83; Spellar, The Seaborne/Airborne Concept, pp. 53–82.

32.   C. Tuck, 'The Royal Navy and Confrontation, 1963–66', in G. Kennedy (ed.), *British Naval Strategy East of Suez, 1900–2000: Influences and Actions* (Abingdon, 2005), pp. 199–220; P. French, 'Dire Straits: The Transit of the Lombok Strait, September 1964', in R. Gardiner (ed.), *Warship 1999–2000* (London, 1999), pp. 115–24; J. Roberts, *Safeguarding the Nation: The Story of the Modern Royal Navy* (Barnsley, 2009), pp. 66–71.

33.   Moore, *The Royal Navy and Nuclear Weapons*, pp. 152–72.

34.   Young, 'The Royal Navy's Polaris Lobby, 1955–62', pp. 56–86; D.J. Gill, 'Strength in Numbers: The Labour Government and the Size of the Polaris Force', *Journal of Strategic Studies*, vol. 33 (2010), pp. 819–45.

35.   G.L. Dyndal, *Land Based Air Power or Aircraft Carriers? A Case Study of the British Debate About Maritime Air Power in the 1960s* (Farnham, 2012).

Chapter 9. Cold War 1964–89

1. Wettern, *The Decline of British Seapower*, pp. 173–346; E. Grove, 'The Royal Navy: The Fleet Comes Home', in M. Edmonds (ed.), *The Defence Equation: British Military Systems, Policy, Planning and Performance* (London, 1986), pp. 79–113; Rees, 'The 1957 Sandys White Paper', pp. 215–29.

2. R. Ovendale, *British Defence Policy Since 1945* (Manchester, 1994), p. 8.

3. D. Healey, *The Time of My Life* (London, 1989), pp. 234–300; Tuck, 'The Royal Navy and Confrontation', pp. 199–220; Gisborne, 'Naval Operations in the Malacca and Singapore Straits, 1964–66', *The Naval Review*, vol. 55 (1967), pp. 43–6.

4. D. Burke, *TSR2: Britain's Lost Bomber* (Marlborough, 2010), pp. 263–97; C. Gibson, *Vulcan's Hammer: V-Force Projects and Weapons Since 1945* (Manchester, 2011), pp. 132–48; *Statement on the Defence Estimates, 1965* (London, 1965), p. 10.

5. I. McGeoch, *Mountbatten of Burma: Captain of War, Guardian of Peace* (Yeovil, 2009), pp. 223–33; P. Ziegler, *Mountbatten: The Official Biography* (London, 1985), pp. 578–89; Healey, *The Time of My Life*, p. 274.

6. Gill, 'Strength in Numbers', pp. 819–45; Dyndal, *Land Based Air Power or Aircraft Carriers?*; E. Hampshire, *From East of Suez to the Eastern Atlantic: British Naval Policy, 1964–70* (Farnham, 2013).

7. A. Gorst, 'CVA-01: A Case Study in Innovation in Royal Navy Aircraft Carriers, 1959–1966', in R. Harding (ed.), *The Royal Navy, 1930–2000: Innovation and Defence* (Abingdon, 2005), pp. 170–92; D. Faddy, 'The Cancellation of CVA-01 and the Initiation of the Future Carrier (CVF)', *Defence Studies*, vol. 9 (2009), pp. 329–53.

8. Healey, *The Time of My Life*, pp. 265–76; R.A. Clarkson, 'The Naval Heresy', *Royal United Services Institute Journal*, vol. CX (1965), pp. 316–20; D.C. Watt, 'The Role of the Aircraft Carrier in Some Recent British Military Operations', *Royal United Services Institute Journal*, vol. CXI (1966), pp. 128–31; A.T. Ross and J.M. Sanderson, *A Historical Appreciation of the Contribution of Naval Air Power* (Canberra, 2008), pp. 21–54; Dyndal, *Land Based Air Power or Aircraft Carriers?*; Hampshire, *From East of Suez to the Eastern Atlantic*.

9. *The Statement on the Defence Estimates 1966, Part I* (London, 1966), p. 16; R. Humble, *The Rise and Fall of the British Navy* (London, 1986), pp. 179–92; Grove, *Vanguard to Trident*, pp. 280–310.

10. *1967 Report by the Defence Review Working Party: Statement on the Defence Estimates, 1968* (London, 1968); *Supplementary Statement, July 1968* (London, 1968).

11. Friedman, *British Carrier Aviation*, pp. 327–61; R. Chesnau, *Aircraft Carriers of the World, 1914 to the Present: An Illustrated Encyclopaedia* (London, 1986).

12. I. Smith, *The Great Betrayal: The Memoirs of Africa's Most Controversial Leader* (London, 1997), pp. 116–58.

13. J. Baylis and K. Stoddart, 'Britain and the Chevaline Project: The Hidden Nuclear Programme', *Journal of Strategic Studies*, vol. 26 (2003), pp. 124–55; T. Robb, 'Antelope, Poseidon or a Hybrid: The Upgrading of the British Strategic Nuclear Deterrent, 1970–1974', *Journal of Strategic Studies*, vol. 33 (2010), pp. 797–817.

14. Grove, *Vanguard to Trident*, pp. 310–42; J. Baylis, *British Defence Policy: Striking the Right Balance* (London, 1989); Dockrill, *British Defence Since 1945*, pp. 104–10.

15. R. White, *Phoenix Squadron: HMS Ark Royal, Britain's Last Top Guns and the Untold Story of Their Most Dramatic Mission* (London, 2009); Naval Staff History, BR 1736(57), *The Cod War: Naval Operations off Iceland in Support of the British Fishing Industry (1958–76)* (London, 1990); A. Welch, *The Royal Navy in the Cod War: Britain and Iceland in Conflict, 1958–1976* (Liskeard, 2006).

16. Ziegler, *Mountbatten*, pp. 698–700.

17. M.H. Fletcher, *WRNS: A History of the Woman's Royal Naval Service* (Annapolis, 1989).

18. Baylis, *British Defence Policy: Striking the Right Balance*; Dockrill, *British Defence Since 1945*, pp. 111–24; Grove, *Vanguard to Trident*, pp. 342–99.

19. C. McInnes, *Trident: The Only Option* (London, 1986), pp. 4–31; Moore, *The Royal Navy and Nuclear Weapons*, pp. 152–84.

20. Ballantyne, *Strike from the Sea*, pp. 52–70; P. McLaren, The Gulf Revisited – Why?', *The Naval Review*, vol. 78 (1990), pp. 196–204.

21. *The United Kingdom Defence Programme: The Way Forward*, Cmnd 8288 (London, 1982).

22. Appendix A to Annex to OD (81)29, 2 June 1981.

23. K. Speed, *Sea Change* (Bath, 1982), pp. 99–116; H. Leach, 'Introduction', in M. Critchley (ed.), *British Warships and Auxiliaries* (Liskeard, 1981), pp. 3–4.

24. Cabinet Documents, Prem 19/416, GR 220 British Embassy, Washington, 19 May 1981; British Embassy, Washington, GR 650, 4 June 1981; C. Weinberger, *Fighting for Peace: 7 Critical Years in the Pentagon* (New York, 1991); J. Lehman, *Command of the Seas* (Annapolis, 2001).

25. FCS/81/70, 5 June 1981; R.N. Lebow, 'Miscalculation in the South Atlantic: The Origins of the Falklands War', *Journal of Strategic Studies*, vol. 6 (1983), pp. 5–35.

26. H Leach, 'Crisis Management and the Assembly of the Task Force', in S. Badsey et al (eds), *The Falklands Conflict Twenty Years On: Lessons for the Future* (Abingdon, 2005), pp. 64–74; M. Thatcher, *The Downing Street Years* (London, 1993).

27. M. Clapp and E. Southby-Tailyour, *Amphibious Assault Falklands: The Battle of San Carlos Water* (London, 1996); S. Woodward, *One Hundred Days: Memoirs of the Falklands Battle Group Commander* (London, 1992); L. Freedman, *The Official History of the Falklands Campaign*: vols I and II (London, 2005).

28. P. Grove, 'The Falklands Conflict 1982 – The Air War: A New Appraisal', in S. Badsey et al (eds), *The Falklands Conflict Twenty Years On*, pp. 265–81.

29. *Lessons of the Falklands Conflict, December 1982* (London, 1982), pp. 15–30; House of Commons Defence Committee, *Defence Commitments and Resources and the Defence Estimates, 1985–86*, vol. 1 (London, 1985), pp. xiii–xxx; G. Puddefoot, *No Sea Too Rough: The Royal Fleet Auxiliary in the Falklands War – the Untold Story* (London, 2007), pp. 187–214; N. Childs, *The Age of the Invincible: The Ship that Defined the Modern Royal Navy* (Barnsley, 2009), pp. 114–25.

Chapter 10. The End of the Cold War to the War on Terror 1989– 2001

1. C.J. Bartlett, *The Global Conflict: The International Rivalry of the Great Powers, 1880–1990* (Harlow, 1994), pp. 384–90.

2. Cm 1022-I, *Statement on the Defence Estimates 1990*, vol. 1 (London, 1990); Cm 1022-II, *Statement on the Defence Estimates 1990*, vol. 2 (London, 1990).

3. Cm 1559-I, *Statement on the Defence Estimates: Britain's Defence for the 90s* (London, 1991); Cm 2270, *Statement on the Defence Estimates 1993: Defending Our Future* (London, 1993).

4. Cm 2550, *Statement on the Defence Estimates 1994* (London, 1994); *Front Line First: The Defence Costs Study* (London, 1994), pp. 5–8; Cm 3223, *Statement on the Defence Estimates 1996* (London, 1996), p. 115.

5. Ballantyne, *Strike from the Sea*, pp. 71–86; C. Symonds, *Atlas of US Naval History* (Annapolis, 2001), pp. 226–9; Childs, *The Age of the Invincible*, pp. 129–30.

6. M. Ranken, 'The Gulf War – Logistic Support and Merchant Shipping', *The Naval Review*, vol. 79 (1991), pp. 198–206; Ballantyne, *Strike from the Sea*, pp. 87–94.

7. Cm 1559-I, pp. 17–28.

8. C. Craig, 'Gulf War: The Maritime Campaign', *Royal United Services Institute Journal* (August 1992), pp. 11–16; Ballantyne, *Strike from the Sea*, pp. 95–130; Ranken, 'The Gulf War – Logistic Support and Merchant Shipping', pp. 198–206.

9. Cm 1559-I, pp. 21, 74; Ballantyne, *Strike from the Sea*, pp. 129–30.

10. Roberts, *Safeguarding the Nation*, p. 215.

11. *Ibid.*, pp. 245–7.

12. Childs, *The Age of the Invincible*, pp. 132–8.

13. E. Kelbie, 'Almost a Year in the Life of an F/A2 Pilot', *Broadsheet* 1995/96, pp. 40–1; D.G. Snelson, 'Naval Poise Operations in the Adriatic – II', *The Naval Review*, vol. 82 (1994), pp. 127–9; N. Richardson, *No Escape Zone* (London, 2000).

14. E. Grove, 'Naval Operations: The Multinational Dimension', *Jane's Navy International* (January/February 1995), pp. 12–17.

15. Cm 3999, *The Strategic Defence Review* (London, 1998); *The Strategic Defence Review: Supporting Essays* (London, 1998).

16. G. Till, 'The Royal Navy in a New World, 1990–2020', in P.P. O'Brien (ed.), *Technology and Naval Combat in the Twentieth Century and Beyond* (London, 2001), pp. 219–37.

17. Interviews with author.

18. G. Till, 'Great Britain Gambles with the Royal Navy', *Naval War College Review*, vol. 63, no. 1 (Winter 2010), pp. 33–60.

19. *The Strategic Defence Review: Supporting Essays*, pp. 6-6, 6-7.

20. Childs, *Age of the Invincible*, pp. 148–9; Roberts, *Safeguarding the Nation*, pp. 258–9; *Broadsheet 1999/2000* (London, 1999), pp. 26–8.

21. Childs, *Age of the Invincible*, pp. 149–50; Roberts, *Safeguarding the Nation*, pp. 260–2; *Broadsheet 2000/2001* (London, 2001), pp. 13–14; M. Critchley, *British Warships and Auxiliaries 2001/2002* (Liskeard, 2001), pp. 2–4; T. Blair, *A Journey* (London, 2010), pp. 246–7; A. Dorman, *Blair's Successful War: British Military Intervention in Sierra Leone* (London, 2009).

Epilogue. The Royal Navy 2001 to Today

1. *Broadsheet 2007* (London, 2007), pp. 2–25; R. Scott, 'Staying Afloat', *Jane's Defence Weekly*, 22 July 2009, pp. 28–31; A. Orchard, *Joint Force Harrier: The Inside Story of a Royal Navy Fighter Squadron at War* (London, 2008); Till, 'Great Britain Gambles with the Royal Navy', pp. 33–60; R. Scott, 'Overland and Sea', *Jane's Defence Weekly*, 19 August 2009, pp. 28–31.

2. D. Snelson, 'Liberating Iraq – the UK's Maritime Contribution', *The Naval Review*, vol. 91 (2003), pp. 323–8; S. Bush, *British Warships and Auxiliaries 2004/2005* (Liskeard, 2004), pp. 2–5; Ballantyne, *Strike from the Sea*, pp. 150–236; Childs, *Age of the Invincible*, pp. 151–9.

3. Snelson, 'Liberating Iraq', pp. 323–8; Childs, *Age of the Invincible*, pp. 151–9; Roberts, *Safeguarding the Nation*, pp. 275–83.

4. J. Newton, *Armed Action: My War in the Skies with 847 Naval Air Squadron* (London, 2007).

5. Scott, 'Staying Afloat', pp. 28–31.

6. Cm 7948, *Securing Britain in an Age of Uncertainty: The Strategic Defence and Security Review* (London, 2010).

7. Cm 5566, vol. 1, *The Strategic Defence Review: A New Chapter* (London, 2002); Cm 6041-I, *Delivering Security in a Changing World, Defence White Paper* (London, 2003).

8. National Audit Office, *Management of the Typhoon Project* (London, 2011), pp. 23–7.

9. Cm 7948, *Securing Britain in an Age of Uncertainty*; HC 1639, House of Commons Defence Committee, *The Strategic Defence and Security Review and the National Security Strategy* (London, 2011); HC 761, House of Commons Defence Committee, *The Strategic Defence Review and the National Security Strategy* (London, 2011).

10. D. Sloggett, 'A Unified Approach: How Naval Agility Helped Win in Libya', *Jane's Navy International* (March 2012); House of Commons Defence Committee, *Operations in Libya* (London, 2012); A. Johnson and S. Mueen (eds), *Short War, Long Shadow: The Political and Military Legacies of the 2011 Libya Campaign*, Royal United Services Institute, Whitehall Report 2012.

11. N. Childs, *Britain's Future Navy* (Barnsley, 2012), pp. 137–58; *Joint Concept Note 1/12: Future 'Black Swan' Class Sloop-of-War: A Group System* (Shrivenham, 2012); R. Scott, 'Aiming High: A Future Ballistic Missile Defence Role for the Type 45?', in *Warship World*, vol. 13 (May/June 2013), pp. 2–3; R. Scott, ;Steady State: Reality Check for UK Procurement Plans', *Jane's Navy International* (September 2009), pp. 12–17.

Bibliography

Unpublished material
British Library: Additional manuscripts

National Archives
Admiralty papers
Cabinet Office papers
Air Ministry and Air Staff papers

National Museum of the Royal Navy
Naval Staff Histories, Second World War
Battle Summaries, Second World War

Naval Historical Branch
Naval Staff Monographs (Historical), First World War
Admiralty Technical Histories, First World War
Naval Staff Histories, Second World War
Battle Summaries, Second World War
Monthly Anti-Submarine Reports, 1939–1945
Pink Lists, 1939–1945
Naval Staff Histories, post-1945

Newspapers and periodicals
British Warships and Auxiliaries (1983–2013)
Daily Mail
Daily Mirror
Daily Telegraph
Jane's All the World's Fighting Ships (1945–2013)
Manchester Guardian
Morning Post
Naval Annual
Naval Chronicle

Scotsman
Standard
Statements on the Defence Estimates (1957–2010)
The Times

Books and articles

Ackermann, P., *Encyclopaedia of British Submarines 1901–1955* (Penzance, 2002)

Agar, A. *Baltic Episode* (London, 1963)

Allen, H.R., *Who Won the Battle of Britain?* (St Albans, 1974)

Babji, O., 'The Royal Navy and the Defence of the British Empire', in K. Neilson and G. Kennedy (eds), *Far Flung Lines* (London, 1997)

Bacon, R., *The Dover Patrol*, vol. II (London, n.d.)

Bailey, C.H. (ed.), *Social Change in the Royal Navy, 1924–1970: The Life and Times of Admiral Sir Frank Twiss* (Stroud, 1996)

Ballantyne, I., *Strike from the Sea: The Royal Navy and US Navy at War in the Middle East 1949–2003* (Barnsley, 2004)

Barnet, C., *Engage the Enemy More Closely* (London, 1991)

Bartlett, C.J., *The Global Conflict: The International Rivalry of the Great Powers, 1880–1990* (Harlow, 1994)

Baylis, J., *British Defence Policy: Striking the Right Balance* (London, 1989)

—— and MacMillan, A., 'The Global Strategy Paper of 1952', *Journal of Strategic Studies*, vol. 16 (1993)

—— and Stoddart, K., 'Britain and the Chevaline Project: the Hidden Nuclear Programme', *Journal of Strategic Studies*, vol. 26 (2003)

Beesly, P., *Room 40: British Naval Intelligence 1914–1918* (London, 1982)

——, *Very Special Intelligence* (London, 2000)

Behrens, C., *Merchant Shipping and the Demands of War* (London, 1955)

Belby, A., 'Ex Africa semper aliquid novi: The Second Boer War 1899–1901', in P. Hore (ed.), *Seapower Ashore* (London, 2001)

——, *The Victorian Naval Brigades* (Dunbeath, 2006)

Bell, C., *The Royal Navy, Seapower and Strategy Between the Wars* (London, 2000)

——, 'The "Singapore Strategy" and the deterrence of Japan: Winston Churchill, the Admiralty and the Dispatch of Force Z', *English Historical Review*, vol. 116 (2001)

——, *Churchill and Seapower* (Oxford, 2013)

Benbow, T., *British Uses of Aircraft Carriers and Amphibious Ships, 1945–2010*, Corbett Paper No. 9 (Watchfield, 2011)

Bennett, G., *Cowan's War* (London, 1964)

Blair, T., *A Journey* (London, 2010)

Blond, A., *Technology and Tradition: Wireless Telegraphy and the Royal Navy 1895–1920* (unpublished PhD thesis, University of Lancaster, 1993)

Bond, G., *The Evans of the Broke Story* (London, 1961)

Boswell, R., *Weapons Free: The Story of a Gulf War Helicopter Pilot* (Manchester, 1998)

Boyce, D., *The Crisis of British Power: The Imperial and Naval Papers of the Second Earl of Selborne, 1895–1910* (London, 1990)

Bridge, C., *Sea Power and Other Studies* (London, 1910)

Brodie, B., *Strategy in the Missile Age* (Princeton, 1965)

Brooks, J., *Dreadnought Gunnery and the Battle of Jutland* (London, 2005)

——, '*Dreadnought*: Blunder, or Stroke of Genius?', *Journal of Strategic Studies*, vol. 14 (2007)

Brooks, R., *The Long Arm of Empire* (London, 1999)

Brown, D., *The British Pacific and East Indies Fleets: The Forgotten Fleets' 50th Anniversary* (Liverpool, 1995)

Brown, J.D. (ed. D. Hobbs), *Carrier Operations in World War II* (Barnsley, 2009)

Burke, D., *TSR2: Britain's Lost Bomber* (Marlborough, 2010)

Burn, A., *The Fighting Captain* (Barnsley, 1993)

Burne, C., *With the Naval Brigade in Natal* (London, 1902)

Butler, J.R.M., *Grand Strategy*, vol. II (London, 1957)

Cagle, M.W. and Manson, F.A., *The Sea War in Korea* (Annapolis, 1957)

Calder, A., *The Myth of the Blitz* (London, 1992)

Campbell, J., *Jutland: An Analysis of the Fighting* (London, 1986)

Carew, A., *The Lower Deck of the Royal Navy 1900–1939* (Manchester, 1981)

Carter, G., *Crises Do Happen: The Royal Navy and Operation Musketeer, Suez 1956* (Falmouth, 2006)

Chesnau, R., *Aircraft Carriers of the World, 1914 to the Present: An Illustrated Encyclopaedia* (London, 1986)

—— (ed.), *Conway's All the World's Fighting Ships: 1922–1946* (London, 1980)

Childs, N., *The Age of the Invincible: The Ship that Defined the Modern Royal Navy* (Barnsley, 2009)

——, *Britain's Future Navy* (Barnsley, 2012)

Clapp M. and Southby-Tailyour, E., *Amphibious Assault Falklands: The Battle of San Carlos Water* (London, 1996)

Cocker, M., *Royal Navy Submarines: 1901 to the Present Day* (Barnsley, 2008)

Coetzee, F., *For Party or Country: Nationalism and the Dilemmas of Popular Conservatism in Edwardian England* (Oxford, 1990)

Coles, M.H., 'Suez 1956: A Successful Naval Operation Compromised by Inept Political Leadership', *Naval War College Review*, vol. 59 (2006)

Collier, B., *The Defence of the United Kingdom* (London, 1995)

Corbett, J., 'Education in the Navy (I)', *The Monthly Review* (March 1900)

——, 'Education in the Navy (II)', *The Monthly Review* (April 1900)

——, 'Education in the Navy (III)', *The Monthly Review* (September 1900)

——, 'Lord Selborne's Memorandum', *The Monthly Review* (February 1903)

——, 'Lord Selborne's Memorandum (III)', *The Monthly Review* (March 1903)

——, 'Lord Selborne's Critics', *The Monthly Review* (July 1903)

——, *Naval Operations*, vol. I (London, 1920)

——, *Naval Operations*, vol. II (London, 1929)

——, *Principles of Maritime Strategy* (New York, 2004)

Craig, C., 'Gulf War: the Maritime Campaign', *Royal United Services Institute Journal*, August 1992

Critchley, M., *Britannia, Beira and Beyond* (Liskeard, 2010)

Cull, B. et al, *Wings over Suez* (London, 1996)

——and Newton, D., *With the Yanks in Korea*, vol. 1 (London, 2000)

Cumming, A., *The Royal Navy and the Battle of Britain* (Annapolis, 2010)

——, 'The warship as the ultimate guarantor of Britain's freedom in 1940', *Historical Research*, vol. 83 (2010)

Curran, T., 'Who was Responsible for the Dardanelles Naval Fiasco?', *Australian Journal of Politics and History*, vol. 57 (2011)

Darling, K., *Blackburn Buccaneer* (Marlborough, 2006)

Daunton, M., '"The Greatest and Richest Sacrifice Ever Made on the Altar of Militarism": The Finance of Naval Expansion, c. 1890–1914', in R. Blyth, A. Lambert and J. Rüger (eds), *The Dreadnought and the Edwardian Age* (Farnham, 2011)

Davidson, R.L., *The Challenges of Command* (Farnham, 2011)

Davis, R., *Bombing the European Axis Powers* (Maxwell, Al, 2006)

Dewar, M., *Brush Fire Wars: Minor Campaigns of the British Army since 1945* (London, 1990)

Dickenson, H.W., *Educating the Royal Navy* (Abingdon, 2007)

Dockrill, M., *British Defence Since 1945* (Oxford, 1988)

Dorman, A., *Blair's Successful War: British Military Intervention in Sierra Leone* (London, 2009)

Dyndal, G.L., *Trenchard and Slessor: On the Supremacy of Air Power over Sea Power* (Trondheim, 2007)

——, *Land Based Air Power or Aircraft Carriers? A Case Study of the British Debate About Maritime Air Power in the 1960s* (Farnham, 2012)

Edmonds, J., *Military Operations 1916*, vol. 2 (London, 1938)

Ehrman, J., *Grand Strategy*, vol. V (London, 1956)

Faddy, D., 'The Cancellation of CVA-01 and the Initiation of the Future Carrier (CVF)', *Defence Studies*, vol. 9 (2009)

Fitzgerald, C.C.P., 'Training of seamen in the Royal Navy', *National Review*, vol. 35 (1900)

Fletcher, M.H., *WRNS: A History of the Woman's Royal Naval Service* (Annapolis, 1989)

Flintham, V., *High Stakes: Britain's Air Arms in Action 1945–1990* (Barnsley, 2009)

Freedman, L., *The Evolution of Nuclear Strategy* (London, 1989)

——, *The Official History of the Falklands Campaign*, vols I and II (London, 2005)

French, P., 'Dire Straits: The Transit of the Lombok Strait, September 1964', in R. Gardner (ed.), *Warship 1999–2000* (London, 2000)

Friedman, N., *The Postwar Naval Revolution* (London, 1986)

——, *British Carrier Aviation: The Evolution of the Ships and Their Aircraft* (London, 1988)

Fullick, R. and Powell, G., *Suez: The Double War* (Barnsley, 2006)

Gardiner, I., *The Flatpack Bombers: The Royal Navy and the Zeppelin Menace* (Barnsley, 2009)

Gardiner R. (ed.), *Conway's All the World's Fighting Ships, 1947–1995* (London, 1995)

Gardner, W., *Decoding History* (London, 1999)

Gibbs, N., *Grand Strategy: Rearmament Policy*, vol. 1 (London, 1976)

Gibson, C., *Vulcan's Hammer: V-Force Projects and Weapons Since 1945* (Manchester, 2011)

Gill, D.J., 'Strength in Numbers: The Labour Government and the Size of the Polaris Force', *Journal of Strategic Studies*, vol. 33 (2010)

Goette, R., 'Britain and the Delay in Closing the Mid-Atlantic "Air Gap" during the Battle of the Atlantic', *The Northern Mariner* (2005)

Gordon, A., *The Rules of the Game: Jutland and British Naval Command* (London, 2000)

Gordon, G.A.H., *British Seapower and Procurement between the Wars* (Annapolis, 1988)

Gorst, A., 'CVA-01: A Case Study in Innovation in Royal Navy Aircraft Carriers, 1959–1966', in R. Harding (ed.), *The Royal Navy, 1930–2000: Innovation and Defence* (Abingdon, 2005)

Goulter, C., 'The Royal Naval Air Service: A Very Modern Air Service', in S. Cox and P. Gray (eds), *Air Power History: Turning Points from Kitty Hawk to Kosovo* (London, 2002)

Grove, E., *Vanguard to Trident: British Naval Policy Since World War II* (London, 1987)

——, 'The Royal Navy, 1945–1990', in P.P. O'Brien (ed.), *Technology and Naval Combat in the Twentieth Century and Beyond* (London, 2001)

——, *The Royal Navy Since 1815* (Basingstoke, 2005)

——, 'The Royal Navy and the Guided Missile', in R. Harding (ed.), *The Royal Navy, 1930–2000: Innovation and Defence* (Abingdon, 2005)

——, 'Air Force, Fleet Air Arm – or Armoured Corps', in T. Benbow (ed.), *British Naval Aviation: The First 100 Years* (Farnham, 2011)

——, 'Seamen or Airmen? The Early Days of British Naval Flying', in T. Benbow (ed.), *British Naval Aviation: The First 100 Years* (Farnham, 2011)

Grove, P., 'The Falklands Conflict 1982 – The Air War: A New Appraisal', in S. Badsey et al (eds), *The Falklands Conflict Twenty Years On: Lessons for the Future* (Abingdon, 2005)

Hackmann, W., *Seek and Strike* (London, 1984)

Hague, A., *The Allied Convoy System 1939–1945* (St Catherines, Ontario, 2000)

Hammond, R., *The British Anti-Shipping Campaign in the Mediterranean 1940–1944: Comparing Methods of Attack* (unpublished PhD thesis, University of Exeter, 2011)

Hampshire, E., *From East of Suez to the Eastern Atlantic: British Naval Policy, 1964–70* (Farnham, 2013)

Healey, D., *The Time of My Life* (London, 1989)

Heathcote, T.A., *The British Admirals of the Fleet, 1734–1995* (Barnsley, 2002)

Herwig, H., *'Luxury' Fleet: The Imperial German Navy 1888–1918* (Amherst, NY, 1987)

Hessler, G., *The U-Boat War in the Atlantic 1939–1945* (London, 1989)

Hezlet, A., *Aircraft and Seapower* (London, 1970)

Hill, J.R., 'British Naval Planning Post 1945', in N.A.M. Rodger (ed.), *Naval Power in the Twentieth Century* (London, 1990)

Hinsley, F., *British Intelligence in the Second World War*, vol. II (London, 1981)

Hobbs, D., 'British Commonwealth Carrier Operations in the Korean War', *Air Power Review*, vol. 7 (2004)

——, 'Naval Aviation 1930–2000', in R. Harding (ed.), *The Royal Navy, 1930–2000. Innovation and Defence* (London, 2005)

——, *The British Pacific Fleet* (Barnsley, 2011)

Hore, P. (ed.), *Patrick Blackett: Sailor, Scientist, Socialist* (London, 2003)

Hough, R., *The Great War at Sea 1914–1918* (Edinburgh, 2000)

Howse, D., *Radar at Sea: The Royal Navy in World War 2* (London, 1993)

Humble, R., *The Rise and Fall of the British Navy* (London, 1986)

Hurd, A., '"Great Ships Or – ?": A Footnote to the *Times* Correspondence', *Fortnightly Review*, vol. 109 (1921)

Ion, H., 'Towards a naval alliance', in P.P. O'Brien (ed.), *The Anglo-Japanese Alliance, 1902–1922* (London, 2004)

Jeans, T. (ed.), *Naval Brigades in the South African War* (London, 1901)

Jerrold, D., *The Royal Naval Division* (London, 1923)

Kennedy, G., 'Intelligence and the Blockade, 1914–1917: A Study in Administration, Friction and Command', *Intelligence and National Security*, vol. 22 (2007)

——, 'The North Atlantic Triangle and the Blockade, 1914–1915', *Journal of Transatlantic Studies*, vol. 6 (2008)

——, 'Strategy and Power: The Royal Navy and the Foreign Office and the Blockade, 1914–1917', *Defence Studies*, vol. 8 (2008)

Kennedy, P., 'The Relevance of the Prewar British and American Strategies of the First World War and its Aftermath', in J.B. Hattendorf and

R.S. Jordan (eds), *Maritime Strategy and the Balance of Power* (Basingstoke, 1989)

——, *The Rise and Fall of British Naval Mastery* (London, 1991)

Ladd, J.D., *By Sea By Land: The Authorised History of the Royal Marine Commandos* (London, 1998)

Lambert, A., 'The power of a name: tradition, technology and transformation', in R. Blyth, A. Lambert and J. Rüger (eds), *The Dreadnought and the Edwardian Age* (Farnham, 2011)

Lambert, N., 'Economy or Empire? The fleet unit concept and the quest for collective security in the Pacific, 1909–14', in N. Neilson and G. Kennedy (eds), *Far Flung Lines. Studies in Imperial Defence in Honour of Donald Mackenzie Schurman* (London, 1997)

——, *Sir John Fisher's Naval Revolution* (Columbia, SC, 1999)

——, 'Transformation and Technology in the Fisher Era: The Impact of the Communications Revolution', *Journal of Strategic Studies*, vol. 27 (2004)

——, 'Strategic Command and Control for Manoeuvre Warfare: Creation of the Royal Navy's "War Room" System, 1905–1915', *Journal of Military History*, vol. 69 (2005)

——, *Planning Armageddon: British Economic Warfare and the First World War* (Cambridge, MA, 2012)

Lansdown, J.R.P., *With the Carriers in Korea: The Fleet Air Arm Story, 1950–1953* (Worcester, 1992)

Larew, K., 'The Royal Navy in the Battle of Britain', *The Historian*, vol. 54 (1992)

Lavery, B., *Hostilities Only: Training the Wartime Royal Navy* (London, 2004)

Leach, H., 'Crisis Management and the Assembly of the Task Force', in S. Badsey et al (eds), *The Falklands Conflict Twenty Years On: Lessons for the Future* (Abingdon, 2005)

Lee, D., *Flight from the Middle East* (London, 1980)

——, *Wings in the Sun: A History of the Royal Air Force in the Mediterranean, 1945–1986* (London, 1989)

Levy, J., *The Royal Navy's Home Fleet in World War II* (Basingstoke, 2003)

Lovering, T. (ed.), *Amphibious Assault: Manoeuvre from the Sea* (Woodbridge, 2007)

McGeoch, I., *Mountbatten of Burma: Captain of War, Guardian of Peace* (Yeovil, 2009)

MacGregor, D., 'The Use, Misuse, and Non-Use of History: The Royal Navy and the Operational Lessons of the First World War', *Journal of Military History*, vol. 56 (1992)

McInnes, C., *Trident: The Only Option?* (London, 1986)

Mackay, R., *Fisher of Kilverstone* (London, 1973)

McLaren, P., 'The Gulf Revisited – Why?', *The Naval Review*, vol. 78 (1990)

Maiolo, J., *The Royal Navy and Nazi Germany* (Basingstoke, 1998)

——, 'Deception and Intelligence Failure: Anglo-German Preparations for U-boat Warfare in the 1930s', *Journal of Strategic Studies*, vol. 22 (1999)

——, *Cry Havoc: The Arms Race and the Second World War 1931–1941* (London, 2010)

Marder, A.J., *From the Dreadnought to Scapa Flow*, 5 vols (London, 1961–70)

——, *The Anatomy of British Sea Power* (London, 1972)

——, *From the Dardanelles to Oran: Studies of the Royal Navy in War and Peace, 1915–40* (London, 1974)

Marriott, L., *Jets at Sea: Naval Aviation in Transition, 1945–1955* (Barnsley, 2008)

Mason, U., *The Wrens 1917–77* (Reading, 1977)

——, *Britannia's Daughters: The Story of the WRNS* (London, 1992)

Massie, R., *Dreadnought: Britain, Germany and the Coming of the Great War* (London, 1993)

Mitchell, B., *British Historical Statistics* (Cambridge, 2011)

Montagu, E., *The Man Who Never Was* (London, 1968)

Moore, J.E. (ed.), *The Impact of Polaris: The Origins of Britain's Seaborne Nuclear Deterrent* (Huddersfield, 1999)

Moore, R., *The Royal Navy and Nuclear Weapons* (London, 2001)

Moretz, J., *The Royal Navy and the Capital Ship in the Interwar Period* (London, 2002)

Morris, A., *The Scaremongers: The Advocacy of War and Rearmament 1896–1914* (London, 1984)

Murfett, M.H., *Hostage on the Yangtze: Britain, China and the Amethyst Crisis of 1949* (Annapolis, 1991)

Nathan, J., *Soldiers, Statecraft, and History: Coercive Diplomacy and International Order* (Westport, CT, 2002)

Neillands, R., *The Battle for the Rhine 1944. Arnhem and the Ardennes: The Campaign in Europe* (London, 2005)

Neilson, K., 'The Anglo-Japanese alliance and British strategic foreign policy', in P.P. O'Brien (ed.), *The Anglo-Japanese Alliance, 1902–1922* (London, 2004)

Newbolt, H., *Naval Operations*, vol. IV (London, 1928)

Newton, J., *Armed Action: My War in the Skies with 847 Naval Air Squadron* (London, 2007)

Nish, I., *The Anglo Japanese Alliance* (London, 1966)

Offer, A., *First World War: An Agrarian Interpretation* (Oxford, 1991)

Orchard, A., *Joint Force Harrier: The Inside Story of a Royal Navy Fighter Squadron at War* (London, 2008)

Osborne, E., *Britain's Economic Blockade of Germany 1914–1919* (London, 2004)

Ovendale, R., *British Defence Policy Since 1945* (Manchester, 1994)

Page, C., *Command in the Royal Naval Division* (Staplehurst, 1999)

——, 'The Royal Naval Division, 1914–19', in P. Hoare (ed.), *Seapower Ashore* (London, 2001)

Peden, G., *Arms, Economics and British Strategy: From Dreadnoughts to Hydrogen Bombs* (Cambridge, 2007)

Penn, G., *Snotty: The Story of the Midshipman* (London, 1957)

——, *HMS Thunderer* (Emsworth, 1984)

Phillipson, D., *Roll on the Rodney: Life on the Lower Deck of Royal Navy Warships after the Second World War* (Stroud, 1999)

Pope, D., *73 North: The Battle of the Barents Sea 1942* (London, 1988)

Price, A., *Aircraft versus Submarine* (London, 1973)

Puddefoot, G., *No Sea Too Rough: The Royal Fleet Auxiliary in the Falklands War – the Untold Story* (London, 2007)

Rahn, W., 'German Naval Strategy and Armament 1919–1939', in P.P. O'Brien (ed.), *Technology and Naval Combat in the Twentieth Century and Beyond* (London, 2001)

Ranft, B. (ed.), *The Beatty Papers*, vol. 1 (Aldershot, 1989)

Ranken, M., 'The Gulf War – Logistic Support and Merchant Shipping', *The Naval Review,* vol. 79 (1991)

Ray, J., *The Battle of Britain: New Perspectives* (London, 1996)

Redford, D., 'The March 1943 Crisis in the Battle of the Atlantic: Myth and Reality', *History* (2007)

——, 'Inter and Intra-Service Rivalries and the Battle of the Atlantic', *Journal of Strategic Studies*, vol. 32 (2009)

——, *Submarine: A Cultural History from the Great War to Nuclear Combat* (London 2010)

——, 'Collective Security and Internal Dissent: The Navy League's Attempts to Develop a New Policy towards British Naval Power between 1919 and the 1922 Washington Naval Treaty', *History*, vol. 96 (2011)

——, 'Naval Culture and the Fleet Submarine', in D. Leggett and R. Dunn (eds), *Re-inventing the Ship: Science, Technology and the Maritime World 1800–1918* (Farnham, 2012)

Rees, W., 'The 1957 Sandys White Paper: New Priorities in British Defence Policy?', *Journal of Strategic Studies*, vol. 12 (1989)

Richards, D., *The Royal Air Force 1939–1945*, vol. 1 (London, 1953)

Richardson, N., *No Escape Zone* (London, 2000)

Robb, T., 'Antelope, Poseidon or a Hybrid: The Upgrading of the British Strategic Nuclear Deterrent, 1970–1974', *Journal of Strategic Studies*, vol. 33 (2010)

Roberts, J., *Safeguarding the Nation: The Story of the Modern Royal Navy* (Barnsley, 2009)

Roskill, S.W., *The War at Sea*, 4 vols (London, 1954–94)

——, 'The Dismissal of Admiral Jellicoe', *Journal of Contemporary History*, vol. 1 (1966)

——, *Naval Policy between the Wars*, 2 vols (London, 1968)

——, *Admiral of the Fleet Earl Beatty: The Last Naval Hero: An Intimate Biography* (London, 1980)

Ross, A.T. and Sandison, J.M., *A Historical Appreciation of the Contribution of Naval Air Power* (Canberra, 2008)

Rowher, J., *The Critical Convoy Battles of March 1943* (London, 1977)

Ruegg, B. and Hague, A., *Convoys to Russia* (Kendal, 1993)

Rüger, J., 'The symbolic value of the *Dreadnought*', in R. Blyth, A. Lambert and J. Rüger (eds), *The Dreadnought and the Edwardian Age* (Farnham, 2011)

Scott, R., 'Steady State: Reality Check for UK Procurement Plans', *Jane's Navy International* (September 2009)

——, 'Aiming High: A Future Ballistic Missile Defence Role for the Type 45?', *Warship World*, vol. 13 (May/June 2013)

Seligmann, M, 'A prelude to the reforms of Admiral Sir John Fisher: the creation of the Home Fleet, 1902–3', *Historical Research*, vol. 83 (2010)

——, *The Royal Navy and the German Naval Threat 1901–1914* (Oxford, 2012)

Simpson, M. (ed.), *The Cunningham Papers*, vol. 1 (Aldershot, 1999)

Skelton, O.D., *Life and Letters of Sir Wilfred Laurier* (Toronto, 1921; abridged ed., 1965)

Slessor, J., *Strategy for the West* (London, 1954)

Sloggett, D., 'A Unified Approach: How Naval Agility Helped Win in Libya', *Jane's Navy International* (March 2012)

Smith, I., *The Great Betrayal: The Memoirs of Africa's Most Controversial Leader* (London, 1997)

Smith, K., *Conflict over Convoys: Anglo-American Logistics Diplomacy in the Second World War* (Cambridge, 2002)

Smith, M., *Britain and 1940: History, Myth and Popular Memory* (London, 2000)

Snelson, D.G., 'Naval Poise Operations in the Adriatic – II', *The Naval Review*, vol. 82 (1994)

——, 'Liberating Iraq – the UK's Maritime Contribution', *The Naval Review*, vol. 91 (2003)

Speed, K., *Sea Change* (Bath, 1982)

Spellar, I., 'The Seaborne/Airborne Concept: Littoral Manoeuvre in the 1960s?', *Journal of Strategic Studies*, vol. 29 (2006)

——, 'Limited War and Crisis Management: Naval Aviation in Action from the Korean War to the Falklands Conflict', in T. Benbow (ed.), *British Naval Aviation: The First 100 Years* (Farnham, 2011)

Stevenson, D., 'War by Timetable? The Railway Race before 1914', *Past & Present*, no. 162 (February 1999)

Stewart, N., *The Royal Navy and the Palestine Patrol* (London, 2002)

Sumida, J., *In Defence of Naval Supremacy* (Boston, MA, 1989)

——, 'Sir John Fisher and the *Dreadnought*: The sources of naval mythology', *Journal of Military History*, vol. 59 (1995)

Syrett, D., 'The Safe and Timely Arrival of SC130, 15–25 May 1943', *American Neptune* (1990)

——, *The Defeat of the German U-Boats* (Columbia, SC, 1994)

Temple Patterson, A. (ed.), *The Jellicoe Papers*, vol. 1 (London, 1966)

——, *The Jellicoe Papers*, vol. 2 (London, 1968)

Terraine, J., *Business in Great Waters: The U-boat Wars, 1916–1945* (London, 1989)

Thatcher, M., *The Downing Street Years* (London, 1993)

Thetford, O., *British Naval Aircraft Since 1912* (London, 1991)

Thomas, G., *Furies and Fireflies over Korea* (London, 2004)

Thompson, J., *The Royal Marines: From Sea Soldiers to a Special Force* (London, 2000)

Till, G., 'Airpower and the Battleship', in B. Ranft (ed.), *Technical Change and British Naval Policy 1860–1939* (London, 1977)

——, *Air Power and the Royal Navy* (London, 1979)

——, 'Passchendaele: The Maritime Dimension', in P. Liddle (ed.), *Passchendaele in Perspective: The Third Battle of Ypres* (London, 1997)

——, 'The Royal Navy in a New World, 1990–2020', in P.P. O'Brien (ed.), *Technology and Naval Combat in the Twentieth Century and Beyond* (London, 2001)

——, 'Corbett and the emergence of a British school?', in G. Till (ed.), *The Development of British Naval Thinking* (London, 2006)

——, 'Great Britain Gambles with the Royal Navy', *Naval War College Review*, vol. 63, no. 1 (2010)

——, 'Competing Vision: The Admiralty, the Air Ministry and the Role of Air Power', in T. Benbow (ed.), *British Naval Aviation: The First 100 Years* (Farnham, 2011)

Tuck, C., 'The Royal Navy and Confrontation, 1963–66', in G. Kennedy (ed.), *British Naval Strategy East of Suez, 1900–2000: Influences and Actions* (Abingdon, 2005)

Tute, W., *True Glory: The Story of the Royal Navy over a Thousand Years* (London, 1983)

Twigge, S.R., *The Early Development of Guided Weapons in the United Kingdom, 1940–1960* (Reading, 1993)

Van Creveld, M., *Supplying War: Logistics from Wallenstein to Patton*, 2nd ed. (Cambridge, 2004)

Van der Vat, D., *Standard of Power: The Royal Navy in the Twentieth Century* (London, 2000)

Walker, S., *Shockwave: Countdown to Hiroshima* (New York, 2005)

Watson, B.W., *The Changing Face of the World's Navies: 1945 to the Present* (London, 1991)

Watt, D.C., 'The Role of the Aircraft Carrier in Some Recent British Military Operations', *Royal United Services Institute Journal*, vol. CXI (1966)

Webster, C. and Frankland, N., *The Strategic Air Offensive Against Germany 1939–1945*, vol. 1 (London, 1961)

Welch, A., *The Royal Navy in the Cod Wars: Britain and Iceland in Conflict, 1958–1976* (Liskeard, 2006)

Wells, J., *The Royal Navy: An Illustrated Social History, 1870–1982* (Stroud, 1994)

Wettern, D., *The Decline of British Seapower* (London, 1982)

White, R., *Phoenix Squadron: HMS Ark Royal, Britain's Last Top Guns and the Untold Story of Their Most Dramatic Mission* (London, 2009)

Wiest, A., 'The Planned Amphibious Assault', in P. Liddle (ed.), *Passchendaele in Perspective: The Third Battle of Ypres* (London, 1997)

Willams, R., *Fly Navy: Aircraft of the Fleet Air Arm Since 1945* (Shrewsbury, 1989)

Williamson, P., *Stanley Baldwin* (Cambridge, 1999)

Winton, J., *Ultra at Sea* (London, 1988)

——, *The Forgotten Fleet: The Story of the British Pacific Fleet* (Wadhurst, 1995)

Woodman, R., *Arctic Convoys* (London, 1995)

Woodward, S., *One Hundred Days: Memoirs of the Falklands Battle Group Commander* (London, 1992)

Wright, P., *Tank* (London, 2000)

Young, K., 'The Royal Navy's Polaris Lobby, 1955–62', *Journal of Strategic Studies*, vol. 25 (2002)

Ziegler, P., *Mountbatten: The Official Biography* (London, 1985)

Index